Murder Two

The Second Casebook of Forensic Detection

Colin Evans

WILEY
John Wiley & Sons, Inc.

Published by John Wiley & Sons, Inc., Hoboken, New Jersey
Published simultaneously in Canada

Photo credits: pages 33, 152, 234, 235, Federal Bureau of Investigation; page 40, U.S. Fire Administration; page 43, Scotland Yard; page 89, Belmont Police Department; page 202, Pinkertons Inc.

For general information about our other products and services, please contact our Customer Care Department within the United States at (800) 762-2974, outside the United States at (317) 572-3993 or fax (317) 572-4002.

ISBN 0-7394-6316-0

Printed in the United States of America

Contents

Acknowledgments

I am deeply indebted to the following, all of whom contributed in many ways during the preparation of this book: David Anderson, Catherine Cooper, William Drennan, Lou Fuller, Dr. Audrey Giles, Jeff Golick, Sue Livingston, Greg Manning, Patti McLendon, Kimberly Monroe-Hill, Devra K. Nelson, Stephen Power, Marge Schultze, Ed Knappman, and all at New England Publishing Associates. My sincerest thanks to everyone.

Introduction

For more than two thousand years humankind has been attempting to solve crimes through the application of scientific knowledge. In Roman times, physicians routinely performed autopsies to find out why people had died, and this was extended to the criminal arena in 44 B.C. when the most famous Roman of all, Julius Caesar, was stabbed to death. On that occasion there was no great secret regarding "whodunit," but the fact that an autopsy took place at all does highlight the way in which human curiosity was beginning to explore the broader aspects of crime investigation.

From this promising birth came only chaos. As barbarian hordes swarmed across Europe, sacking Rome and plunging the entire continent into the Dark Ages, all this early knowledge was trampled underfoot, with most of it lost forever. For the next millennium, science was a dim memory at best. The revival, when it came, occurred on the other side of the world. In 1248 a Chinese book, *Hsi Duan Yu* (The Washing Away of Wrongs), laid out a rudimentary description of how to distinguish the symptoms of drowning from those of strangulation, and also how to determine if a body was already dead before immersion in water. It wasn't much, but with its emphasis on careful study of the crime scene, this volume marked the first time that anyone had set down guidelines to what we would nowadays call forensic science.

Europe took centuries to catch up. Gradually, though, the notion that science, rather than plunging a suspect's hand into fire or a vat of boiling water, might be a more reliable means of determining guilt did take hold. This was a concept that really blossomed in the Victorian Age, particularly in France and Germany and later in Britain, and from there it spread across the Atlantic to America. Since that time a barrage of forensic advances—each building on the last—has moved crime solving into another dimension. From ballistics to toxicology to brain fingerprinting to anthropology to computer-enhanced digital imagery and all points between, the crime laboratory has led the fight in the war against wrongdoing.

This book is an attempt to chart that progress. Like its predecessor, *The Casebook of Forensic Detection* (1996), it highlights a wide array of criminal cases, all medico-legal classics, and all fascinating. They range across four continents and are presented alphabetically for easy reference. Each contains some forensic quirk or wrinkle that elevates it above the humdrum. It might be a flash of intuitive brilliance, more likely the result of painstaking research and study. They demonstrate how, from the first fumbling attempts to identify poisons and bullets through to the modern miracle of GPS satellite technology, with its ability to pinpoint anyone's whereabouts on the planet, the battle has been multifaceted; for, while no one would seriously dispute that fingerprinting and DNA are the major-league all-stars of the forensic world—each deservedly garnering the biggest headlines when it came along—elsewhere there have been scores of developments, no less important collectively, and they, too, are given due recognition.

As the title suggests, this book is predominantly devoted to the solving of murder cases. There is a sound reason for this: cutting-edge forensic science is prohibitively expensive, and law enforcement agencies have budgets, the same as anyone else. Inevitably this means that resources are targeted at the most heinous crimes. But dig a little deeper and you will find numerous examples where the crime laboratory has triumphed in other fields.

Interspersed among the individual cases, cross-referenced in bold type, and signaled by an icon of a magnifying glass, are accounts of the primary scientific developments and procedures that gave life to much of this progress. (Any discipline also covered in the previous volume has been considerably revised and enlarged.) Because this book is written primarily for the layperson, technical jargon has been kept to a minimum. You won't need a degree in physics or chemistry to understand the many fascinating technologies that bring criminals to justice, and there is also a useful timeline to help put these advances in context.

A common thread among the many readers who so kindly wrote to me following publication of *The Casebook of Forensic Detection* was their obvious fascination with the lives of the great forensic pioneers—Heinrich, Lacassagne, Helpern, and the like—those scientists, inventors, and detectives whose discoveries and occasionally sheer cussedness have revolutionized the fight against crime. For this reason I have included profiles and case details of twenty-five such luminaries, once again fully cross-referenced and signaled by an icon in the text. Hopefully this will put some flesh on the bones of these often shadowy individuals, and reveal the personalities and often bitter rivalries that hallmarked (some might say blighted) their careers.

Such an impressive array of forensic might and muscle does, of course, raise one vital question: Why is it, with so much scientific brilliance on tap, that the prison populations of the world are bulging as never before? Surely, the fledgling criminal would realize the inevitability of detection and settle, however grudgingly, for a lawful existence? The answer lies mainly in the fact that most serious crime is committed by a handful of inveterate recidivists who have neither the inclination nor the incentive to pursue any other lifestyle. But there is another reason: mankind's capacity for malevolent inventiveness. The modern criminal, like the society around him, has moved on. Nowadays such a person is driven by fanatical zeal to topple skyscrapers; he grooms unsuspecting young victims in Internet chat rooms, trafficks drugs on street corners and in boardrooms, or siphons off millions of dollars with the click of a mouse. He kills on one continent, hops on a plane, flies halfway around the world, and kills again. In short, modern criminals are able to practice a level of hard-core lawlessness far beyond anything their forefathers could have imagined; and with no sign of this trend being arrested, forensic science will forever be playing catch-up.

On a more prosaic level, the battle is remorselessly nonstop. Consider the following: figures published by the FBI in 2001 show that every thirty-four minutes someone is murdered in America; violent crimes occur at five-second intervals; and each hour, thirty women are raped or sexually assaulted (most incidents, it is thought, go unreported). These are horrifying numbers. Just imagine how much worse they might be were it not for the forensic laboratory.

A quick caveat: we don't just need more science, we need more *good* science. Elsewhere I have dealt with some of the murkier episodes in the history of forensic science (see *A Question of Evidence*, Wiley, 2003)—overly compliant "expert witnesses" shading the evidence is a recurring bugbear—and there are, happily, few such incidents within these pages. This is, overwhelmingly, a testament to cleverness and decency.

Even though the core of this book is devoted to great scientific triumphs, its intensely human element should never be overlooked. Each case mentioned here has its own victim or victims; a life snuffed out, a woman hideously assaulted, someone bilked or duped, a family left grieving. For all these victims the miracle of the test tube, the scanning microscope, and all the related paraphernalia of the modern crime laboratory is not just a topic of jaw-dropping awe but also their only hope of obtaining a grain of justice in what must seem a cruelly unjust world. They deserve nothing less.

John Allan

Date: 1998
Location: Luxor, Egypt

Two days before she was due to fly home to England, Cheryl Lewis, a forty-three-year-old vacationing lawyer from Liverpool, enjoyed one last shopping spree in the souk at Luxor, Egypt. As evening drew in, she returned to the New Winter Palace Hotel, where, with her fiancé, John Allan, she enjoyed a meal before they retired to their room. Sometime later, Allan called reception to say that Cheryl was seriously ill and needed a doctor.

An American tourist trained in first aid, Pamela Black, volunteered assistance. Entering the darkened room, she found Cheryl naked on the bed, foaming at the mouth, and drenched in sweat, her skin a hideous blue color. Pamela did what she could, but was puzzled by Allan's diffidence, in particular his point-blank refusal to attempt mouth-to-mouth resuscitation on his distressed fiancée. That same day—October 9, 1998—Cheryl Lewis died.

The Egyptian death certificate recorded "heart and circulatory failure and acute coronary thrombosis," but when Cheryl's body was returned to the United Kingdom, her relatives insisted on a full autopsy. This was performed by the Home Office pathologist Edmund Tapp. He found no evidence of natural disease and noted that the top of the stomach was raw, as if she had ingested some corrosive agent, yet the mouth and windpipe were undamaged. He suspected that Cheryl had been poisoned.

Such a finding didn't surprise Cheryl's family, who had long nursed suspicions about John Allan. Despite calling himself a businessman, he had sponged off Cheryl for years and following her death had continued to occupy her expensive house in Liverpool, even driving her Mercedes. (He had the personalized license plate changed to one resembling his own name.) When the police learned that Allan was the major beneficiary of Cheryl's £400,000 ($672,000) estate, they decided to investigate more closely.

Allan had a checkered background. Twice married, twice divorced, he'd worked as an industrial chemist in Zambia's copper mines. One night in Chingola, his second wife had been mysteriously shot and wounded while driving to a restaurant. Even though she insisted that Allan had nothing to do with the incident, he was arrested. Freed on bail, Allan literally carried his wife out of the hospital and then fled with her to South Africa. From there they traveled back to England, where, after his divorce, he met Cheryl Lewis.

As a first step in their inquiries, investigators impounded the Mercedes. In a compartment between the front seats, they found a bag containing four off-white briquettes of hard powder. Laboratory analysis revealed that Allan was driving around with enough cyanide to kill six hundred people!

Since February 8, 1924, when Gee Jon, a Chinese tong assassin executed in Nevada, became the first person to die in a U.S. gas chamber, cyanide has been the poison of choice for those states that still employ this method of capital punishment. It is horribly effective. As it meets the gases in the stomach, the resulting hydrocyanic acid has a catastrophic effect, preventing the body from using any oxygen, effectively causing suffocation.

Allan knew all about the deadly poison. According to his first wife, in Zambia he had been an avid butterfly collector who'd killed his specimens by placing them in a jar containing cyanide.

Ordinarily cyanide disappears quite quickly from the body, making it difficult to detect. Here there was another complicating factor: Cheryl had been embalmed. Despite these drawbacks, analysts still managed to detect traces of the poison in Cheryl's system. This, so police believed, explained Allan's curious reluctance to administer mouth-to-mouth; he didn't want to run the risk of inhaling any cyanide fumes that might be emitted from the dying woman's mouth.

Oblivious to the fact that he was now a murder suspect, Allan resumed a normal life. Indeed, within a week of Cheryl's death, he was answering lonely hearts ads in local papers. Simultaneously, he began dating a friend of Cheryl's, Jennifer Hughes, a wealthy divorcée, and in November presented her with a gold bracelet—the same bracelet that had gone missing from Cheryl's hotel room in Luxor.

When Mrs. Hughes returned from a world trip in January 1999, Allan was there to greet her. In the weeks that followed she suffered two mysterious illnesses, but that didn't prevent her from agreeing to visit Egypt with Allan in February. Just one week before they were scheduled to leave, he was arrested.

Cheryl's will, ostensibly dated 1993, had been exposed as a forgery. Typeface irregularities between the final page and the rest of the will provided the initial clue that something was amiss; soon, detectives sifting through scores of floppy disks at Allan's home found the "smoking gun." Allan had typed the contents of the will into a word processor, then effected changes to make himself the principal beneficiary. When, at the third attempt, he was satisfied with the results, he had printed out the amended sheets and slipped them in front of the original and all-important final page, which contained Cheryl's original signature and those of the witnesses. Foolishly, he hadn't realized that the computer recorded the three amended versions as having been prepared on August 20, 1997.

This date was just two months before the couple's first planned visit to Egypt, which had been canceled due to terrorist outrages. Whether Allan had homicide in mind on this trip is mere conjecture, but one year later, having decided it was now safe to travel, Cheryl set off for Egypt and her doom.

When arrested on February 5, 1999, and charged with murder, Allan first tried to blacken Cheryl's name, saying that for several months prior to her death, she had been abusing drugs and had died from a heroin overdose.

When hair analysis exposed this lie, he then accused Cheryl's first husband and her family of pursuing a vendetta, claiming that they had framed him.

In March 2000 the final act in this real-life *Death on the Nile* was played out when Allan was convicted of murder.

Lowell Amos

Date: 1994
Location: Detroit, Michigan

Just before Christmas 1994, a group of executives was gathered at the Atheneum Hotel in Detroit for a company party. Among those present were Lowell Amos, a fifty-two-year-old former General Motors plant manager from Anderson, Indiana, and his wife, Roberta. After socializing with friends until 4:30 A.M., the Amoses retired.

The next morning, at 8:30, another executive, Norbert Crabtree, received a phone call in his room from Amos, who sounded agitated and pleaded for help. When Crabtree and another guest, Daniel Porcasi, reached the room, Amos dropped a bombshell: Roberta was dead.

There had been a tragic accident, he explained, and he needed time to clean up before he contacted the authorities. Could they do him a big favor? He handed over a small leather case, which he asked them to hold for him. Crabtree agreed. When he later checked, he found it contained a foul-smelling washcloth, a sport coat, and a syringe without a needle. (Although Amos later reclaimed this bag, its contents subsequently vanished.)

When Amos did call the police, he had a lurid tale to tell. After returning to their suite, he and Roberta had engaged in cocaine-fueled sex games. These lasted for some time. Roberta, he said, was still taking the coke when he fell asleep. When he awoke, he found her dead. In a panic, he'd flushed the coke down the toilet and tried to clean up the room. Investigators noticed that the bed linen was soiled and smeared, which was odd because Roberta's body looked very clean, without any hint of makeup.

When detectives pressed Amos about the cocaine usage, he explained that because of sinus trouble, Roberta didn't snort the drug but instead found other means of ingestion. This was confirmed at autopsy, when vaginal swabs showed unmistakable traces of coke. The absence of external signs of the drug was still baffling, however, since the body contained more than *fifteen times* the lethal amount—so big a dose, in fact, that she'd died before even half the drug had been broken down.

This set alarm bells ringing. Acute cocaine poisoning invariably causes violent fits before death, and it seemed inconceivable that Amos could have slept through such disturbances. Besides, what was the likelihood, after his own admitted cocaine binge, that he would sleep, anyway?

It was time to examine the evidence more closely. The forensic scientist Dr. Phyllis Goode was given the bed linen for analysis. Nothing in Amos's story accounted for the strange staining. Because the body was so clean, it was suspected that Amos had washed it before calling police. This was borne out by test samples from the pillowcase, which showed traces of cosmetics, even though, when found, Roberta was not wearing any. Even more ominous were the imprints of teeth marks and lipstick found on the pillowcase, such as might result if the pillow had been pressed over someone's face.

Turning her attention to the sheet, Goode found coke traces all over the material, even on those parts tucked under the mattress. Although this provided clear evidence of crime scene manipulation, it was scarcely proof of murder.

While investigators struggled to unravel this mystery, Amos found a novel means of easing his grief. Just two days after Roberta's death, he spent $1,000 on dinner and drinks with two women and had sex with both. Curiously enough, it was Amos's amorous adventures that proved his undoing. Sparked by publicity surrounding the case, various women now came forward with stories of having dated Amos, and all felt that they had been drugged before sex. These revelations prompted an in-depth examination of Amos's background. What investigators discovered was horrifying: women close to Lowell Amos had a habit of dying out of turn.

His first wife, Saundra, age thirty-six, had been found dead in the bathroom in 1979. According to Amos, she had mixed a sedative with wine, collapsed, and hit her head on the bathroom counter. Despite misgivings, the cause of death was ruled indeterminate, and Amos received a $350,000 insurance payout.

Shortly thereafter he married his longtime mistress. According to friends, Caroline Amos argued constantly with her new husband over the large insurance policies he kept buying on her life, and, when he refused to cancel them, she threw him out in 1988. In a curious move, he went to live with his seventy-six-year-old mother. Just a couple of weeks later, she was rushed to the hospital, seemingly stupefied. Doctors were unable to diagnose the problem, and when she soon recovered, she went home. Each day Caroline called to check on her mother-in-law, but one day Amos answered, and he had bad news: he'd just found his mother; she'd been dead for several hours.

Caroline rushed to the house, to find Amos throwing his belongings into his car. He said that he didn't want anyone to know he had been living with his mother. Because of her age, the death wasn't considered suspicious, and there was no autopsy. Amos inherited more than $1 million.

Perhaps believing herself to now be better insulated against Amos's avarice, Caroline let him back into the house. Nine months later she, too, was dead. According to Amos, he'd taken her a glass of wine to the bathroom, where she was blow-drying her hair. Later he found her dead in the bath and thought she had been electrocuted, but no cause of death was ever determined. Significantly, the wineglass was missing from the bathroom and later found rinsed out in the dishwasher. Caroline's death netted Amos another $800,000 insurance payout.

It was a damning litany, and on November 8, 1998, Amos was arrested for murder. In 1994, Michigan had changed the law to allow details of previous incidents to be introduced into trials. This enabled prosecutors to show that although Amos had no direct financial motive for killing Roberta, his marriage was on the rocks. Roberta had already bought a house of her own and wanted him out of her life. Amos killed her because he couldn't stand the rejection, first injecting her with cocaine, then smothering her with a pillow when the fits began. He was sentenced to life imprisonment.

Anthropology (Forensic)

Although often required to draw on elements of archaeology and pathology in their work, forensic anthropologists are primarily concerned with the 206 bones that make up the human skeleton. In the average male these bones weigh twelve pounds; for females, it is closer to ten. To the trained eye, they form an illuminating guide to the body they inhabit. They can show how the person lived, any debilitating illnesses such as rickets or polio, healed fractures, whether that person was right- or left-handed, and even possible clues as to occupation (for instance, waitresses show signs of their arm strength in their bones; their strong side is more developed than the other side).

Several basic questions arise with the discovery of any skeletal remains:

1. What was the person's age at the time of death? Two features—the long bones of the arms and legs, and the skull—are studied closely. In infancy, the ends of the long bones are attached to the main shaft by cartilage, called epiphysis. Gradually this attachment disappears, and the two pieces of bone fuse together, a process that usually ends at about age thirty. The different states of fusion can give an indication of age that is accurate within two or three years. After age thirty, these changes cannot provide an estimate closer than some ten years. Detectable skull changes are also more noticeable in childhood. The infant skull is made up of pieces, marked by sutures, that close up in stages. The frontal suture is the first to close, usually early in life. Other sutures normally close between ages twenty and thirty, but some can remain open or only partially closed to age sixty, making this form of age estimation progressively imprecise later in life.

2. What was the sex of the skeleton? The clearest indicators are the skull and the pelvis. The male pelvis is narrow and steep, but much broader and shallower for a woman (a divergence further accentuated by childbirth).

3. What was the person's race? Using variation in eye socket shape and the nose, forensic anthropologists categorize people in one of three racial groups: Mongoloid (Asian), Negroid (African), and Caucasoid (European). In Negroids and Mongoloids the ridge of the nose often is broad in relation to height; in Caucasoids, it is narrower.

4. What was the person's height? When a corpse is intact, measurement presents little difficulty, but in cases of dismemberment, where a body or skeleton is incomplete, a measurement can be calculated because of a relationship between the limbs and the total height of the body.

This relationship was first noted by Dr. Mildred Trotter, a professor of anatomy at Washington University in St. Louis. After World War II Trotter assisted the U.S. Armed Forces in Hawaii, helping to repatriate the remains of servicemen killed in action. By studying the long bones of hundreds of servicemen, she calculated a formula that is generally accurate within plus or minus three centimeters. For a male Caucasoid the formula is:

Length of femur x 2.38 + 61.41 cm = height
Length of tibia x 2.52 + 78.62 cm = height
Length of fibula x 2.68 + 71.78 cm = height

Additional tables that attempt to provide some indication of the corpse's build (slender, medium, or heavy) also are employed. The most practical applications for these calculations has been in the area of passenger identification after airline disasters or terrorist action.

In modern times, undisputed leadership in the field of corpse aging belongs to the Anthropological Research Facility at the University of Tennessee in Knoxville. Founded by Dr. William M. Bass in the early 1980s, this research facility is an outdoor laboratory established to scientifically document postmortem change. Known locally as the "Body Farm" and surrounded by razor wire, the facility has, at any one time, dozens of corpses (most are willed to science) dotted about its two and a half acres.

They arrive in various states—some headless, some embalmed, some naked, many unidentified—and are placed in a variety of locations: in car trunks, under canvas or plastic, buried in shallow graves, covered with brush, or submerged in ponds. The newly dead may lie alongside piles of disintegrating bones. They are exposed to wide extremes of temperature, either refrigerated in total darkness or else left in direct sunlight. And then they are studied.

When a person dies, the body starts to decay immediately, as enzymes in the digestive system begin eating the tissue. Then insects and climate take over. Attracted by the smell of putrefaction, blowflies begin their ravages (see **entomology [forensic]**), followed by small rodents and other animals. When these factors are combined with high temperatures, total decomposition can be startlingly fast. At the height of summer, for example, a body can deteriorate from fully intact to bare bones in a mere two weeks.

Each stage of decomposition is recorded and analyzed, then added to the growing databank that is made available to law enforcement. Sometimes attempts are made to duplicate the circumstances of a particular crime, but the research is mainly directed toward the collection of general data that might help in future cases. The more precisely the researchers can measure decomposition in identifiable conditions, the more solid is their contribution to solving and prosecuting a crime.

Close attention is paid to soil samples, because as bodies decompose, they leak fatty acids into the ground beneath them. Analysis of this soil makes it possible to determine how long a body was lying in a particular area or whether it was placed somewhere and then moved. The soil can also reveal the presence of a corpse, even if the body itself has been removed or destroyed. The "stain" left by the fatty acids, which also suppresses plant life around it, can last as long as two years, leaving a kind of phantom fingerprint in the earth.

The FBI is just one investigative agency with close links to the "Body Farm." Every February, agents descend on the Knoxville facility to dig for bodies that assistants have prepared to simulate crime scenes. They excavate the burials and look for the evidence that has been deliberately planted.

Troy Armstrong

Date: 1992
Location: Lubbock, Texas

On a raw winter day in early 1994, two hunters tracking game outside Lubbock, Texas, pursued their quarry into a remote area known as Yellowhouse Canyon. They didn't find the prey they were seeking, but they did stumble across some skeletonized human remains. Only the skull and a few bones remained; the rest had been scattered by animals. Close by lay a white high-heeled shoe.

When Harold Gill-King, the director of the University of North Texas Health Science Center's Human Identification Laboratory, examined the body, he had no doubt that this was a case of murder. Gouged deeply into the ribs and vertebrae were no fewer than eleven marks made by knife thrusts.

The body was that of a white female, aged between eighteen and twenty-four, and, to judge from weathering of the bones, she had been dead for approximately two years. But apart from the shoe, there was nothing to identify the body. X-rays of the victim's teeth were compared with dental records of local women reported missing, but this line of inquiry drew a blank.

With the inquiry floundering, Karen Taylor, a forensic artist with the Texas Department of Public Safety, was brought in and asked if she could produce a drawing of the dead woman's face from just the skull.

It was the Russian anthropologist Mikhail Gerasimov (see **facial reconstruction**) who first drew up the complex tables detailing the thickness of facial soft tissue, based on averages of sex, race, and size, that inform facial reconstruction. Although designed initially to assist in the creation of actual busts, these tables are equally useful to the forensic artist who seeks merely to produce a two-dimensional likeness. They enabled Taylor to cut out rubber pegs that matched the average depth of skin for a young white woman. These were then glued onto the skull at twenty-one landmark sites, such as the cheeks and chin. Once the markers were in place, photos of the skull were taken. Great care was necessary at this stage; for an accurate representation of the face, the photos have to be life-sized and in perfect focus.

Up until this point, much of the work had been academic, following tables, exercising great caution. Now it was time for Taylor's artistic side to take center stage. Placing transparent paper over the photos, and using the rubber pegs as guidelines, she sketched out the facial contours. In doing this, she was hindered by the absence of the victim's clothing, which is often an excellent indicator of body weight and, by extension, of facial size as well.

As always in facial reconstructions, the eyes and nose posed special problems. The eye color is unknowable, and while the average human eyeball measures approximately one inch in diameter, there is no such uniformity when it comes to the eyelids. Again, this is where the artist's individual skill shines through. It's a similar story with the nose. One can glean hints from the nasal cavity, but nothing definite. Indeed, a 60 percent accuracy rate is thought to be excellent. In this case, because the victim was a white female, Taylor drew a nose, adding roughly one-fifth of an inch to each side of the nasal cavity. The nasal spine at the base of the nose is a good clue to the angle of tilt of the nose, up or down. Here Taylor arrived at a smaller-than-average nose with a slight uptilt.

In any facial reconstruction the hardest element to capture is the hair, particularly when dealing with female skulls. With every shade from ebony to platinum, cropped to waist length, straight, curled, thick, or fine, the variety is infinite. This is pure guesswork. Most forensic artists opt on the side of neutrality, which is what Taylor did here: medium length, medium thickness, brownish in color.

The finished drawing, depicting a young woman with high cheekbones and a broad chin, was presented to the media. Within a week, two calls came in with positive identifications, including one from the dead girl's mother, who had lost touch with her daughter.

Belynda Kay Tillery, a seventeen-year-old nightclub dancer, was last seen alive on July 24, 1992, when a coworker dropped her off outside a fast-food restaurant, where her boyfriend's truck was parked. When compared to the photo on Belynda's driver's license, the drawing provided a good match, and the identification was verified by checking dental records. Despite her reliance on nothing more concrete than tables of averages, Taylor had achieved a quite remarkable similarity with her forensic drawing.

Now that the authorities had the victim's name, they went looking for her boyfriend.

Troy Armstrong had a string of convictions in Colorado for burglary, theft, and trespass before moving to Texas. A skilled outdoorsman, he regularly camped in Yellowhouse Canyon and always carried a large hunting knife. Acquaintances described a violent relationship between him and Belynda, one that had become more abusive still when Belynda announced that she was pregnant. There seemed to be some confusion over the paternity of the child, but one thing was certain: Belynda was dead, and Troy Armstrong was missing.

The thirty-year-old truck driver was eventually tracked to Roswell, New Mexico, but there the trail grew cold. Tipped off that the police were after him, Armstrong had fled.

Six months passed. Then, in January 1995, came news that Armstrong was holed up with a trucker friend in California. By a stroke of good fortune the friend's truck was equipped with GPS tracking (see **Albert Walker**), which allowed his employer to determine that, at that moment, he was driving through the Midwest. A phone call to the Nebraska state police was all it took to get a roadblock set up, and Armstrong was arrested.

At his trial, Angie Allen, Belynda's rival for Armstrong's affection, testified that six months after Belynda's disappearance, he had admitted stabbing her to death. Armstrong's fate was sealed, and on December 5, 1996, he was convicted of murder and imprisoned for life.

Arson

Arson and **explosives** are closely related. The chemical processes are very similar, and an explosion is often followed by fire, and vice versa. Each can be an indiscriminate killer, and each can wreak massive psychological damage. Figures published by the National Fire Data Center show that each year in the United States there are close to two million fires. Of those, roughly one in four is deliberate. In human terms the cost is appalling—more than five hundred lives lost in 2000—while the monetary value of property damage exceeds $3 billion per annum. Setting aside wanton vandalism and those happily few incidents triggered by mental disorder, arson usually has one of three motives: insurance fraud; revenge; or concealment of another crime, such as robbery or murder.

Fire has always exerted a powerful appeal for the criminal anxious to conceal evidence of nefarious activity. The assumption is that a raging blaze consumes all, but this is not necessarily true. For instance, the murderer anxious to dispose of his or her victim will find that a human corpse is astonishingly fire-resistant and that the enormous temperatures essential for total destruction of teeth and bone are rarely encountered outside of a crematorium.

Another consideration for the criminally disposed to bear in mind is that a suspicious fire receives merciless investigation. Generally at least three independent agencies are involved: fire officers, specially trained to locate the seat and cause of the blaze; the police, whose interest lies in discovering the perpetrator or perpetrators of any crime; and insurance adjusters, who are naturally eager to protect the interests of their employers.

In any fire, the following equation applies: fuel + oxygen + heat source = combustion; and it is the arson investigator's job to determine if any of these three ingredients is present in a quantity that would raise suspicion.

Often the first clue to arson is provided by smell, particularly accelerant odor. An accelerant is any substance, nearly always a liquid, that has been placed at the fire scene to facilitate the spread of a fierce and fast blaze. Gasoline and kerosene are the most common accelerants; others include acetone and ethanol. Any time a fire scene reveals the presence of an accelerant where one is not normally present, it is powerfully compelling evidence of arson.

The human nose is still the primary source of odor identification. Trained dogs come next, and then we have portable electronic gas detectors called "sniffers." Although capable of identifying the presence of accelerants at just ten parts per million, and indispensable in situations where poisonous fumes might abound, sniffers are still viewed with considerable skepticism in some quarters.

The next clues tend to be visual. Is there any sign of a break-in? Or bare wires on an electrical appliance? Maybe a dropped cigarette? If the answer to any of these or similar questions is no, the investigator will broaden the search to look for the classic signs of arson: faster and more widespread burning than normal; multiple points of origin; some kind of time-delay device (typical examples include a matchbook and cigarette, a twisted piece of paper, or a scrap of fabric); and the nearby presence of cans and containers. Often an unusually heavy concentration of debris and ash is a good indication of where flammable material has been piled in a heap to start the fire.

Because fires burn upward in an inverted conical shape, the point of origin is usually the lowest place where burning has occurred. From there, as the flames leap upward and outward, they tend to produce distinctive V patterns along walls. Air currents play a huge role in this development and help to explain why flames can hurtle with terrifying speed up stairways and in the hollow spaces between walls.

There is a widely held belief among arsonists that most if not all accelerants are consumed in a fire or else evaporate. This is a gross misconception. Traces invariably remain, and to find these, the investigator will once again direct his or her attention to the lowest point of ignition. Wooden floors and beams, for example, tend to carbonize in a checkerboard pattern, the checks being smaller nearer the seat of the blaze. Also, any accelerant used to start the fire has a tendency to be absorbed by the charred wood or seep into cracks in the flooring, where it often fails to burn from lack of oxygen.

Good-quality control samples—the kind that scientists prefer—are best harvested from these low locations and from any porous surfaces such as carpet and furniture. Once these samples are in the laboratory, analysis can take the form of **chromatography,** or if more sophisticated testing is required, mass spectrometry. Whatever the method employed, identifying the accelerant used is a relatively simple procedure.

Given the sophistication of modern chemical analysis, concealing arson is virtually impossible. Catching the arsonist is another matter. In the United States, just 16 percent of arson offenses lead to arrest, and of those arrested, just 2 percent are convicted. Disgruntled ex-employees, ex-renters, transients, and juveniles—in 2000, under-eighteens accounted for approximately 50 percent of all arson arrests—make up the bulk of suspects. Perhaps less surprisingly, records also show that most deliberate fires are started in the hours of darkness or on a quiet weekend. And there tends to be a socioeconomic dimension: when the business cycle is in decline and small companies are failing, the number of arson cases soars, as desperate owners torch premises in the hope of a lucrative insurance payout.

Whatever the source, whatever the reason, arson continues to be one of the most insidious and dangerous of all crimes, and one that is fearfully difficult to solve.

Frank Atwood

Date: 1984
Location: Tucson, Arizona

When eight-year-old Vicki Lynn Hoskinson failed to return to her Tucson home after cycling to the mailbox with a letter, her elder sister, Stephanie, went looking for her. All she found was Vicki's pink Stingray bicycle, abandoned in the middle of a quiet road.

Once twenty-four hours had passed without any sign of Vicki, the case was assessed a probable kidnapping and referred to the FBI. Among the many people they interviewed was a teacher at Vicki's school. Sam Hall recalled that on the day of Vicki's disappearance—September 17, 1984—he had seen a long-haired, unkempt man in a Datsun 260Z with California plates parked outside the school playground. Concerned by the stranger's behavior, Hall had shouted out, and the man immediately drove off but not before Hall was able to note the car's license number—1KEZ608—on a piece of paper.

Records showed the car as being registered to Frank Atwood, a twenty-seven-year-old ex-con, recently paroled in California after serving time for sex offenses and kidnapping a young boy. Freed in May 1984, Atwood had violated the terms of his parole by moving to Tucson—just two weeks before Vicki vanished.

On September 20 Atwood was arrested some seven hundred miles away, in Kerrville, Texas. However, an exhaustive search of the car's interior failed to disclose any evidence—hair, fingerprints, fibers—that could be linked to Vicki, despite the fact that traces from previous occupants of the car were found.

With the investigation seemingly stuck in neutral, FBI agents went back and reexamined the area where Vicki's bicycle had been found. Only now did they notice that a mailbox belonging to a nearby house had been bent over, as if it had been struck by a car. Was it possible that the kidnapper, in his haste to escape, had hit the post? A closer inspection showed that the impact was obviously fresh and only twelve inches from the ground, a height consistent with having been struck by a low-slung sports car such as a 260Z.

Now, instead of concentrating on the car's interior, investigators checked the bodywork for signs of damage. On the front bumper they found a thin smear of pink paint. To the naked eye it appeared identical to the color of Vicki's bicycle, but only laboratory analysis could provide an iron-clad match.

In the meantime, a specialist in accident reconstructions went over every inch of the Datsun, looking for evidence of a recent collision. Underneath the car, on the protective gravel pan, he found his first clue: some recent scratches. There were similar scratch marks on the pedal of Vicki's bike, and he found that when the bicycle was laid on the ground beneath the car—as might happen in an accident—the bike's pedal was at exactly the same height as the scratched gravel pan. All the indications were that Atwood deliberately knocked Vicki off her bicycle while going no faster than 5 miles per hour; then he bundled her into his car before fleeing. Such a slow impact speed would account for the absence of blood at the crime scene and the fact that no one heard the accident occur.

This was the hypothesis. What did the laboratory say? FBI scientists subjected the paint from the Datsun's bumper and paint from a scratched area of Vicki's bicycle to a battery of tests. Both microscopically and chemically, the samples displayed similar characteristics. A higher degree of sophistication and accuracy was achieved by placing the samples in a gas chromatograph mass spectrometer, then heating them to 760°C, to vaporize and separate the organic compounds. The components of each sample were indistinguishable. However, when viewed under a scanning electron microscope, the sample from Vicki's bike did show one highly unusual element: it contained a trace of nickel. This was highly significant, as the gouge on the Datsun's bumper had revealed its nickel underplating. When analyzed, the chemical composition of both nickel samples was found to be identical.

While it looked very much as though Atwood had abducted Vicki, there was still no sign of her whereabouts. Then in April 1985, fully seven months after Vicki's disappearance, a hiker found a skull in the desert some twenty miles from where Vicki was last seen.

The physical anthropologist Walter H. Birkby of the Arizona State Museum used comparative dental radiography to match these teeth to Vicki's dental records. But the remains were too ravaged to reveal the cause of death. Atwood's attorney claimed that since his client had been in custody from three days after the disappearance, and since it was impossible to state with any certainty when the body had been dumped in the desert, this at least introduced an element of reasonable doubt into the equation. However, another factor now came into play: traces of adipocere had been found on the skull.

Adipocere, a whitish, suetlike substance, is formed when human fat comes into contact with bacteria, moisture, and, to a lesser extent, heat. Clearly the Arizona desert is exceptionally hot for several months of the year, and during the summer months rainfall is virtually unknown, but a check of weather records showed that in the forty-eight hours after Vicki's disappearance there had been unseasonably heavy rain in the region where her body was found. Then the desert had reverted to its habitual aridity. In order for adipocere to have formed on Vicki's remains, according to the prosecution, her body must have been dumped before or during this forty-eight-hour time frame. With this revelation, Atwood's final chance of evading justice evaporated.

On May 8, 1987, Atwood was sentenced to death. At the time of writing, his sentence is under review, following the U.S. Supreme Court's ruling in *Ring v. Arizona* (2002), which mandated that in capital cases juries and not judges should determine the final sentencing.

Autopsy (Postmortem)

Evidence suggests that the first autopsies were conducted by the Egyptians in the third century B.C. These were primarily illness-related, and not until Roman times do we find bona fide medico-legal autopsies. The most famous was performed by Antistius, on the body of Julius Caesar in 44 B.C. His conclusion? Only one of the twenty-three stab wounds—a thrust between the first and second ribs—was fatal.

Not much happened for another thousand years, not until the Chinese started the systematic investigation of suspicious death. By the late Middle Ages, though, it was Europe that held sway. In France, Italy, Austria, and Scotland, pioneering doctors and scientists added to the collective knowledge, and in 1813, America gained its first professor of medical jurisprudence with the appointment of James S. Stringham at Columbia University. In the wake of these developments, forensic pathology flourished as never before, so that many early twentieth-century practitioners, especially in Europe, became media celebrities.

The duties of the pathologist go beyond the mere cause of death; they must establish all the facts, both lethal and nonlethal, that might have any bearing on criminal or civil litigation. Above all, they must pay scrupulous attention to detail, measurements, descriptions, and documentation. They know that although performed in isolation, the autopsy is inextricably tied to the crime scene. What might cry out "murder" in the mortuary could easily be explained as suicide if the circumstances lead ineluctably to such a conclusion.

Such demands have brought about drastic changes in the way autopsies are performed. The days when the famed British pathologist **Francis Camps** —working barehanded and with ash drooping from the cigarette clamped between his teeth—would blaze through an autopsy in ten minutes are long gone. Reputations are heavily guarded in this litigious age. In present-day autopsies, but especially in potentially criminal cases, findings are dictated to a stenographer or else recorded during the actual procedure, rather than written up later, as used to be the case. The record often becomes legal evidence and therefore must be complete and accurate.

Although all pathologists and all autopsies vary to some degree, the following ten-step process is typical of most criminal autopsies:

1. The body arrives at the mortuary in a bag, with the extremities wrapped in plastic to ensure that evidence is not lost in transit. A general description of the body is made, covering height, weight, general condition, and any obvious external wounds. Any clothing is then removed and handed to attending assistants, who will bag it for further analysis.

2. A full external examination of the body now takes place. This can be highly informative, giving many clues to the person's lifestyle. Typically this examination might start at the head and neck, then proceed to the chest, abdomen, upper limbs, lower limbs, and genitalia. The whole procedure is repeated for the back.

3. Trace evidence is now gathered from the body. Fingernail scrapings or clippings are taken at this time. In sex crime cases, swabs are taken of key locations such as the vagina, rectum, breasts, and mouth. Swabs also figure prominently in gunshot cases, as samples from around the wound might reveal powder residue, which may help establish the range at which the shot was fired.

4. Each individual is photographed as a permanent record. A scale is included in every photograph so that the size of the wound is obvious, to prevent any subsequent disputes.

5. The body is opened using a Y-shaped incision from shoulders to mid-chest and down to the pubic region.

6. This incision enables easy access to the thorax and neck, and exposes any subcutaneous bruising that might not be apparent on the surface of the skin. Very close attention is paid to the neck, always one of the body's most vulnerable and informative regions. At this stage of the examination, the first clues to the nature and depth of any stab wounds are now apparent.

7. To examine the organs of the chest, the breastbone must be cut through. This can be achieved with a scalpel in persons under thirty, but older bones generally require a saw. The internal organs thus exposed can now be examined. Tissue from the organs is saved and sent for histological examination. The major solid organs (heart, lungs, brain, kidney, liver, and spleen) are weighed on a grocer's scale; smaller organs such as the thyroid and the adrenals usually require a chemist's triple-beam balance.

8. To examine the skull, a single incision is made across the vertex of the head, and the scalp is pulled forward and backward to reveal the bone. (When the incision is sewn back up, it will be concealed by the pillow on which the dead person's head rests.) A special vibrating saw that cuts bone but not soft tissue is used to cut through the skull, and the dome is pried off by means of a chisel-headed key.

9. Once the skull is open, the brain can be carefully cut free from its attachments and removed. The inside of the skull can reveal a pattern of old injuries, giving a clue to the victim's lifestyle. In cases involving blunt instruments, skull fragments should match damage to the meninges—the membrane around the brain—and to the surface of the brain itself.

10. After completion of the autopsy, it is necessary to reconstruct the body by reversing the dissection process. The breastbone and ribs are usually replaced in the body; the skull and trunk incisions are sewn shut, using the trademark "baseball stitch"; the body is washed, and responsibility is then passed to the undertakers.

Michael Baden (1939–)

Bronx-born and Brooklyn-bred, Baden has become one of America's most recognized and experienced pathologists. After receiving his degree in 1959 from New York University School of Medicine, he interned at Bellevue Hospital until 1961, then joined the office of the chief medical examiner (CME) in New York City. There, under the tutelage of **Milton Helpern,** he prospered. At the time, forensic pathology was not a popular career choice for young doctors—the pay was abysmal, and many found the work distasteful—so Helpern was delighted to have such a keen student.

Throughout the 1960s and 1970s in New York, Baden gained priceless experience of violent death in all its infinite varieties, and during that period he probably autopsied more murder victims than any other pathologist in the world. In 1978 he was finally offered the coveted top position. His tenure as CME lasted barely a year. Then, like so many of his contemporaries, he fell afoul of the vicious political infighting that so often blights this office. In taking on Mayor Edward Koch and Manhattan District Attorney Robert Morgenthau, Baden couldn't be accused of fighting below his weight. But the contest was hopelessly lopsided. Baden's highly public and acrimonious demotion led to a subsequent lawsuit for wrongful dismissal (which he ultimately lost on appeal), and while awaiting its outcome, he was appointed deputy chief medical examiner for Suffolk County, New York. Since 1983 he has largely restricted himself to private practice.

Besides handling a busy private caseload, he also served as chairman of the Forensic Pathology Panel of the U.S. Congress Select Committee on Assassinations, which investigated the deaths of President John F. Kennedy and Dr. Martin Luther King Jr. He later autopsied victims of the TWA Flight 800 crash, and was closely connected with the forensic examination of the remains of the Russian royal family who were murdered in 1918. Such credentials have led to his being consulted in some of recent history's most notorious criminal cases.

Throughout it all, Baden remains firmly entrenched in the public eye. Unlike many medical examiners, he is pragmatic about the perennial scrutiny that accompanies his profession. Controversy is never far away, and much of his work nowadays is conducted in the full glare of the media spotlight. This clearly doesn't worry him. Talking of his early days in New York, he says, "I liked the reporters and the television cameras. The fact that they were covering my work added importance to it, an extra dimension."

With medico-legal affiliations too numerous to mention and a hectic lecture schedule, Baden is rarely far from the headlines. In recent times he had brought his vast experience and knowledge to his position as host of the HBO program *Autopsy.*

Significant Cases

1918	The Romanovs
1963	John F. Kennedy
1963	Frank Falco and Thomas Trantino
1976	Wilbur Howard*
1976	Catherine Fried
1977	Shlomo Tal
1979	Carmine Galante

1980	Joseph Christopher
1980	Claus von Bulow
1982	John Belushi
1983	Richard Kuklinski
1990	Christian Brando
1994	O. J. Simpson
1998	Sandy Murphy and Rick Tabish

*Profiled in this book.

Ballistics

Although, strictly speaking, ballistics is the science that deals with the motion of projectiles and the conditions that affect that motion, in criminal investigation it has come to mean the specific study of firearms and bullets. The first firearms were introduced into Europe from Arabia in about A.D. 1300, but another two centuries would pass before the next great ballistics milestone was reached. This came when engineers realized that by etching a spiral groove into the gun barrel—a process called rifling—they could impart spin to the projectile and thereby vastly improve its accuracy. This was first mentioned in a book that discussed gunsmiths employed by Emperor Maximilian of Germany between 1493 and 1508.

Rifling not only enhanced the lethal nature of firearms, it also made them identifiable. Each bullet that passes through a gun barrel sustains distinctive scratch marks unique to that barrel. The raised parts of these marks are called "lands," while the valleys are termed "grooves," and they are caused by an unavoidable defect in gun barrel construction. After being smooth-bored, the gun barrel blank is reamed to a specification diameter, then rifled. Because the machine tools used to manufacture barrels wear minutely with each succeeding gun, uniformity is a physical impossibility; hence the unique rifled gun barrel.

The realization that rifling might assist in matching a bullet to a firearm took time to catch hold. In 1900 a groundbreaking article titled "The Missile and the Weapon" was published in the *Buffalo Medical Journal.* Written by Dr. Albert Llewellyn Hall, it dealt with methods of systematically measuring land and groove markings on bullets, the examination of gunpowder residues in barrels of firearms, and the physical changes that take place over time after the weapon is fired. Sadly, Hall declined to pursue his research in this field, with the consequence that he remains one of the great unsung heroes of ballistics history.

Those who followed in his footsteps soon realized that other factors besides the barrel contribute to bullet individuality. When fired, a bullet is driven forward through the barrel; simultaneously, its shell casing hurtles back against the breech face. Any imperfection on that breech face will impress itself on the case head. Something similar happens with the firing pin, the extractor, and the ejector post; all may etch distinguishing marks on the head or shell casing.

After exiting the muzzle, a bullet must compete with its surroundings. If it strikes human bone or any hard object, severe distortion may result. For this reason, it is often more reliable to compare test firings with casings taken from a crime scene, if available, rather than with the bullet itself.

The distance from which a weapon was fired often figures significantly in criminal cases, and this can be determined—up to several feet—by examining the form and size of the hole in a target, the extent of burning around the hole, the amount of embedded powder grains, and the presence of mercury or lead from primers. Such information can be vital in determining whether a gunshot wound was self-inflicted. Infrared, X-ray, and chemical tests are used to clarify the extent of powder residues.

The modern cartridge was invented in France in 1835 and consists of a casing with a soft metal cap holding the primer charge. When struck by the gun's firing pin, the primer ignites the main propellant charge, expelling the bullet from the gun and leaving the case behind. The invention of smokeless powder at the beginning of the twentieth century caused havoc with the old lead bullets. Unable to cope with the new powder's greater propellant velocity, they were too soft to be gripped by the rifling and tended to get stripped, fouling the barrel. This led to the introduction of the metal-jacketed bullet, usually cupronickel.

In 1912 Victor Balthazard, professor of forensic medicine at the Sorbonne, devised a means of matching bullets to firearms by use of photographs. Images were made of bullets fired from the suspected firearm, as well as the reference bullet. The photographs were then carefully enlarged, so that Balthazard could inspect the lands and grooves in microscopic detail. These same specialized photographic techniques were also applied to the examination and identification of cartridge casings using firing pin, breech face, ejector, and extractor marks.

Undoubtedly the greatest single advance in firearms identification came in the 1920s when Philip O. Gravelle, who together with Charles Waite had founded the Bureau of Forensic Ballistics in New York, designed the comparison microscope (see **microscopy**). This allowed the firearms examiner to study the reference bullet and the suspect bullet side by side to determine if they were fired by the same gun. If there is agreement in the width, depth, and spacing of a significant number of striae (surface marks) on both bullets, an identification can be made.

Nowadays the firearms examiner finds that assistance is often little more than a mouse click away. DRUGFIRE, run by the FBI, is an automated

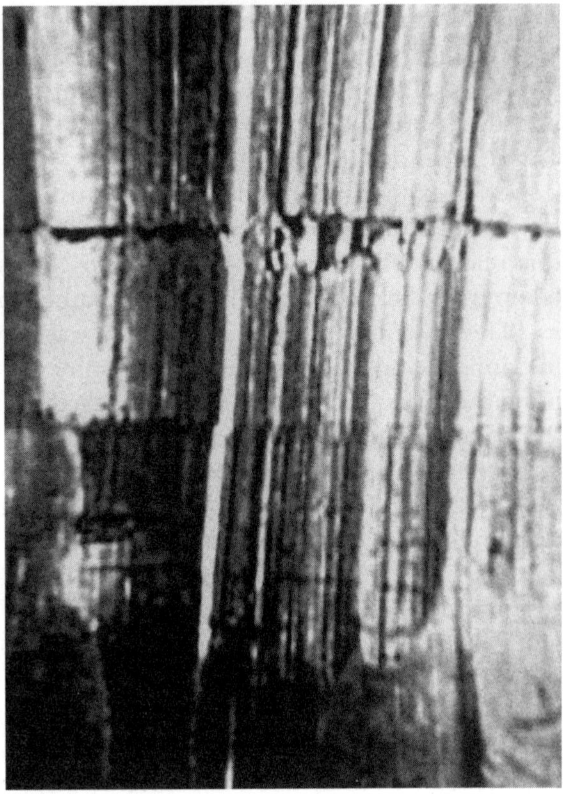

Image of two bullets viewed simultaneously through a comparison microscope. The right side of the photo shows the test bullet fired from the suspect's gun; the left side displays the bullet recovered from the crime scene. The matching marks or striations on each bullet indicate that they were fired from the same weapon.

computer program that links firearms evidence from different serial shooting investigations. Digital images of bullets from crimes are fed into computers and can be accessed instantly by any law enforcement agency that is hooked up to the system. Currently it is used by more than 450 firearms examiners and technicians worldwide, and as of October 1, 1999, there were more than 225,000 images in the system, which have led to more than 3,700 "cold hit" identifications.

IBIS (Integrated Ballistics Identification System), developed by Forensic Technology of Montreal, works along similar lines. Photographs of the surface areas of a bullet and the primer/firing pin area of fired cartridge cases are stored in databases, along with such details as caliber, rifling specifications, date of crime, and date of entry. The program then spits out possible matches, listing the results with the highest score at the top. An examiner can then call up the relevant images and compare them side by side on a monitor. If a possible match is found during this screening process, it is still only a guideline. The final determination must be made on a comparison microscope.

Roy Beck Jr.

Date: 1996
Location: Columbia, South Carolina

An autopsy on a woman found in the Owens Field district of Columbia, South Carolina, at dawn on November 13, 1996, revealed that she had been shot three times in the head with a .38-caliber pistol, most likely between 9:00 P.M. and midnight the previous night. The victim's handbag had been emptied and its contents strewn about. Two purses were found by the body. One contained just two dollars in change; the other was empty, suggesting that robbery had been a possible motive.

Other items recovered from the crime scene included three shell casings and two used bullets—strong evidence that the shootings had occurred here—and two empty Michelob Light beer bottles, which were sent for fingerprint analysis.

By chance the victim had a record for drunk driving. Her name was Virginia Russell, age thirty. On the last night of her life she had been visiting a friend's baby in the hospital when she was paged at 8:54 P.M. As she returned the page, she was overheard mentioning Jaco's, a bar in the Olympia area of Columbia.

Irregular phone calls were Virginia's stock in trade. As her family grudgingly admitted, she was a high-priced call girl who regularly carried several hundred dollars in her purse, thereby confirming suspicions that robbery had played at least some part in her murder.

The next day, Virginia's car was found dumped in Olympia. There was blood on the dashboard, and in the backseat there was yet another bottle of Michelob Light, still in its six-pack container. Like the other two bottles, this was also tested for fingerprints and any other trace evidence, but it proved to be equally uninformative.

At this point detectives noted similarities between this murder and a rape case that they were already investigating. At 4:00 A.M. on November 10, another prostitute had received a call through her escort service. The customer did not identify himself but gave his address as an apartment on Whitney Street in the Olympia area, close to where Virginia's body had been found.

After entering the apartment, the prostitute was jumped by a man wearing black, military-style boots who held a knife to her throat. When she asked if he had a gun, the man "smirked" and said, "Don't make me use it." He dragged her into the bedroom, sexually assaulted her, then stole $300 from her purse before throwing her out of the house.

The assailant had obviously gambled on the young woman not contacting the police, but he was mistaken, and she was able to lead them to the apartment where she had been assaulted. It was leased to Roy Beck Jr., a petty criminal with numerous convictions for burglary. When shown a computer-generated photo layout of men of similar age and appearance—white, midtwenties, about five feet, five inches, with dark hair—the victim had no hesitation in picking out Beck.

When police went to arrest Beck, they found the apartment abandoned. The power had been turned off because of nonpayment, and everywhere was littered with garbage and beer bottles. There was also ammunition for various guns, but none that matched the bullets that killed Virginia Russell.

Beck was eventually tracked to the apartment of a friend, Richard Bullard. This assumed greater significance when phone company records revealed that the customer who had paged Virginia Russell did so from this very apartment. Bullard unhesitatingly allowed police to search the place. He even pointed out a loaded .38 pistol, hidden beneath a sofa cushion, as well as a Rambo-style hunting knife that the rape victim identified as the one carried by her assailant. Bullard freely admitted that the gun was his but claimed he had lent it to Beck. It was the same story with a pair of black military-style boots that Beck often borrowed.

Ballistics tests confirmed that this was the firearm that had killed Virginia, and traces of her blood were found on the boots. Arrested and charged with murder, Beck swore that the real killer was Bullard. After all, the gun was registered in his name, and the boots belonged to him as well.

Having anticipated this line of defense, detectives had been busily pursuing another avenue of investigation: the beer bottles. Each year, Anheuser-Busch distributes about two hundred million bottles of Michelob Light, and each bottle is coded according to its source. The code for the bottles found at the crime scene was *17 Oct 96 WF58*. The first part of the code was self-explanatory: *W* stood for the Williamsburg plant; *F* for a particular line; while *58* specified that this beer had been bottled during the fifty-eighth fifteen-minute period of production that day. The bottles found at the crime scene and in Virginia's car shared the same code, meaning they had been bottled in the same fifteen-minute time slot, as did a bottle found at Beck's apartment.

This was the vital link connecting Beck to the death of Virginia Russell. When a human hair found on Virginia's skirt was found to match Beck's, it sealed an already damning case, especially as Bullard was able to provide a complete alibi for the time of the murder.

It transpired that Beck was previously acquainted with his victim. Police speculated that he had contacted Virginia and arranged to meet her at his old apartment, where they drank a couple of beers before driving to Owens Field. There, after guzzling yet more beer, Beck shot Virginia in the head, dragged her out of the car, and shot her twice more. Beck received a life sentence.

This had been no spontaneous crime. Four months earlier, on July 10, 1996, Beck had urged an acquaintance, Larry Barlow, to join him in a scheme to rape and rob employees of escort services. Barlow had told him it was "a crazy idea" and that he would have nothing to do with it.

Alphonse Bertillon (1853–1914)

Although Alphonse Bertillon's place in the annals of forensic detection is undisputed, his actual influence was of surprisingly limited duration. His father was president of the Paris Anthropological Society, while his brother Jacques became an eminent statistician, and it was through a combination of these two disciplines that Alphonse made his name. An undistinguished scholar—he was expelled from school in his teens—he fared no better in his first job, being dismissed from a Paris bank, and only parental intervention secured him a post as assistant clerk in the records office at the Prefecture of Police.

His duties included itemizing the particulars of arrested felons and entering them on a record card. The work fascinated him. He became obsessed with the notion that no two humans share exactly the same physical characteristics, and he evolved a system of recording bodily measurements that he called anthropometry.

He first categorized a person in one of three main head size types. Next, they were subdivided according to the dimensions of the bony parts of the body, in an eleven-step process. Special attention was paid to distinguishing marks such as moles, tattoos, and scars, and especially eye color. The hundreds of calculations that resulted provided the ammunition for Bertillon's boast that the chances of two people sharing identical physical characteristics were fewer than one in four million. Finally, he refined traditional photo mug shots to include two views—frontal and profile—a system still in use throughout the world.

In 1879 he published his findings. His employers were not impressed. Another three years of fine-tuning were demanded before the Paris police condescended to give what became known as bertillonage an extended trial. Given the absence of any coherent means of criminal identification, such official resistance is hard to fathom, but gradually Bertillon prevailed. In its first three years of use anthropometry was responsible for more than eight hundred arrests as criminals found that they no longer could hide their real identities from Bertillon's calipers and compasses.

One great advantage of bertillonage was the ease with which a criminal's details could be telegraphed to various parts of the country. Such speed led to the cracking of many cases that would otherwise have gone unsolved.

Bertillon's star shone brilliantly through the 1880s as police forces around the world embraced his revolutionary method. Appointed director of the Judicial Identification Service, his finest hour came in 1892 when he identified the notorious anarchist called "Ravachol" as mass murderer François Claudius Koenigstein. For this, Bertillon was awarded the Legion of Honor.

Such triumphs were head-turningly dangerous. Convinced of his forensic omnipotence, Bertillon meddled disastrously. It was his unhesitating

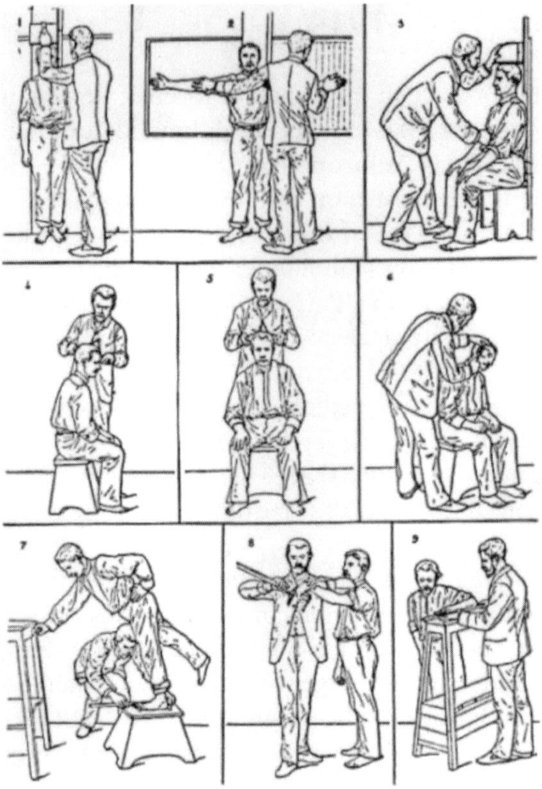

Left, diagram detailing Bertillon's instructions for accurately taking a *portrait parle* (speaking likeness). *Below,* a typical index card with the tabulated results.

identification of Alfred Dreyfus, a French army officer accused of passing secrets to Germany, as the author of a traitorous letter that led to the wholly innocent Dreyfus spending twelve years on Devil's Island before the real culprit was named. Other blunders followed.

By 1912 Bertillon was a spent force, having seen his beloved anthropometry swept aside by the superiority of **fingerprinting** as an identification tool. Marginalized and increasingly ignored, he faded into embittered obscurity until dying in Switzerland at age sixty.

Blood Spatter Analysis

Despite the pioneering groundwork of the Austrian criminologist **Hans Gross** as early as 1893—research that **John Glaister** improved upon in *Medical Jurisprudence and Toxicology* (1942)—only in recent years has blood spatter analysis entered the forensic mainstream. Much of the credit for this revival must go to the U.S. scientist Herbert Leon MacDonell.

The human body is a veritable bladder of blood. Puncture it, and the consequences can be unexpected and overwhelming. When Lady Macbeth, tormented by dreams of her victims, mused, "Yet who would have thought the old man to have had so much blood in him?" she was merely echoing the sentiments of countless killers through the ages. Shooting, stabbing, or blunt-force trauma—the three primary causes of crime scene spatter patterns—may all produce astonishing quantities of blood. It can flow from a wound, it can drip, it can fly through the air. Because blood is a uniform substance that responds well to the physics of fluid motion, the exit pattern it produces can often provide a revealing insight into just how the tragedy unfolded. When reviewing a crime scene, the skilled blood spatter interpreter will seek information regarding seven points:

1. The distance between the target surface and the origin of blood at the time of the bloodshed.
2. The point or points of origin of the blood.
3. The movement and direction of a person or an object.
4. The number of blows, shots, etc., causing the bloodshed and/or the dispersal of blood.
5. The type and direction of impact that produced the bloodshed.
6. The position of the victim and/or object during bloodshed.
7. Movement of the victim and/or object after bloodshed.

No matter how it exits the body, blood will always form some kind of pattern. This is largely dictated by the speed of impact and the distance of spatter travel, and it is usually classified in three ways.

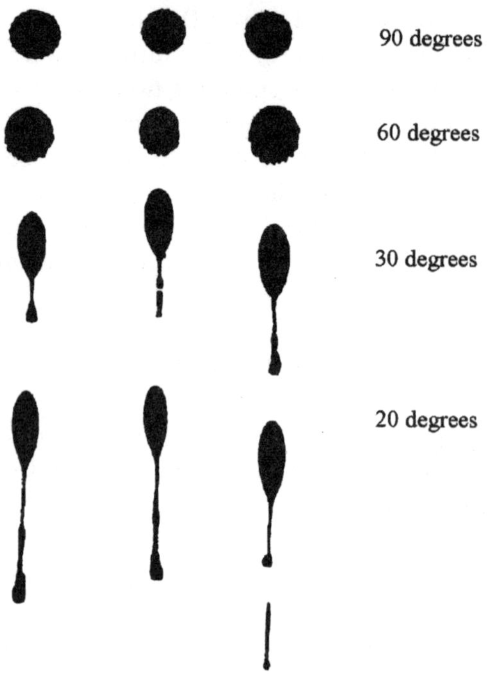

This diagram demonstrates how the angle of impact affects the stain shape. The tails on the stains point in the direction of travel.

Low-Velocity Spatter

Caused by an impact of fewer than 5 feet per second; blood cast off from a fist or a small weapon, in a dripping or splashing pattern. The resulting blood spots are mostly 4 to 8 millimeters in diameter.

Medium-Velocity Spatter

Caused by an impact of 25 to 100 feet per second; blows with a baseball bat, hammer, ax, or similar instrument. This produces blood spots typically about 4 millimeters in diameter.

High-Velocity Spatter

Caused by an impact of 100 feet per second; almost always gunshot but occasionally generated by contact with high-velocity machinery. The smallest of all, these blood spots are typically fewer than 1 millimeter in diameter, producing a fine, mistlike spray, much like an aerosol.

Another key factor in determining spatter type is surface texture. Blood hitting a hard, nonporous surface such as a varnished table tends to form smooth-edged stains. Jagged edges form when blood hits an absorbent surface such as a carpet.

When an assailant uses either a knife or a blunt object to strike someone, the first blow will often cause an open wound, and blood will adhere to the weapon. As the attacker withdraws the weapon in preparing to strike again, blood will fly from its surface. Blood also will be cast off the weapon as it is brought forward. In both instances the cast-off blood spatter pattern appears linear and the droplet size is generally quite small.

Gunshot wounds are equally illuminating. Here, there are two discrete patterns to look for. Forward spatter—the kind most often associated with exit wounds—is the product of blood traveling in the same direction as the bullet. Backspatter occurs when blood is blown back from an entrance wound by increased pressure from inside the tissues as the bullet impacts them. Often, with a firearm held in close proximity to the target, the inside of the barrel, as well as the outside of the gun, may sustain heavy backspatter.

The impact angle made by the blood as it strikes a flat surface can be highly informative. A droplet falling vertically will create a much more circular stain than one that falls obliquely. And the more the angle decreases, the more the stain is elongated. The angle of a given pattern can be determined fairly simply, as there is a mathematical relationship between the shape of the bloodstain and the angle at which it impacts a surface.

The shape of the individual drops in the overall pattern can reveal the direction from which the blood originated, as well as the trajectory of each drop. In the distinctive "teardrop" bloodstain the pointed end of the stain faces the direction in which the stain is traveling. When a blood drop strikes a surface with considerable force and at an oblique angle, a smaller droplet, or satellite, is cast off from the larger, "parent" drop, much like a breaking wave. This small wave travels close to the surface and in a very short distance begins to streak the surface in a straight line. Usually this stain appears as a very fine straight line, with a round end marking the point at which the droplet's forward motion was terminated.

Arterial bleeding can create a unique staining pattern. Because the heart is still beating, pressure in the arteries forces blood to pulsate from an open wound, causing an indiscriminate spurting pattern, rather than the flowing or dripping associated with other wounds.

When blood leaves the body, it may be transferred by direct contact to a weapon, another person, or an article of clothing. Transferred stains often appear as smears rather than distinct drops of blood. This can be very helpful in identifying the weapon used in an assault.

Even though blood spatter analysis is as much art as science, it does rely heavily on physics and the basic principles of geometry. Once all the answers to certain basic questions are in place, an experienced analyst usually can generate a three-dimensional model of the attack, often finding a key piece of information that may corroborate or contradict a suspect's story.

Hyppolyte and Lydie de Bocarmé

Date: 1850
Location: Mons, Belgium

Like many impoverished noblemen before him, Count Hyppolyte de Bocarmé decided that the best means of reviving the family's flagging fortunes and maintaining his lavish lifestyle was to marry a rich wife. His predatory gaze settled on Lydie Fougnies, the daughter of a local businessman, and in 1843 she joined him at his château near Mons, Belgium.

Unfortunately for Hyppolyte, his new bride's income was nowhere near as substantial as anticipated—just a few thousand francs a year—certainly not enough to satisfy his profligate appetites. Lydie shared his frustration over their mutual impecunity, and plans were hatched. The death of Lydie's father did bring about some improvement in her financial position, but the bulk of her father's fortune had passed to her brother, Gustave. There was one beacon of hope for the disappointed couple, however. In the event that Gustave died unmarried, his entire estate would pass to Lydie. Since Gustave was a sickly individual whose fragile health had been further undermined by the amputation of a leg, the count and countess prepared to bide their time, certain that before long, nature would aid their cause.

Then disaster struck: Gustave announced he was getting married.

On November 20, 1850, Gustave arrived at Château Bocarmé, eager to elaborate on his good fortune. That evening as they dined, Lydie had decided to forgo the help of the servants and serve the food herself. Sometime later a loud thud was heard. Lydie rushed from the room and cried out to a maid, "Gustave has fallen ill—I think he is dead." He had suffered, she said, a stroke.

Alarmed servants crowded into the room and witnessed the extraordinary sight of Hyppolyte forcing glass after glass of vinegar down his brother-in-law's throat, all to no avail. Gustave was quite plainly dead. Lydie busied herself by stripping her brother naked, rushing to the laundry with his soiled clothes, then returning to help her husband as he sluiced Gustave's body with yet more vinegar.

All night long, Lydie scrubbed the dining room floor. Behind her came Hyppolyte, scraping every inch of the wooden floorboards with a knife. Finally, on the following afternoon, the exhausted couple collapsed into bed. While they slept, the servants discussed the alarming events of the past twenty-four hours, eventually contacting a local priest who, in turn, summoned an examining magistrate, a man named Heughebaert.

Assisted by three doctors, Heughebaert visited the château and demanded to see the dining room. He found the fireplace filled with ashes from the mountain of books and papers that had been burned there, and the floor still littered with hundreds of wood shavings. Only after stern cajoling did Hyppolyte reluctantly agree to let the doctors see the dead body. It had been laid in a darkened bedroom, and Lydie did her best to keep it that way. Annoyed by her intransigence, Heughebaert pushed past and drew the curtains himself. Still, Hyppolyte attempted to cover the dead man's face. The reason for his coyness was soon apparent: black marks around the mouth and deep weals across the face provided ugly evidence that this was anything but a natural death.

An impromptu autopsy, held in the coach house, revealed burns in the mouth, throat, and stomach, and convinced the doctors that Gustave had died from ingesting some kind of corrosive liquid, most likely sulfuric acid. After placing the count and countess under arrest, Heughebaert ordered the removal of the bodily organs. The samples were sealed in jars of alcohol and sent to the man widely regarded as the greatest chemical analyst of the nineteenth century.

Belgian-born Jean Servais Stas had studied in Paris before taking up a position in 1840 as a chemistry professor at the École Royale Militaire in Brussels. His lifework was the accurate determination of atomic weights, but it is as the inventor of a method to identify the presence of alkaloid poisons in human tissue—a method that remains fundamentally unaltered to the present day—that forensic science remembers him best.

Stas speedily dismissed sulfuric acid as a cause of death, convinced that the vinegar had been used to mask some toxic alkaloid. But what? And how to find it?

Contemporary toxicology was then still in its infancy. Scientists knew how to identify metallic poisons such as arsenic in human tissue, but this required the tissue itself to be destroyed. Unfortunately, with alkaloid poisons a similar process destroyed the poison as well. What Stas did was to dissolve the substance of the stomach and intestinal tissues with alkaline solution and to isolate this matter by repeated washing and filtration. After this continual refinement, the samples were treated with ether and then evaporated. He labored throughout the winter of 1850 and into the following year, until finally he recovered an oily substance with the characteristics of nicotine.

Europe had been addicted to tobacco for almost three centuries before anyone realized that nicotine was a wonderfully efficient poison. Named after Jean Nicot, the sixteenth-century Frenchman who introduced tobacco to his homeland, nicotine was first isolated in 1828. It belongs to the alkaloid group of poisons that include morphine and strychnine, and it can kill in minutes. Symptoms include burning in the mouth and throat, confusion, nausea, and vomiting, followed by convulsions and respiratory arrest. A dose of 40 to 60 micrograms—roughly the amount found in two cigarettes—taken intravenously is enough to kill an average-size adult.

Stas was certain that Gustave had been murdered with nicotine, and he told Heughebaert to investigate whether the Bocarmés ever had nicotine in their possession. Proof was soon forthcoming. A gardener recalled helping the count prepare a type of eau de cologne using enormous quantities of tobacco leaves, and local pharmacists remembered Hyppolyte badgering them with questions about the toxic qualities of nicotine. The bodies of cats and ducks, which were discovered on the grounds, were sent to Stas for analysis—all contained nicotine. When Hyppolyte's secret laboratory was discovered behind some wall paneling, the game was up.

In May 1851 the couple stood trial for their lives. Each blamed the other. Lydie threw herself on the mercy of the court, pleading that Hyppolyte had forced her into the murderous conspiracy. He merely sniffed his disdain. The jury, reluctant to consign a woman to the guillotine, set Lydie free. Hyppolyte wasn't so fortunate: he lost his head to the triangular blade the following July.

The Booth Deringer

Date: 1997
Location: Washington, D.C.

One of the FBI's strangest modern-day cases was, ironically, inspired by the most notorious assassination of the nineteenth century. On April 14, 1865, an actor named John Wilkes Booth made his way to the state box at Ford's Theatre in Washington, D.C., and fired a single shot into the head of President Abraham Lincoln as he sat watching a play. In fleeing the crime Booth broke his leg, yet still managed to make his escape. The next day Lincoln succumbed to his injury. Another eleven days and Booth also was dead, shot by a Unionist soldier.

Before fleeing, Booth had dropped the murder weapon, a silver-inlaid Deringer, in the box where Lincoln lay bleeding. The gun was recovered and, in time, came to form a central exhibit at the Ford's Theatre National Historic Site, which had been established to commemorate the tragedy. For the thousands who visit the exhibition each year, it seems scarcely credible that such an insignificant scrap of metal and wood, fewer than six inches in length, could have so profoundly affected the course of history. And there was another question: by the mid-1990s some had begun to doubt whether this really was the murder weapon at all.

The misgivings had been sparked by bitter wrangling over the estate of a deceased New Englander who had once been a member of a burglary ring that operated throughout the northeast between the late 1960s and early 1980s. According to underworld scuttlebutt, the gang had actually broken into Ford's Theatre at some time in the 1960s, when security was far less stringent than is now the case, stolen the Booth Deringer, and left a replica in its place. If true, it meant that the genuine murder weapon was, in all likelihood, stashed in some private collection or locked away in a bank vault.

The Deringer pistol that killed Abraham Lincoln. Doubts about its authenticity were quashed by FBI forensics experts in 1997.

By the summer of 1997 the agency in charge of Ford's Theatre, the National Park Service, was sufficiently concerned to contact the FBI to request their assistance. Could they prove that the weapon on display really was the same pistol that killed Lincoln?

The pocket Deringer had a brief but colorful history. Manufactured by the Henry Deringer firearms factory in Philadelphia in the early 1850s, it became a favorite of gamblers and civilians seeking a compact, easily concealed firearm for use in personal defense. Its light weight and small size more than offset its single-shot limitations, which Deringer circumvented by selling the guns in pairs.

One drawback that Deringer could not overcome was the lack of a standardized caliber for its bullets. Each set of matched pistols came with its own bullet mold specific to that caliber—lose the mold, and the pistols were virtually useless. The Civil War only magnified this handicap. Overnight, repeating firearms and standardized ammunition were all the rage, tolling the death knell for single-shot percussion pistols such as the Deringer. By 1870 the factory had ceased production of the pocket pistol, which was soon relegated to the status of historical curio.

On July 28, 1997, the Booth Deringer pistol was removed, under guard, from its case in Ford's Theatre, and hand-carried the short distance to the FBI laboratory for examination. The Deringer that the Firearms-Toolmarks Unit of the FBI received was a typical example. It had a black walnut stock with checkering, a barrel with an octagonal upper portion and a round lower portion, an S-shaped trigger guard, a hammer, and fancy scrollwork on the metallic surfaces.

Because of the pistol's age and historical value, it was not possible to test-fire the weapon to obtain rifled bullet samples. Instead, the interior of the barrel, breech plug, and flash port of the firearm were cast with Mikrosil, a dental material used to reproduce three-dimensional impressions. From the resulting cast, FBI examiners determined that the barrel of the pistol was rifled with seven grooves in a left twist. This was extremely unusual, as most Deringers had a right-twist rifling pattern. How frequently this rifling aberration occurred during the production run of the original pistols is unknown. Land and groove impression measurements of 0.100 inch and 0.085 inch, respectively, were recorded.

The Firearms-Toolmarks Unit also examined the lead bullet that was extracted from Lincoln's brain during the autopsy. Though determined to be consistent in size and weight to the .41-caliber lead balls common to Deringers of this type, the lethal bullet had suffered too much corrosion and oxidation for accurate comparison with the Booth Deringer. Clearly, the scientists needed to look elsewhere.

Ever since the 1930s the Deringer had been photographed regularly, and technical descriptions of its construction and condition were ubiquitous. These noted a number of imperfections unique to the firearm, foremost of which was a significant fracture or crack in the forestock of the firearm, which bore evidence of previous repair. Impression toolmarks in the barrel above the fractured portion of the stock and an S-shaped defect in the metal of the pistol's barrel were additional discrete features found on the Deringer. Variations in the shading and grain of the pistol's black walnut stock were also noted for comparison purposes.

At this point the FBI's Special Photographic Unit was brought in to perform photographic superimpositions, using the Deringer and the historical images of the pistol. These showed a very close correspondence. All of those unique identifying characteristics—the swirl patterns in the grain of the stock, pit marks on the barrel, and other damage to the wood of the pistol—were plainly visible on the historical photographs.

The upshot of all this forensic wizardry was that the FBI was able to state, beyond a reasonable doubt, that the Deringer pistol currently displayed at Ford's Theatre is the same weapon that was photographed during the 1930s. It was a finding that laid to rest all those outlandish underworld claims that some master gang had stolen the pistol from the theater, then replaced it with a replica.

Brain Fingerprinting

One of the newest and most controversial tools in the battle against crime, brain fingerprinting, has been developed by an Iowa-based neuroscientist, Dr. Lawrence A. Farwell, and is predicated on the belief that the brain itself can be accessed much like a computer hard drive, to retrieve data stored there. The forensic theory of brain fingerprinting works like this: When people commit a crime, even if they go to quite extraordinary lengths to ensure that they leave no physical evidence, the one thing they can't do is erase the memory of that crime. It stays with them, logged in the brain. In the ordinary course of events this knowledge remains hidden from investigative view, but Farwell believes he has discovered the key that will unlock this secret and provide a window into someone's past visual experience.

A typical brain fingerprinting test requires the subject—not necessarily a suspect, the technology works equally well with witnesses—to don a headband equipped with sensors and then sit in front of a computer screen. A series of words or pictures pertaining to the crime in question is then displayed on the VDU, together with other, irrelevant words or pictures. As the exhibits flash by, the subject's electrical brain activity is monitored by the sensors and recorded by a sophisticated computer program.

The intention is to generate a specific brain-wave response called a MERMER (Memory and Encoding Related Multifaceted Electroencephalographic Response). This is elicited when the brain processes noteworthy information it recognizes. Contained within the MERMER is a well-known and scientifically established brain response known as a P300, and it is this that the examiner is focusing on. A P300 is a specific electrical brain wave, activated when a person sees a familiar object.

If a person looks at random pictures of weapons without activating a P300 wave, in all likelihood these objects are unknown to him or her. But say a suspected killer is shown a murder weapon, and a P300 wave is generated; then, according to proponents of brain fingerprinting, that person had some prior knowledge of the weapon. The fundamental difference between a perpetrator and an innocent person is that the perpetrator, having committed the crime, has the details of the crime stored in his brain, and the innocent suspect does not. This is what brain fingerprinting purports to detect scientifically.

Brain fingerprinting has nothing to do with lie detection. Rather, it is a means of determining whether someone has committed a specific crime or other act. No questions are asked and no answers are given during a brain fingerprinting test; it is a purely visual experience.

Of course, for the P300 wave to be truly effective, the prosecutor would have to show that the tested person didn't see that murder weapon in some other, innocuous way, such as in media accounts or as a result of being a bystander. This could be problematic, given the disturbing frequency of hoaxers and other time wasters.

Another significant drawback is that brain fingerprinting relies on utter compliance from the subject. Farwell concedes that brain-wave data can be obtained only if a person sits reasonably still and looks at the computer screen. Anyone seeking to skew the results would only have to act in an agitated fashion to render the test useless. Also, brain fingerprinting can be regarded only as an exclusionary tool, one that may eliminate but not implicate.

Despite lavish claims made for its success rate in detecting stored memory, thus far brain fingerprinting has received a cool response from U.S. courts. Only Iowa has permitted its introduction. In 1978 Terry Harrington was convicted of murdering a security guard, largely on the evidence of someone whose involvement in the crime was beyond doubt. As part of his application for a retrial, Harrington, who has always claimed he was elsewhere at the time of the crime, agreed to undergo a brain fingerprint test.

Farwell testified that Harrington did not have a P300 wave when showed key parts of the crime scene, but he did emit the P300 wave when shown scenes from his alibi, suggesting that he was unfamiliar with the crime. "Scientifically, we can conclude with a 99.9 percent confidence that the critical details of the crime are not stored in Harrington's brain," said Farwell. "This is like finding that Harrington's fingerprints or DNA do not match the fingerprints or DNA found at the crime scene."

After reviewing arguments from all sides, the judge, while conceding the possibility that P300 brain-wave measurement may have some scientific merit, felt that the totality of the evidence presented was insufficient to warrant overturning the original conviction. On March 12, 2001, Harrington's motion for a new trial was rejected.

Farwell continues to promote brain fingerprinting and claims many governmental allies, mostly in the field of national security. The FBI, appalled by the ease with which superspies Aldrich Ames and Donald Hansen repeatedly hoodwinked **polygraph** experts over several years, has allegedly sunk millions into the new technology. Other U.S. agencies, such as the CIA and various arms of the military, are also rumored to be exploring its uses. Given the current reluctance of courts to permit testimony based on this technology, it remains to be seen whether brain fingerprinting will emerge from its shadowy role as a security screening device to become a full-fledged crime-fighting tool, or if it is destined to remain a peripheral idiosyncrasy.

Earl Bramblett

Date: 1994
Location: Vinton, Virginia

On a Monday morning in August 1994, firefighters were called to a blazing Cape Cod–style house on East Virginia Avenue, a quiet thoroughfare in Vinton, Virginia. Inside the burned-out shell, on a couch, lay the charred and strangled body of Teresa Hodges, age thirty-seven. Upstairs, entwined on a bed, were her two daughters, Winter, age eleven, and three-year-old Anah. Each had been executed with two shots to the head. Their father, Blaine, was found in the master bedroom, his body partially hidden by a pile of laundry, a single bullet wound to his left temple.

Initial questioning raised the possibility of a murder/suicide scenario. One year earlier, Blaine Hodges had been convicted of embezzling from his employer, the U.S. Postal Service, and was facing a six-month prison term. It certainly seemed plausible: Hodges, depressed by the prospect of imminent jail, slaughtering his family, then torching the house before shooting himself in the head.

Except that, according to medical examiner Dr. David Oxley, Blaine had been dead for at least twelve hours when the rest of his family was murdered. And then there was the pistol found by Blaine's body. Although it was .22-caliber—as were the murder bullets—its barrel was missing. Clearly, Blaine could not have killed himself, then disassembled the weapon, nor could Teresa have shot the rest of her family, then strangled herself, which could mean only some third-party involvement.

As it was, the pistol was virtually unrecognizable. Despite the serial number having been filed off, it was identified as an Arminius. Made in Germany, Arminius handguns are rare in the United States, and they have an unusual feature: bullets fired from its barrel show eight lands and grooves, but the bullets that killed the Hodges family showed *six* lands and grooves. Therefore, it could not be the murder weapon. Seemingly, the killer had planted a red herring to throw off his pursuers.

Already police attention was focused firmly on just one man. Earl Bramblett was a close friend of the Hodges. On the Sunday afternoon before the fire, he had taken Teresa and the girls out fishing near Blue Ridge Parkway before dropping them off at home.

When interviewed, he unleashed a bilious tirade against Blaine Hodges: "The sorry son of a bitch! Had a beautiful family. He did them and he did himself." Since details of what happened inside the murder home were still privileged information, police wondered how Bramblett had acquired this knowledge. As the questioning intensified, Bramblett became confrontational, challenging the police to charge him with murder.

There wasn't sufficient evidence to do that, but investigators kept digging. A witness who'd passed the Hodges residence at 4:50 A.M.—when the fire started—described seeing an old pink pickup truck with a black tailgate speeding off. Coincidentally, Bramblett owned just such a truck, except his was white, though when seen under the street lighting outside the house, it did assume a pinkish hue. Inside the driver's compartment, police found .22-shell casings, of the same brand used in the murders.

When a bullet is fired, not only does the barrel impart distinctive and unique marks to the slug itself, but also the gun's firing pin makes an equally unique impression on the shell casing. In this instance a ballistics expert was able to find enough similarities to identify them as having been fired from the same gun that killed the Hodges.

Detectives now needed to know if Bramblett had the opportunity to commit the murders. He worked for a local silk-screen company called Brewco, and on the morning of the fire he had been scheduled for duty at five o'clock. His punched time card for that day had been crudely inked over. By applying infrared light, examiners were able to see through the obliterating ink and read the original entry: 5:08 A.M. Obviously Bramblett had been delayed that particular morning.

Piece by painstaking piece, the evidence mounted. When a fellow employee discovered a pair of Bramblett's jeans in a solvent tank at work, they were fished out and sent for analysis. After being soaked in a substance called pentane, the solvent was allowed to evaporate and the remaining chemical compounds were analyzed in a gas chromatograph. This showed the presence of an accelerant.

Behind the printing company, in a trash can, detectives found notes written by Bramblett about the Hodges family and an illustration with four stick figures; two of the figures were large, and two were small. One of the large figures and both of the small figures had arrows pointing at the head.

The oddest feature of this bizarre case were six dozen cassette tapes that Bramblett had given to his sister for safekeeping. An oral diary, they revealed his pathological hatred for Blaine Hodges: "I'm beginning to realize what a backstabbing, cheap motherfucker I got for a friend. He's trying to set me up." These accusations harked back to 1977, when Bramblett had been a suspect in the disappearance of two girls who were never found. Seven years later he had been charged with but acquitted of child molestation. Somehow Bramblett got it into his head that Blaine—desperate to escape his upcoming prison time—was hoping to get his sentence reduced by accusing him of molesting his daughter Winter. In Bramblett's twisted imagination Winter was a sexual temptress and a willing accomplice to this plot.

Elsewhere, developments took a startling turn when it was realized that the gun found at the scene *was* the murder weapon. Originally misidentified, it was actually an H & R model, with six lands and grooves, and its firing pin made the impressions on shell casings found at the crime scene and in Bramblett's truck.

At Bramblett's trial prosecutors portrayed a brutal killer who had already murdered Blaine Hodges when he took the family fishing on the Sunday. That night he finished them off one by one, then set the fire. The long-suspected sexual element in this case was confirmed when DNA analysis of a pubic hair found on the bed between Winter and Anah matched it to Bramblett.

Convicted of four murders, Bramblett was eventually put to death in the electric chair on April 9, 2003.

Gregory Brown and Darlene Buckner

Date: 1995
Location: Pittsburgh, Pennsylvania

Just after midnight on February 14, 1995, the Pittsburgh Fire Department was summoned to the Buckner family household at 8361 Bricelyn Street. Of the firefighters who rushed bravely into the blazing building, three never came out alive. Another three were grievously injured. None of the Buckners were injured. Because fatalities were involved, the Bureau of Alcohol, Tobacco, and Firearms (ATF) investigated the blaze, as is standard procedure in the death of firefighters.

The house was built on three levels, and most of the damage occurred in the basement and attic. The basement was where the fire appeared to have started. Once it had consumed all the available oxygen and combustible material, it had then shot to the top of the house through gaps between the walls. As there was no obvious electrical cause for the fire—no frayed wiring or burned-out appliances—attention centered on a pile of charred laundry found on the basement floor. Directly above this mound, the basement ceiling joists were burned out in a circular pattern about twelve feet in diameter. Such a distinctive burn pattern immediately aroused suspicions.

All burning materials produce energy at varying rates. Using a table of known values for burning textiles, ATF agents calculated that a pile of laundry that size would generate 176 kilowatts of energy. Another mathematical formula gave them the maximum height that flames from such a blaze would reach. In this case it was just thirty inches, several feet short of the ceiling. Clearly there was something wrong here. Even if the clothes had been stacked right up to the ceiling, they still could not have generated enough heat to cause such damage to the joists.

However, add a single gallon of gasoline to the laundry pile and suddenly there would be 1,300 kilowatts of energy at work, enough to project a flame thirteen feet in the air, right where the blackened joists showed the trademark "alligatoring effect" typical of gasoline.

Right, rear view of 8361 Bricelyn Street, the house in which three Pittsburgh firefighters tragically died. The sectional shot, *below,* gives some idea of the difficulties faced as fire swept up the stairs and between the walls.

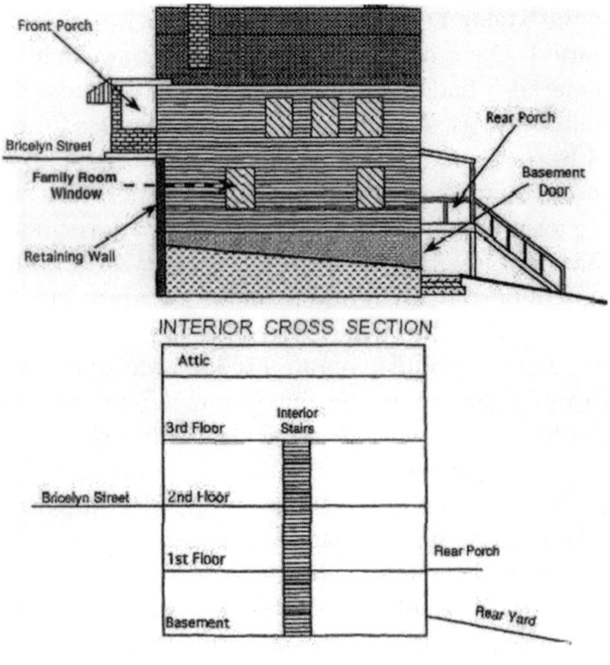

While investigators unraveled the mysteries of the increasingly suspicious fire, they learned that the Buckners were busy house hunting. They had rented 8361 Bricelyn since November 1990, but in the summer of 1994 they had tried to buy their own property, only for the deal to fall through because they lacked the necessary deposit. After four years of living without insurance, in November 1994, Darlene Buckner took out a renters' policy for $20,000. Just ten days after the blaze, she put down a deposit on the very house that had so taken her fancy the previous summer.

On February 27, Dr. James Quintere, of the University of Maryland, examined the fire scene and determined that the fire was incendiary in nature. Four days later, scientists at the ATF National Laboratory in Rockville, Maryland, confirmed what investigators had suspected: this was no accidental blaze. They had analyzed samples of laundry, wood, and cement chips from the burned-out house by heating them with charcoal-coated strips, which capture any hydrocarbon molecules, the main component of accelerants such as gasoline. Next, the charcoal strips were placed in a gas chromatograph. This would provide the chemical profile of the substance. No fewer than six samples showed clear traces of accelerant.

This finding put the Buckners under heightened scrutiny. What had begun as an attempted insurance fraud now looked very much like triple murder. By coincidence the Buckners' daughter had a history of minor skirmishes with fires, but she was eliminated as a suspect as investigators zeroed in on Darlene Buckner and her seventeen-year-old son, Gregory Brown.

On the night of the fire, Buckner said she and Brown had driven at about midnight to a nearby supermarket in her Dodge Dynasty, and had returned at 1:05 A.M. to find the house ablaze. But a neighbor, when interviewed, recalled seeing Brown standing in front of the Buckner residence, with smoke billowing from the rear basement window, prior to 12:22 A.M., when the first emergency vehicles arrived. In addition, a police officer distinctly remembered seeing Buckner alone in her car at a time when she claimed that Brown was accompanying her.

As the holes began to appear in Darlene's story, investigators worked up the following scenario: Sometime on February 13 Buckner removed a crate containing a one-gallon gasoline can from the trunk of her car and placed it on the front porch of her residence, saying she needed to make space so she could transport relatives to the doctor the next day. At the same time she said she had also removed a car seat and placed it inside the house.

That night, at approximately 1:05 A.M., she returned alone—not with Brown, as claimed—to find the street full of emergency vehicles. Forced to park some way off, she ran down Bricelyn Street toward her residence. Quite by chance, a police officer happened to glance inside Buckner's car at this time and noticed a car seat in the front of the vehicle. He inspected the car thoroughly to ensure that a baby had not been left behind. This was the same car seat Buckner claimed she had removed from the vehicle earlier in the day.

On March 15 Brown was jailed on unrelated narcotics and firearms violations. While behind bars, he allegedly bragged to other inmates of having set the fire that earned his family a $20,000 insurance payout.

Investigators needed another year to make their case, but on April 12, 1996, Buckner and her son were arrested and charged with three counts of homicide, arson, conspiracy, and insurance fraud. The following January they stood trial for triple murder. The court heard how an attempted insurance scam had backfired and left three officers dead. Brown was convicted on all charges and imprisoned for life. His mother was more fortunate. Acquitted of murder, she was found guilty of insurance fraud alone, for which she received three years probation, five hundred hours of community service, and a $5,000 fine.

Edwin Bush

Date: 1961
Location: London, England

Producing images of wanted criminals has always been one of the most difficult aspects of crime detection. In earlier times it generally meant a professional artist sitting down with either victims or witnesses, listening to their descriptions, and sketching out suggestions, all the while striving to create the closest possible likeness. The resulting "Wanted" poster, which was then circulated among the general public, has become one of the most enduring images from that era.

This rudimentary system, with added refinements as the skill level of police artists improved, survived well into the twentieth century. The first really significant advance didn't occur until the 1950s, when an American named Hugh MacDonald developed what came to be called Identikits. Instead of having someone draw a picture from scratch, MacDonald's method relied on hundreds of predrawn transparent sheets. The face was divided into different sections—hairline, forehead, eyebrows, eyes, nose, mouth, chin—and numerous line drawings were made of each physical feature. These separate face parts could then be fitted together according to the witness's description, much like a jigsaw puzzle. This system was not only much quicker than the old manual method but also allowed for far greater refinement of detail. This revolutionary idea quickly caught on with law enforcement agencies around the world. Although the first arrest ever made through use of the Identikit took place in Paris in 1959, its most notable early success came in London two years later.

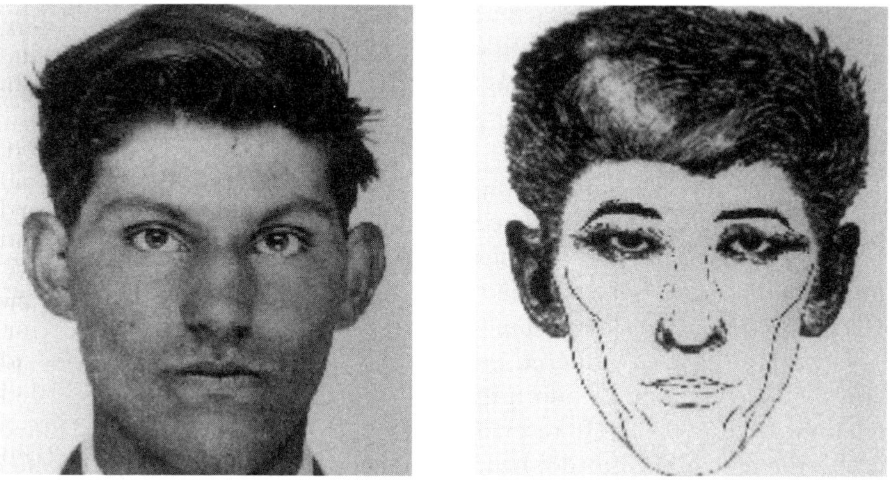

As a mug shot of the killer shows *(left)*, the first use of an Identikit in a British murder case produced a remarkable likeness *(right)*.

On March 3, 1961, the body of Elsie May Batten was found at the antiques shop where she worked in central London. She had been stabbed three times. An ivory-handled dagger remained in her chest, with its blade buried to a depth of eight inches. Police spoke to the store owner, Louis Meier, who recalled that the previous day an Asian customer had expressed considerable interest in a curved sword and several daggers, saying that he was looking for a present for his girlfriend. "He told me his father was an Indian," said Mr. Meier, "and that it was a common thing to carry a dagger in India." The man had left without buying anything, but on checking his inventory, Meier now realized that the sword was missing.

Meier was asked if he would assist in the compilation of an Identikit, a new addition to Scotland Yard's crime-fighting armory, one it had only recently taken delivery of, and which they were anxious to try out on a genuine case. While Meier trawled his memory cells, Detective Sergeant Raymond Dagg juggled the various transparencies until he came up with a finished likeness that Meier thought strongly resembled the customer.

In the meantime, a nearby gun dealer, Paul Roberts, had come forward to say that on the day of the killing, a young man had entered his store clutching a large curved sword that he wanted to sell. Roberts, too, agreed to work on an Identikit of the suspect. His resulting image so closely matched that derived from Meier's description that the police decided to circulate a photograph of both Identikits, side by side, to every police force in the country as well as to the media.

Publication of the Identikits caused enormous interest, both in the national press and among police forces, and it was a member of the latter who first put the system to practical use. On March 8, Police Constable John Cole was patrolling the red-light district of Soho, not far from where the murder had occurred, when he spotted a young man who he thought strongly resembled the Identikit picture. Immediately, Cole detained the man and his female companion.

The man gave his name as Edwin Bush, a twenty-one-year-old petty criminal with a long string of sentences for minor offenses. During interviews, he conceded that the Identikit pictures being circulated in newspapers did look a bit like him, but he denied anything having to do with the murder. His girlfriend was quickly eliminated from inquiries and released.

The investigation gathered pace. Bush's mother also was interviewed, and she stated that on the morning of the murder she thought her son had left for work at 7:30 A.M. However, unknown to her, Bush had already claimed that at the time of the murder he was at home with her. Unwittingly, she had destroyed her son's alibi and with it his only chance of escaping the gallows.

Bush was placed on an identity parade. Louis Meier, brought in to view the lineup, failed to make a positive identification. Paul Roberts, however, had no such doubts. He immediately picked out Bush as the man who had tried to sell him the sword. After being charged with murder, Bush decided to make a full statement, admitting everything.

At his trial, Bush admitted killing Elsie Batten but claimed he had been provoked beyond endurance. He had, so he said, returned to the store fully intending to buy one of the daggers, only to fly into a rage when Batten had chided him for the amount of time he was taking. During an exchange of words, said Bush, Batten had resorted to a vicious racial slur, whereupon he had grabbed the knife instinctively and stabbed her. The jury refused to swallow any of this and convicted Bush of murder. He was hanged on July 6, 1961.

Since that time, the basic Identikit system has been largely superseded by more advanced methods. One of these—Photofit—uses not drawings but actual photographs of facial areas. This provides for a much more realistic image. In the latest update—E-FITs—the whole process has been computerized, allowing for literally millions of individual colors, shades, and shapes to be blended together until a reasonable likeness is achieved. Whatever the name and whatever the system, the standardized compilation of images of wanted persons continues to be one of the most useful crime-fighting tools yet devised.

Brian Calzacorto

Date: 1990
Location: Largo, Florida

Neighbors who lived at Laurie Colannino's apartment complex in Largo, Florida, knew her as a fun-loving twenty-three-year-old cocktail waitress and aerobics instructor who was absolutely devoted to her cats. They became used to seeing her front door left wide open so the cats could come and go as they pleased. Some questioned the wisdom of such a cavalier disregard for one's personal security. Those fears came to grim fruition on the afternoon of January 2, 1990.

Laurie was talking on the phone with a friend, Scott Kelley. As they chatted, something obviously startled her. Kelley heard a scream, followed by a muffled male voice in the background, then the line clicked dead. Frantic with worry, he raced to Laurie's apartment complex and persuaded the manager to open her door, which was ominously closed. Inside, they found Laurie facedown in a pool of blood. She had been raped, strangled, and stabbed fifteen times through the heart.

With no obvious solid suspect in the case, initial inquiries slowly fizzled out and the crime was put on the back burner. And then in 1994, prompted by recent advances in DNA microtesting, a "cold case" team revived the investigation. Detectives returned to the apartment complex and interviewed more than 170 males who knew or lived near Laurie. All were eliminated except one.

Brian Calzacorto had lived across the courtyard from Laurie at the time of her death—in direct eye line of her apartment—and he lived there still. But he proved to be maddeningly elusive. Each time detectives called, he was out. Nor did he respond to their written requests that he contact them. And then he disappeared.

In July 1994 his brother, Alfred Jr., filed a missing-persons report. Seven weeks later Brian, a shoe salesman, was arrested on a charge of stealing from the store where he worked in Clearwater, Florida. When asked to provide a DNA sample so he might be eliminated from the Colannino inquiry, he refused, saying that his experience at the time of his father's death in Donora, Pennsylvania, in 1986 had left him with a residual distrust of police pressure.

On October 27 of that year, Calzacorto's father, Alfred Sr., a sixty-year-old police officer, had been found dead in bed at home. Initial indications that the cause of death had been a brain hemorrhage altered drastically when a funeral director found a bullet hole in the dead man's skull. The next day Brian Calzacorto fled to Florida. At a subsequent inquiry various family members invoked their Fifth Amendment right against self-incrimination no fewer than 133 times, and Alfred Jr. was charged with tampering with evidence, but the case was left unresolved. Shortly thereafter, Alfred Jr. had also moved to Florida and was living in Tampa at the time of Laurie's death.

Frustrated by Brian Calzacorto's annoying and wholly constitutional intransigence, investigators were once again obliged to temporarily close the file on the death of Laurie Colannino.

Five more years passed, and then it was decided to put Brian Calzacorto under intense surveillance. Investigators staked out his Tampa apartment and watched as Calzacorto carried two bags of trash out to a Dumpster. Rummaging through the bags, investigators struck paydirt: a protective screen from an electric razor and several Marlboro cigarette butts. When subjected to DNA testing, all these items provided a match with semen found on the body of Laurie Colannino. Apparently the killer of Laurie Colonnino had been caught at last.

But there was just one problem: Brian and Alfred Calzacorto were identical twins. And this meant that they shared the same DNA. Unlike a fingerprint, which is unique to every individual regardless of genetic makeup, **DNA typing**—normally so conclusive when dealing with personal identification—comes completely unstuck when confronted by identical twins. It cannot differentiate between the two. In DNA terms they are one person sharing two chemically identical bodies (this does not apply to non-identical twins).

Back in 1994 Alfred, made aware that his brother was a homicide suspect, had declined to provide a DNA sample. Now, years later, a similar raid on *his* garbage yielded a rich harvest of DNA material, most notably a toothbrush and several disposable razors. These also provided a DNA match with samples from the crime scene with a certainty put at 1 in 1.49 quintillion (a colossal number that has sixteen zeros).

Detectives knew that one of the twins was a brutal killer. But which one?

Everything pointed toward Brian; he lived within one hundred yards of the victim, and he worked just a few blocks away. Alfred, by contrast, lived more than twenty miles away. A check at the Tampa credit union where Alfred worked showed that although worker attendance records for the day of Laurie Colannino's death had long since been destroyed, the supervisor confirmed Alfred as a "model employee," with an exemplary attendance record. He could scarcely recall him ever taking a day off.

Brian's place of work had similarly disposed of its worker records, but he was known as a far more erratic employee. On April 18, 2001, detectives decided they had enough to charge Brian Calzacorto with the murder of Laurie Colannino.

At Calzacorto's trial, prosecutor Bill Loughery told the jury, "This is an extremely unique situation. . . . I don't think there is another case in the country, maybe even the world, like it." It was his job to convince the jury that the state was trying the right man.

Both twins testified, and both denied knowing the victim. Neither could account for how their DNA material came to be on the victim's body.

Defense attorney Michael Schwartzberg, while admitting that DNA found on Laurie's body pointed toward his client, noted ominously, "Except in this case . . . I can walk out the door and get a guy who has the exact same DNA as Brian Calzacorto." He then turned his guns on Alfred Calzacorto, citing his refusal to provide a DNA sample all those years before as the act of a guilty man.

Under cross-examination, Alfred remained steadfast, and on April 25, 2003, after five hours of deliberation, the jury convicted Brian Calzacorto of first-degree murder. Following the penalty phase of this unique trial, he was sent to prison for life.

Stuart Campbell

Date: 2001
Location: East Tilbury, England

In the United Kingdom, about 76 percent of the population owns a cell phone, with few realizing that the familiar instrument in their hands is now a major crime-fighting tool. Never was this more vividly highlighted than in the summer of 2001. Danielle Jones was a typically avid teenage user of the technology, using it to send text messages to her friends and to keep in touch. One of those acquaintances was her uncle, Stuart Campbell, age forty-three. At first, fifteen-year-old Danielle was flattered by the attention that he lavished upon her, and she regularly replied to the avalanche of text messages he fired her way, but then doubts began to creep into her mind, and she tried to put some distance between herself and her persistent uncle.

And then Danielle vanished. On the morning of June 18, she left her home in East Tilbury, Essex, en route to St. Clere's School, where she was a pupil. She never arrived. Witnesses later came forward to say that they had seen her talking to a man in a blue Ford van, one very like the van that Campbell used in his job as a self-employed builder. Campbell denied all knowledge of Danielle's whereabouts, insisting that he had been buying equipment at a builders' merchant some thirty minutes' drive away, an alibi supported by his wife.

In the meantime, concerned family members and friends bombarded Danielle's cell phone with text messages, pleading for her to contact them. Only two replies were sent, both to Campbell. In one she claimed to have run away because of trouble at home. The other said, "I'm fine. Thanks for being the best uncle ever. Tell Mum I'm sorry. Love, Dan."

Discreet inquiries soon revealed a sinister side to Campbell's character. For months he had been fixated on Danielle, pestering her to pose for photographs, maybe even enticing her into an illicit sexual relationship. It wouldn't have been the first time that Campbell had shown an appetite for young girls. In 1976 he had been convicted of robbing a sixteen-year-old; then, in 1989, came a suspended jail sentence for improperly detaining a fourteen-year-old.

Eventually there was enough suspicion to warrant searching Campbell's house. In the loft officers found a green canvas bag containing lingerie (including a pair of stockings stained with blood), camera equipment, sex toys, condoms, and handcuffs. While these were dispatched for analysis, the search continued. Hidden around the house were more than fifteen hundred photographs of girls aged under sixteen, mostly taken by Campbell, who had duped his victims into posing by telling them that they were destined to become models.

His computer was also packed with pedophile pornography downloaded from the Internet. There was also a diary that recounted in intimate detail his obsession with the girl he called "Princess," even down to chronicling the number and content of text messages that he and Danielle had exchanged.

It all painted a damning picture; yet, even when analysis of the lingerie revealed traces of Danielle's DNA mingled with that of Campbell's, there was still nothing concrete to link him to her disappearance.

Without a body or a crime scene, police turned to cell phone records to find the evidence they felt sure would convict Campbell. Each time a cell phone is used, it leaves a "radio footprint," one that experts can track to the location of that phone. In this instance telecommunications specialists were able to say that Danielle's phone was in the same location as the phone used by Campbell when the two messages ostensibly from Danielle were received by him. Everything pointed to Campbell having faked the messages in hopes of throwing off the investigators.

The radio footprint on Campbell's phone was also crucial in destroying his alibi for the time of Danielle's disappearance. Once confronted with this evidence, and made fully aware of the horror of her husband's activities, his wife abandoned the misplaced loyalty she had shown earlier and retracted the statement corroborating his alibi.

Danielle's two alleged phone calls kept coming back to haunt Campbell. In a landmark decision in a British murder trial, forensic linguistics testimony was introduced regarding the content of the text messages purportedly sent by Danielle. In these two messages, small but significant differences were noted when compared to Danielle's normal texting style. For example, she normally spelled the word "what" as "wat" when texting; but after she vanished, the spelling changed to "wot."

These discrepancies, combined with a wealth of circumstantial evidence, were enough for the jury. On December 19, 2002, Campbell, dressed in a somber blue suit, showed no emotion as the guilty verdict and sentence were returned. He paused only to pick up a file before being led away to begin a life sentence. The body of Danielle Jones has still not been found.

The radio footprints left by cell phones are becoming an increasingly common feature of British trials as unwitting criminals use cell phones during illegal activities. Not only can telecommunications experts establish where a handset was used, they also can uncover deleted text messages. Generally, cases involving phone threats, reckless driving, or calls made by bragging offenders are among the most likely to rely on phone analysis.

A new system known as Celldar adds yet another crime-fighting dimension to cell phone technology. It works by using receivers attached to cell phone masts. These "see" the shapes made when radio waves emitted by cell phone masts meet an obstruction. Signals bounced back by immobile objects, such as walls or trees, are filtered out by the receiver, thus allowing anything mobile, such as cars or people, to be tracked. Users will be able to focus on areas even hundreds of miles away and bring up a display showing any moving vehicles and people. An individual with a portable unit little bigger than a laptop computer could even use it as a "personal radar" covering the area around the user. Researchers are working to give the new equipment X-ray vision: the ability to "see" through walls and look into people's homes.

Obviously such intrusive capabilities will cause concern and outrage in certain quarters, but the likelihood is that cell phone technology will play an increasingly important part in the fight against crime, especially if, as expected, all cell phones will eventually have built-in satellite-locating devices.

Francis Camps (1905–1972)

Forensic pathology has never seen anyone like Francis Camps. In the mortuary he was a whirlwind, operating at breakneck pace—no more than ten minutes for a "regular" autopsy—often eschewing basic standards of hygiene and sanitation in a reckless, almost foolhardy fashion that made observers blanch and rivals seethe. Being paid per corpse turned Camps into a human conveyor belt and helped finance an exotic lifestyle populated by top-quality restaurants and fine wines. He was fast, erratic, vindictive toward his colleagues, and ill disposed to having his opinion contradicted. He was also capable of quite exceptional brilliance.

He was born into a comfortable middle-class family in southwest London, the son of a general practitioner with a lucrative practice, and there was never any doubt that Camps would maintain the medical connection. After graduation he qualified as a doctor at Guy's Hospital Medical School, then joined a thriving clinic in Chelmsford, Essex. There he took his first tentative steps in police work—minor cases mostly, but it was enough to convince him where his true vocation lay.

Like every other forensic pathologist in England at this time, Camps's early years were spent in the shadow of the legendary **Sir Bernard Spilsbury.** In the race to fill the great man's shoes following his suicide in 1947, Camps soon emerged as a leading candidate, together with his close friend **Keith Simpson.** At first the two worked harmoniously, but relations soon soured as Camps grew resentful of the way in which major cases tended to gravitate in Simpson's direction. This was no accident. The police and the courts preferred Simpson's cool, urbane witness stand manner, with no histrionics and above all no surprises. On the other hand, Camps, flashy and mercurial, was thought to be untrustworthy. Camps never forgave Simpson, whom he felt had deliberately engineered this fall from grace, and for the next twenty years the two feuded bitterly.

No one ever accused Camps of being pleasant; he was a bully to those who worked under him, and arrogant and overbearing to his peers. The one incongruity in what was an otherwise wholly self-centered personality was a laudable willingness to fight for the underdog. He investigated miscarriages of justice—both real and imaginary—with a bulldog-like tenacity. Ultimately this led to his downfall, when his disastrous foray into the Steven Truscott case (see *A Question of Evidence,* Wiley, 2003) resulted in a very public humiliation at the hands of his mortal enemy, Keith Simpson.

Camps never recovered from the mauling handed out to him in that Canada courtroom in 1966, and he retired just over three years later. By the end of his career he had performed close to 88,000 autopsies. His final years were marred by bad health and by an irrational fear that he would be autopsied by the hated Simpson. The end, when it came in 1972, was the result of a stomach ulcer. No post mortem was necessary.

Significant Cases

1949	Brian Donald Hume
1949	Nora Tierney
1953	Frederick Emmett-Dunne*
1953	John Christie
1953	Albert Kemp
1953	Ernest Elmes
1953	William Pettit
1954	Styllou Christofi
1955	Michael Queripel
1957	Mary Wilson
1958	Marcus Marymont
1958	Edith Chubb
1959	Ronald Marwood
1960	Sarah Jane Harvey
1961	Willis Boshears

1961	Hendryk Niemaszes
1966	Steven Truscott

*Profiled in this book.

The Sir Roger Casement Diaries

Date: 2000
Location: London, England

On April 21, 1916, at a time when millions of Allied soldiers were dying in the mud of Flanders, a fifty-one-year-old former British consul and human rights campaigner, Sir Roger Casement, was arrested in his native Ireland on charges of high treason. He had just been set down on Irish soil by a German U-boat, and in his possession were details of an impending shipment of arms from Germany and information concerning how to contact German spies in Britain.

At his trial in London, Casement, having made little attempt to deny that he had sought to foster an Irish uprising against the ruling British government, was sentenced to death. Because of his standing and achievements, he attracted significant support from such luminaries as George Bernard Shaw and Sir Arthur Conan Doyle, both of whom campaigned for clemency. But the British government was determined that the law should follow its course. Other German agents were executed without demur or public clamor, and the authorities were anxious to fend off any accusation that there was one law for the influential and another for the insignificant.

In what can be described only as a shameful act of political manipulation, the British government covertly provided various dignitaries of the times—including King George V—with extracts from five diaries allegedly recovered from Casement's lodgings in London. This was literary dynamite! Packed with highly graphic accounts of homosexual encounters with Amazonian Indians and male prostitutes, they utterly destroyed Casement's reputation and with it any hope for a reprieve. On August 3, 1916, he was hanged at Pentonville Prison in London.

Only in 1936 did rumors of the so-called Black Diaries surface publicly, when William J. Maloney, an American doctor, made a direct allegation of foul play in *The Forged Casement Diaries.* At its heart was an allegation that the British intelligence service (MI5) had forged the diaries to discredit Casement, an accusation that strengthened and persisted throughout the remainder of the century. In his homeland, where Casement was revered as a freedom fighter, and where any hint of homosexuality was viewed with horror, the diaries were perceived as yet another disgraceful attempt by the British to stain a great Irish hero. The martyrdom was complete in 1965 when Casement's remains were reinterred in Dublin.

Sir Roger Casement was hanged for treason in 1916. After decades of doubt and distrust, the authenticity of his notorious "Black Diaries" was finally proved in 2002.

Still the argument raged. Only in 1959 did the British government actually admit to the existence of the diaries, when they were made available to historians. They were finally released by the Public Record Office in 1994, with their authenticity still in question. Certainly MI5 had the political motivation to fake the diaries—and the technical expertise, as well—but there was one glaring anomaly: why go to the time and considerable trouble of producing five volumes of highly detailed homoerotic ramblings when just a couple of incriminating letters would have been equally damning?

In May 2000 the Irish prime minister, Bertie Ahern—a longtime supporter of the notion that Casement had been gravely traduced—requested that an independent forensic examination of the Black Diaries be made, to establish once and for all whether Casement had written them.

The investigation was headed by Bill McCormack, a professor of literary history at Goldsmith's College at the University of London. He assembled a seven-person team for the project and delegated primary responsibility for handwriting comparisons to Dr. Audrey Giles, an internationally recognized figure in the field of document forensics.

In reviewing the diaries Giles was faced with three possibilities: Casement had written the diaries in their entirety; they were a total forgery; or—and this was the most popular view among conspiracists—the existing Casement diaries had been doctored by MI5 to include the homosexual passages.

Undisputed examples of Casement's handwriting came in the form of letters held by the London School of Economics, and even a superficial analysis revealed several similarities between these and the diaries. There was the idiosyncratic manner in which Casement wrote the letter "e," for instance, almost in the Greek form, and the way he flattened out the letter "s," but most distinctive of all was his habit of joining words together. In time Giles would inspect every single character in the five-volume diary, but nothing in the initial examination suggested any fraudulent hand at work.

By great good fortune, Casement had kept another contemporaneous account of his activities—the so-called White Diary, a two-hundred-page account held by the National Library of Ireland, and a few pages from this were sent to Giles to assist in her efforts. These permitted direct comparisons of entries made on the same day. As an example, Giles chose October 10, 1910. When mixed electronically, by overlaying one image on top of another, the handwriting was shown to be uniform throughout.

More than a year of detailed forensic tests were carried out, not only on the handwriting and the ink but also on the paper on which the diaries were written. The individual pages were subjected to ESDA analysis (see **questioned documents**). This found no evidence to indicate that the diaries had been tampered with in any way—no impressions, deletions, or disguised amendments.

On March 12, 2002, the team revealed its findings. Professor McCormack declared the diaries to be "exclusively the work of Roger Casement's hand, without any reason to suspect either forgery or interpolation . . . the diaries are genuine throughout." Oddly enough, an identical conclusion had been reached by the Irish Republican leader Michael Collins when he inspected the diaries in 1921.

For the final word on this thorniest of topics, we need only turn to Casement himself. In a letter to his uncle on June 6, 1916, from his prison cell, he wrote: "Some day a rather interesting account of my doings will see the light, I hope, although I shall not be able to revise the proofs, but it will show a side to the picture that people now in this jaundiced time don't understand—I have left a pretty full record."

Chromatography

Most samples (including trace evidence) submitted to the forensic chemist for analysis are in a contaminated or impure state—that is, they are a mixture of several different substances. To identify and quantify these individual chemical compounds, scientists turn to the process known as chromatography. Although nowadays a highly sophisticated laboratory tool, chromatography has its origins in much humbler surroundings. Early European dye makers were the first to adopt its principles, albeit in a rudimentary and unintended fashion. They found that they could test their dye mixtures by dipping strings, pieces of cloth, or filter paper into a dye vat, then watching closely as capillary action drew the solution up the inserted material. At various intervals, bands of differing colors appeared on the material, and by studying these, the manufacturers could gauge the strength of their dyes.

This phenomenon was further explored by chemists in nineteenth-century Germany, but it wasn't put on a firm scientific footing until the Russian botanist Mikhail Tsvet began a series of experiments in 1906. Eager to find a method of separating plant pigments, he developed the basic principles that apply to this day.

Tsvet's technique was very simple. He packed a vertical glass column with an adsorptive material such as alumina, silica, cellulose, or charcoal; added a solution of the plant pigments to the top of the column; and washed the pigments through the column with an organic solvent. As they traveled through the column, the pigments separated into a series of discrete colored bands divided by regions entirely free of pigments. Because Tsvet worked with colored substances, he called the method chromatography (from the Greek meaning "color writing").

In principle, all chromatography involves two phases: a mobile phase, in which the substance is dissolved in an appropriate solvent; and a stationary phase, in which the sample is passed through a finely divided adsorbent. As the sample migrates, its molecules become the subject of a fierce battle between the stationary phase and the mobile phase, which ends with elements in the sample attaching themselves to the adsorbent. Because each compound has its own distinctive adsorption rate, this adherence takes place at different times. By plotting these variances on a chart, then comparing that chart with a set of known reference values, the compound can be identified.

This, then, is the broad definition of chromatography. Modern improvements have refined the basics into many subdisciplines, such as paper chromatography, thin-layer chromatography, and gas chromatography.

Paper chromatography uses a sheet of filter paper as the stationary phase. The lower end of this paper is impregnated with a suitable solvent, which moves upward by capillary action. A spot of the sample to be analyzed is placed alongside it. As the solvent passes over the sample spot, it carries with it the various components of the sample. When the solvent finally reaches the top, the paper is dried, and the separate spots are located by spraying with a suitable reagent, or illuminating with UV light. Once again reference values are brought into play. If a spot from the unknown sample has moved the same distance as a known substance, this particular component of the mixture can be readily identified. There are two significant advantages with paper chromatography. The first is cost—it is inexpensive. The second lies in the fact that it will work on minuscule quantities of material.

Although thin-layer chromatography was first discussed in Russian studies in 1938, it did not receive wide scientific recognition until 1956, when the German chemist Egon Stahl began intensive research on its application. In this variation a glass plate or plastic sheet is coated with a thin layer of a finely ground adsorbent, usually silica gel or alumina, that is mixed with a binder such as starch or plaster of Paris. The test sample is deposited at a spot near one end of the plate, and a suitable solvent is allowed to rise up the plate by capillary action. Components of the sample become separated from one another because of their different degrees of attachment to the coating material on the plate or sheet. The solvent is then allowed to evaporate, and the location of the separated components is identified, usually by application of reagents that form colored compounds with the substances. Thin-layer chromatography has a distinct advantage over paper chromatography in that the slide is able to withstand strong solvents and color-forming agents.

Gas chromatography, first carried out in Austria in 1944 by the chemist Erika Cremer, is used for the separation of mixtures of liquids and gases. As such, this makes it highly suitable for toxicological analysis, identifying suspected poisons. This format dictates that the stationary phase is coated on fine clay or glass beads, which are packed in a steel tube, and the mobile phase is the actual mixture to be analyzed. Liquids must be heated above their boiling point, and the steel tube must also be heated. Various types of detectors measure the emerging fractions.

An offshoot of this method, called pyrolysis gas chromatography, is used to analyze solid samples such as fibers and paints. The sample is heated to a temperature at which it decomposes in gaseous components. The resultant trace from the detecting device is usually sufficiently characteristic to be compared with that from known materials and thus identified. Pyrolysis gas chromatography is especially useful in arson cases, to test for the presence of accelerants.

No matter what the sample—be it semen, sweat, blood, explosive residues, poison, hairs, fibers, fragments of paint, glass, paper, ink, earth, or sand—it can be identified by this technique. Such ubiquity has made chromatography an ever-present tool in the fight against crime.

Robert Churchill (1886–1958)

Right from his earliest days, this Londoner was surrounded by guns. At age fourteen he went to work at the shop owned by his uncle, E. J. Churchill, a West End gunsmith who had already begun to dabble in ballistics on behalf of Scotland Yard. When his uncle died in 1910 he inherited the company, only to find that it was virtually bankrupt.

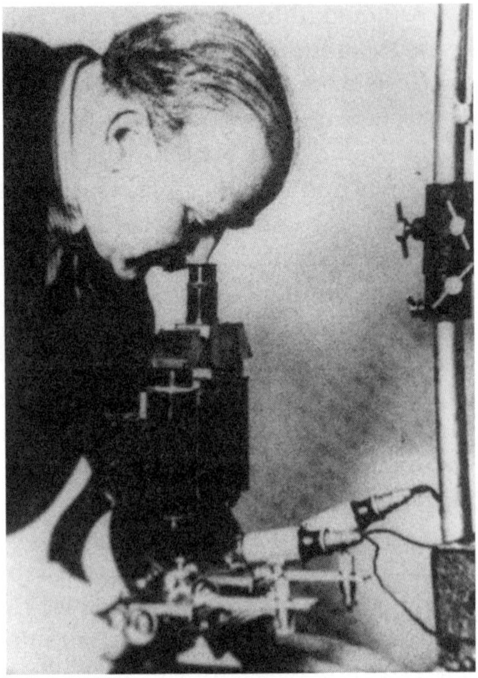

Robert Churchill, one of the earliest ballistics experts, seen here examining bullets through a comparison microscope.

Churchill threw himself wholeheartedly into saving the business he loved. A born salesman, he primarily sold sporting guns for use on the pheasant and grouse moors, to customers who included the cream of British society. He himself was a fine shot—but if shooting was his passion, then ballistics was his avocation. Churchill studied firearms as no one had before him, logging their quirks and characteristics, determined to become the greatest authority the world had yet seen.

In the soundproof basement of his London gun shop, he must have test-fired thousands of rounds of ammunition in the course of his long career, measuring distances and angles, squirreling away his results in the filing cabinets that lined the walls, alongside photographs of dead bodies, test bullets, and yellowing press clippings.

Many of those clippings featured himself. He surfaced at a time when science was performing near miracles in the courtroom, and newspapers were hungry for forensic celebrities. Churchill suited their needs perfectly, as they suited his. An unabashed egoist, he reveled in the recognition that came his way, and as his fame grew, so did the sale of his exquisite handmade shotguns, to the point where Churchill became a very wealthy man. He was proudest of the fact that he rarely received a penny for his testimony. He asked only for expenses; the opinion came gratis. And the courts were only to glad to hear it.

Like other forensic pioneers, he was not immune to an occasional lapse in judgment, and many of the utterances that colored his testimony would nowadays be unthinkable, but in the British courtroom he invented the ground rules for ballistics testimony. Squatly built and ferociously competitive, he feuded constantly with other gunmakers and ballistics experts, most of whom resented his public status. On many of his greatest cases he worked in tandem with **Sir Bernard Spilsbury,** and between them they made a terrifying duo, implacable and unbending in their opinions, unshakable in their confidence.

Churchill's later years were a disappointment. As courts and juries became more skeptical of the kind of blinkered dogmatism that earlier expert witnesses had routinely delivered as gospel truth, the telephone stopped ringing. Resentful of this diminished status, he retreated to the grouse moors, comforted only by the knowledge that at least no one could undermine his hard-won status as the undisputed father of British ballistics analysis.

Significant Cases

1912	George Mackay ("John Williams")*
1919	Ronald Light
1922	Abbe Delorme
1926	Stella Maris Affair
1926	John Donald Merrett
1927	Frederick Browne and William Kennedy
1928	Frederick Stewart
1932	Elvira Barney
1933	Theodosius Petrou
1940	Udham Singh*
1947	Christopher Geraghty, Charles Jenkins, and Terence Rolt

*Profiled in this book.

Hadden Clark

Date: 1992
Location: Bethesda, Maryland

Warren Houghteling was worried. He'd just received a call from the Washington, D.C., office where his sister, Laura, worked, reporting that she hadn't showed up that particular Monday, October 19, 1992. Nor could they get any answer at Laura's house. Warren drove to where Laura lived with their mother, Penny, who had been away on business for the weekend.

He found the back door unlocked, but no sign of Laura. A cursory inspection revealed nothing out of place or taken. When police interviewed neighbors, one, who'd been waiting for a bus nearby, recalled seeing Laura leaving the house at 8:20 on Monday morning. She had been dressed in slacks and a trench coat as she hurried off toward the railroad station. Atypically for Laura, she made no attempt to acknowledge the neighbor.

It was all very baffling. And still there was no sign of Laura. A closer examination of the house revealed that a fitted sheet and mattress underblanket were missing from her bed. Concern hardened to fear four days later with the discovery in nearby woods of a bloodstained pillow and pillowcase. A police bloodhound, given the scent from Laura's clothing and released in the vicinity, ran immediately to where the pillowcase was found. It then tracked the scent, through a church yard, right to the back door of the Houghteling's house. Curiously, the dog didn't go around to the front of the house, where Laura had last been seen.

Using a variant of DNA typing called restriction fragment length polymorphism, experts demonstrated that the blood on the pillow came from an offspring of Penny Houghteling and a sibling of Warren. Therefore it belonged to Laura. More extensive testing of the mattress with luminol revealed heavy blood staining along its length. And there was another discovery: among the several identical hairs removed from Laura's hairbrush was a single wig fiber. As Laura didn't wear wigs, this assumed major significance.

The big breakthrough came with what appeared to be a partial thumbprint on the bloodied pillowcase. Treatment with amido black, then a wash solution, followed by distilled water, provided a print that was good enough for comparison. Police records matched it to a part-time gardener who had recently worked at the Houghteling residence, Hadden Clark. Just one week before Laura's disappearance, Clark had left in a temper after getting into an argument with Penny Houghteling over some missing tools. Warren now remembered that on the night of the disappearance, he had been outside the house when Clark drove by slowly. When Warren called out to ask him if he had seen Laura, Clark just gunned the engine and raced off.

Clark had a troubled history. Brain damaged from birth, in 1985 he had been discharged from the navy as a paranoid schizophrenic and soon fell afoul of the law, acquiring convictions for burglary. More ominously, in 1986 he had been a suspect in the then-unsolved disappearance of six-year-old Michele Dorr, last seen outside her father's Silver Spring, Maryland, home on May 31 of that year.

Clark was living in his old truck when arrested. A check of his activities revealed that just after the fight with Penny, he had purchased duct tape and rope from a hardware store, paying with a personal check. On the stub he'd written "Laura." As detectives dug deeper into Clark's background, they learned of a rented storage unit hundreds of miles away in Rhode Island, where site records showed a visit by Clark just two days after the disappearance.

Officers rushed to the unit. What they found did nothing to lead them to Laura, but it did provide a chilling insight into the bizarre world of Hadden Clark. They entered an Aladdin's cave of dresses, bras, panties, and other items of female apparel, the physical expression of Clark's appetite for cross-dressing. Also, there were several wigs.

One of the wigs appeared to be a color match for the fiber found in Laura's hairbrush. Microscopically it was indistinguishable. To make doubly sure, the fiber was sent to the FBI forensics laboratory, for analysis using a microspectrophotometer. This passes a beam of light through the sample, which then absorbs light. The darker the color, the more light it absorbs. The results are then compared to a database of reference values for the more than seven thousand commercially available dyes in the United States. There could be no doubt about it: the dye on the fiber was identical to that on the wig.

It was the clinching evidence. Even if a slick defense counsel managed to explain away the bloody thumbprint on the pillowcase, this fiber placed Clark inside Laura Houghteling's bedroom. In reconstructing the crime, officers believed that Clark let himself in the house, murdered Laura, and took her body out the back door to its hiding place, inadvertently dropping the pillowcase along the way. He had then returned to the house and attempted to clean up behind him. To make his escape, he had dressed in women's clothes, donned the wig, and given it a quick flick with the hairbrush before letting himself out the front door, bamboozling any possible witnesses into thinking they were seeing the real Laura leave for work.

That same day, he had purchased a king-size bedsheet and was, so officers believed, on his way back to the house that night to replace it, only to be scared off by Warren Houghteling. Overwhelmed by an avalanche of evidence, on day one of his trial, June 14, 1993, Clark abruptly changed his plea to guilty of second-degree murder and received a thirty-year prison term. In return for this leniency he led detectives to the shallow grave off Interstate 270, about half a mile from the house, where Laura was buried.

In October 1999, Clark was finally convicted for the murder of Michele Dorr and sentenced to another thirty years. Shortly thereafter, he wiped this particular slate clean by revealing the whereabouts of Michele's skeletonized remains.

Martin Colwell

Date: 1925
Location: Vallejo, California

Shortly before six o'clock on December 19, 1925, John McCarthy, a foreman for the Vallejo Street Department, was seen to enter his small house on Pennsylvania Street. Moments later a gunshot rang out. Shortly thereafter, McCarthy staggered outside the house and collapsed in front of friends. From the spreading stain on his shirtfront, it was obvious that he had been shot in the chest. He died before reaching the hospital but managed to mutter several times, "I fired Colwell."

Attending detectives took this to be a reference to Martin Colwell, a fifty-nine-year-old local troublemaker and drunk with more than twenty jail sentences in his record, whose latest bleary-eyed attempt to go straight had faltered just weeks earlier when he had been dismissed from a street laboring gang by none other than John McCarthy. Since then, Colwell had hit the bottle hard and had often been heard making threats on McCarthy's life.

While officers raced to the waterfront and the dilapidated scow that Colwell called home, Police Chief W. T. Stanford ordered a search of McCarthy's house. This uncovered a single bullet that had apparently passed right through McCarthy's body and embedded itself in the living room wall. Curious neighbors milling around outside described someone who closely resembled Colwell as having fled the scene just after the shooting. That same day Colwell, rolling drunk as usual, was tracked down and arrested without incident. In his pocket was a .38-caliber revolver with one chamber empty. He was also carrying three bullets of similar size.

When questioned, Colwell claimed that he had been drunk at the time of the shooting and had no recollection of anything that happened that day. In the meantime, officers searching his houseboat uncovered a box of ammunition with four bullets missing. This box of shells was sent, together with the murder bullet and the gun found on Colwell, to **Edward O. Heinrich.**

Heinrich first established that the murder bullet was, indeed, a .38-caliber. Then he made test firings of eight further bullets: one from the three shells found in the accused man's pocket, another from the box in Colwell's home, and six more from a batch of the same make and size. Microscopic examination confirmed that the markings on the bullets were identical to those found on the bullet that had killed McCarthy. But the prosecutors wanted more. Word had filtered through that Colwell had hired some sharp lawyers, and the state was anxious to seal off every possible legal loophole.

Heinrich reckoned he had the solution. Although a superb witness, fluent on the stand and easily understandable by any jury, he also knew the truth of the old adage that "a picture is worth a thousand words." For some time he had been experimenting with the stereoscopic microscope, an instrument with two lenses that enabled the user to peer at two photographs placed side by side and to view the result as a single three-dimensional image. Was it possible, he wondered, to substitute camera lenses for his eyes, take a photograph through the dual microscope lenses, and thus obtain a picture of the single three-dimensional image?

After many frustrating failures, he finally found a way of rigging his test equipment so he could click the two camera shutters simultaneously and thereby produce the much-prized single image. It was a fantastic achievement. When prosecutors saw Heinrich's photographs, they were dumbfounded. The photograph of the murder bullet and that of a test bullet merged seamlessly.

Details of Heinrich's latest coup—which he likened to "bullet fingerprinting"—soon leaked out, leading one newspaper to proclaim excitedly, "[This will be] the first use of the fingerprinted bullet test ever introduced in an American court. . . . If Colwell is convicted on Heinrich's testimony, it will establish a new precedent in American legal procedure."

A tense hush fell over the court as Heinrich took the stand. With customary authority and conciseness, he explained his methods in great detail; then, with a conjurer's timing and flair, he produced the already famous photographs. Everyone craned forward for a closer look, especially the jury. It appeared damning. But Colwell's defense team had been busy rounding up their own experts, including a longtime and implacable foe of Heinrich's named Chauncey McGovern, whose vehement insistence that Colwell's revolver had *not* fired the murder weapon instilled just enough doubt to secure a hung jury.

Six weeks later, the state retried the case, and this time something quite remarkable happened. The jury foreman stood up and requested on behalf of his fellow jurors that they be permitted to see, with their own eyes, what exactly was visible through Heinrich's microscope. Heinrich agreed at once to provide a demonstration. One by one the jurors trooped down into the well of the court and peered into the microscope lens. Nods of agreement confirmed that the photographs did, indeed, match the specimen. Still not satisfied, they asked if Heinrich could replicate his feat—shoot the picture, develop it, and produce it for all to see—this time, in court. It was a bizarre request, but Heinrich declared himself up to the challenge.

After taking the photographs, he was accompanied by a court bailiff to a nearby darkroom, where he developed the negatives. Later that same day, he returned to court with the result of his latest picture-taking—a photograph identical to the one he had exhibited earlier in his testimony.

It was all the jury needed. Within an hour they found Colwell guilty of murder, and he was sentenced to life imprisonment. He later died in Folsom Prison.

Heinrich's great innovation worked just as he had thought, and even today his basic method, albeit with far more sophisticated equipment and considerable modification, is still used by forensic laboratories around the world.

Coroner

The office of coroner is one of the oldest and most significant in the field of law enforcement. Although the post probably originated in England sometime during the ninth century A.D., it did not achieve the full recognition of the law until September 1194, when a conclave of judges sitting in Kent stated in the Article of Eyre, "In every county of the king's realm shall be elected three knights and one clerk, to keep the pleas of the crown."

The king in question was the impecunious and quarrelsome Richard I, a swaggering spendthrift with an appetite for expensive wars. The coroner's primary function was to ensure that funds traditionally funneled into the notoriously deep pockets of local sheriffs were now redirected to the royal coffers. A principal source of this revenue was the property of convicted felons, all of which became forfeit to the crown. It was this royal association that earned the new job its title of "crowner," or "coronator," derived from corona, meaning "crown." From there, it was but a short linguistic step to its present term.

As the British Empire spread around the globe, it exported the office of coroner to all its overseas colonies, including North America. At home it was a different story. All through the nineteenth century, legislation gnawed away at the English coroner's traditional powers, most of which were now obsolete. The *Coroners (Amendment) Act* (1926) completed the emasculation. This limited the coroner's duties to conducting an inquest, with the aid of a jury, into all deaths occurring within his district by violent or unnatural means or from some unknown cause. The act also established strict qualifications for the office, requiring that the incumbent be a barrister, solicitor, or legally qualified medical practitioner. In this modified form the coroner system in England persists to the present day.

Early immigrants to America embraced the English coroner system they had brought with them. In 1635 a coroner's inquest in the colony of New Plymouth, New England, found that one John Deacon had died as a result of "bodily weakness caused by fasting and extreme cold."

Following the Revolutionary War, the post of county coroner became an elected position, with the only requirement for office being an absence of any criminal convictions. Political allegiance was paramount, with most campaigners for the office being nominated on party lines. Such a climate bred open corruption. For about $10, many coroners could be persuaded to ease a family's grief and shame by ruling a suicide to be a natural death. In New York certain shady operators were even rumored to gloss over an inconvenient homicide for no more than $50. Corruption this widespread and this pernicious survived until the early 1900s.

Clearly something needed to be done. A few decades beforehand, in 1877, the Commonwealth of Massachusetts had attempted to clean house by deciding to abolish the role of coroner and replace it with a system of qualified medical examiners. In practice very little changed, as the first batch of medical examiners proved every bit as inept and corrupt as their predecessors.

New York City seemed particularly ill served by those elected to the post of coroner. With death certificates earning a coroner's fee of $11.50, it was not unknown for corpses to pass through several coroners' offices before final disposal. Everybody wanted a cut. General revulsion with this situation led to the Wallstein Report (1914), which confirmed what New Yorkers had known for decades: coroners were hopelessly ill-qualified. Most had been either bartenders or tradesmen without a jot of medico-legal experience, and many were prone to signing death certificates with their own "favorite" causes of death.

The outrage triggered by this report led to a bill passing the New York legislature in 1915 that abolished the office of coroner in New York City and created instead the post of chief medical examiner. The law passed into effect on January 1, 1918, when **Charles Norris** was appointed chief medical examiner by Mayor John F. Hylan.

Elsewhere in America, the role of the coroner not only remained undiminished but actually flourished, with high-profile coroners in states such as Ohio acquiring considerable notoriety for their sometimes overzealous prosecutions. Even today in these jurisdictions, a coroner can issue a warrant for the arrest of persons who may have caused the death of another by criminal means, and coroners possess all the powers of a magistrate to hear testimony.

Today in the United States two main types of medico-legal investigative agencies exist side by side: the coroner's office and the medical examiner. As of 2003, ten states retained the traditional coroner; twenty-two states (plus the District of Columbia) had switched to medical examiners; while eighteen states opted for a combined medical examiner and coroner system.

Selection and qualification criteria for coroners vary enormously from state to state. Most coroners are elected to office but not all. Some states require the holder to be a qualified pathologist; others are happy to appoint laypeople. Where the latter applies, the coroner invariably has the power to employ a physician to conduct an autopsy, should one be required. The only universal qualification seems to be one of age: coroners must be twenty-one years of age or older.

As the business of law enforcement becomes ever more scientific and professional, it is likely that the slow erosion of coroners' powers in the United States will continue, and that a time will come when all suspicious deaths are investigated by properly qualified medical examiners.

Frederick Crowe

Date: 1968
Location: Ladue, Missouri

August Sunnen lived with his wife and four sons in the St. Louis suburb of Ladue. As the eponymous head of a large manufacturing company, life was comfortable and unruffled for the middle-aged businessman—until a phone call at 10:00 P.M. on July 22, 1968. Sunnen picked up the receiver. A man, whose voice he later described as ordinary, told Sunnen that unless he handed over $40,000, "one of your boys will be killed—maybe even your wife. Get the money out of the bank. I'll call you later and tell you exactly what to do."

In seconds it was over. Sunnen stared at the receiver in disbelief for a moment, then dialed the police. He told them he had no enemies, nor was he very wealthy. In answer to their most important question—no, he had not recognized the voice.

The police took this threat very seriously. A six-man team moved into the Sunnen household to provide round-the-clock protection, while experts hooked up a tape recorder to the phone. The next night, at approximately the same time, the phone rang again. This time the caller reeled off a list of instructions. Sunnen, under orders to prolong the call as long as possible in hopes that it might be traced, jotted down the directions: "Drive to the Ramada Inn on Natural Bridge Avenue and wait there at the public telephone for a call. I'll tell you then what we'll do from there. And remember, you and no one else. Okay?"

Sunnen set off in his Lincoln. Some way behind, Detective Pete Vasel, an officer well versed in the way of extortionists, followed in his own car. Sunnen parked by the public phone. It rang almost immediately. The caller had more directions. "Drive to the gas station around the corner. There you'll fill up your tank, and be sure to leave open all four doors so I'll know there's no one else in the car. Then go over to the garage of the Nantucket Cove Restaurant and I'll meet you there. And, once more, be sure you're alone or you know what will happen."

At this point, Sunnen switched cars covertly with Vasel and then drove home. As instructed, Vasel drove to the restaurant in the Lincoln and parked. An hour passed, but apart from an occasional passing pedestrian, no one showed. Discouraged, Vasel made his way back to the Sunnens' house. Within minutes of his arrival the phone rang again. It was the anonymous caller. "You tipped off the police," he growled at Sunnen. "Now I'm really going to get you."

For several days the caller stepped up the pressure, with a nonstop barrage of calls, all threatening violence. None of the calls lasted long enough to permit a trace. Police stationed at the house were constantly on the alert, but nothing happened. And gradually the calls diminished. Weeks went by, then months, finally a year. When a second year passed without incident, the Sunnen family could be forgiven for thinking that the nightmare was behind them. Perhaps it had been just a crank caller after all.

Sunnen certainly hoped so; he had a business to run, and part of that business involved complex labor negotiations. On a July morning in 1970 he was reviewing those talks with several of his employees. One, Fred Crowe, age thirty-five, seemed particularly bellicose, carping over some petty grievances. Sunnen listened to the litany of complaints with an attentive ear until suddenly a warning bell in the recesses of his brain began shrilling: Crowe's voice sounded remarkably similar to that of the caller who had made his life a misery two years ago!

This was not an easy concept for Sunnen to grasp. Over the past two years he had heard Crowe speak dozens of times; not once had it occurred to him that this was the anonymous caller. But the more he listened, the more convinced he became. As a way of double-checking, Sunnen arranged for Crowe to see the company nurse about an old injury. Crowe spoke freely, unaware that every word was being recorded on tape.

That night Sunnen reviewed the tape nonstop, certain that Crowe was the mystery caller. The police agreed and brought him in for questioning. As anticipated, Crowe hotly refuted any such suggestion. How come, he sneered, Sunnen had suddenly recognized his voice after all this time? But beneath the bluster, Crowe showed signs of being visibly jarred, and soon his statements began to creak under all the contradictions.

Because the St. Louis police at this time had no facilities for the controversial technique of **voiceprint** analysis, they contacted Lieutenant Ernest W. Nash, head of the Michigan Voice Identification Unit. He ran spectrographic tests on the tapes recorded at Sunnen's house and the one recorded by the nurse. The resulting patterns provided conclusive evidence, in Nash's opinion, that both tapes had recorded the voice of the same person.

Largely on the basis of this analysis, Crowe was arrested and sent to trial. Much of the testimony was taken up with the validity or otherwise of voiceprint identification. Defense attorney Samuel Vandover reserved his greatest onslaught for Nash, but the detective remained unmoved, firm in his conviction that the findings were accurate.

Finally, on January 20, 1972, almost three and a half years after the phone calls began, Crowe was found guilty of extortion and sentenced to a two-year jail term. This was later suspended, and Crowe was granted probation on condition that he undertake psychiatric counseling.

Although voiceprints still struggle to gain acceptance in American courts, their use in cases such as this highlights an area where they have achieved success. And while the anonymous caller may never be wholly eliminated, voice identification procedures and modern telephone tracing techniques have greatly reduced the incidence of this cowardly and invasive crime.

James Robert Cruz

Date: 1993
Location: Bellefonte, Pennsylvania

It was just after first light on the morning of March 24, 1993, when a motorist spotted something unusual lying in a snowbank just outside

Bellefonte, Pennsylvania. A closer inspection confirmed his worst fears. The young woman—half naked and trussed like a hog—had been strangled with a length of rope. Beneath the ligature was a single dark hair, in marked contrast to the victim's own strawberry blond tresses. There were no personal effects on the body, nothing to identify her. Alongside the body was a set of tire tracks. Judging from their size and configuration, they belonged to a tractor-trailer. Photographs and plaster casts made of the tracks were compared with reference manuals and identified as low-profile Michelins, a rare type.

The autopsy suggested that the victim had been dead for fewer than twelve hours and that she had had sex shortly before she died. And there was something else. On the palm of her left hand—very faint and almost illegible—were some numbers written in ink. Because of the delicate nature of this evidence, the skin was excised from the hand and sent to the FBI laboratory for digital enhancement. A check of the victim's fingerprints failed to produce any leads.

While these time-consuming procedures went ahead, local detectives visited truck stops in the vicinity, showing the victim's photograph and asking if anyone recognized her. No one did. There was a similarly frustrating outcome to a check of the missing-persons records.

Some light at the end of the identification tunnel came when FBI scientists established that the digits on the hand were a telephone number with what looked like a Florida area code. But when this number was dialed and found to be disconnected, it forced investigators to widen their search. Using the crime scene as a central point, they drew a twelve-hour driving distance radius on a map—a zone that took in northernmost New England, as far south as Georgia, and across to western Illinois—then dispatched information packs to every law enforcement agency in that catchment area.

One month after the body was found, a sheriff in Poland Spring, Maine, studied the request for assistance, reached for the phone, and dialed the local number written on the victim's palm. He reached Mark Rosenberg, a guidance counselor at a local school for children with emotional problems. A few minutes of conversation prompted a fast visit. Rosenberg studied the proffered photograph and sadly nodded his head.

Her name was Dawn Marie Birnbaum, and at age seventeen, she had already lived a hard life: a broken home, more foster parents than she could remember, trouble at every turn. Rosenberg remembered her calling from a pay phone just days before she was found dead. He'd told her to call back, and she had written his number down on the palm of her hand. A comparison of dental records removed any remaining vestige of doubt that the victim was indeed Dawn.

Detectives pieced together Dawn's final days. According to a friend, she had decided to track down a truck driver named John Hoffpower, whom she'd met a year previously. On that occasion the childcare authorities had caught up with Dawn and returned her to Maine. For several months Hoffpower kept in touch, and then he mysteriously disappeared. Dawn's dream never died, and on March 22 she had gone to Dysart's Truck Stop in Hermon, Maine, to ask around and maybe hitch a ride down south to Mississippi, where Hoffpower lived.

The police, too, were desperate to track Hoffpower, who was suddenly a strong suspect. Then they discovered that Hoffpower hadn't been seen in more than seven months, not since his bullet-riddled car was found abandoned. In all probability he'd been killed in a drug deal gone bad.

As there was now an interstate dimension, jurisdiction passed to the FBI. Their agents went to Dysart's Truck Stop, where a cashier remembered seeing Dawn making calls on a pay phone a few weeks earlier. She'd also been seen asking truckers for rides.

Because the distance from Dysart's to where Dawn was found dead was approximately 650 miles, agents surmised that a trucker might well fill up in Maine and again in Pennsylvania. Gas purchase records at Dysart's for a four-day period covering the time Dawn was known to be there were compared with similar records taken from the three truck stops nearest to where the body was found.

It was grueling work, with thousands of names to compare and eliminate. There was just one hit. On the morning of March 22, right when Dawn was using the nearby phone, James Robert Cruz, a thirty-six-year-old truckdriver from Waterford, Ohio, bought fuel at Dysart's. Two days later he filled up again at the Bestway Truck Stop in Milesburg, Pennsylvania, on I-80, just a few miles from where Dawn's body was found. When it was found that Cruz had a previous conviction for attempted murder, he became the prime suspect. Unknown to him, agents scoured every inch of the eighteen-wheeler he had driven on this trip. One fact jumped out at them: the tires were low-profile Michelins.

The second lead proved much harder to find and was almost overlooked. Right when the criminalists were ending their work, one of them noticed a single blond hair trapped in carpeting at the foot of the passenger door. Microscopically, it was indistinguishable from the hair on Dawn's head. When agents found that the driver's log Cruz was obliged by law to keep had been altered on each occasion when he bought gas, they had probable cause to arrest him. The final piece in this remarkable investigative jigsaw puzzle was slotted in when DNA testing matched hair and blood samples taken from Cruz to the hair found under the ligature and to semen left at the scene.

On June 14, 1994, Cruz was convicted and sentenced to life without parole. Although not charged, he is strongly suspected of involvement in the death of several other young women whose bodies were found alongside freeways in his home state of Ohio. Following Cruz's arrest, these killings stopped abruptly.

Joann Curley

Date: 1991
Location: Wilkes-Barre, Pennsylvania

In August 1991 a young Pennsylvania electrician named Bobby Curley suddenly fell ill. His symptoms—burning feet, a beet-red face, and sweating and numbness in his hands—led doctors at the hospital he attended to diagnose Guillain-Barré syndrome (GBS), an acute inflammation of the nervous system that causes numbness in the extremities. GBS is usually not fatal, although in extreme cases the weakness may become so severe that the patient needs mechanical help in breathing, but as long as further complications do not occur, the disease remits spontaneously, and most patients recover. Which is what happened to Bobby Curley.

Discharged from the hospital, Bobby returned home, only to suffer a relapse. This time he was taken to another hospital, the Hershey Medical Center. Specialists there doubted they were dealing with GBS, and blood tests confirmed this. Bobby, meanwhile, went into fast decline: he lost weight, and his hair fell out by the handful. A urine test found the cause of the problem: Bobby Curley had been poisoned with thallium. Thallium is a rare heavy metal that nowadays has no commercial use. Before being banned in the early 1970s, its extreme toxicity made it a common ingredient in rat poison. There is no known antidote.

On September 26, 1991, Bobby lapsed into a coma, and his wife, Joann, gave consent for the life support system to be turned off. He died the following day. The couple had been married for only thirteen months, and Joann was distraught and at a loss to explain what might have caused the poisoning, which was confirmed at autopsy. Then she recalled that back in May of that year, Bobby had started work on a laboratory renovation and him telling her that several of the workers were unhappy being around so many old bottles of chemicals. Had Bobby been the victim of a tragic industrial accident?

When interviewed, a company spokesman denied that there were any thallium traces in the laboratory but admitted that there were five bottles of thallium in a storage room. Air and dust samples were taken, counters were swabbed, and they were all taken for analysis.

When Joann remembered that Bobby had brought home some cabinets from the lab, common sense dictated that she and her young daughter from a previous marriage be tested for thallium exposure. The results were positive but in such minute traces that it did not require treatment. As the search broadened, traces of thallium were found in two thermos flasks that Bobby took to work each day, usually filled with iced tea. This brought Bobby's workmates into the equation, and the possibility of a practical joke having gone horribly wrong. But close questioning revealed nothing.

Then a curiosity arose. A third flask at the Curley household—one that Bobby never took to work—was also found to contain traces of thallium. Joann hurriedly remembered pouring some leftover iced tea from Bobby's work flask into this one, in order not to waste any.

It sounded suspicious. Already, Bobby's family harbored doubts about Joann; they knew the marriage had been volatile right from the outset. At the funeral Joann had been dry-eyed, and she had snapped at Bobby's mother, who was crying, to be quiet. Also fueling doubts was the knowledge that Bobby had made Joann the sole beneficiary of his $300,000 life insurance policy just months after getting married. In light of these circumstances an order was obtained authorizing the exhumation of Bobby's body for a second autopsy.

Samples of the hair were subjected to atomic absorption spectrophotometry to show which sections of hair contained thallium and which did not. The human hair is a marvelous barometer of toxicological misdoing. Any poison present in the system will migrate into the hair, and because hair grows at a fairly predictable rate—approximately 0.04 inch every 2.7 days—it is possible to plot a graph of roughly when poison was ingested.

Working together, toxicologist Dr. Frederic Rieders and **Cyril Wecht,** the Allegheny County coroner, were able to compile a timeline of Bobby Curley's long, slow death. The tip of his hair, nearly five inches long, showed traces of thallium: 0.5 part per million. Hair of that length could be dated to October or November 1990. By late November the level of thallium had risen to 3.5 parts per million. After dropping in December, the thallium level rose steadily in January through March 1991.

This posed a baffling question: why did Bobby Curley show no overt signs of thallium poisoning earlier, if his poisoning was so lengthy? Wecht put it down to the fact that many people are "asymptomatic . . . That's one of the problems with diagnosing thallium poisoning. Some people never complain." The early symptoms such as nausea, loss of appetite, or numbness could have been overlooked, while the trademark thallium symptom of hair loss occurs "rather late in the game," said Wecht.

By July and August 1991 Curley was being systematically poisoned. His hair showed relatively consistent levels of 7.5, 8, and 9.5 parts per million. The thallium level dropped briefly to 3 parts per million on September 11, 1991, then rose again to 6 and 7 parts per million later in the month.

Then came a shocking find: Rieders learned that Bobby Curley had received a massive dose of thallium even as he lay dying at Hershey Medical Center. The concentration of thallium in the intestine was a thousand times higher than that found in his blood or autopsy tissues. Close examination of this eleven-month timeline allowed investigators to eliminate suspects by seeing who had access to Bobby Curley on the poisoning dates and who didn't. As the dust cleared, one name stood out: Joann Curley.

Charged with first-degree murder and facing the death penalty, Joann Curley pleaded guilty to third-degree homicide in return for a twenty-year sentence. As part of her plea bargain, she wrote a forty-page confession in which she admitted poisoning her husband on at least seventeen occasions with some old rat poison. Asked why, she replied, "For the money."

DNA Typing

Even though the discovery of chemical DNA can be dated to 1869, it was the Russian-born biochemist Phoebus Levene, in 1911, who first discerned that individual cells each contain a nucleus made of nucleic acid. There are two types of nucleic acid, which he called ribonucleic acid (RNA) and deoxyribonucleic acid (DNA), according to whether they contain ribose or deoxyribose. Within each nucleus are twenty-three pairs of chromosomes made up of DNA. Within each pair, one chromosome comes from the father's sperm, the other from the mother's egg. By the 1940s scientists realized that DNA forms the building blocks of life and is the substance that dictates our hair and eye color and also everything else about our physical makeup.

So how does DNA issue its instructions? Scientists knew it had to be in some kind of code and that each code is unique to each individual. The answer came in 1953 when two scientists based at Cambridge, England, James Watson and Francis Crick, determined that the structure of DNA is a double-helix polymer, a spiral consisting of two DNA strands wound around each other. Together with the biophysicist Maurice Wilkins, whose work on X-ray diffraction had proved crucial to Crick and Watson, all three men were awarded the 1962 Nobel Prize in medicine for their work in this field.

There are four chemicals that make up DNA: adenine (A), guanine (G), cytosine (C), and thymine (T). Strung together in an extremely long sequence, the chemicals on one chromosomal strand always align with the chemicals on the other strand; that is, A always joins with T, and C always joins with G. Thus a section of DNA code might be arranged thus:

C A G T T C A
G T C A A G T

Although large chunks of DNA are universal (because each of us has the same body parts and organs), some sections of DNA vary from individual to individual. By studying these polymorphic segments, scientists can determine whether a particular strand of DNA could have come from a given individual. By comparing prints of several different polymorphic sequences from different specimens to one another, scientists can tell whether the specimens match.

This, in necessarily brief form, is the science of DNA. Development of the so-called DNA fingerprint, with its enormous forensic implications, can be credited to the British geneticist **Sir Alec Jeffreys,** who, in 1984, noticed the existence of certain sequences of DNA (called minisatellites) that do not contribute to the function of a gene but that are repeated within the gene and in other genes of a DNA sample. Jeffreys also determined that each organism has a unique pattern of these minisatellites, the only exception being multiple individuals from a single zygote (identical twins).

The procedure for creating a DNA fingerprint in a criminal investigation can best be shown in the following steps (the sample used is blood, but it could equally be any bodily fluid or item of human tissue):

1. Blood samples are collected from the victim, the defendant, and the crime scene.
2. White blood cells are separated from red blood cells.
3. DNA is extracted from the nuclei of white blood cells.
4. A restrictive enzyme is used to cut fragments of the DNA strand.
5. DNA fragments are put into a bed of gel with electrodes at either end.
6. Electric current sorts DNA fragments by length.
7. An absorbent blotter soaks up the imprint, the imprint is radioactively treated, and an X-ray photograph (called an autoradiograph) is produced.

Once the autoradiograph has been analyzed and an apparent match found, it is then a question of probabilities: what is the statistical likelihood of two people sharing this DNA profile? According to Jeffreys, the answer is fewer than 1 in 1 nonillion (1 followed by thirty zeros)—a figure many trillions of times greater than the current world population.

If only a small amount of DNA is available for fingerprinting, a polymerase chain reaction (PCR) may be used to create thousands of copies of a DNA segment quickly and accurately. Developed in 1983 by the Nobel Prize–winning American biochemist Kary B. Mullis, PCR allows the investigator to obtain the large quantities of DNA necessary for high-quality forensic analysis. It is a three-step process carried out in repeated cycles, and it requires as little as a single DNA molecule to serve as a template.

The initial step—denaturation or separation of the two strands of the DNA molecule—is achieved by heating the sample to approximately 95°C (203°F). Each strand is a template on which a new strand is built. Steps two and three involve cooling and reheating the sample, a process that doubles the number of copies. At the end of the cycle, which lasts about five minutes, the process begins again. Usually twenty-five to thirty cycles produce sufficient DNA for analysis. The technique has also been used to amplify DNA fragments found in preserved tissues, such as those of a 40,000-year-old frozen woolly mammoth, and of a 7,500-year-old human found in a peat bog.

Begun in 1990, the Human Genome Project, to which researchers all over the world have contributed, holds out the promise of a radical new direction for crime fighting in years to come. If the project's stated goals—to identify all the approximately 30,000 genes in human DNA, to determine the sequences of the 3 billion chemical base pairs that make up human DNA; and to store this information in databases—are achieved, then criminal identification might soar to new plateaus.

In the meantime, despite problems with overzealous laboratories scrimping on their test procedures to produce quick and profitable results, DNA fingerprinting has survived the most rigorous courtroom scrutiny and continues to prosper. With its unparalleled ability not only to convict the guilty but also to free the innocent—no fewer than twelve U.S. death row inmates exonerated by the end of 2003—it is nothing less than the greatest advance in forensic science since the advent of **fingerprinting.**

Howard Elkins

Date: 1969
Location: Long Island, New York

Two homebuyers viewing property in Jericho, Long Island, in the fall of 1999 ran an approving eye over the large split-level house on Forest Avenue. With an asking price of about $450,000, it was within their budget and appeared to be just what they were looking for, but before closing the deal they asked the current owner if he would get rid of the unsightly fifty-five-gallon oil drum jammed into a crawl space beneath an addition. Ronald Cohen had no objections. He'd inherited the drum from the previous occupants, nine years earlier, and just had never gotten around to moving it. On September 2, watched by a real estate agent, he pried the lid off the rusted steel drum. Seconds later he was scrambling for the phone.

When Detective Robert Edwards arrived and peered inside the drum, he saw "what appeared to be a human hand with a ring on it" sticking out from a barrel that had been inserted into the drum. Closer examination revealed the mummified, fully clothed remains of a young woman with long black hair and two gold teeth, sat cross-legged on the bottom of the inner barrel. A shawl was draped across her shoulders, and there also was some jewelry, along with the business card of a New Jersey doctor, Frank D'Allberti.

The drum's interior showed traces of a green chemical dye. Moisture-absorbing pellets, stuffed into the space between the barrel and the drum, accounted for the body's remarkable, albeit shrunken state of preservation. When found, the body measured four feet, nine inches and weighed fifty-nine pounds. An autopsy showed that she was aged between twenty and thirty, in an advanced stage of pregnancy, and had been bludgeoned to death.

Edwards managed to trace all the previous owners of the property back to 1972. Arthur Ebbin had bought the house in October of that year, and he, too, recalled the drum. It had thwarted all his efforts to shift it, because "it weighed a ton." With the identity of the woman still a mystery, detectives tracked the barrel to a factory in Linden, New Jersey, that began making that style of container in 1963 for companies that used dyes. This dated the murder to sometime between 1963 and 1972. Dr. D'Allberti, now retired, could recall no one who fit the dead woman's description.

Among other items recovered from the barrel was a three-inch thick address book. Its pages were pulped together, rendering all the entries unreadable to the naked eye, but painstaking restoration and manipulation under a video spectral comparator (see **questioned documents**) saved the day. Very faintly, some names emerged. One, clearer than the rest, was Katy Andrade, and when interviewed, this former charity volunteer was able to shed some light on the mystery.

When Reyna Marroquin left her native El Salvador in August 1966, she was twenty-five years old and determined to put a broken marriage behind her. Her future, she decided, lay in New York City. For two years she wrote home regularly to her mother; and if the streets that she described were not exactly paved with gold, then at least she seemed to be getting by. She had a room at the Jeanne D'Arc home, a Catholic residence for working women on West Twenty-fourth Street, and she held a steady job. And then, in early 1969, the letters suddenly stopped. Her family, alarmed by the strange silence, placed ads in newspapers, pleading for knowledge of Reyna's whereabouts, but as the months and then years passed without word, they reluctantly reconciled themselves to the fact that Reyna was missing for good.

Katy Andrade could now fill in some of the gaps. As a volunteer at Jeanne D'Arc, she knew Reyna well and recalled the tearful episode in November 1968 that ended with Reyna leaving the home because she didn't want the nuns to discover that she'd become pregnant. She wouldn't name the father, other than to say he was one of the bosses where she worked, a married man who had promised her an apartment. The last contact Katy had with Reyna was a distraught phone call during which Reyna said she had made a "horrible mistake" by going to her lover's house and confronting his wife. This had enraged the man. "He's going to kill me!" cried Reyna, and then she hung up. Katy never heard from her again.

When detectives learned that Reyna had worked at Melrose Flowers, a company that made fake plastic flowers and trees for department store displays, their curiosity was piqued. Inside the barrel they'd also found the stem of a plastic flower. Ex-employees of the now defunct company identified the drum, the dye, and the moisture-absorbing pellets as products regularly used at Melrose Flowers. They also recalled factory gossip that named the father of Reyna's baby as the company's boss, Howard Elkins. This was the third time that Elkins's name had cropped up during inquiries: first as a faint diary entry, now as Reyna's employer, and—most vitally of all—as owner of the house on Forest Avenue from 1957 to 1972.

In 1972 Elkins had sold Melrose Flowers and moved to Florida, and he was still living in a Boca Raton retirement community, affluent and respected, when detectives came calling on September 9, 2000. Calm at first and adamant that he knew no Reyna Marroquin, the seventy-year-old ex-businessman grew agitated as the questioning got tougher, and he angrily refused to supply the DNA sample that would establish whether he was the father of the fetus Reyna was carrying when she met her death. At this point the detectives left, saying they would return with a warrant for the DNA sample.

But Howard Elkins forestalled them. Unwilling to face the shame of being exposed as a callous murderer, the next day he went to a nearby Wal-Mart, paid $247 cash for a shotgun and two boxes of shells, drove home, and blew his head off. At Elkins's autopsy, police got the DNA they wanted. The probability of paternity was determined to be 99.93 percent.

Frederick Emmett-Dunne

Date: 1953
Location: Duisberg, West Germany

The first day of December 1953 was but a few hours old when the body of Sergeant Reginald Watters was found hanging in a British army barracks at Duisberg, West Germany. Dr. Alan Womack, a civilian pathologist attached to the army, examined the corpse and found bruising of the larynx and trachea, consistent with hanging, but confessed himself puzzled because the groove caused by the rope was some way above the bruising. Also, Watters had eaten a large meal less than one hour before death, and in Womack's experience suicides rarely gorged themselves with food before taking that last, irrevocable step. Somewhat uneasily, he recorded a verdict of suicide.

Friends of the dead man were stunned. Watters didn't seem the suicidal type at all; quite the contrary, everyone knew him as unfailingly cheerful, despite all those rumors concerning his attractive German-born wife, Mia, and a burly fellow soldier named Sergeant Frederick Emmett-Dunne. For months, barracks gossip had linked the two romantically, but through it all Watters had kept up a brave face. Emmett-Dunne, by contrast, was deeply unpopular. Cocky and swaggering, he was fond of throwing his weight around, and he worked hard at consolidating his reputation as an army base gigolo.

When, barely six months later, he and Mia married, what had previously been a trickle of rumor now turned into a tidal wave, enough to persuade Lieutenant Colonel Frank Elliott, who had supervised the inquiry, that some sort of reinvestigation was in order. His request to Scotland Yard, in London, was answered with the dispatch of Superintendent Colin MacDougal to Germany. After familiarizing himself with the facts of the case, he authorized a second autopsy of Watters's body, this time to be conducted by **Francis Camps** of the London Hospital Medical School.

This was exactly the sort of high-profile case that Camps thrived on. He flew to Cologne and supervised the exhumation of Watters's body from the service cemetery. First, he made a visual inspection of the larynx, trachea, and cricoid before removing the larynx for microscopic examination. What he saw left him in no doubt that Watters had been dead before being hanged. "In my view he died from shock caused by a blow to the neck," he later testified, adding that it was the kind of injury likely to be inflicted by someone skilled in martial arts—someone like Emmett-Dunne, who, earlier in his army career, had served as a commando and who was proficient in lethal hand-to-hand combat.

By this time Emmett-Dunne was back in England with his new bride. His denials of any involvement in the death of Watters, protesting that he was being victimized because of his premature marriage to the dead man's widow, were seriously undermined by an intervention from an unexpected quarter. What ex-Private Ronald Emmett, the half brother of Emmett-Dunne, now had to say to police led to the sergeant being taken into custody and returned to Germany, where he was charged with murder. The trial commenced in Düsseldorf on June 27, 1954.

The court heard how on the evening of November 30, Emmett-Dunne, in response to a telephone call received in the sergeants' mess, had logged out of the camp at 7:05 P.M. After twenty minutes he was back, although the time shown on the guardroom time sheet was subsequently altered to make it appear later. At about 7:30 P.M. a bundle approximately five feet long—Watters was five feet, two inches tall—was seen just inside the entrance to Barracks Block 4. Emmett-Dunne deflected queries about the bundle by giving orders that this entrance was not to be used.

Half an hour later he approached his half brother, Ronald, for help. There had been a terrible accident, he said. Watters had flown into a jealous rage and attacked him. "I just gave him a tap to shut him up," claimed Emmett-Dunne, but the man had fallen down dead. Now he wanted help to make it appear like a suicide. Trembling with fear, Private Emmett limited his assistance to fetching a bucket, whereupon his half brother hoisted the body up on a rope from the banister before tipping the bucket on its side to simulate suicide.

By the time of the trial, and perhaps mindful of the fact that he was almost a foot taller than the diminutive Watters, Emmett-Dunne amended his story to now claim that Watters had threatened him with a revolver. But every attempt by his counsel to prove that the blow that had killed Watters was delivered in self-defense received short shrift from Camps. Holding aloft the actual larynx of the dead man, he launched into a lengthy exposition of how attack and defense blows vary in character, and what type of blow had shattered Watters's neck.

Earlier, Emmett-Dunne had attempted to demonstrate for the court how he had merely struck Watters in a defensive fashion. Camps now tore this version of events to shreds, showing how the defendant's account would have resulted in a blow being delivered to the side of the neck. "The injuries I found must have been inflicted by a central blow—quite definitely," he said. Delivered with enough force to fracture the thyroid cartilage that covers the Adam's apple, it had caused death, maybe instantaneously but certainly shortly afterward. Forced to endure the full weight of Camps's often lengthy explanations, the defense counsel sighed, "I quite understand your theory—"

"This is not a theory," Camps broke in belligerently. "This is straightforward mechanics!"

Camps's testimony clinched the case. Emmett-Dunne was convicted of murder and originally sentenced to death, but because the killing had occurred in West Germany, where capital punishment had been abolished, this was later commuted to life imprisonment.

Entomology (Forensic)

Insects represent by far the largest single group of living organisms on earth. Upwards of 900,000 different species have already been identified, though it is generally agreed that the true total is at least twice that figure, with some estimates putting the figure as high as 30 million. Even more startling is a study that suggests there are *200 million insects* for each human on the planet!

The numbers are clearly mind-boggling. Yet only in recent times have insects come to be regarded as a valuable forensic resource. It all stems from their role as nature's garbage collectors: they have a ravenous appetite for dead bodies. And it is this craving for putrefaction that makes them so useful when it comes to estimating the **time of death.**

When a corpse begins to decompose, its stench acts as a powerful entomological magnet. Blowflies *(Calliphoridae)* are generally the first to arrive. The females lay their eggs, and after a short time—the exact period depends on the species—the larvae emerge and begin gorging on the remains. In due course the larvae pupate and, again after a specific period, appear as newborn flies. If the body remains undiscovered, the cycle repeats itself, with other insects joining the feast. Because the behavior and the life cycle of each insect species are so well documented, they can provide a reasonably accurate estimate of the time that has elapsed since death, or the postmortem interval (PMI)—accurate to the nearest day or week, however, rather than hours.

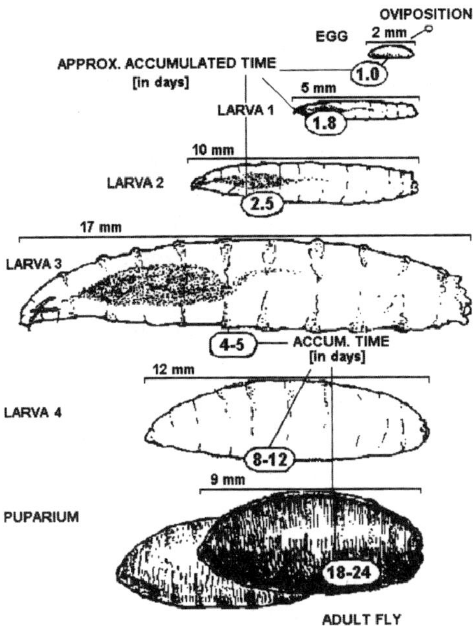

Depiction of typical immature blowfly development.

In the open air, a body can be invaded by as many as eight successive waves of insects. After the blowflies come the staphylinids; and as putrefaction develops, more species arrive at the scene, with most groups present just before the body is drying out due to seepage of liquids. After the body has dried out, dermestids, tineids, and certain mites will be the dominant groups on the body, and blowflies will gradually vanish. Last of all are the beetles, with their preference for exposed bone.

The life cycles of all these species vary, but the blowfly can be used as a representative example. Blowflies tend to lay their eggs on wounds, the eyes and lips, and in the bodily orifices, most often during daylight, and preferably in warm sunlight around the middle of the day. It is much less common—although not unknown—during the winter months. Between eight and fourteen hours later, depending on the air temperature, the eggs hatch, and the first tiny maggots appear.

This stage of development—the first instar—lasts another eight to fourteen hours, during which time the maggot reaches approximately five millimeters in length, then sheds its skin. The second instar lasts two to three days, giving the maggot time to grow to ten millimeters long. By the third instar, the maggot is now a creamy white color, and feeds voraciously for some six days, reaching some seventeen millimeters in length.

When the larva is fully grown it becomes restless and begins to wander. It is now in its prepupal stage. The prepupa then molts into a pupa but keeps the third larval instar's skin, which becomes the so-called puparium. Typically it takes one to two weeks from the egg to the pupa stage. Once again, the exact time depends on the species, the ambient temperature, and humidity. It then migrates some distance from the body and burrows into the ground, where it pupates for some twelve days before emerging as a fly. As bluebottles prefer fresh flesh, the fly is unlikely to return to the dead body. Even a covering of earth is no guarantee against insect infestation, as the "coffin fly" may burrow into the ground and can even find its way into closed caskets.

Seasonal variations also have an enormous impact on the course of insect infestation. Bodies found in the winter are far less likely to have suffered insect depredation than their summer counterparts. Geographic and habit considerations also play a big part. Has the body been found in a rural or an urban area? Insects, too, have their residential preferences, and the presence of an urban dweller on a body found by a forest lake is a strong indicator that the corpse has been moved.

It is one of the great anomalies of forensic science that insects—generally so useful for determining the time of death—can also play havoc with this determination. This happens when swarming maggots infest a decomposing body in such numbers that they can actually raise the temperature of the body, to the point where it becomes perceptibly warm. Such activity can accelerate the rapid formation of the fatty substance known as adipocere. Usually adipocere forms when a body is immersed in water or buried in moist surroundings, and it generally takes several months to develop. Nevertheless, cases are recorded in which maggot infestation has produced adipocere in as few as three weeks, making it appear that the body has lain undiscovered for much longer.

In addition to their well-known use as indicators of when someone died, insects occasionally provide clues as to *how* a person met his or her end. In most cases poisons are traced by analysis of blood, urine, and stomach contents, but after a while all of these degrade to the point of uselessness as specimens. If there are maggots, empty puparia, or larval skin casts present, these may be tested instead. Cocaine, heroin, malathion, and mercury are just a few of the substances that have been found in maggots.

But there is a trade-off. These substances affect the insects as well. High doses of cocaine can accelerate the life cycle of some sarcophagids, while the presence of antidepressants such as amitriptyline have been known to prolong the developmental time of the same species by up to seventy-seven hours. Therefore a knowledge of the victim's drug use is imperative not only in finding the cause of death but also in estimating the time.

Explosives

The criminal use of explosives falls into two categories: as an aid in furtherance of theft, such as attacking the locks of safes and strong rooms (though this is becoming increasingly rare); and as a means of attacking persons or property, usually in pursuit of some political agenda, sadly an ever-increasing threat in the modern world. Whatever the motivation, explosions remain among the most terrifying of modern experiences.

An explosion is produced by combustion accompanied by the creation of heat and gas, and it is the sudden buildup of expanding gas pressure that causes the violent blast at the center of the explosion. Bombs can be classified as "low explosive" or "high explosive" depending on the speed of detonation (the chemical reaction time). The earliest known low explosive—black powder—is thought to have originated in China, where it was used in the tenth century A.D. for fireworks and signals. During the Middle Ages black powder was supplanted by gunpowder, the composition of which typifies all the requirements for an explosive. It is a mixture, principally of potassium nitrate and charcoal, together with some sulfur. The potassium nitrate is a very rich source of oxygen, which combines with the carbon of the charcoal to form carbon dioxide.

If widely dispersed or loosely packed when detonated, low explosives (LE), although still dangerous, lose much of their destructive power. It is the container that gives LE its deadly dimension. A simple pipe bomb can be constructed by emptying the black powder from a few shotgun shells into a pipe, closing the ends, and adding a fuse. When detonated, the compressed black powder produces a large volume of gas that expands violently, forcing the walls of the pipe to bulge and stretch and ultimately fragment, launching shrapnel in all directions. But it's the shock wave that does most of the damage, hurtling outward at 3,000 feet per second.

High explosives, such as TNT (trinitrotoluene), dynamite, and PETN (pentaerythritol tetranitrate), are safer to transport and handle than their LE cousins, and for this reason they are favored by the military and industry. To detonate, high explosives require some kind of primer or blasting cap. The destructive power can be colossal, as high explosives explode almost instantaneously, at a rate of up to 20,000 feet per second, shattering their targets.

When investigating an explosion, experts will first define the area of debris fallout. This is critical. A commonly employed method is to estimate the distance from the center of the explosion to the farthest piece of debris, then seal off an area with a radius 50 percent greater than this. Everything within this zone should be investigated thoroughly.

Dents, or even more revealing, holes and scars, in vertical surfaces can help pinpoint the center of the explosion. From there, visual inspection of the damage will normally indicate the direction of the shock wave. Long metal objects such as piping, railings, and window frames—even long nails, screws, or bolts—bend away from the direction of the blast. Metal surfaces on items such as refrigerators or washing machines show a "dishing" effect, as do other empty metal containers. If, however, a metal container is full—a water tank or radiator, for instance—it will retain its shape, because the liquids inside are virtually incompressible. By subjecting similar objects to laboratory tests, it is usually possible to determine the amount of pressure that caused the damage and, from this, the nature and quantity of the explosive involved.

Embedded fragments help determine whether the explosive was in some kind of container, and, if so, what form that container took. Pieces of the detonator, such as wires and the crimping cap, mechanical detonating devices, or small fragments of a timing device also may be found. Laboratories that specialize in explosives analysis maintain a comprehensive collection of commercial products, from which it is often possible to identify the manufacturer and source of the explosive and its detonator.

The blast from an explosion is notoriously unpredictable. Ordinarily, structural elements tend to be blown outward, as do most movable objects. But anomalies do occur. For instance, when the area of low pressure that follows the shock wave passes over horizontal surfaces, such as kitchen worktops, it will often suck them upward. To the untrained eye this might give the erroneous impression that the original explosion took place beneath them.

As noted earlier, explosives are nowadays rarely seen in burglaries. The modern thief prefers thermic lances or a plasma cutting torch to gain access to some troublesome safe, and it is in the febrile world of international terrorism where explosives have assumed their most lethal incarnation.

Bombs are inexpensive to construct, easy to conceal, and virtually impossible to guard against. They can slaughter thousands and profoundly affect the lives of millions more. Whether domestic or international, the dedicated terrorist has easy access to a frightening array of explosive devices. The fertilizer-based bomb that worked with such abominable efficiency in Oklahoma in 1995 was similar in construction to the device used at the World Trade Center two years earlier. On that occasion the twin towers withstood the assault, but as the ghastly events of September 11, 2001, demonstrate, nowadays the suicide bomber doesn't even have to construct his own device; others do it for him. Twenty thousand gallons of high-octane jet fuel encased in pressured containers, traveling at several hundred miles per hour, need only the intervention of a deranged hand to convert them into the deadliest criminal use of explosives yet seen.

Facial Reconstruction

There is evidence to suggest that the art of facial reconstruction may be more than nine thousand years old. Skulls uncovered at Jericho in 1953, and dating back as far as 7500 B.C., were found to have been built up with

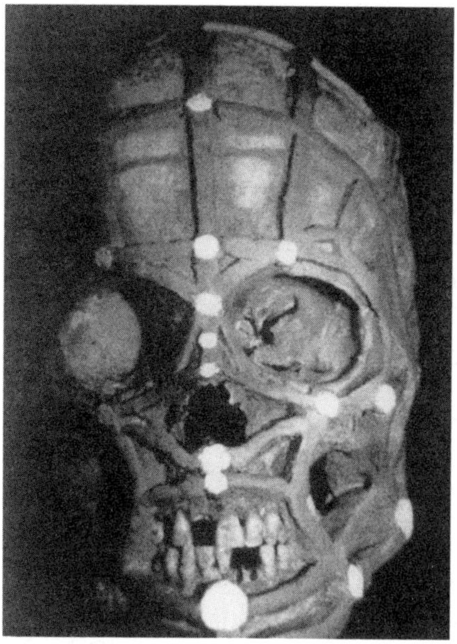

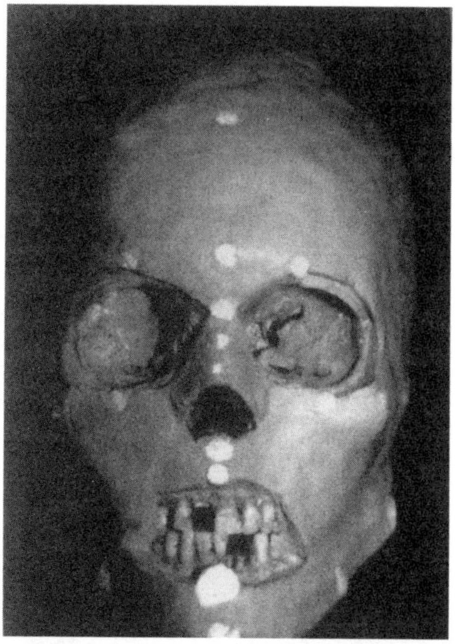

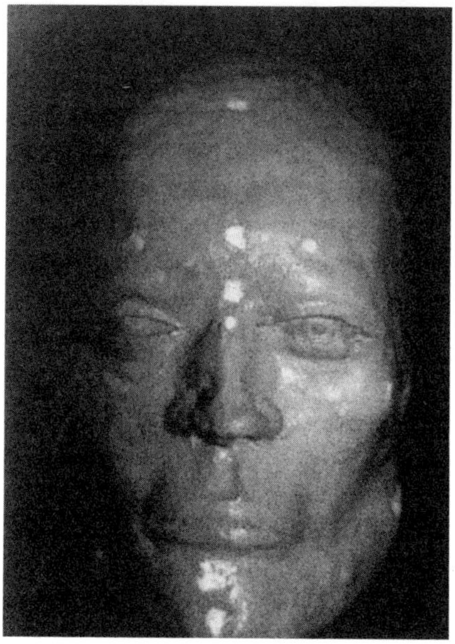

This series of photographs demonstrates one method of how facial reconstructionists set about creating a likeness.

plaster and to have shells set into the eye sockets to simulate eyes. Although probably a form of artwork, because the artists worked directly on the skull, the practice provides an indication of what our ancestors may have looked like. And this is exactly what the modern facial reconstructionist is seeking to achieve when asked to put a face to skeletonized remains.

Although the relationship of the skull to the human face has been clearly recognized for several millennia, no scientifically controlled reconstructive work was undertaken before 1895. That was the year when a Swiss-born anatomist, Wilhelm His, was given a skull rumored to be that of Johann Sebastian Bach. Through analysis of the cadavers of twenty-four males and four females, as well as experiments with soft tissue thickness measurements, His succeeded in modeling a face that confirmed that the skull did indeed belong to the great composer. Obviously, eye and hair color remained areas of guesswork—as they do to this day—but His felt confident that bone conformation alone would provide him with a clear idea of what a face should look like.

After this promising beginning, facial reconstructions were dealt a near deathblow in 1913, when two anthropologists, each given the same Neanderthal skull and asked to re-create a facial likeness, produced reconstructions of such startling dissimilarity that it beggared belief. The ensuing rift in the scientific community set back facial reconstruction research by several years.

Its revival, and the current status it enjoys, are due primarily to the Russian paleontologist Mikhail Gerasimov, whose work was featured in the 1983 movie *Gorky Park*. In 1927, while still only twenty years old, he was placed in charge of the Department of Archaeology at the Irkutsk Museum. Over the next four decades he developed the technique that still bears his name, though some term it the "Russian Method." In this, the development of the musculature on the skull and neck is regarded as being of fundamental importance. This contrasts with the so-called "American Method," which relies on the measurements of the soft tissue.

When dealing with a human skull, both schools follow similar basic protocols. After making a cast of the skull, the first step is to determine skin thickness. Using tables first formulated in the nineteenth century, the sculptor will cut small rubber pegs, all cut according to average tissue thickness, and cement them to the skull at various locations. These thicknesses vary according to the race and health of the individual, and differ for males and females. Also factored in are clues gleaned from the skeleton and any associated clothing and/or preserved soft tissue.

With the markers in place, the artist centers the eyes in the sockets and roughs out the size of the nose and mouth. The American Method estimates the projection of the nose at three times the length of a bony spur located beneath the nasal opening in the skull. The width of the nostril wings is a set distance from the lateral edges of the nasal openings: six millimeters for Europeans and Asians, and eight millimeters for Africans.

Gerasimov's disciples create the nose by extending one line from the bridge and a second line from the floor of the nasal opening, then rounding their point of intersection to make the tip of the nose. They estimate nose width as 1.67 times the width of the nasal opening.

Where the schools differ most is in tissue placement. The American Method relies heavily on the skill of the artist and less on the underlying structure of the skull. Strips of clay are placed between the tissue-thickness markers, creating an open, gridlike pattern, which the artist then fills in with more clay until a mannequinlike face begins to emerge.

Practitioners of the Russian Method tend to build up the face muscle by muscle. Most have a background in osteology and anatomy, and they begin by closely studying the bones of the face and observing asymmetries in bone structure and variations in the development of muscles. These are clues to the personal characteristics of the dead. Heavily used muscles, for example, leave prominent spurs or ridges in facial bone and show what expressions the person most often held.

Next, after siting the tissue thickness markers, the Gerasimov artist fashions eighteen major muscles from clay and places them on the face, according to their standard thickness in human beings. Using these muscles as a secondary framework, the artist applies a thin layer of clay over the face to represent subcutaneous tissue and skin. The resultant face is immediately quite lifelike and gives the artist less latitude in crafting the finished image.

The greatest difficulty comes in determining the facial features, such as the wideness of the mouth, the form of the eyelid folds, the thickness of the lips, the heaviness of the eyebrows, the shape of the ear, and the hairline on the forehead. All of these are highly subjective and rely heavily on the skill and experience of the sculptor.

An interesting recent development involves the use of high technology. A skull is set on a turntable and revolved; at the same time, a laser beam scans the skull and feeds information to a computer, where it is compared with data obtained from the head of a living person with similar skull measurements. From these comparisons, a three-dimensional likeness is developed. Currently this is not thought to be as accurate as a human-generated reconstruction.

Because facial reconstruction is so subjective—bear in mind that the overall shape of the nose can be predicted with only about 60 percent accuracy and that this drops off to 40 percent at the very tip of the nose—the technique is destined to remain an art, albeit an increasingly informed one.

Fingerprinting

Each fingerprint is unique. They develop on a fetus at about the sixth month of interuterine life and remain unchanged until the body decomposes after death. When one considers the vast array of physical changes that a human body will go through during its span, this constancy at the tips of the fingers is truly remarkable.

Although fingerprint individuality had been suspected since biblical times, it was the Czechoslovakian physiologist Jan Evangelista Purkinje who, in 1823, first recognized and described the basic patterns of fingerprints. The earliest practical application of fingerprints as an identification medium came in 1858 when a young administrative officer in India, William Herschel, adopted a local Bengali practice whereby illiterate workers "signed" for pay by leaving a thumbprint. This was done by Herschel to help stamp out pension fraud. (Apparently some wily ex-soldiers had taken to doubling, even tripling, their pensions by scribbling a mark when they were paid, then rejoining the line at the back and being paid all over again.) As soon as Herschel made a record of each pensioner's fingerprints, the scam stopped overnight. Convinced that fingerprints could be a worthwhile aid in identifying criminals, Herschel approached the local inspector general of prisons, only to be brushed off. Disillusioned, he returned to England in 1879.

That same year, a Scottish physician working in Japan, Henry Faulds, became involved in what is generally considered to be the first crime solved through the use of fingerprints. A burglar making his escape from a Tokyo house had left a dirty handprint on a whitewashed wall. When the police quickly arrested a suspect, Faulds inspected the man's prints and declared him wholly innocent, much to the amusement of skeptical investigators. Three days later Faulds was vindicated. Not only did another felon admit to the burglary, but also his handprint matched exactly the one left on the wall.

Eagerly, Faulds published his findings in the British scientific journal *Nature,* in 1880. Herschel, understandably miffed by Faulds's proprietorial exuberance, fired back a riposte, sparking off one of those bitter literary feuds that so excite the scientific world.

As tempers cooled, pragmatic analysis took over, and an English scientist, Sir Francis Galton, applied himself to the task of turning theory into practical reality. Painstakingly he laid out the ground rules for a basic classification system, putting the most commonly observed features into three groups—arches, loops, and whorls. His monumental work *Finger Prints* (1892) lit the beacon, but it was left to yet another police officer in India, **Sir Edward Henry,** to complete the task of classification.

Basically, fingerprint impressions fall into three types: latent, legible, and plastic. By far the most frequent is the *latent* print. These are formed by sweat, either from the hands themselves or by unconscious contact between the fingers and the face or other parts of the body where sebaceous glands are situated. If a criminal touches any surface, he is likely to leave a latent print, invisible to the naked eye, but this is more pronounced on smooth surfaces such as glass or polished wood.

Latent prints can be "developed" by a variety of means. The most common method is to dust the print with a high-contrast powder—white or gray/black, depending on the background—then to either photograph the print or lift it physically from the surface by means of a rubber "lifter" or transparent tape. This can then be stored and recorded. When latent prints are found on multicolored surfaces, it is customary to use fluorescent dusting powder.

The *legible* print, resulting from fingers dipped in either blood, grease, dirt, or some other contaminant, is rarely found at the crime scene, and shares its scarcity with the *plastic* print, which is an impression made on a soft surface such as tar, soap, or putty.

Although the life of a latent print is variable and can be degraded by atmospheric conditions and humidity, if made on a hard, protected surface and left untouched, it is virtually permanent. Latent prints have been found and developed from objects in ancient tombs.

Of course, a fingerprint is worthless without a reference database. This used to mean long, tedious hours spent poring over card indexes. Computerization has changed all that. The world's major law enforcement agencies all maintain huge, ever-expanding fingerprint databases, and what once may have taken weeks or even months is now accomplished in seconds.

For most of the twentieth century the sanctity of a fingerprint identification remained unchallenged; it was the one item of evidence that police, courts, and juries agreed on. But recent developments on both sides of the Atlantic have raised doubts. At issue is one fundamental question: is the identification of fingerprints—especially partial or smudged prints—a science or an art? Concerns arose in the United States when a 1995 proficiency test of 156 examiners conducted with the approval of the International Association of Identification, the profession's certifying organization, found that one in five examiners made at least one "false positive" identification—linking a mock crime-scene print to the wrong person. In the real world a 1997 burglary trial in Britain collapsed when it was learned that a Scotland Yard expert had erroneously identified the defendant's fingerprint as being identical to one found at the break-in.

While lawyers believe that courts in the future will demand a higher standard of identification—with more points of similarity—than has previously been permitted, it should be emphasized that this argument concerns only impaired prints. What is not in dispute is the principle of fingerprint individuality—it remains inviolate. In more than a century of use, in every country on earth, no two people have ever been shown to share the same fingerprint.

Jake Fleagle

Date: 1928
Location: Lamar, Colorado

Shortly after the First National Bank in Lamar, Colorado, opened its doors on May 23, 1928, four bandits burst in with guns drawn. The next few seconds were a frenzied blur as the gang stuffed cash and bonds totaling $219,000 into bags. The elderly bank president, A. N. Parrish, reluctant to relinquish the funds without a struggle, suddenly grabbed a gun from a desk drawer and began firing. One of the bandits reeled back, blood pouring from a facial wound. His gun cracked once, and Parrish fell lifeless to the floor. As Parrish's son rushed to help his stricken father, he, too, was shot dead.

At gunpoint, E. A. Lungren, a teller, and Everett A. Kessinger, the assistant cashier, were forced into the gang's waiting automobile, which raced out of town, heading west. Though hopelessly outgunned, Sheriff Lloyd Alderman set off in pursuit. So began a wild chase along the highway. With shells flying, the bandits hurled Lungren, lifeless, from their car; Kessinger they kept, to use as a human shield. After a few miles, Alderman's bullet-riddled car wheezed to a halt, and he could only pound the wheel in frustration as his quarry vanished into the distance.

Later that day, some 150 miles away, Dr. R. W. Weininger of Dighton, Kansas, received a caller at his home. The man said that his friend had been injured in a tractor accident and needed urgent medical attention. Weininger grabbed his bag, and the two men set off in the doctor's car. When Dr. Weininger failed to return home that night, his family became alarmed.

Concerns were also growing for the safety of Everett Kessinger. These proved to be well grounded when a search party found his body dumped in an abandoned shack: he had been shot several times. Not far away lay the body of Dr. Weininger, his wrecked automobile nearby. Investigators speculated that the doctor had been lured from his home to treat the wounded bandit and had then been murdered. Confounding the inquiry, though, were the contents of a note in Weininger's pocket. Apparently penned by the killer, it amounted to a bitter diatribe against the entire medical profession. Only later would its significance become clear.

The wrecked car was examined by R. S. Terwilliger, a fingerprint officer with the Garden City, Kansas, Police Department. First results were not encouraging; it had been thoroughly cleaned inside and out. But Terwilliger kept looking, and eventually his persistence was rewarded. On the passenger side rear window was a solitary partial fingerprint. Carefully he removed the glass and took it to Garden City to develop the print.

Two months later, and still unable to put a name to the print, Terwilliger sent enlarged photographs to the FBI Identification Division. At that time the division's files were classified on the Henry ten-fingerprint card system, which meant that a single print had to be manually compared with more than two million files, a vast undertaking far beyond staffing capabilities. All the FBI fingerprint experts could do was memorize the Lamar bank robbery print, on the off-chance that it might one day crop up in some other investigation.

Meanwhile, the contents of the note found in Weininger's pocket led police to Charles Clinton, a small-time crook who had developed an obsessive hatred of doctors ever since his wife died during an operation. Unable to provide alibis for the time of the bank robbery, Clinton and three of his criminal associates were arrested. Their fate seemed assured when dozens of eyewitnesses identified them as the Lamar bank robbers. But others were unconvinced. Court officials, skeptical of Clinton's involvement, kept delaying their trials.

The impasse lasted for almost a year and ended in a most unlikely fashion. Albert B. Ground, an FBI fingerprint expert, was collating a stack of identification requests when he came across a card from the sheriff's office in Stockton, California. It contained the full prints of one William Harrison Holden, who had been arrested as a train holdup suspect. Since there was no one by that name on record, Ground had been ordered to check the fingerprint file. He found that they belonged to a Jake Fleagle, taken when Fleagle had served a term for robbery at the Oklahoma State Penitentiary in 1916.

Aliases being an everyday occurrence, Ground thought nothing more about it; he would inform the Stockton sheriff's office of their suspect's true identity, and that would be that. But then something stirred in his memory. He studied the card again. That right index fingerprint seemed vaguely familiar. After several false starts he finally placed it—the partial print from that Colorado bank robbery! Comparison of the photograph and the card from Stockton left no room for doubt: the fingerprint on Weininger's rear car window had been left by Jake Fleagle.

By the time Ground telegraphed Stockton, Fleagle was no longer in custody, but a massive police sweep of Colorado and Kansas did net Ralph Fleagle, brother of Jake, as well as Howard Royston and George Abshier. All three confessed to the Lamar bank robbery and the subsequent murders. Ralph Fleagle also admitted writing the vitriolic note found in Weininger's pocket; it had been a deliberate attempt to frame his mortal enemy Charles Clinton, who was now released.

Jake Fleagle was finally run to ground as he was about to board a train in Branson, Missouri. Ordered to surrender by police, he chose to shoot it out and was killed. His brother and the other two gang members were later hanged.

Only an FBI agent's phenomenal memory prevented a miscarriage of justice, and it was clear that the unwieldy nature of fingerprint identification needed overhauling. As early as 1921, Scotland Yard's Charles Collins had published a booklet on a single-print identification system: *A Telegraphic Code for Fingerprint Formulae.* But it was not until 1928 that two other Scotland Yard officers, Frederick Cherrill and Harry Battley, refined the single-print system that was to revolutionize the war against crime.

Nowadays the automated fingerprint identification system (AFIS) employed by most U.S. law enforcement agencies would most likely have matched Fleagle's print in a matter of minutes, if not sooner. Under ideal conditions, AFIS computers have achieved comparison rates of 100,000 prints per second, which is just as well when one considers that the FBI fingerprints database now runs to more than 200 million records in civil and criminal categories.

David Frediani

Date: 1985
Location: Del Mar, California

In 1977 a young biochemist, Dr. Helena Greenwood, moved with her husband from their native England to the United States, and began a new job in California's Silicon Valley. It was the kind of life they had always dreamed of, until one day in 1984 when an intruder broke into their home in Atherton, a suburb of San Francisco, while thirty-four-year-old Helena was alone. Over a period of three hours she was sexually assaulted at gunpoint. Throughout her ghastly ordeal, Helena kept talking. Displaying immense courage and considerable common sense, she not only persuaded the attacker to let her live but also somehow managed to convince him that she would not contact the police. However, as soon as the intruder left, Helena dialed 911.

When criminalists examined the house, they found a fingerprint on a teapot that had been moved to gain entrance to the house through a window. Several months would pass before they were to match this fingerprint. It belonged to an accountant, David Frediani, who had been arrested for exposing himself to a thirteen-year-old girl. At an initial court hearing he was granted bail, and his trial was scheduled for 1985.

In the meantime Helena, eager to put this grim episode behind her, had moved to Del Mar, close to San Diego, where she had taken up a position with GenProbe, a biotech company that specialized in the burgeoning new science of DNA research. This was groundbreaking work, with Helena herself convinced that forensic DNA would one day play a vital role in crime-solving. Always at the back of her mind, though, was the unsettling thought that she would soon have to return to northern California to testify against Frediani. Then, on August 22, 1985, just three weeks before Frediani was due to stand trial, tragedy struck in the worst possible way. Helena's body, strangled and beaten, was found by her husband in the front yard of their home.

Helena had fought like a demon for her life. The evidence of that struggle was found beneath her fingernails, traces of blood and skin that she had gouged from her attacker. Immediately checks were made on Frediani's whereabouts. When detectives learned that the accountant had been involved in a traffic accident in the Los Angeles area just one week before the attack, it only hardened their suspicions that he had traveled to southern California to silence the only witness against him.

Unfortunately, under the technology of the time—DNA typing was still some way off—there was nothing that scientists could do to link the finger-

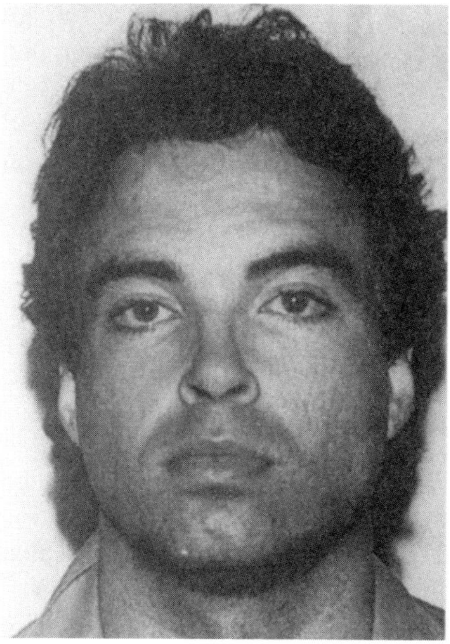

David Frediani, brutal sex attacker who tracked his victim and murdered her sixteen months later to prevent her from testifying against him.

nail scrapings to Frediani, who insisted that at the time of the murder he had been lounging by the pool of his condominium complex in San Francisco, some four hundred miles away.

After Helena's murder the assault case went to jury trial, and her pretrial testimony was admitted into evidence. Although Frediani was convicted of the assault and the burglary, the case was appealed, and the convictions were overturned. A second trial produced identical outcomes. Then, just before the third trial, Frediani pleaded no contest and, in 1989, he was sentenced to six years in prison.

Despite a huge cloud of suspicion hanging over him, Frediani, gloating and cocksure, had escaped a charge of murder. He wound up serving just three years in prison. On his release, he obtained a master's degree in business and found work as a financial analyst.

And there the story might have ended. Except that nowadays most major police departments have what is called a "cold cases" division, set up to investigate older, unsolved crimes, and in 1999, San Diego police reopened about three hundred unsolved murders, applying the very latest scientific techniques. Among those cases selected for review was the murder of Helena Greenwood. By a strange quirk of fate, the branch of DNA genetic typing that she herself had been promoting at the time of her death—obtaining usable forensic DNA material from minute samples—had now come to fruition. Suddenly those skin particles found under her nails took on a new resonance.

Using the recent advances, scientists were now able to isolate foreign DNA from the particles, and they were able to state categorically that it had originated from David Frediani. Colleagues who had worked alongside Helena at the time of her death were quick to appreciate the bitter irony of the situation. It was as though, said one, "Helena pointed her finger from the grave at her murderer."

When detectives arrested Frediani on December 15, 1999, and told him they had evidence that conclusively linked him to the killing, he had lost none of his swaggering arrogance. "Did you misplace it or something?" he sneered. "It took so long." Helena's husband didn't live to see Frediani's arrest. He had died just six months earlier, from cancer. Friends insisted that the awful tragedy that had befallen Helena hastened his end.

During Frediani's trial prosecutors told the jury that Frediani killed Helena because he was afraid he would lose his job as an accountant and be humiliated in front of his family if he was convicted of sexually assaulting her a year earlier. But it was the blood from Helena's fingernails that sealed the case. According to Gary Harmor, an expert with the Serological Research Institute, "Nobody else in the world, in my opinion, could produce that DNA profile." When asked to place a statistical likelihood to his conclusion, Harmor put the odds of a wrong match at 2.3 quadrillion to 1, "to the exclusion of everyone on the face of the earth, now and forever."

On January 31, 2001, Frediani, now age forty-six, was finally convicted of murder and subsequently sentenced to life imprisonment. It had taken almost sixteen years for Helena Greenwood's family to get justice. But the cost had been enormous. Just hours after being told the verdict, Helena's lone surviving relative, her eighty-eight-year-old father, died at his home in England.

Terry Gibbs

Date: 1999
Location: Bournemouth, England

Acting in response to concerned storekeepers on a busy street in Bournemouth, England, police went to investigate why one business was mysteriously closed. The heavily tinted windows of the Adult Fantasies sex shop were designed to keep out prying eyes, and in this respect they worked admirably, denying officers any view of the store's interior. Ordinarily on this Monday afternoon in January 1999, the store would have been open for several hours, but since lunchtime the front door had been ominously locked.

Eventually officers forced the lock and entered the premises. It was like walking into a slaughterhouse. The store manager, Adam Shaw, lay sprawled by the empty cash register, dead from a horrific knife attack. Twenty-four stab wounds to the face and upper body had sent blood spraying in all directions, up walls and across the floor. It was safe to assume that whoever had wielded the knife must have been drenched in his victim's blood.

Judging from the tangle of bloody footprints on the floor of a small kitchen at the back of the store, the killer had washed himself in a sink. Because the footprints were smeared and overlapping, it was very difficult to get a clear photograph of the tread pattern, but they appeared to have been made by some kind of sneaker.

The discovery of the front door key on the floor by the counter gave some insight into how the crime had probably unfolded. In all likelihood the killer had grabbed the key and locked the front door to prevent anyone entering while he cleaned himself up. After ransacking the cash register, in his confusion he had then dropped the key, only for it to slip out of sight by the counter. When he was unable to find it, panic set in as he realized that the store had no rear exit, which effectively meant that he was locked in with a dead body. A bloody trail showed his frantic struggle to find a way out of the store. Eventually he managed to rip a sheet of wood off some ductwork and make his escape. Traces of blood found on an outside wall raised hopes that the killer had injured himself, only for these to be dashed when the blood was matched to Adam Shaw.

Logic dictated that police were searching for the store's last customer, someone who had entered by the front door, then left though the makeshift exit at the rear. As fortune would have it, directly across the road from the crime scene, fixed high above a pub, were two CCTV (closed-circuit television) cameras that scanned the length of Old Christchurch Road.

First introduced as a crime-reducing measure in the 1970s, the use of CCTV exploded across Britain in the 1990s, to the point where it has the largest network of CCTV cameras in the world. It is estimated that at least 2.5 million cameras scan the country's mainly urban areas, and that in the course of a typical day the average city-dweller can expect to be filmed at least eight times. In some areas of London, with its more than 150,000 cameras, the capture rate on video can exceed three hundred times per day.

The effect CCTV has on crime is debatable. Advocates who point to reductions in urban crime figures are countered by critics' claims that the main impact of CCTV has been to disperse the problem, so that previously unaffected rural areas now suffer as criminals seek to avoid the camera's watchful gaze.

Regardless of the ethics or merits of CCTV, the fact remains that in this instance it offered the very real possibility of identifying the killer. Except that, by a cruel stroke of fate, neither camera actually covered the store's front door, which fell between the twin fields of vision.

But all was not lost. As both cameras were checked and found to be functioning correctly, it was a question of scouring every frame of footage, searching for anyone who left the field of vision of one camera, yet failed to reappear in the next. Eventually they found the fuzzy image of a young man seen walking down Old Christchurch Road at 12:13 P.M. by Camera One, who passed out of vision briefly, then could just be seen in the top left corner of the second camera angle as he abruptly turned around. Since he didn't reappear in the first camera shot, he could only have entered Adult Fantasies.

The man, dressed in a leather jacket with long sleeves that covered most of his hands, had a distinctive gait, wore bulky sneakers, and appeared to be studying each store as he passed, possibly assessing its suitability as a robbery target. By examining other CCTV footage from the top of Old Christchurch Road, police managed to track this young man's path toward the crime scene. But at no stage were they able to obtain a really clear image of his face, and despite public appeals, when a photograph was issued, it failed to produce any leads.

This led detectives to concentrate on the man's footwear. By combining photographs of the bloody footprint at the shop with images of the sneakers in the video, they were able to identify the make of sneaker, and that it was probably a size 10/11. At this point they contacted the manufacturers and requested a list of retail outlets for their products. Undaunted by the fact that the sneakers were sold worldwide, detectives were able to compile a list of about nine hundred people known to have purchased size 10/11 sneakers of this particular make. They decided to begin their questioning with those purchasers who lived nearest the crime scene, then radiate outward.

In one of those strokes of immense good fortune that happen all too infrequently in crime detection, the very first door they knocked on belonged to Terry Gibbs, age nineteen, who lived in a nearby town. Known to be heavily in debt from a trip taken the preceding Christmas, he also owned a leather jacket identical to that seen in the video. When he tried it on, the sleeves hung down over his hands. Even before his clothes could be sent for analysis, Gibbs confessed and admitted that the robbery had netted him just £35 (about $57 in 1999).

John Glaister (1892–1971)

The younger half of a quite remarkable father and son team who between them dominated Scottish forensic science for the first half of the twentieth century, John Jr. inherited the rank of regius professor of forensic medicine at Glasgow University from his father in 1937 and held it for another thirty-two years.

Curiously, given such a strong forensic pedigree, Glaister was originally disinclined to follow in his father's footsteps. After leaving school in Glasgow, he yearned for a life on the stage, a career choice that met with the sternest of parental disapproval. A rather one-sided compromise was agreed on: first, Glaister would qualify in the law; then he would study medicine.

But history played its hand, and in 1916, with millions of casualties littering the battlefields of western Europe, the young man found himself commissioned into the Royal Army Medical Corps. At the end of the war he returned to work as assistant in the Department of Forensic Medicine at Glasgow University. At the same time he pursued his legal studies, and in 1926 he was called to the bar at the Inner Temple, one of the London Inns of Court.

When, in the following year, **Sir Sydney Smith** resigned his chair at Cairo and returned to Edinburgh, Glaister took over Smith's official and academic posts in Egypt, confirming the high reputation of Scottish medico-legal experts abroad.

A pioneer in the identification of hair and fibers using the comparison microscope, Glaister published *Hairs of Mammalia from the Medico-Legal Aspect* (1931), which remained for several years the standard reference on the subject. At the same time he worked tirelessly to expand the horizons of forensic science. He conducted landmark research into the tricky field of estimating the time of death, analyzed skull sutures as a means of revealing age, devised a table for tracking the onset of decomposition in the human body, and was among the first to conduct intensive research into **blood spatter analysis.**

It was a hugely impressive body of work, one that found expression in *Glaister's Medical Jurisprudence and Toxicology* (1941), the editorship of which he had inherited from his father. One of the biggest fans of Glaister's monumental treatise was the American crime novelist Erle Stanley Gardner, who regularly scoured its pages for plot ideas, background research, and fact checking. In 1964 Gardner repaid the debt in some measure by dedicating his book *The Case of Horrified Heirs*—loosely based on the Buck Ruxton case (see *The Casebook of Forensic Detection,* Wiley, 1996)—to the eminent scientist.

Glaister was a kindly person, with none of the mean-spirited competitiveness that has so often marred the British medico-legal scene. Indeed, in 1952 he wrote a paper deploring the vendettas then rife between certain of his colleagues, complaining that it impaired their ability to act as a group and therefore retarded progress.

In 1969 Glaister finally relinquished the chair at Glasgow University, retiring with the honor of professor emeritus of forensic medicine.

Significant Cases

1934	Jeannie Donald
1935	Buck Ruxton
1947	Stanislaw Myszka
1950	James Robertson*

*Profiled in this book.

George Green

Date: 1938
Location: Melbourne, Australia

Annie Wiseman was a woman of regular habits. Each Saturday night the sixty-five-year-old retired at approximately eight o'clock, so that she might be up bright and early for church on Sunday morning. November 12, 1938, was no different, except that Annie's teenage niece, Phyllis, was also staying at her modest brick-built home in Glenroy, a suburb of Melbourne.

The next morning, as arranged, a friend, Mrs. Rowland Barrett, arrived to accompany the two women to church. Getting no answer to her knock, she entered the house, then stared about in utter horror. The house had been ransacked, drawers yanked out, furniture overturned, and in the midst of all the mayhem lay Annie and Phyllis on the carpet. Each had been strangled with either a lighting cord or bare hands.

The killer had been enormously powerful. As Mrs. Wiseman fought for her life, he had ground her arms so savagely into the carpet that a coin lying there had become so embedded in the flesh of her wrist that it could only be pried out with a knife blade.

That same Sunday morning, the government analyst **Charles Anthony Taylor** was summoned from his home to examine the bodies when they reached the city morgue. Double murders in Melbourne were always newsworthy events, all the more so when the victims were such law-abiding citizens, and the authorities didn't want any slipups in such a high-profile case.

Taylor's inspection of the bodies told him little beyond the fact that Mrs. Wiseman had the pure white hair that only comes with age. Then he made his way to the crime scene, where detectives had already uncovered an important clue. On the carpet between the two bodies was the torn-off corner of an old milk delivery bill, together with several coins and some dead matches. Taylor saw something else: buried deep in the carpet pile were a few grains of black powder, which smudged easily when rubbed.

Taylor finished scrutinizing the crime scene and returned to his laboratory. He soon established that the grains were household soot. Furthermore, microscopic examination of the torn bill also showed a dark smudge or smear across one corner of that scrap, again made by soot. As it seemed inconceivable that either of the fastidious Wisemans had left these traces on the bill or the carpet, in all probability the scrap had been brought to the house by the killer.

A check of local dairies produced the names of several hundred potential customers who might have received such a bill. Painstaking door-to-door inquiries finally paid off when one woman recognized her own handwriting on the fragment of paper. And she had an interesting tale to tell. Just over a week before the murders, she had moved to a new house. Four days later, on November 7, a handyman had called at her new home, asking if she needed the chimney swept. When she said no, he asked about the people who had bought her previous house: might they be interested? Thinking that this was, indeed, highly likely, she wrote out the address on a milk bill, tore off the receipted part to keep, and gave the other piece to the man, whom she described as about forty years old.

Inquiries soon led police to a chimney sweep named George Green, who lived in the Melbourne suburb of Heidelberg. He hotly denied the crimes but did admit to being given the scrap of milk bill, adding that, unable to do the job himself, he had passed the scrap to two itinerant sweeps in search of work. When pressed for names, he drew a blank. Nor could he deny that on the day of the murders he had been drinking heavily since lunchtime. At 6:00 P.M., witnesses saw him staggering from a bar, blind drunk.

Although police were convinced that Green was the killer, without hard physical evidence there was no hope of a conviction. Taylor redoubled his efforts. He wanted to know more about exactly how Mrs. Wiseman died. Pathologist Dr. Crawford Mollison told him that she had fought valiantly for her life, sustaining severe bruising to the back of her head as the killer savagely jerked it from side to side. Armed with this knowledge, Taylor hurried back to the crime scene.

He noticed that the heavy pile of the carpet where Mrs. Wiseman's head had lain was slightly flatter and a little more tangled than the surrounding parts. Deep in the disturbed pile he came across a few short pieces of pure white hair. From the lapel of the dead woman's dressing gown, he also removed a couple of dislodged white hairs. Judging from the indentations in the carpet, this had obviously been a violent, convulsive attack, one that quite possibly had left its mark on the killer.

This led him to examine Green's frayed coat, the horsehair stuffing of which protruded through the outer material. As Taylor had thought, the bristly lining had picked up and retained all manner of foreign material, including some short hairs. He harvested one strand from inside the worn lapel; another was plucked from the right side pocket of the coat, and another from Green's trouser cuff. These were not horsehairs; they were fine human hairs that tapered to a point—and they were pure white. In length, shade, texture, and other pertinent characteristics, each was microscopically indistinguishable from those found in the carpet pile and on Annie's dressing gown and with the samples that Taylor had taken from the deceased's head of white hair.

During the trial, defense claims that the hair could have come from any white-haired person, especially a young child, were dismissed by Taylor. He lucidly explained how only old people (or albinos) have pure white hair without any pigmentation. Even the blondest hair is actually a shade of cream, and these hairs had absolutely no pigmentation.

The robbery had netted just 1A£, about $2. For this paltry sum, two women lost their lives and so did Green. On April 17, 1939, he was hanged.

Hans Gross (1847–1915)

A true giant of forensic science, Gross had virtually no formal academic training, and yet he virtually invented what is nowadays termed criminalistics. Born in Austria, at age twenty-two he left Graz University, where he had studied law, to work as an examining magistrate, traveling the villages of his native Styria region, listening to cases, passing sentences, and assisting the police in investigating unsolved crimes. He was a fastidious collector of details, both physical and psychological, and for almost three decades used his courtroom as a kind of social laboratory.

In 1893 he distilled all these observations into *System der Kriminalistik* (translated into English as *Criminal Investigation*). In this groundbreaking volume Gross laid out the first truly scientific system for tackling crime, employing such radical new techniques as fingerprints, microscopy, and serology.

With its chapters on such diverse subjects as "Ciphers and Other Secret Writings" and "Cheating and Fraud," the book revolutionized crime detection and established Gross as Europe's foremost criminologist. He trained judges and police forces in his methods, and under his tutelage the Austrian police became the most advanced in Europe. Earlier than anyone else, he saw the need for meticulous organization. This led him to assemble his *Untersucherkoffer,* a detective's briefcase, with compartments holding everything an investigator might need, including rubber gloves, a measuring tape, scissors, test tubes, a magnifying glass, and various fingerprint powders. With this one innovation, Gross predated his British counterparts by several decades (see Patrick Mahon in *The Casebook of Forensic Detection,* Wiley, 1996).

In 1902 he was honored with the chair in criminology at the University of Prague (where his students included Franz Kafka). Two years later Gross was appointed professor of penal law at the university in his home city of Graz. Besides his academic duties, he continued to assist the police on several difficult cases. The culmination of his career came in 1912, at Graz University, when he founded the world's first criminological institute. Inside its museum were housed carefully mounted exhibits of murder weapons, bloodstained garments, and the other detritus of crime. It was, according to one reporter, where "all the vileness, all the wickedness, all the unalterable cruelty of mankind" could be found beneath one roof.

A bull-necked, powerful, and, from all accounts, ferociously intimidating individual, Gross came badly unstuck when he turned his attention from crime to criminals. Viewed through his mercilessly unforgiving gaze, what he termed "degenerates"—homosexuals, tramps, pederasts, career criminals, revolutionaries, and the like—were considered to be so far beyond redemption as to warrant either castration or transportation to the remote parts of Africa!

Whatever human failings may have afflicted Gross, they cannot diminish his contribution to the business of catching criminals. By the time of his death in 1915—at age sixty-seven he had enlisted to fight in World War I and contracted a fatal lung illness in the line of duty—his classic *Criminal Investigation* had become the definitive international standard on the subject, translated into several languages. Fascinating, repulsive, and informative in equal measure, it remains one of the great books on forensic science.

George Gwaltney

Date: 1982
Location: Barstow, California

On the evening of January 11, 1982, an aspiring actress named Robin Bishop had just left Barstow on the final leg of her journey home to Las Vegas, when she was pulled over by Officer George Gwaltney of the California Highway Patrol (C.H.P.). He said she had been speeding. But instead of just writing a ticket, he led her in handcuffs back to his cruiser, drove along the lonely access road off U.S. 91, then raped her on the backseat. Confident that Robin would be too scared to say anything of her ordeal, he removed the handcuffs and accompanied her back to her car. At about the same time, he radioed in a report on her vehicle. Just then another patrol car passed by and caught Gwaltney in its lights. Rattled by this intrusion—or perhaps Robin may have threatened to blow the whistle—Gwaltney made her lie on the ground and shot her in the back of the head. She was just twenty-three years old.

In a panicky voice the normally phlegmatic Gwaltney called in that he'd found a body, possibly a suicide. Then, before other officers arrived, he searched frantically beneath Robin's head for the bullet, aware that it could be matched to his revolver. To his dismay, the bullet was nowhere to be seen. (It had lodged inside the skull, near the jaw.)

Investigating officers were puzzled. There seemed no obvious reason why Robin had stopped at this deserted place: her car was well maintained, there was no evidence of robbery, and then they spotted her registration and driver's license on top of her bag, as if recently produced during a traffic stop. All eyes now swiveled in Gwaltney's direction. He described finding the body and checking for a pulse but could not account for the number of footprints he had left at the scene, in direct contravention of C.H.P. procedures.

That night Gwaltney worked fast. He removed the barrel from his revolver and the next morning went to a local gun shop to get a replacement, only to learn that the barrel wasn't in stock and would need to be ordered.

His other attempts to compromise any possible trace evidence included having his uniform dry-cleaned and his holster redyed and restitched.

In the meantime, the autopsy found marks on Robin's wrists consistent with her having worn handcuffs, and it confirmed that she had had sex shortly before death. There was one other significant finding: the bullet was not standard police issue ammunition.

All local law enforcement officers on duty that night were ordered to surrender their weapons for ballistics inspection. Gwaltney was the only one to refuse. When visited at his house, he tried vainly to bluff investigators by producing another gun, then claimed his service revolver had been stolen in a recent burglary. In a bedroom closet bullets of the same nonstandard issue ammunition as that used in the killing were found. Gwaltney denied ownership of the ammunition, saying it had been planted.

The missing .357 Smith & Wesson magnum, minus all the identifying parts, including its barrel, was eventually found in his truck. Toolmarks etched into the gunmetal surface may have come from wrenches and a pipe vise found in Gwaltney's garage—all showed signs of metal transfer—but, inexplicably, a proper comparison was not made.

Most C.H.P. officers rallied behind Gwaltney, a well-respected patrolman and father of five, refusing to accept that he was a killer, especially after he passed a polygraph exam. Even when semen was found on the backseat of the cruiser and in Robin's jeans, they still supported his claim that he was the victim of a frame-up. So did local gun shop owners, none of whom recalled serving Gwaltney recently.

State prosecutors were convinced they had enough to try Gwaltney for murder, but they had not reckoned on his excellent witness stand demeanor. It was enough to deadlock the jury and win a mistrial on December 14, 1982. A second trial produced an identical outcome, after which the judge dismissed all charges.

There was one option still open to the authorities: federal court. Under recently enacted legislation, Gwaltney could still be charged with violating Robin Bishop's civil rights. With this in mind, control of the investigation passed to the FBI. Almost immediately, agents noticed something that earlier investigators had missed. A photograph of Gwaltney's patrol car trunk taken at the time of the crime showed a box of nonstandard issue ammunition, which he'd denied ever owning. When enlarged, it was identical to that found in his bedroom closet. In related tests, chemical analysis of the lead in this ammunition found it to be identical to that found in the bullet that killed Robin Bishop.

FBI scientists also examined fifteen tools from Gwaltney's garage, to see if they had been used on the dismantled gun. A broken tooth on one pipe wrench was found to leave a $\frac{1}{16}$-inch mark when used, which corresponded exactly to a blemish left on the gun.

One unusual twist came from the fact that Gwaltney had undergone a vasectomy reversal, a procedure that can lead to the formation of antisperm antibodies. Samples from the backseat of the cruiser, Robin's jeans, and Gwaltney's sperm all showed this identical trait, which occurs in fewer than 1 percent of the population.

The investigation now began to snowball. Every woman who'd received a ticket from Gwaltney in the past two years was now contacted. A dozen reported some kind of sexual abuse. Elsewhere, a gun shop owner now admitted lying under oath, when store phone records showed that, on the day after the killing, the owner had called around, looking for a Smith & Wesson revolver barrel.

Legal history was made when Gwaltney became the first California law officer to be charged under the federal civil rights statute. This time he didn't escape justice. On June 25, 1984, he was sentenced to ninety years for violating Robin Bishop's civil rights. He died in prison twelve years later.

John Haigh

Date: 1949
Location: Crawley, England

It was a quiet Sunday afternoon in February 1949 when a man and a woman called at a London police station to report the disappearance of Mrs. Olive Durand-Deacon, an elderly fellow resident at the Onslow Court Hotel in South Kensington. The man, dapper and neatly dressed, with a trim mustache, and who gave his name as John Haigh, told of arranging to meet Mrs. Durand-Deacon two days earlier, to take her to his place of business in Sussex, but she had failed to keep the appointment. Haigh's air of oily superiority grated so much on the woman police officer who logged the report that she informed her superiors. They ran a check of criminal records that revealed a checkered past: the thirty-nine-year-old self-professed inventor had three convictions for swindling. Significantly, he had no visible means of income.

Acting on suspicion and not much else, officers visited Haigh's business premises, a grimy warehouse in Crawley, to the south of London. Here they discovered a .38 revolver and a receipt for a fur coat from a firm of dry cleaners. When it was learned that the coat had belonged to Mrs. Durand-Deacon, and that Haigh had sold some of her jewelry to a local store, he was taken into custody.

After first attempting—and failing—to convince his interrogators that Mrs. Durand-Deacon was a society blackmailer, Haigh suddenly looked up and blithely inquired as to the chances of anyone being released from Broadmoor, Britain's best-known asylum for the criminally insane. He then gloated, "If I told you the truth you wouldn't believe me. . . . Mrs. Durand-Deacon no

Professor Keith Simpson sifting through human remains found at the workshop of serial killer John Haigh.

longer exists. . . . I have destroyed her with acid. . . . You'll find the sludge that remains at Leopold Road [Crawley]. . . . How can you prove murder if there is no body?" While serving one of his previous sentences, Haigh had scoured the prison library for law books, wherein he had come across the legal term *corpus delicti.* Like others before and since, he had misunderstood it to mean that without a corpse it was impossible to prove murder, whereas the expression actually refers to the body of an offense or crime having taken place.

Oblivious to his blunder, Haigh went on to detail an incredible career of murder, six victims since 1944—he later increased the tally to nine—all killed for profit and all dissolved in drums of sulfuric acid. Afterward he had disposed of the sludge down the drain. On February 18 he had duped Mrs. Durand-Deacon into visiting his "factory" at Crawley, ostensibly to discuss the manufacture of plastic fingernails, and killed her.

As a means of hedging his defense bets, Haigh laid the groundwork for a plea of insanity, by claiming that the murders had been motivated by a morbid bloodlust. After each killing he would toast his success with a glassful of his victim's blood. For good measure he also claimed that the murders had been divinely inspired. While on remand, perhaps to foster belief in his mental instability, he began drinking his own urine.

The Home Office pathologist **Keith Simpson** examined the Crawley premises, aware that if Haigh's smug admission that he had poured the Durand-Deacon "sludge" over the ground several days earlier were true, then evidence of murder would indeed be hard to come by. He found the sludge easily enough, covering an area about six feet by four, to a depth of three inches.

He also found something else, no larger than a cherry pit, lying among some pebbles: a gallstone. Wearing thick rubber gloves to combat the still corrosive acid, searchers sifted the sludge in steel trays. Their efforts were rewarded with the recovery of a partially dissolved left foot, a full set of dentures, two more gallstones, twenty-eight pounds of animal fat, eighteen corroded bone fragments, the handle of a red plastic handbag, and a lipstick container. Far from obliterating the body, Haigh had left more than enough to hang him.

Specks of blood on the wall above a workshop bench were shown to be human, as were other bloodstains on the fur coat and on one of Haigh's shirts. The red plastic strap was identified as belonging to the handbag carried by Mrs. Durand-Deacon when she left to keep her appointment with Haigh on February 18.

In his laboratory at Guy's Hospital in London, Simpson identified most of the bone fragments as human; in some joints he detected the presence of osteoarthritis, an ailment known to have afflicted Mrs. Durand-Deacon. Meanwhile, the police had made a plaster cast of the left foot and checked it against a shoe belonging to Mrs. Durand-Deacon; the fit was perfect. The missing woman's dentist examined the dentures and confirmed that she had fitted Mrs. Durand-Deacon with them two years earlier. Unknown to Haigh, they were made of acrylic and therefore unusually resistant to acid. The identification was complete. Nor was Simpson impressed by Haigh's claims of insanity. "A tough, shrewd little businessman" was Simpson's characterization, and it is difficult to argue with the assessment.

After a trial lasting fewer than two days, Haigh was found guilty of murder and later hanged. Ironically, it was his determination to feign madness that secured the noose around his neck. Had he not decided to confess and pin his hopes on a plea of insanity, then in all likelihood the sludge would have remained undiscovered for weeks; and, as Simpson later admitted, by that time the acid might well have consumed everything but the gallstones and the human fat, which, in themselves, would have constituted insufficient evidence of identity.

Hair and Fibers

Whether left at a crime scene by the perpetrator or carried away on his person, hairs and fibers have provided some of the most crucial evidence in countless cases. Because of their relative similarity, they are often considered jointly.

Hair

The significance of hair in the investigation of crime has been recognized for many years. As early as 1857, a paper on the subject was published in

France; then came **John Glaister**'s *Hairs of Mammalia from the Medico-Legal Aspect* (1931)—still a highly regarded reference book on the subject.

Hair can be defined as slender outgrowths of the skin of mammals. Composed of protein, mostly keratin, it grows from follicles, which house the bulb or root. From there, the hair has two other parts, the shaft and the tip. Viewed microscopically in cross section, the three-piece inner section can be seen: the cuticle or outer sheath, formed of overlapping scales; the cortex, containing the pigment granules that give hair its natural color; and the hollow medulla, the central core, which contains air. Hair is exceedingly durable, and unless destroyed by some outside agent, it often remains identifiable on a corpse long after the flesh has decomposed. Similarly, it can adhere to a murder weapon for a gratifyingly long period of time.

In a mature adult scalp hair grows at approximately half of one inch per month. Unsurprisingly, the male beard grows much faster than this; conversely, other bodily hair has a far slower growth rate. Because we shed up to one hundred hairs each day, and because hairs are often transferred during physical contact, their presence can link a suspect to a crime scene.

The comparison microscope is the means normally used to reveal similarities and differences between two sample hairs. Distinguishing between human and animal hair is relatively straightforward. Each species of animal possesses hair with characteristic length, color, shape, root appearance, and internal distinctive microscopic features. These have been logged in recognition charts that permit quick identification of the species involved.

Forensic examiners can differentiate among hairs of Caucasoid (European ancestry), Mongoloid (Asian ancestry), and Negroid (African ancestry) origin, all of which exhibit microscopically distinguishable characteristics. To some extent they can hazard a guess as to the age of the person concerned—as we get older, hair undergoes pigment loss and changes in the configuration of the hair shaft, so that it becomes much finer and more variable in diameter.

What is still beyond forensic absolutism is the ability to identify the sex of the donor, unless the bulb is still intact and DNA analysis can be employed. (As a very rough rule of thumb, longer hair, particularly if it has been treated with dyes or other chemicals, is generally regarded as female.) Nor is the examiner able to state unequivocally that a particular hair came from a particular individual. The best that can be said is that the two samples closely resemble one another.

Fibers

According to the *World Directory of Manufactured Fiber Producers,* 34.2 million tons of fiber were produced worldwide in 2000. Of this, more than half of all fibers used in the production of textile materials are man-made. Some originate from natural materials such as cotton or wood; others are made from synthetic materials. Polyester and nylon fibers are the most commonly encountered man-made fibers, followed by acrylics, rayons, and acetates. There are also many other less common man-made fibers. The scarcity of any particular fiber increases its probative value as evidence.

Wool is the most common natural fiber, and a knitted sweater, or any similar garment, sheds fibers constantly. It also acts as a fiber magnet. When two people come in contact, or when contact occurs with an item from a crime scene, there is a likelihood of fiber transference. This does not mean that a fiber transfer *will* always take place. Much depends on the type of fabric; some closely woven fabrics do not shed easily, and others do not retain fibers well. Age is another factor. Newer fabrics tend to shed more readily because of an abundance of loosely adhering fibers on the surface of the fabric. Damaged areas of fabric are also more likely to shed easily. For instance, if a car hits a pedestrian, the bodywork is almost certain to retain fibers from clothing, which can be discovered with a magnifying glass and removed with sticky tape for examination.

Once in the forensic laboratory, the fiber has very little chance of escaping identification. Comprehensive registers that list all types of natural and artificial fibers make this a relative formality. The problem lies in statistical frequency: how often does this particular fiber crop up in everyday life?

A white cotton thread, for example, might have come from literally thousands of different garments. On the other hand, a rare acrylic—especially if it has been dyed an unusual color—would have a much lower incidence in general life. The investigator is constantly searching for the lowest possible frequency. This is because, as with hair, it is impossible to state with certainty that a fiber originated from a particular garment. "Microscopically indistinguishable" is all the examiner can commit himself to. Thereafter it becomes a question of statistical probabilities: just how rare is this particular fiber?

It has been said that hair and fiber evidence is primarily corroborative, only of value when used in conjunction with other evidence. While this may be accurate, it should be made clear that this does not, in any way, diminish its importance. Too many crimes have been solved using this form of trace evidence for it to be disregarded.

James Hanratty

Date: 1961
Location: Slough, England

Britain's longest-running and most highly publicized "miscarriage of justice" began on the evening of August 22, 1961, when a car containing lovers Michael Gregston, a married man, and Valerie Storie was parked in a cornfield overlooking the River Thames, near Slough. At about 9:30 P.M. a man tapped on the window and threatened the couple with a gun. He said he was on the run from the law and, getting into the backseat, ordered Gregston to drive off. Over the next five or six hours the car weaved an erratic journey across northwest London, onto the A6 road, and into Bedfordshire. At a spot known as Deadman's Hill, the gunman instructed Gregston to pull into a lay-by.

After they had been parked for some time, the gunman told Gregston to hand him a bag from the front seat. Suddenly he opened fire, killing Gregston instantly. After a hysterical fifteen-minute hiatus, during which the gunman garbled that he had been startled by the abruptness of Gregston's movements, he ordered Valerie into the backseat and raped her. Afterward he and Valerie dragged her dead lover out of the car. Once this was accomplished, the gunman fired a salvo of bullets that cut Valerie down. Leaving her for dead by the side of the road, he made off in the car.

Miraculously, Valerie Storie survived, though she would remain paralyzed. Throughout the six-hour ordeal she had managed just a single, brief glimpse of the killer, and it must be said that her subsequent descriptions of him were wildly conflicting. Because of this confusion, two different Identikit pictures were compiled and published. Eventually, investigative leads steered the inquiry in the direction of a twenty-five-year-old petty criminal named James Hanratty, who had gone missing from his usual haunts in London. There was just one problem: Hanratty did not resemble either Identikit picture.

At this point Valerie Storie honed her description of the "A6 Killer" to include "staring icy-blue eyes," a singular characteristic of Hanratty's. Reinforcement for the police view that Hanratty was the killer came when two .38 cartridge cases from the murder weapon were found in a London hotel room occupied on the night before the murder by a "Mr. J. Ryan," an alias used by Hanratty. (The murder weapon had subsequently been discovered, hidden beneath a seat on a London bus.)

However, on the night after the murder, the same hotel room was occupied by an odd character named Peter Louis Alphon, who in some areas resembled the Identikits. When he was placed in a lineup, not only did Valerie Storie fail to recognize him, she actually picked out someone else—an entirely innocent person—as the killer.

Eventually Hanratty was arrested in Blackpool on October 9, identified by Storie at yet another lineup, and sent for trial. Given Storie's contradictory descriptions of the killer and her misidentification, grave doubts attended her testimony, but it was impossible not to feel sympathy for a young woman who had to be carried on a stretcher into court. Hanratty, by contrast, came across as brash and stupid. Suicidally garrulous, he first claimed to have been in Liverpool—some two hundred miles away—on the night of the murder, visiting some criminal friends whom he declined to identify. Then, in a breathtaking volte-face, he switched his alibi to say that

The body of gunshot victim Michael Gregston, as it was found at Deadman's Hill. Hanratty was hanged for the murder. Four decades later DNA profiling confirmed that there had been no miscarriage of justice.

he had not been in Liverpool after all but rather in Rhyl, North Wales. Such an inexplicable change of story—as idiotic as it was unnecessary—coupled with his witness-box braggadocio, completely obliterated Storie's evidentiary shortcomings and led to his being sentenced to death.

Even before his execution, there was a public groundswell of unease about the verdict. In a letter to his brother on the night before he was hanged, he wrote, "I would like you to try and clear my name of this crime. Someone, somewhere, is responsible for this crime and one day . . . the truth will come out."

Throughout the 1960s, the view that Hanratty had been the victim of a grave miscarriage of justice gained impetus. John Lennon was just the most famous of many public figures who aligned themselves with the Hanratty cause. But the Home Office was implacable in its refusal to reopen the case, despite the belated appearance of a dozen or so people who claimed to have seen Hanratty in Rhyl on the fateful night. Peter Alphon also stoked the flames, first boasting that *he* was the A6 killer, then withdrawing the claim.

For decades Hanratty's family fought to clear his name. Rumors had filtered through of evidence from the original inquiry—a handkerchief that the killer had wrapped around the gun and semen stains on Valerie Storie's underwear—still surviving, and they wondered if modern science could finally prove Hanratty innocent.

After protracted lobbying, in 2000 the Home Office yielded to pressure and allowed DNA tests to be made. In the first trials samples were taken from Hanratty's brother, Michael, and compared to the evidence. The results delivered a bombshell. They showed that Hanratty, or someone very closely related to him, *was* the A6 killer, with a probability put at "2.5 million to 1." Hanratty's family fought back angrily, with Michael publicly dismissing the tests as "flawed."

Determined to lay this ghost once and for all, the authorities permitted Hanratty's body to be exhumed. On March 21, 2001, his remains were disinterred and tissue samples were taken. This time the results were even more unequivocal, with a "1 in 100 million chance" that the DNA came from someone other than James Hanratty.

Even this failed to silence the pro-Hanratty campaign. But noisy protestations that poor evidence storage resulted in cross-contamination between items retrieved from Storie and Hanratty were destroyed when new techniques were able to distinguish between primary and secondary contamination. For many, DNA profiling's greatest triumph has been the way it has exonerated those people who have innocently fallen foul of the legal system. James Hanratty was not one of them.

On May 10, 2002, the Court of Appeal finally drew a line under this case when it dismissed the family's appeal for the last time.

Lewis Harry

Date: 1986
Location: Tempe, Arizona

The case that Maricopa County deputy district attorney Cleve Lynch described as "the most interesting of my career" began in the offices of the Transamerica Title Insurance Company in Tempe, Arizona, on a Monday morning in 1986. Julie Anne Williams, age forty-six, was in the break room, helping herself to some water from the fountain. As she sipped it, she instantly grimaced: it tasted awful. Bad enough, in fact, to send her running to the bathroom. When she had not reappeared sometime later, concerned employees went to investigate. They found her comatose on the floor. Despite urgent medical attention, she died in the hospital without regaining consciousness.

The remaining staff were in shock. For one, Diane Harry, the tragedy was doubly unnerving. Just a few days earlier something similar had happened to her. She had noticed a strange smell in the break room and felt instinctively that something was amiss with the coffee or creamer. Anxious and distraught, she now rushed to the phone to pour out her concerns to her husband.

Lewis Harry, a regular visitor to the office, responded immediately. When he arrived he first consoled his wife, then tried to assist officers in their efforts to gather samples for analysis. They good-naturedly refused his offer of help before taking away the coffee, creamer, and sugar for analysis, along with the water cooler. They also began dusting the scene for fingerprints that didn't belong there but found nothing irregular.

Diane, meanwhile, was amplifying her account for detectives. She told how, on the previous Friday—March 21—she had become ill at home after taking a sip of scotch. That, too, had smelled bad, similar to the break room odor, which was why she hadn't drained the glass. Even so, she'd still spent the entire weekend in bed, suffering from cramps and a stomachache. A cup of tea had affected her similarly. At this point Lewis voiced his belief that someone was trying to poison Diane, that she was the intended target, and that poor Julie Anne Williams had been the inadvertent victim of a sadistic murderer.

Lewis gave his reasons. Just recently he'd received two threatening letters from the obsessive boyfriend of a woman he'd known. He had no doubts that the jealous ex-lover had tried to gain revenge by poisoning his wife, except that it had all gone horribly wrong. Lewis was sent home to collect the letters, the scotch bottle, and the teakettle so that they might be chemically analyzed.

Toxicologists read carefully through the reports of the victim's symptoms. They were clearly looking for a fast-acting poison, in all likelihood either strychnine or some kind of cyanide. It didn't take long for their suspicions to be confirmed. All the samples—from both the office and the Harrys' home—revealed the presence of potassium cyanide in massive quantities. The water dispenser alone contained enough to kill 150 people.

Police suspected that whoever planted the poison did so over the weekend. A check of the office's security system showed that only one pass card had been used to gain access in that time. It belonged to Diane Harry. She protested that at the time her card had been used—10:18 A.M. on Saturday—she was home in bed, and the card was in her purse, where it remained all weekend.

But what about her husband? Diane grudgingly admitted that she couldn't account for his whereabouts on Saturday morning. Nor could he, other than to say he'd been out running errands until returning home around 12:30 P.M. The police got a break. A person who worked just across the road from the Transamerica Title Insurance Company recalled seeing a black male, in his early thirties, parking a blue sports car nearby at about 10:15 A.M.

Since Lewis Harry was black, drove just such a car, and was thirty-two years old, police felt they had enough to apply for a warrant to search his workplace, the sports department of a local college. What they found in his office amounted to forensic gold dust. In the trash can was a label from a chemical supplies company; there was some white powder on a shelf, along with a small plastic knife that also showed white traces. In both instances the powder was identified as potassium cyanide.

As suspicious as this sounded, it still did not provide conclusive proof against Harry. A smart defense attorney would have little difficulty persuading a jury that all this evidence could easily have been planted by the jealous boyfriend in order to frame Harry. But the forensic clues kept on coming. A legal pad found in Harry's office showed handwritten versions of the very letters that Harry claimed had been sent by the boyfriend. Handwriting comparison with known exemplars of Harry's writing left no doubt as to the authorship. After correcting the letters in longhand, he had then typed the two letters and mailed them to himself.

When detectives called at the chemical company whose label had been found in the trash can, a clerk recalled selling cyanide to someone who matched Harry's description. The purchaser had given his name as Charles Holly, but when no one with this name could be found, Harry was asked to supply a sample of his own handwriting. It matched the sales receipt. At this point Lewis Harry was charged with murder and attempted murder.

Prosecutor Lynch was able to show that Harry had, in fact, received threatening letters from the ex-boyfriend of a woman he was having an affair with, and it was this that inspired him to write his own letters, implicating the boyfriend.

Diane refused to believe that her husband had tried so hard to kill her just so he could be with another woman. Even when, on February 12, 1987, he was imprisoned for life, she still stuck by him. For twelve months her support never wavered—not until her brother, rummaging through the attic at her home, stumbled across a box of potassium cyanide hidden among some other effects. Only then did Diane Harry realize how gravely she had misjudged the man she married.

Eric Hayden

Date: 1995
Location: Kirkland, Washington

On the morning of May 14, 1995, the body of Dawn Fehring, a twenty-seven-year-old old Bible student, was found on the bedroom floor of her apartment in Kirkland, Washington. Apart from the top bedsheet and a T-shirt, which were wrapped around her head and neck, she was nude. There were bloodstains on the carpet near her body and what looked like bloody handprints on the fitted bedsheet covering the mattress. An autopsy revealed that Dawn had died from asphyxiation, most likely the previous Friday evening, and that the source of the blood was a torn hymen.

Despite the fact that she had been raped, there were no DNA traces of her attacker (many rapists nowadays use condoms). In fact, the crime scene was remarkably clean, apart from some cigarette ash and tobacco found near the bed. Since Dawn was a nonsmoker, it was reasonable to assume that this came from the killer.

During routine interviewing of the other residents in the apartment building, a strong suspect began to emerge. Eric Hayden, who had a criminal record and lived upstairs from Dawn, seemed unnaturally nervous when asked to account for his whereabouts on the Friday evening. Instinctively he grabbed a cigarette before answering. His recollection was hazy and consisted of a claim to have been out drinking with some friends, but when asked to provide names, he drew a blank. According to his girlfriend, Hayden said he'd been too drunk to remember where he'd been.

Being drunk to the point of amnesia hardly amounted to proof of murder, and at first glance there seemed to be nothing to connect Hayden with the crime—except, perhaps, those smudged handprints.

Trying to lift prints from any fabric is fiendishly difficult, which is why Daniel Holshue, a King County latent print examiner, opted to employ a revolutionary procedure. After cutting out the five areas of the bedsheet that contained the most blood and prints, he treated these samples with amido black, a dye stain that reacts with organic proteins such as blood. At the back of his mind was one overriding concern: what if such a drastic technique destroyed the only piece of genuine evidence? At first this anxiety seemed justified as the whole sample turned navy blue, but rinsing in pure methanol gradually lightened the background, to the point where protein-based handprints became faintly visible. As a final step Holshue dipped the samples in distilled water to set the prints.

Even after all these chemical processes were completed, the contrast between the latent prints and the pieces of bedsheet was still too subtle for Holshue to isolate the requisite number of points of comparison necessary for a positive identification. It was like peering into a maze, as the weave of the fabric and the whorls and ridges of the prints themselves merged into one amorphous whole.

At this point Holshue enlisted the assistance of Erik Berg, an imaging expert at the Tacoma Police Department, which had begun using forensic digital enhancement just a few months earlier, in January 1995.

Open any modern magazine and chances are that it will contain digitally enhanced or restored photographs. This is especially true in the advertising sections, where photographic editors tweak and airbrush their way to the desired effect. The technique evolved from NASA programs in the 1960s, as scientists sought to isolate galaxies and receive signals from satellites. It is expensive and time-consuming, two reasons why law enforcement agencies have been reluctant to embrace it. Then there is the question of veracity. The whole point of digital enhancement is to alter an existing image. Ordinarily this would be anathema in any court of law, which is why, when Berg received the samples, his first course of action was to encrypt and store the original of the print, using government standard software, to negate any potential claim of photo tampering.

The digital photographs are enhanced using software that improves sharpness and image contrast. In addition, pattern and color isolation filters remove interfering colors and background patterns. Working with copies of the original, Berg struggled at first to make any headway. It was a poor image, with the ridge patterns and the fabric pattern intermingled, but after persevering with various programs, he managed to filter out the weave pattern. While this did blur the background, it also reduced the contrast of the image. To compensate, Berg employed another program, which raised the tonal values of the ridge details, much like increasing the contrast on a television set. Finally he had a usable print.

Using the enhanced photographs of the latent prints, Holshue was now able to locate twelve points of comparison on one of the fingerprints and more than forty on a palmprint, conclusive proof that prints on the bedsheet belonged to Eric Hayden.

On June 5, 1995, Hayden was charged with murder. At his trial, defense counsel claimed that digital enhancement was an unproven technique and tried to have the prints evidence thrown out. To counter this charge, Berg set up his equipment in court and demonstrated how he had obtained his results. He explained that digital photography's big advantage over its analogue film cousin is that it can capture no fewer than 16 million different colors and differentiate among 256 shades of gray.

Most important of all, Berg was able to demonstrate that digital enhancement is a subtractive process in which elements are removed or reduced; nothing is added. His software package prevented him from adding to, changing, or destroying the original image. In contrast with "image restoration," a process whereby details not present are added to achieve the desired end result, "image enhancement" merely makes what is there clearer and more usable.

After hearing that the Los Angeles County Sheriff's Department had been using digital image processing as a means of enhancing latent fingerprints since 1987, the judge decided that there was plenty of precedent for the technique and admitted the evidence. This left the outcome in no doubt, and Hayden received a life term.

Steven Heflin

Date: 1976
Location: Rainier, Oregon

When a twenty-five-year-old Oregon school bus driver named Vicki Brown failed to show up for work at the Rainier Union High School on February 10, 1976, her place on the morning run was taken by Steven Heflin, a young bus mechanic, who had arrived at work much earlier than usual that day. Later that morning, when another driver noticed an ominous stain on the bus barn wall, everyone present, except Heflin, agreed that it looked like blood. His skepticism persisted when yet more reddish spots turned up on a gravel drive outside the repair shop. "Transmission fluid," he jeered, even when a colleague poured transmission oil onto the ground and it seeped into the gravel, unlike the coagulated stain. Fears of foul play skyrocketed, though, with the discovery in the bus barn of numerous blond-brown hairs and a dental bridge identified as belonging to Vicki Brown.

The lead detective assigned to investigate the strange disappearance, Inspector Dean Renfrow, noticed Heflin's edginess under questioning, as well as his exaggerated eagerness to help when volunteers were asked to man a search party. At dusk, just as the search was about to be abandoned for the day, Heflin announced unilaterally that he would make one last pass through some nearby woods. Minutes later he was back, breathless from running, brandishing a woman's sodden handbag on the end of a stick. He'd found it, he gasped, in a small pond. Inside was a wallet bearing Vicki Brown's name.

Renfrow studied Heflin closely. Already he had learned that Vicki Brown, single and fun-loving, was a free spirit who had enjoyed sexual relations with several fellow employees, with the notable exception of Heflin, whom she'd pointedly avoided. A motive, perhaps? Renfrow wondered.

A teacher at the school produced a strong lead. She recalled that the previous evening, at approximately six forty-five, she had heard scuffling sounds, followed by a scream and a gunshot. Initially she had assumed that the disturbances had come from students rehearsing a Western play; now she wasn't so sure. At about the same time, a student had seen someone with thick sideburns and a drooping mustache, dressed in a dark motorcycle jacket, driving off in a pickup truck. The description fitted Heflin exactly.

Heflin's pickup was a forensic bonanza. There were bloodstains in the carrying compartment as well as on its plywood bedliner, the bench seat, and on a pair of gloves. Also found were some strands of blond-brown hair. Extending the search to Heflin's home, Renfrow recovered a .22 Ruger revolver, its grip covered with a sticky substance that resembled blood. He also caught Heflin attempting to conceal a black vinyl motorcycle jacket and a pair of leather gloves. Both were soaking wet, as though recently washed.

All the blood found was type O with a positive Rh factor. Approximately 85 percent of the population is Rh positive, and about half of these have type O blood. Included in both categories was Steven Heflin. However, one stain found in the barn and another on a shovel discovered near Heflin's house contained a relatively minor "c" factor. This factor was missing from Heflin's blood. If Vicki's blood was also type O positive *and* contained the missing "c" factor, a link would be made.

Unfortunately, no one knew Vicki's blood type, so it was impossible to compare the samples found.

At this point, Heflin's gun and a section of blood-streaked board from the barn wall were sent to the renowned criminalist Herbert MacDonell for analysis. His preliminary examination located blood inside the gun's muzzle, on its barrel, and in the empty cylinders. He attributed the external staining to backspatter caused by blood from the bullet wound splashing back over the gun. Ordinarily, internal muzzle staining happens in the same way, often up to a distance of 2 feet, but in this instance MacDonell felt that the Ruger's tight .22 muzzle was unlikely to have admitted blood from anything like that range. He believed it had actually been sucked back into the muzzle by the contraction of the hot explosive gases as they cooled, an action likeliest to occur if the bullet struck bare skin at very close range.

Through a series of experiments on sick and diseased animals already scheduled for humane destruction, MacDonell was able to compile a unique table. After each test, all from varying ranges, he measured how far down the muzzle the blood was drawn. Eventually he established a direct correlation between gun-to-target distance and the depth of muzzle contamination. With the Ruger, blood had been drawn roughly 0.33 inch down into the muzzle. According to MacDonell's table, this placed the muzzle no more than 3 inches away from the skin when fired, possibly less.

By studying a floor plan and photographs of the barn, MacDonell was also able to sketch out the likely crime scenario. After driving her bus into the barn, Vicki had been jumped by a gun-wielding assailant. Fighting back furiously, she had received a savage pistol-whipping that dislodged her dental bridge and tore out strands of hair. MacDonell reasoned that the assailant then pinned Vicki against the wall and fired. Judging from the wide blood pattern on the board, the bullet struck bare skin. Had it traveled through clothing, most of the spraying blood would have been absorbed by the fabric. He further concluded that Vicki had been shot in the skull, because on a cold winter's evening the two bodily areas most likely to be exposed were the head and hands, and no hand wound could have produced such a fountain of blood. Afterward, he figured, Heflin hauled Vicki the entire length of the garage, threw her into the rear of his truck, then drove off and dumped the body.

Analysis of the hair found in Heflin's truck and hair from Vicki's brush revealed thirty points of similarity, but the technology of the time did not allow for a positive identification; so it was with considerable trepidation that Oregon prosecutors decided to try Heflin for murder. Not since 1904 had the state attempted to prove a homicide case without having a body. But on September 8, 1976, their faith was vindicated. Heflin was convicted and later sentenced to death (commuted to life imprisonment).

Edward O. Heinrich (1881–1953)

America's greatest forensic scientist of the early twentieth century, this tall, unassuming doctor at the University of California became known as the

"Wizard of Berkeley" for the almost preternatural way in which he managed to solve countless crimes during his long career. When Heinrich entered the world of crime-fighting, it was plagued by shoddy technology and world-class charlatans. Almost single-handedly, he restored the reputation of the expert witness in the American courtroom. With uncanny feats of deduction that seemed to spring from the pages of fiction, Heinrich acquired legendary status, earning a forensic celebrity that extended far beyond his homeland.

He was born in Clintonville, Wisconsin, the son of German immigrants. At age eight he left the Midwest forever when his family moved to Tacoma, Washington. Industrious and inquisitive in equal measure, he combined school studies with part-time work in a pharmacy, where he kept up a nonstop barrage of questions. He soaked up knowledge like a sponge, to the point that at age eighteen, without any formal training, he was able to pass the state pharmacy examination.

Still dissatisfied, he yearned to become a chemist. But with tuition fees far beyond his slender means, it looked to be a forlorn hope. Salvation came in a most unusual form: wheat futures speculation. Heinrich risked every penny he owned on a string of highly leveraged positions that paid off big-time, enough to put the ambitious young man through the University of California School of Chemistry at Berkeley.

In 1908 he received his B.Sc. and decided to return to the Northwest. In that same year he married and took up a job as city chemist for Tacoma, a post he kept for eight years. He soon discovered a knack for crime-solving. Before long he was handling much of the investigative work for the local police and coroner, not just in the laboratory but in the field as well. A brace of well-publicized murder cases added luster to his growing reputation and gave him opportunities to hone his courtroom skills.

Unlike many "experts" of the time, Heinrich made no attempt to talk down to the jury or blind them with scientific jargon. Factual and precise, he kept his testimony simple. Juries appreciated this directness as much as they admired his jaw-dropping scientific talents. There seemed to be no forensic discipline beyond his capabilities: **microscopy,** of course; **ballistics,** too; and enough skill in the field of **questioned documents** to make him a world-renowned handwriting expert. In one celebrated case he even studied Hindi dialects for almost a year in order to pass an opinion in court! Less well publicized but equally important were his pioneering attempts at traffic accident investigation and **blood spatter analysis.**

By 1916 the city of Alameda felt confident enough to appoint Heinrich as its chief of police. Despite an utter lack of administrative experience, he was enormously successful in the job, overseeing the first police force in the United States to be trained in the scientific gathering of crime scene evidence.

At the conclusion of World War I he was appointed city manager at Boulder, Colorado, but the sudden death in 1919 of a friend, the San Francisco handwriting expert Theodore Kytka, allowed Heinrich to return to that city, where he assumed his former friend's practice. When he was also appointed a faculty member of the University of California, it marked the resumption of what would be a lifetime association with Berkeley.

Word soon spread about the bespectacled doctor-detective who, with pipe gripped firmly between his teeth, brought his massive intellect to bear on a string of baffling criminal cases. Although by no means the first of his spectacular forensic successes, it was the D'Autremont Brothers case in 1923 (see *The Casebook of Forensic Detection,* Wiley, 1996) that made Heinrich a household name and earned him yet another nickname, the "American Sherlock Holmes." It was a soubriquet that always made him scowl. He snorted that he never played "hunches," like Conan Doyle's creation; all his decisions were firmly rooted in science, which, perhaps, explains why he never complained at all when other admirers dubbed him "the Edison of crime detection."

As Heinrich's reputation grew, he traveled across America, even to Europe, as a consultant. More than a thousand cases of every description, criminal and civil, passed through his hands. He once reduced his crime-fighting philosophy to five basic questions: "Precisely what happened? Precisely when did it happen? Precisely where did it happen? Why did it happen? Who did it?"

Always he stressed the importance of circumstantial evidence—properly evaluated and interpreted—as against direct testimony. In particular he set little store in the often erroneous impressions of eyewitnesses. Another subject guaranteed to raise his hackles was any accusation that he was merely a "prosecution man," and he could quickly reel off a string of cases in which his evidence had resulted in an innocent person being set free.

Heinrich was a deeply religious man who believed implicitly in the Old Testament concept of retributive justice, but he never allowed this to cloud his scientific judgment. By the time of his death in 1953 he had lived to see many of his innovations become standard police procedure. His proudest achievement was overseeing the introduction of fully equipped and properly funded forensic laboratories. Certainly some states lagged behind, but the "Wizard of Berkeley" had shown what was possible with scientific observation and controlled experimentation.

He will be remembered as a powerful force in revolutionizing police methods right across America, and as a pathfinder who helped change the art of crime detection into a science. But mostly he will be remembered for the brilliance of his intuition. That was peerless.

Significant Cases

1916	Hindu Ghadr plot
1921	William A. Hightower*
1921	Edward Trease
1923	D'Autremont brothers

1925	Martin Colwell*
1925	Charles Schwartz
1925	Jack Ryan
1927	Jessie Watkins
1929	Eva Rablen
1932	Frank Egan
1939	Nathan Housman

*Profiled in this book.

Milton Helpern (1902–1977)

Probably no pathologist in history has had greater experience of homicidal death than the former New York City chief medical examiner (CME) Milton Helpern. As his colleague and great friend **Keith Simpson** put it, "When the recent history of legal medicine comes to be written . . . the name of Milton Helpern will tower above those of his fellows."

He was born just after the turn of the twentieth century in a tenement house on 114th Street, next to Central Park. By his own description his upbringing was "typical working class"—his father worked as a cutter in a cloth factory—and Milton was pretty much left alone to get on with what he called "the interesting job of growing up." An early and abiding fascination with science led him to City College, where he majored in biology, and in 1922 he gained a B.Sc. From there, it was on to Cornell University Medical College.

After graduating in 1926 he became an intern at the Cornell Medical Division of Bellevue Hospital, and it was here that his interest in pathology first flowered. Even so, he made no conscious effort to enter the world of legal medicine, but rather drifted into it during the Depression, when funding shortages sealed off so many other avenues of medical research. In a stroke of immense good fortune, he was befriended by **Charles Norris,** the first chief medical examiner (CME) of New York, and on April 15, 1931, he joined Norris's loyal and devoted staff.

The annual salary was nothing spectacular—$4,000 slashed to $3,600 at the depths of the Depression—but it was regular money at a time when millions of Americans were on breadlines, and Helpern counted himself lucky indeed to have a job and such a good teacher.

When Norris died in 1935, Thomas A. Gonzales took over the top job, a position he retained until his retirement in 1954. Then it was Helpern's turn. For the next twenty years, until 1974, he served as the CME for New York.

It was a period that delivered enormous changes. Most were cosmetic, like the way in which he united all the previously disparate medical office's buildings under one roof in 1961, but the old values were under siege. In the early days of Helpern's tenure the CME's word was accepted without

Milton Helpern *(left)* and Keith Simpson—two titans of forensic pathology.

question. Gradually, though, a more inquisitorial attitude took hold, due in no small measure to Helpern's willingness to dispute the findings of other, less qualified pathologists. There was an excellent reason for this. As incredible as it may now seem, during the mid-1950s Helpern was one of the very few full-time forensic pathologists in the United States. Most states still relied on clinical or academic pathologists, part-timers who merely moonlighted in the medico-legal field. Helpern's dismay at this deplorable situation led to some memorable courtroom battles when he was consulted by out-of-state jurisdictions. In particular he always harbored grave misgivings about what he sourly termed "New England justice," and the way that prosecutors in that part of the world seemed to pursue certain defendants with Salem-like zeal, often shamelessly manipulating inexperienced pathologists for their own ends.

He had his homegrown concerns, also. By the early 1970s the job of New York CME had become increasingly politicized, and the avuncular Helpern found himself embroiled in one cause célèbre after another. He was invariably up to the challenge. Like most renowned expert witnesses, Helpern was a consummate and compelling courtroom performer. He had the facts at his fingertips and knew how to ride the punches of wily advocacy. His slow manner of speech duped many an inexperienced attorney into believing that here was some malleable pushover, but there was nothing dull about the razor-sharp mind, as his testimony in dozens of headline-making cases admirably demonstrated.

Away from the front pages, Helpern worked tirelessly to improve the standards of his profession. In 1937, together with his colleagues Thomas

Gonzales and Morgan Vance, he published an authoritative textbook, *Legal Medicine and Toxicology*. Besides contributing greatly to the text, Helpern also provided the photographs. The book remains a classic in its field.

On a personal level, he was always eager to pass on the knowledge he had gleaned from the twenty-five thousand autopsies he had personally conducted, and the many thousands more he had supervised. According to one of his students, **Michael Baden,** Helpern "liked the old European concept of the professor with a retinue of students learning from him and beholden to him."

An interesting insight into Helpern's philosophy came when the New York medical examiner's department moved into new quarters in 1961. At his insistence the following was inscribed on the marble wall: *Taceant colloquia. Effugiat risus. Hic locus est ubi mors gaudet succurrere vitae.* (Let conversations cease. Let laughter flee. This is the place where death delights to help the living.)

It was this desire to spread the gospel of forensic pathology that led Helpern, in 1966, to cofound the National Association of Medical Examiners (NAME). To honor his name, each year since 1991, the Milton Helpern Laureate has been awarded to that member of the association who is judged to have best met four distinct qualifications:

1. Should have enjoyed a long, outstanding career as a medical examiner.
2. Should have made outstanding contributions to the promulgation of a modern medico-legal investigative system.
3. Should have obtained professional recognition and respect among his or her colleagues.
4. Should have adhered to the high principles and standards set by the National Association of Medical Examiners and contributed to the goals of the organization.

In short, the winner has to live up to the exacting standards set by Milton Helpern.

Significant Cases

1935	Vera Stretz
1943	John Noxon
1949	Herman Sander
1959	Willem van Rie*
1963	Richard Robles
1965	Carl Coppolino
1965	Alice Crimmins
1965	Louis Montesi
1966	Steven Truscott

1969	John Hill
1970	Ronald Cohen
1970	William Moore
1973	Peter Reilly

*Profiled in this book.

Sir Edward Henry (1850–1931)

Although not the first to recognize the individuality of fingerprints, it was Edward Henry who devised the method that turned a physiological quirk into a devastatingly effective crime-fighting tool. Like many of his predecessors in this field, Henry's interest in dactylography was stimulated by his time in India. As a young man he joined the Indian civil service and was assigned to Bengal. After a lengthy spell as an assistant magistrate collector, presiding over tax disputes, in 1891 he was appointed inspector general of the Bengal Police.

Although Bengal adopted bertillonage in 1892 as a means of criminal identification, Henry was already intrigued by the possibilities of fingerprints. A lengthy correspondence with dactylography pioneer Sir Francis Galton led to an order that, henceforth, all Bengali criminal records would not only display that person's anthropometric measurements but his rolled fingerprint impressions as well.

Between July 1896 and February 1897 Henry, together with two assistants, Azial Haque and Hemchandra Bose, devised a revolutionary system of classification that imposed order on chaos, enabling fingerprints to be easily filed, searched, and traced against thousands of others.

In March 1897 a commission set up in Calcutta to examine the comparative merits of bertillonage and fingerprinting sided unanimously in favor of the latter, and that July, Henry's system was introduced across India.

His fame began to spread. Three years later he returned to London to address the Belper Committee which had been set up to explore the problems faced by police when dealing with criminal identification. Then came a lightning visit to South Africa, which resulted in the establishment of an outstandingly successful fingerprint bureau at Pietermaritzburg. In 1900 Henry wrote *Classification and Uses of Fingerprints,* a groundbreaking manual that grouped the ridge patterns of prints into five basic patterns. To this day it forms the basis of fingerprint identification around the globe.

In 1901 Henry was recalled to Britain and appointed assistant commissioner of Scotland Yard in charge of the Criminal Investigation Department. A month later he founded Britain's first fingerprint bureau, and in its first six months of operation it made ninety-three identifications (by 2000 that figure had risen to more than ten thousand annually). The following year brought two significant events: the first British conviction obtained through fingerprints and the announcement that New York City intended to adopt the Henry system. Recognition for Henry included his appointment as commissioner of Scotland Yard in 1903, and a knighthood in 1906.

Ironically, Henry fell victim to his own system. In 1912 Alfred Bowes, disgruntled because he had been refused a cab license after a fingerprint check revealed his criminal record, shot Henry on the doorstep of his Kensington house. Although three shots were fired, only one hit the commissioner, and he survived.

On February 19, 1931, Henry died from a heart attack. His grave in a Berkshire churchyard lay neglected for many years, until it was discovered by a Metropolitan Police fingerprint officer. After an international appeal was launched by the Fingerprint Society in 1994, the grave was renovated.

William A. Hightower

Date: 1921
Location: Colma, California

Late on the night of August 2, 1921, a man with his head buried deep in the collar of a large overcoat and wearing driving goggles hurried up to the rectory of Holy Angels Church in the small town of Colma, a few miles south of San Francisco. Please come quickly, he begged the pastor, his friend was dying of tuberculosis and wanted the last rites. Father Patrick Heslin immediately grabbed his bag containing a stole, holy oils, and the other paraphernalia of his office, jumped into the stranger's car, and the two men disappeared into the darkness.

When Father Heslin had still not returned the next morning, his housekeeper contacted the police. For several hours, search parties combed the route Father Heslin was thought to have taken, all to no avail. That evening, a manila envelope arrived at the residence of San Francisco archbishop Edward J. Hanna. Inside was a long, semicoherent letter, partly typed and partly handwritten, demanding a ransom of $6,500 for the pastor's safe return. The note ended ominously: "Had to hit him four times and he is unconscious from pressure on brain so better hurry and no fooling."

This was clearly no hoax. A check of the postmark confirmed that the letter had been mailed in San Francisco just four hours after the kidnapping, long before Heslin's abduction became public knowledge. When a promised second letter failed to materialize, anxious local police decided to call the University of California at Berkeley and request the assistance of **Edward O. Heinrich.** He arrived within the hour. After a cursory examination of the ransom note he looked up and said, "Whoever wrote that letter revealed his trade." While incredulous detectives looked on, he explained that the florid style of writing was similar to that used by bakers when decorating a cake.

A chorus of suppressed chuckles greeted this announcement as officers speculated on just how many bakers lived in the Bay Area, but Heinrich did not allow himself to be deflected by the sarcasm. In the early days of most investigations, he'd found, skepticism was invariably the order of the day, particularly among hard-bitten detectives unconvinced that some university egghead might succeed where they had failed.

A week passed. In that time there was no sighting of Father Heslin, whose disappearance was now making headlines coast to coast. As apprehension mounted, a reward of $7,000 was offered for clues leading to the finding of the priest, dead or alive. Among a whole host of opportunists flushed out by the promise of this windfall was a man who appeared at Archbishop Hanna's office, claiming he knew the whereabouts of the missing priest's body. The tale he told sounded fantastic. He said a young lady "of loose ways" had told him that Father Heslin had been kidnapped by bootleggers, then murdered and buried beside a billboard that showed a miner frying flapjacks over a campfire. The stranger—a lanky, balding Texan who gave his name as William Hightower—said he had gone to the famous Albers Rolled Oats billboard at Salada Beach, where he'd found something buried.

Reporters who'd crowded into the interviewing room eyed Hightower curiously. After a few seconds, one asked what he did for a living. Hightower looked taken aback. "What difference does that make?" he snapped. "But if you must know, I'm a master baker."

With their investigative antennae by now twitching on full alert, detectives accompanied Hightower to Salada Beach (present-day Sharp Park in Pacifica). Despite the pitch blackness, Hightower's surefootedness through the shifting dunes and treacherous drop-offs made it clear that he knew this region well. After some while he pointed to a patch of loosened sand. "That's the spot."

A few minutes' digging and the search for Father Heslin was over. He had been shot twice, and his head had been crushed. Nearby was a long board, about which were tied two loops of white cord, and some other pieces of lumber. Also buried in the ground was a tent peg, again fastened to a length of white cord.

Hightower was now the number one suspect, worthy of closer investigation. A search of his home revealed a rolled-up canvas tent. When opened out, written over one side was the word TUBERCULOSIS. The tent was sent, along with the other trace evidence and a jackknife taken from Hightower's pocket, to Heinrich's laboratory.

At first glance the knife appeared to be clean, but under Heinrich's microscope it began to reveal its secrets. On one of the blades were two nicks, and trapped in these were shreds of white cotton. Microscopically they were indistinguishable from the cord found wrapped around the tent peg and the piece of wood—the same number of strands to the ply, the same number of plies to the cord. From beneath the knife's hilt, Heinrich recovered a few grains of sand. Petrographic analysis matched them to sand from the crime scene, and sand recovered from the folds of the canvas tent.

Next, Heinrich brought his handwriting analysis skills into play. He found distinct similarities in the formation of the letters in TUBERCULOSIS with writing in the ransom note. When compared with known exemplars of Hightower's writing, he had no doubt as to their authorship. Heinrich speculated that Hightower had pitched the tent on the beach and used it to store the body, pending its ultimate disposal. The warning TUBERCULOSIS had been added to deter the curious.

Quite why Hightower engaged in such a hopelessly bungled venture remains a mystery. A few years earlier and it was conceivable he might have escaped scot-free, but Heinrich's all-seeing microscope had changed the ground rules in Californian courtrooms forever.

At Hightower's trial, his lawyers did their best to discredit Heinrich's testimony, but in totality it was damning stuff, enough to ensure that the accused was sent to San Quentin for life. After forty-one years and twenty-six unsuccessful parole applications he was finally freed in 1962, at age eighty-six.

David and Joy Hooker

Date: 1993
Location: Palmdale, California

After a long and distinguished career with the Los Angeles Police Department, Thomas Hooker had retired, only for chronic illness—he was diabetic, legally blind and required thrice-weekly dialysis treatment—to leave him bedridden and broke. Each day brought more bills and debt collectors to the house in Palmdale, California, that he shared with forty-nine-year-old wife, Joy, and adopted son, David, age thirty.

Then disaster struck. Sometime after midnight on April 19, 1993, Hooker's daughter, DeAnne Eldridge, who lived across the street, was awakened by the sound of Joy pounding at her door, pleading for her to call 911. There had been a fire, she cried. When DeAnne's husband, Robert, ran across the street to the smoke-filled Hooker house, David was in the living room, hosing down a burning sofa.

Robert asked where Thomas was, and David said he didn't know. Crawling through the smoke, Robert reached Thomas's bedroom and found him unconscious on the floor. Five minutes elapsed before David joined Robert in revival efforts. By the time paramedics arrived and rushed Hooker to the hospital, he was dead from smoke inhalation.

David explained that the family had gone to bed and left a fire in the fireplace. He'd been awoken by the smoke detector. After wrenching the alarm from the wall, he had bundled his adoptive mother, Joy, to safety, then ran back into the burning house to save his dog. His attempts to save Thomas had been thwarted by the choking smoke.

Arson investigators confirmed that the source of the fire had been in the living room. Wallpaper had peeled off, plastic objects had melted, the sofa had been consumed, and carpeting around the sofa was scorched. Heavy soot and smoke deposits on the ceiling and walls extended out along the hallway into Thomas's bedroom. Yet the bedrooms occupied by Joy and David showed no smoke damage whatsoever. This didn't make sense. Had either bedroom door been opened after the blaze began, a wall of smoke would have rushed in, leaving a distinctive pattern.

Another puzzling feature was David's claim that the fire must have been started by an ember jumping from the fireplace onto a pile of newspapers stacked nearby. Try as they might, investigators were unable to find any way in which an ember could have managed this 90-degree jump.

Background inquiries exposed the Hookers as a family in crisis, snowed under with debt. Yet even with mortgage payments several months in arrears and the bank threatening foreclosure, Joy still lavished money on expensive purchases. David, too, had caused problems—in and out of juvenile homes nonstop. In 1981 he had received a ten-year prison term for bank robbery and had picked up an extra year when caught mailing threatening letters to the White House.

Paroled just four months before the blaze, he had moved back in with his father, where Joy had taken him under her wing. Before long, neighbors wondered whether her interests were solely maternal. DeAnne Eldridge confirmed that her father had expressed fears that Joy and David wanted to get rid of him so they might continue their affair unhindered, a story corroborated by Thomas's nurse, David Creson. Someone else with a story to tell was Joy's son by an earlier marriage, who until recently had also lived at the house. He had been kicked out on the streets after inadvertently catching his mother and David naked on the living-room couch.

Just three weeks before the fire, Joy had tried to borrow $4,000 from her ex-husband, Robert Laughton, to prevent foreclosure. When he confronted her with allegations about the affair, she made no attempt to deny it, explaining that she was worn out after so many years of nursing Thomas and just wanted to be rid of him.

Arson investigators had already reached this same conclusion. The damning evidence was the smoke detector. Its securing clips on the wall had melted from the extreme heat. Tests demonstrated that a temperature of 300°F was needed to replicate this melting; yet David, who claimed to have yanked the alarm off the wall with his bare hands, had no burns on his hands—or anywhere else, for that matter—while the undamaged smoke detector, which had been tossed into the hallway, had ominous smoke marks on its interior. The conclusion was inescapable: Someone had removed the smoke detector from the wall before the fire started.

On June 1, Joy and David Hooker were taken in for separate questioning. When told she would be charged with murder, Joy broke down and confessed. Prior to putting Thomas to bed at the usual time—about midnight—she had given him an extra sleeping tablet. Sometime after 2:00 A.M., she said, David had lit the fire, waited till it was blazing, then rolled a log onto the newspapers, setting the lethal inferno.

At first David persisted in his denials, but when played Joy's taped confession, he finally admitted setting the blaze. The intention, he said, had been to collect on the house insurance; Thomas's death had been a dreadful accident.

More than two years elapsed before either defendant was tried. The interim allowed some defense fine-tuning. David withdrew his confession, to no avail. On June 6, 1995, he was found guilty of arson and murder and given twenty-five years to life.

Joy, too, engaged in legal sophistry, claiming that Thomas had actually died of natural causes and that they had merely been opportunistic. It was a feeble defense, easily disproved by the high levels of carbon monoxide in Thomas's blood, proof he was alive when the fire began. She also received a twenty-five-to-life prison term.

In an ironic twist, the medical examiner who autopsied Tom Hooker said that murder was unnecessary—he probably would have died inside a month, anyway, due to bad health.

On appeal, Joy Hooker's murder conviction was overturned on grounds that her confession was improperly introduced into evidence. A deal was worked out: in return for a guilty plea to manslaughter, she was released with time served, just two years. She is currently suing to obtain the insurance money on her dead husband's life.

Wilbur Howard

Date: 1976
Location: Greenwood Lake, New York

In the spring of 1976 a woman's decapitated body was hauled from scenic Greenwood Lake, which straddles the border between New York and New Jersey. The hands were also missing, and beneath her left breast a strip of flesh had been gouged away, but strangest of all was the corpse's color—bright green, caused by algae in the water. The medical examiner judged that she had been dead for about three weeks and, from the lean and athletic appearance, estimated her age at no more than thirty. Posters and media broadcasts containing these details failed to produce a single worthwhile lead. Disappointed by the lack of response, the state troopers Dan Reidy and Jimmy Curtis asked New York City's chief medical examiner, **Michael Baden,** to examine the body. Perhaps his more seasoned eye might detect something that the first examiner had missed?

As one of the world's foremost pathologists, Baden was well used to death in all its different forms, but even he had never seen a green corpse before. After his initial surprise he got down to work. He soon realized that the woman was much older than originally thought. Calcium deposits in the cartilage and bone spurs on her spine put her well into middle age, while the ovaries allowed Baden to further refine his calculations. Similar in size to a walnut, an ovary shrivels as it gets older; these were like prunes. Factoring all of these variables into the equation, Baden arrived at an approximate age of fifty-five.

Judging by the half-digested fruits and vegetables in the stomach, the woman had eaten a substantial meal shortly before death. What had caused that death was unknowable, though some kind of trauma to the missing head was the likeliest solution. As Baden examined the severance wounds he was struck by their neatness. They appeared to have been made with a band saw, the kind used by butchers, and yet in the midst of all this skilled dismemberment was that ugly and incongruous gash beneath the breast. It didn't require any great Holmesian feats of imagination to deduce that its purpose was to obliterate a blemish or scar so distinctive that it would have identified the victim, even without her head and hands.

Baden suspected that original notions of the woman having been dead for three weeks were gross underestimations of the truth. To gain a more accurate impression, he turned to the algae, scraping a sample off the torso and submitting it for biological analysis. Microscopic examination revealed two distinct generations of algae: fresh green from this year and dead algae from the year before. This meant that the body had been in the water for at least eighteen months.

When Reidy publicly released these new details of the corpse, the response was immediate. Within twenty-four hours a woman called to say that the body sounded very much like that of her sister, Katherine Howard, a Nassau County housewife, who had been missing for the past two years. Asked if Mrs. Howard had any distinguishing marks, the sister mentioned a scar under her left breast. Oddly enough, the last time she had seen Katherine was over a meal of fruit and vegetables. On one point the sister was unshakable: Katherine had been murdered by her husband.

Wilbur Howard was in his sixties and ice cool under questioning. At the time of his wife's disappearance, he had flunked a routine polygraph test, but without a body, the police were reluctant to proceed against him. He explained Katherine's abrupt departure from the marital home as due to mounting animosity; after countless years of arguments and fighting, she had simply decided to leave him.

This time when detectives returned to Howard's large home in Elmont, New York, they were far less ready to be appeased. Howard, though, refused to be shaken, and he demanded to know how they could be certain that the body in the lake was Katherine. He had a point. Baden had performed forensic miracles but still could not categorically identify the corpse, as Katherine Howard had left no medical records. Even when a podiatrist who had treated the missing woman declared himself 90 percent certain that the feet on the torso belonged to Katherine Howard, the lack of corroborating X-rays still left that niggling element of doubt.

There was other circumstantial evidence to indicate Howard's culpability. A search of his house uncovered all of the equipment necessary to dismember and dispose of a body, including a band saw, a workbench, a boat, and a station wagon. Carpeting in the station wagon had stains that looked like blood, but heavy and repeated cleaning with a detergent had rendered them unreliable from a forensic point of view.

Howard maintained his enigmatic silence, aware he was beyond the law's grasp. Although everything matched—the scar, the amount of time she had been missing, the last meal, and the feet—Reidy was helpless. Frustrated almost beyond endurance, he approached Howard with an extraordinary request. In order to let him (Reidy) close the book on this case, would Howard leave a confession in his will under lock and key, only to be opened after his death? The old man merely shrugged.

Two years later he died of a heart attack. Reidy traveled to Maine to identify the body, more to allay fears of a possible insurance fraud than anything else. Afterward, Reidy was there when Howard's lawyer opened the safe deposit box. There was no confession.

Since the body is still officially unidentified, Wilbur Howard's guilt or otherwise must remain a matter of conjecture. What is certain is that had these events occurred a decade later, DNA typing would have removed all identification uncertainties, one way or another.

The Iceman

Date: 1991
Location: Bolzano, Italy

High in the Alps, on the Austrian-Italian border, two hikers in September 1991 came across the frozen body of a man, slumped facedown in some meltwater. At 10,000 feet such discoveries are not uncommon, and usually result from a climbing accident, but this didn't bear the usual hallmarks. Most puzzling of all were some ancient-looking objects lying around the corpse. The finds were taken to the Forensic Medical Institute in Innsbruck, for examination by the archaeologist Konrad Spindler.

Judging from the artifacts and the leathery skin, Spindler began to suspect that the corpse might be incredibly old, maybe even prehistoric. Carbon dating confirmed it. The body was 5,300 years old, making it the oldest frozen mummy ever discovered. For the first time archaeologists had a Stone Age man, complete with clothes and a copper ax—the only complete Neolithic ax ever found—a bow six feet long, a quiver packed full of arrows, and a flint knife tucked inside a small pouch.

Dubbed Ötzi, after the Ötztal region where he was found, the man became an international sensation. Spindler reckoned that he had died in late fall. He deduced this from his belief that the body had been entombed in ice for thousands of years, and that ice contained pollen from plants that only flowered at that time of year. But there was nothing on the body to indicate *how* Ötzi had died.

Using X-rays and CAT scans, Spindler examined Ötzi internally. He found a brain that had shrunk to half its normal size, evidence of frostbite on the feet, and what looked like unhealed rib fractures. From these, Spindler evolved what became known as the "disaster theory." This had Ötzi as a shepherd, returning to his village with his animals in the fall, only to suffer an accident that left him stranded in the mountains until he died from hypothermia.

It sounded a credible hypothesis, and it persisted until 1998, when Ötzi was transferred to the northern Italian town of Bolzano (the body had actually been found just inside the Italian border). Intending to put the mummy on display in a specially built museum, officials asked the British forensic pathologist Peter Vanezis if he could reconstruct Ötzi's face. Vanezis normally works from the skull itself, but in this case, of course, that was impossible.

To remedy this lack, the original Austrian team created a detailed life-size replica of Ötzi's skull using CAT scan data and a rapid prototyping machine. Vanezis scanned this replica into his computer, then selected a face that anthropologically matched the skull, someone of the same age, race, and sex. The software stretched the selected face over the skull to reveal the shape of Ötzi's face: flat cheekbones, with a jutting chin and a receding forehead.

Vanezis now knew what Ötzi looked like, but he wanted to know how he had met his death. In September 2000 he got his chance to examine the frozen body. It showed no obvious signs of injury, nothing to indicate the cause of death.

Another scientist working on the Iceman project, Professor Klaus Oeggl, a botanist from Innsbruck, managed to remove a tiny sample from Ötzi's gastric tract, part of his final meal of bread, dried meat, and vegetables. Mixed in with this food was fresh pollen from a tree called the hop hornbeam, which still survives in the valleys below the Alps. What made this so significant was the fact that the hop hornbeam flowers only between mid-

March and June. This implied that Ötzi had most probably died in early summer, and not fall, as Spindler had thought.

Central to the disaster theory was the assumption that Ötzi had been frozen in a layer of ice until his discovery, with the scene remaining unchanged for thousands of years. Oeggl now challenged that belief. He spotted that, of the fourteen arrows found packed into Ötzi's quiver, thirteen were of a similar length, but one was much shorter. This had gone unnoticed before, yet when Oeggl studied the remaining fragments from the site, he found another piece that fit exactly into the broken arrow. Curiously, this sliver of wood, together with other splinters, had been located about thirteen feet away from the quiver. Something had obviously moved these fragments, and Oeggl suspected it was the ice itself, forming and then melting over thousands of years.

Was it possible that the body itself had also been moved? Vanezis had no doubt that this was the case. He'd found a pressure mark on the back of Ötzi's head, caused by lying on something hard, and yet the body had been found facedown. Also, an ear was bent into a position inconsistent with that in which the body was found. Nor were the ribs fractured, as Spindler had thought, but merely bent out of shape, most likely from the weight of snow or rocks sometime after death.

In light of these revelations, in June 2001 Bolzano General Hospital decided to X-ray the body again. The radiologist Dr. Paul Gostner immediately spotted something unusual: a foreign object near the left shoulder, something much denser than bone. Hurriedly the Austrians went back to their CAT scans, and sure enough, there it was: a flint arrowhead! In the earlier tests they'd missed it completely.

But was the injury new or old? This time the Iceman was thawed out to the point where pathologists could actually locate and probe the wound in Ötzi's shoulder, thus confirming that it had been inflicted shortly before death.

It was now obvious: Ötzi had been murdered.

In all probability, he had been struck by the arrow and then fled into the mountains to escape his pursuers, until, weakened by loss of blood, he eventually collapsed and died. Obviously it is impossible to say who killed Ötzi, but just the fact that this remarkable case could be recognized as a homicide after so many thousands of years is achievement enough.

Mark Jarman

Date: 1990
Location: Winnipeg, Canada

For most of the twenty years that Shirley and Ed Andronowich were married, they'd drunk hard and fought often. The evening of May 19, 1990, was no different from hundreds of others. Drinks at the Grant Motor Inn, a bar in Winnipeg, had ended with a violent showdown, and Ed stumbling off into the darkness, saying he was going home. Shirley, age forty-two, hung around drinking till almost midnight before she, too, headed home. Neither temper had been improved by the hiatus. Following another bitter fight, Shirley stormed from the house to cool off.

At six o'clock the next morning her battered body was found, along with the strewn contents of her purse, on the grounds of Grant Park School. She had been beaten, kicked, gnawed on like a piece of meat, and partially strangled. The death blow had come when the killer took a fifty-five-pound concrete slab and crushed her head to a pulp. Where this bloodstained slab originated from was a mystery. Then someone mentioned that many Canadians habitually carry large chunks of stone in their car trunks, to act as ballast on snowy winter roads.

Ed Andronowich was such a person. Several fragments of concrete were found in the trunk of his car, but none appeared to have come from the murder weapon, and their presence might easily have been explained by his job as a construction worker.

Still, there was plenty about Ed Andronowich to keep investigators interested. By his own admission he had been hopelessly drunk that night, and, in a written statement, he admitted fighting with Shirley, only to then disclaim all knowledge of what happened after she left the house. The more he was questioned, the fuzzier he became. Then, abruptly, he confessed.

It was a strange confession. Some parts held the ring of truth; others were littered with troubling discrepancies, lapses that detectives attributed to Ed's acute alcoholism. On May 24 he was charged with second-degree murder.

Problems soon developed with the case. Ed wore dentures, and although it was determined that he was capable of inflicting powerful bites, the pattern of teeth marks just didn't match. Puzzled scientists now went back and took swabs from around the bite marks. These showed clear traces of saliva and were therefore suitable for ELISA analysis.

Enzyme linked immunosorbent assay is a powerful tool that types blood in the traditional ABO groupings. First, a tray well is coated with the antibodies of various blood types; then the saliva sample is introduced. After being heated in an incubator, the saliva attaches itself to the appropriate blood type antibody; for instance, A only attaches to type A antibody, B to type B, and so on. It can be a lengthy process, taking up to three days to complete, depending on the quality of the test samples. In this instance the ELISA test identified the attacker as belonging to blood type B—unlike Ed Andronowich, who was blood type A.

Why people confess to hideous crimes is a complex, baffling conundrum. Here it was attributed to a combination of remorse and alcohol-induced blackouts. Whatever the reason, after two months behind bars, Ed Andronowich was released and eliminated from inquiries.

With the investigation back to square one, the geologist Richard Munroe was asked if he could determine the source of the concrete slab. He returned to the crime scene at midnight in an attempt to reconstruct the chain of events. Standing in the deep shadows where the body was found, his attention was drawn to an illuminated area about five hundred feet away. Moving closer, he saw two pieces of concrete, both superficially similar to the murder weapon.

Concrete is made by pouring sand, cement, water, and aggregates into a mold. As it dries, the mixture assumes a distinctive pattern unique to that particular concrete block. Munroe used petrographic analysis to positively match the minerals in the murder weapon and the two pieces of concrete; then he took all three pieces and slotted them together like a jigsaw. When intact, the complete block resembled the kind of bumper curbstones seen in parking lots.

Munroe now had an idea: what if the block held the killer's fingerprints? Obtaining prints from porous surfaces is fiendishly difficult, and Jarman decided to use the cyanoacrylate—or Super Glue—method. This works by heating the sample in a small chamber with a blob of Super Glue for about six hours. The fumes given off adhere to biological material such as the oil in fingerprints. Under a laser, this biological material fluoresces, producing a clear image of print. Unfortunately, the cyanoacrylate was the same color as the concrete. Gut instinct told Munroe the prints were there; he just couldn't see them. What he needed was a chemical that would attach itself to the cyanoacrylate. After numerous fruitless attempts he found a biological stain called Sudan Black that produced smudged but discernible prints.

Despite this promising development, no leads accrued, and it was not until the local media ran one-year anniversary stories on the case that a major breakthrough came. An informant told police that on the night of the crime, his roommate, Mark Jarman, a twenty-nine-year-old unemployed construction worker, had come in wearing bloodstained jeans and boots. The next day he'd burned his clothes.

Jarman lived within a block of the crime scene. When arrested, his bodily samples showed type B blood, and odontologists found seventeen points of similarity between his irregular teeth and bite marks on the body. His presence at the crime scene was clinched by the discovery of his fingerprint on a shopping list found there.

He eventually confessed, claiming he'd met Shirley outside a bar and that they'd had sex. Jarman said he turned violent only when Shirley threatened to tell her husband. Afterward, he had emptied the contents of her handbag to make it appear like robbery.

But the evidence made a liar out of Jarman. **Blood spatter analysis** showed that the purse contents had been up to twelve feet away when splashed with medium-velocity-impact spatter, proving that the bag had been rifled before his murderous attack. Jarman was sentenced to life imprisonment.

Sir Alec Jeffreys (1950–)

Immortalized as the "Founder of DNA Fingerprinting," Alec Jeffreys first became fascinated with genetics while still a postgraduate student at Oxford University. At the core of his work was a belief that by comparing two people's DNA, it would be possible to identify an almost unlimited number of genetic differences. Jeffreys knew that the short chunks of DNA that vary most between individuals—called "minisatellites"—are repeated over and over again. But this created a problem: how could these sequences be located in the vast, unmapped tracts of the human genome?

Jeffreys wrestled with this conundrum as he continued his studies in Holland. In 1977 he returned to the United Kingdom to take up a post as lecturer in genetics at the University of Leicester. More years of frustration followed, and then came his great breakthrough.

The time was nine o'clock on the morning of September 15, 1984. Jeffreys had left some X-ray film in a developing tank over the weekend; now, as he held the film aloft and saw the distinctive display of stutter sequences—similar to a supermarket bar code—a single thought raced through his mind: "My God, what have we done here?!" Almost by accident he'd stumbled across a way of establishing a human's genetic identification. (Twenty years later, that first DNA fingerprint still hangs on his office wall.) By that afternoon he and the rest of his team had named the discovery "DNA fingerprinting."

The first practical application of DNA fingerprinting came with the settlement of a British immigration dispute. It was Jeffreys's technology that allowed a Ghanaian woman and her son to be reunited after he had established their biological connection beyond all reasonable doubt.

Although Jeffreys was quick to realize the forensic implications of DNA fingerprinting, he also recognized its pitfalls. In the early days a great deal of high-quality DNA was required to obtain a good DNA fingerprint, and all too often at crime scenes there was insufficient biological evidence to attempt a match with the DNA of a suspect. Also, old DNA can degrade, leading to problems of interpretation in court.

In 1985 Jeffreys and his team developed a technology that overcame these limitations. Called DNA profiling, it enabled them to isolate individual minisatellites and produce a pattern on X-ray film with just two bands per individual: one from a person's mother and one from his or her father.

Simpler to read and interpret, DNA profiles also can be stored on a computer database. Most significant of all, they can be obtained from much smaller samples.

It was this technology that Jeffreys employed when consulted in the brutal Narborough killings in 1986, when DNA profiling first proved one man's innocence, then convicted the actual murderer, Colin Pitchfork. Overnight, the quiet academic from Leicester University became an international celebrity. Since that time, the technique he pioneered has gone on to revolutionize crime solving in every corner of the globe.

Significant Cases

1986	Colin Pitchfork
1988	Ian Simms
1992	Josef Mengele

Clayton Johnson

Date: 1989
Location: Shelburne, Canada

Clare Thompson watched the school bus pick up the two Johnson girls outside their home at 7:40 A.M. on February 20, 1989, then reached for the phone. Across the street, Janice Johnson took the call on the basement extension, and the two neighbors chatted for several minutes. At some point during that call, Clare heard Janice kiss her husband good-bye and say, "See you later, hon," to Clayton Johnson as he left for the seventeen-mile drive to the high school in Shelburne, Nova Scotia, where he taught.

At 7:50 A.M. Janice broke off the call, saying that she was expecting a friend. Just minutes later, that friend arrived and found Janice Johnson unconscious at the foot of the basement stairs, with one foot on the bottom step, blood pumping from an ugly wound to her head, car keys still clutched in her hand. The emergency call to paramedics was timed at 7:54 A.M.

When Clayton reached the school at 8:11 A.M., he was told of the tragedy and rushed immediately to the hospital. He was at his wife's bedside that day when she died, having never recovered consciousness.

The coroner, Dr. Roland Perry, had little doubt that the death was a flukish and dreadful accident. The way he figured it, Janice had toppled forward down the steps, trapping her head in the six-inch gap between the stairs and the wall, before coming to rest at the foot of the stairs. Local police, satisfied that this had been just a tragic trip and fall, let the matter rest.

For a fifty-two-year-old father struggling to raise two young daughters, life was tough. At first, the closely knit community of Shelburne rallied around the bereaved husband, but all that changed when, just three months later, Clayton began dating Tina Weybrett, a woman thirty years his junior.

Gossip intensified with news that two months before the accident, Clayton had taken out a $120,000 insurance policy on Janice's life, money he needed badly to get himself out of a financial hole. When Clayton married Tina, he was unaware that investigators had quietly reopened the case.

At the time of the tragedy two neighbors had misguidedly volunteered to wash out the basement before it could be properly photographed. Their original statements mentioned seeing a large amount of blood on the wall by the third step and a small stain on the floor, comments that had informed Dr. Perry's findings. Thirty months later, back in the basement with police videocameras rolling, it was a very different matter. Now these neighbors recalled a virtual abattoir, with blood drenching the floor, and splashing up the walls.

When police referred this new testimony to the pathologists Charles Hutton and David King, both felt, given the amount and distribution of blood, that Janice Johnson had been bludgeoned at the foot of the stairs, probably with a two-by-four, then fell back on the wall. Detectives now reasoned that before leaving for work that morning, Clayton Johnson had battered his wife to death, then disposed of the weapon in the basement furnace. In light of these findings, Dr. Perry changed his verdict to one of murder.

Setting aside the neighbors' revised stories, it hardly seemed likely or even possible that Johnson could have killed his wife. According to Clare Thompson, Janice hung up the receiver at 7:50 A.M. Four minutes later, the ambulance was summoned. In those four minutes, Clayton had to bludgeon Janice, knowing that she was expecting company at any moment, dispose of the weapon, clean himself up, and get out of the house. All of these might just have been possible had it not been for the fact that at 7:50 A.M. witnesses saw Clayton filling his truck at a gas station. Desperate to paper over this glaring crack in its case, the prosecution retaliated by claiming that Clare Thompson had been confused over the phone timings and that her call had actually finished at 7:40 A.M., thus allowing Clayton ten more minutes for murder.

This was good enough for the jury. On May 4, 1993, Johnson was convicted of first-degree murder and sentenced to life.

After years of disquiet, his case was referred to the Association in Defense of the Wrongly Convicted, a Canadian organization with a distinguished record for investigating miscarriages of justice. First they discovered that the allegedly damning $120,000 insurance policy had actually been a blanket policy taken out by 40 percent of the teachers at Clayton's school; they then enlisted the assistance of the noted blood spatter expert Herbert MacDonell, director of the Laboratory of Forensic Science in Corning, New York. He reviewed an examination of the case papers made by a pathologist, Dr. Linda Norton, in which she gave her opinion that Janice had actually fallen backward down the stairs, not forward, as everyone had assumed. And she was sure it was an accident.

MacDonell struggled to find a way to physically flesh out Norton's hypothesis. Then inspiration struck. He built a full-scale replica of the stairwell, and, using a model of the same height and weight as Janice Johnson, he attached her to a harness of the kind used in theatrical productions to make stage performers "fly" on wires.

Next, he placed blue chalk on the wall and step where blood had originally been reported, then he flipped the model backward from the top of the stairs. Even in a slow-motion descent, the model's head struck the wall and step exactly where MacDonell had placed the chalk, leaving blue marks on her head that corresponded with the wounds found on Janice Johnson's head. The videoed reconstruction allowed MacDonell to conclude, "There is no question in my mind that the death of Mrs. Johnson was the result of an accident. It was not a homicide."

When it was learned that a Royal Canadian Mounted Police report that found that any conclusion made on the bloodstains "would be questionable at best" had been deliberately withheld from the defense, demands for a retrial were too loud to ignore.

After six years behind bars, Clayton Johnson was set free. When the prosecution announced that it had no new evidence to present, all charges were dropped. At the time of writing, he is suing over his wrongful conviction.

Bryan Maurice Jones

Date: 1985
Location: San Diego, California

By May 1986 it became horribly clear that a serial killer was at work in East San Diego. In less than a year four prostitutes had been found murdered within a two-block area. Three were left in Dumpsters, two were set on fire—all had been violently assaulted sexually. The first victim, Tara Simpson, was found on August 29, 1985, discarded like so much garbage in an alley in the 5100 block of El Cajon Boulevard. Over the next few months, more bodies were found nearby, leading investigators to conclude that the murderer probably lived in the neighborhood. But it was not until the death of Joanne Sweets in May 1986 that investigators got a break.

Like the other victims, she had several broken ribs—a trademark of the San Diego killer—and had been strangled. Her body, wrapped in two black plastic bags joined together with masking tape, had been left in the Dumpster of an apartment block. And on that Dumpster was a fingerprint. Initial excitement soon turned to frustration. When compared manually with existing records, the print failed to provide a match.

Following this murder, curiously, the killings suddenly stopped. With this cessation came an understandable waning of interest as homicide detectives were assigned to other, more current cases. But in 1989 it was decided to revisit the evidence. New techniques were being evolved all the time in the field of fingerprint identification, and one of the latest was the use of gentian violet to obtain prints from surfaces previously thought unsuitable for testing. Scientists speculated that the killer might have left his prints on the masking tape used to bind Joanne Sweets. By applying gentian violet to the adhesive surface they hoped to expose any prints that were present. Despite repeated applications, they failed to isolate a single print.

But there was an unexpected offshoot: the print recovered from the Dumpster was now scanned by the automated fingerprint identification system (AFIS), which had not been in use when the investigation was first under way. Almost immediately it spat out a match.

At the time of the killings, Bryan Maurice Jones lived with his mother in an apartment at Fifty-first Street and El Cajon Boulevard, almost next to the alleyway where Joanne Sweets and Tara Simpson had been found. His present whereabouts were no mystery; he was currently serving a twenty-two-year term at Corcoran State Prison for rape, robbery, and kidnapping a prostitute. In 1986 he didn't have a record, which explained why his fingerprints were not on file at the time, but shortly thereafter he had been convicted and imprisoned, coincidentally right around the time when the killings stopped.

But even though Jones's fingerprint had been found on the Dumpster, there was still nothing to link him to the killings. Living so close to the Dumpster, he had in all probability used it on several occasions—or could at least claim to have done so—and prosecutors knew that no jury would convict on such a flimsy connection. Stronger evidence was needed.

San Diego forensic experts wondered about the plastic bags themselves. Was it possible that the killer had left his prints on the shiny surface? Unfortunately, they had no technology that could isolate any such prints. In a quandary they contacted the FBI and were told of a new technique being used in Europe, Australia, and Canada that was enjoying great success in exposing fingerprints on difficult-to-analyze surfaces.

Vacuum metal deposition (VMD) has a proven track record of succeeding where all other analytical techniques fail. Not only can it lift latent prints from plastics, but it also does so with higher quality and greater definition than that of other techniques. Although VMD works best on smooth, nonporous surfaces such as polyethylene, glass, and magazine paper, it also can be used on paper towels and even tissues. In Australia, where they have recently introduced polymer banknotes, fingerprint laboratories that have struggled to lift prints from the semiporous surface now regularly employ VMD to assist them in identifying the possibly criminal handling of money.

The beauty of VMD lies in the fact that prints are developed using the smallest of materials, the atom. This provides the highest resolution and is able to produce marks of the highest quality on both new and old samples. Critically, VMD is able to recover marks from only trace amounts of the substances that comprise every print. The sample is placed in the top of a small decompression chamber. A few milligrams of gold are then laid in metal containers on the floor of the chamber. Once the chamber is sealed, the air is pumped out and a vacuum is created. The gold is then heated until it melts. As the fumes rise they condense on the surface of the sample in an exceedingly fine layer—just one atom in depth. If no print is present, the layer will be uniform; but if a print is found, the gold will sink into its valleys, leaving the oily ridges uncoated.

This process is then repeated with a few milligrams of zinc. Like the gold, the zinc vaporizes inside the chamber, but its chemical properties mean that it only condenses onto other metals; therefore it sticks to the previous layer of gold. Because zinc won't adhere to any oily ridge, a high-contrast negative fingerprint is developed.

Because, at this time, VMD was little used in the United States—its high cost made it feasible only in exceptional circumstances—the plastic bags were sent to the Royal Canadian Mounted Police forensic laboratory in Ottawa. Their results were conclusive: Bryan Maurice Jones's prints were all over the plastic bags used to dispose of Joanne Sweets.

On June 25, 1992, Jones, still in prison and now age thirty, was charged with four murders. His protestations of innocence fooled no one, least of all the jury. In September 1994 he was sentenced to death.

Theodore Kaczynski

Date: 1978
Location: Chicago

For two decades, the terrorist who came to be known as the Unabomber waged a one-man campaign against what he perceived to be the domination of technology over culture. The madness began on May 25, 1978, when a wooden box packed tightly with the heads of matches was addressed to a professor at Northwestern University. It was opened instead by a security officer, who was injured but survived.

Over the next seven years, another ten attacks occurred. Because they seemed to target universities and airlines mostly, the FBI dubbed the case *UN*(university)*A*(airlines)*BOM*, hence the Unabomber. The first fatality came on December 11, 1985, when a Sacramento computer store owner, Hugh Scrutton, was killed after picking up a bomb placed outside his business.

All the bombs showed a recognizable "signature," with most of the pieces carefully crafted by hand. The Unabomber made his own boxes, hinges, and switches, cut wire to make nails, and filed off any identifying tool marks on

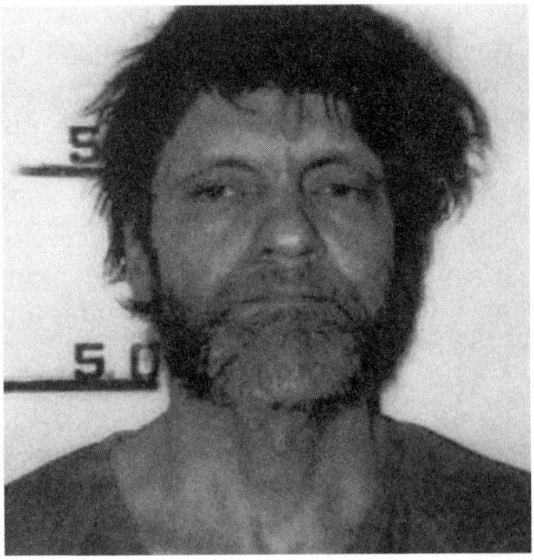
Mug shot of the Unabomber, taken shortly after his arrest.

screws. He used old electric wiring and pieces of domestic plumbing that might be found in any hardware store. He also scratched "FC" on the devices.

Clarification of this logo came in a letter to the *San Francisco Examiner* in which the writer identified himself as "FC," a terrorist who belonged to a group called the Freedom Club, dedicated to taking a stand against technology and science. The initials FC were then used on the bombs and in future communications.

On February 20, 1987, a witness in a Salt Lake City computer store saw a man placing a bomb in the parking lot. Described as white, about six feet tall, about forty years old, with a medium build, ruddy complexion, and reddish-blond hair, he wore a hooded sweatshirt and aviator glasses.

Following this close brush with capture, the Unabomber laid low for more than six years, long enough for investigators to consider the possibility that he was incarcerated for some other offense or else had died. But in 1993 he emerged from retirement with awful consequences, blitzing the old, familiar types of targets with newfound ferocity. By the time of his final outrage, on April 24, 1995, which killed a Californian timber industry lobbyist, Gilbert Murray, the Unabomber had murdered three people and injured twenty-nine others.

In June 1995 a rambling, thirty-five-thousand-word manifesto claiming to be from the Unabomber was sent to the *New York Times* and the *Washington Post,* promising that the bombings would cease if the document was published in full. Both newspapers ran the antitechnology diatribe, and there were no more attacks. What looked, superficially, like a victory for the Unabomber turned out to be his downfall.

In Schenectady, New York, Linda Kaczynski, the wife of a social worker, had read the article with mounting concern. She showed her husband,

David, and he agreed that in tone and phraseology it sounded a lot like his estranged brother.

Theodore Kaczynski was a fifty-three-year-old Harvard graduate who, in 1978, had turned his back on society and gone off to live as a hermit in a remote part of Montana, hunting rabbits, growing vegetables, and receiving occasional handouts from his family.

The more David read the manifesto the more convinced he became that Linda's assessment was correct. Finally, after suffering agonies of conscience, he contacted the FBI.

They were similarly torn; one couple's suspicion was hardly enough to obtain a warrant to search Kaczynski's isolated cabin. Instead, they requested a textual analyst, James Fitzgerald, to examine the Unabomber manifesto to see how its content and structure compared with known examples of Kaczynski's writing.

Forensic linguistics is a new tool, predicated on the belief that no two people use language in quite the same way. All of us have our idiosyncrasies and preferences, especially when writing, and it is this identifiable individuality that the expert is seeking. On this occasion, Fitzgerald's opinion that there were significant similarities was sufficient for a judge to grant a search warrant.

On April 3, 1996, Kaczynski was arrested in his isolated cabin in Montana. Inside, FBI agents found an abundance of writings that matched the sentiments of the Unabomber, along with materials for making bombs.

Once Kaczynski's lawyers heard of Fitzgerald's work for the prosecution, they went searching for an expert of their own. The obvious candidate was the Vassar literary professor Donald Foster, who had gained considerable acclaim (and abundant criticism) for his purported identification of a previously unattributed work of William Shakespeare's. Even those who roundly rejected Foster's claims in the Shakespeare affair were silenced by his next piece of literary sleuthing—identifying the anonymous author of the best-selling political novel *Primary Colors.* Within a week, Foster had fingered Joe Klein, a reporter for *Newsday.* Despite some initial blustered denials, Klein eventually admitted responsibility, and Foster's reputation soared.

Foster reviewed the materials given him by Kaczynski's defense team and came up with some bad news: he could find nothing wrong with Fitzgerald's analysis. Once the prosecution heard this, they immediately asked Foster if he would jump ship and testify for the government. He readily agreed.

At Kaczynski's trial, Foster explained his methodology. He begins by scouring text databases, searching for similar language habits that will help him "establish the writer's age, gender, ethnicity, level of education, professional training, and ideology." This is complex work. Linguistic clues typically include not just vocabulary, spelling, grammar, and syntax, but also word usage such as slang, professional jargon, regionalisms, even punctuation. No matter how we may try to disguise the fact, claims Foster, "human beings are prisoners of their own language."

Foster's evidence was crucial, and it went some way toward persuading Kaczynski in January 1998 to accept a plea bargain that will guarantee he remains behind bars for the rest of his life.

Although Foster's claim that "forensic linguistics is about where DNA evidence was a few years ago" might be viewed as a triumph of self-interest over hard-nosed reality, there can be no doubt that this is a significant and interesting new discipline, one likely to feature ever more prominently in the future.

Gene Keidel

Date: 1966
Location: Phoenix, Arizona

A colleague of DiAnne Keidel, alarmed by her nonappearance at work on Monday, September 19, 1966, decided to call the Phoenix police. "DiAnne," she explained, "is getting a divorce and has expressed fear that her husband may harm her." It had been a bad marriage littered with extramarital affairs. Both DiAnne and Gene Keidel were heavy drinkers, and both had violent tempers.

As it happened, the missing thirty-one-year-old's estranged husband had already reported her disappearance, saying he'd last seen her the previous Friday. After finalizing details of their upcoming divorce, they went out drinking until 11:15 P.M., when DiAnne had dropped him off at his father's house, where he was living temporarily.

Later that night, Gene said, he'd phoned his eldest daughter, Susie, at the family home in the 4200 block of Citrus Way, to check if DiAnne had arrived home safely. When told that there was no sign of her, he'd gone over to baby-sit. The next morning, DiAnne's car was in the drive, her purse and keys were in the house, but she had seemingly vanished.

Police discovered that after leaving Gene, DiAnne had gone to a bar, where she met another man. When interviewed, Bob Marlin couldn't shed any light on the mystery, and in a bizarre twist of fate, fewer than forty-eight hours later, he died of a heart attack.

Meanwhile, Gene moved back full-time into the house, a strong indication that he wasn't expecting DiAnne to return, and one week later the missing-person inquiry was closed.

To the outside world, life at Citrus Way appeared to be settling into some kind of normality when, just before midnight on January 9, 1967, tragedy struck: the house was engulfed in flames. Two sisters, Susie and Kelly, died in the blaze; nine-year-old Greg and his youngest sister, Lori, age five, managed to scramble to safety. Gene had been at a local Laundromat at the time of the ostensibly accidental fire. The disaster made national headlines. But if DiAnne Keidel read the horrifying accounts, they failed to flush her out of hiding, and Gene was left to bring up what remained of his shattered family alone.

And there the story lay for more than a quarter of a century—until one June day in 1993, when Lori Romaneck, as she was now named, walked into a Phoenix police station with an extraordinary tale.

On the night of her mother's disappearance, Lori said, she and her sister Susie had cringed on an upstairs landing as their father, enraged by DiAnne's promiscuity, beat her unconscious. That same night, unaware that his every move was being watched by his two daughters, he dug a grave for his wife's lifeless body, next to the backyard swimming pool. Over the next few days he submerged his misdeeds beneath a thick layer of concrete.

Lori had lived with this nightmare for more than twenty-six years; now she wanted to unburden her soul.

At first the Phoenix police were deeply skeptical, and more than fifteen months passed before they agreed to act. Since the house on Citrus Way had changed hands, there was an understandable reluctance to dig up the entire backyard, which is why they contacted NecroSearch International.

A nonprofit organization open for membership by invitation only, NecroSearch relies on a wide range of sciences, from anthropology and botany to entomology and geophysics, to find the hidden burial sites of murder victims. Its members are largely drawn from the laboratories of Colorado universities, scientists who volunteer their time, stepping in whenever a law enforcement agency asks for their help. Since its formation in 1989, NecroSearch has aided investigations in twenty-seven states and has been consulted by police in seven foreign countries.

G. Clark Davenport, a longtime NecroSearch team member, flew down to Phoenix armed with ground-penetrating radar. GPR operates by transmitting pulses of ultra-high-frequency radio waves down into the ground through a transducer or antenna. The transmitted energy is reflected from various buried objects or different earth materials, bounced back up through an antenna, and then stored in the digital control unit.

Using the GPR, Davenport scanned the entire backyard and identified an area of unusual ground disturbance approximately six feet by two feet, right where Lori claimed her mother was buried. When police broke through the concrete patio, ten inches down they unearthed a human skull, then a full skeleton with bra and girdle, and stockings still wrapped around the neck.

It was a remarkable discovery, but was it the body of DiAnne Keidel?

Anthropology (forensic) confirmed that the skeleton was that of a white woman, about five feet, four inches tall, who, judging from the pelvic bones, had had at least two children and was between twenty and forty years old at the time of death—all details consistent with DiAnne Keidel. As was the discovery in the grave of part of a blue zipper. Lori remembered that her mother had been wearing a blue dress on the night of her disappearance.

Bacteria had eliminated any hope of DNA testing. Even the tooth pulp—often a rich source of DNA material—was too badly damaged to test. Another setback came with news that DiAnne's dentist no longer practiced, and that her dental records had been destroyed, thus blocking off that avenue of identification.

But there was something else that might indicate how long the body had been buried. A tree root had grown through the skull, and by examining a section of this root, Thomas Harlan, a dendrochronologist at the University of Arizona, judged it to be fifteen years old. This meant that the body had to have been in the ground prior to 1979. All that was left was for the anthropologist Dr. Laura Fulginiti to perform a skull and photo superimposition, and there could be no doubt that these were the mortal remains of DiAnne Keidel.

Gene Keidel had dodged justice for almost thirty years, but on April 17, 1995, now age sixty-one, he was convicted of first-degree murder and jailed for life.

Roger Kibbe

Date: 1986
Location: Sacramento, California

In the middle of a July night in 1986, Stephanie Brown, a nineteen-year-old Sacramento bank teller, answered a phone call for help from some friends who were having car trouble. After dropping them off at their house, she asked for directions home. They pointed her back toward the freeway and told her to take I-5 north. Tragically, she missed the turn and instead headed south.

Some days later a fisherman in a remote region outside Sacramento discovered the half-naked body of a young woman in a flooded drainage ditch. Stephanie Brown had been strangled. Both straps of her tank top had been severed, and the back was sliced from top to bottom, most probably with a pair of scissors found nearby. Judging from the way he'd hacked off Stephanie's hair, the killer appeared to have some kind of cutting fetish. He'd left semen traces, but these were too degraded to type.

As the search radiated outward from the crime scene, Stephanie's abandoned yellow Dodge Colt was found some twenty miles away. It was mechanically sound, suggesting that she had probably stopped to ask directions and then been abducted.

This was the second time in a few months that a young woman had gone missing along I-5. In March, Charmaine Sabrah and her mother, Sabri, had also broken down on the freeway at night. A man driving a dark sports car had pulled alongside and offered assistance. He shouted over that since his car was just a two-seater, he could take only one of them for help. Reluctantly, Charmaine got into the stranger's car, and it drove off. She was not seen again for three months, not until a hunter some fifty miles away, in adjoining El Dorado County, stumbled across her badly decomposed remains. Like Stephanie, Charmaine had been strangled and her clothes were neatly cut. Judging from the absence of any obvious incriminating evidence, the killer—described as white, middle-aged, and with a big nose—appeared to have some familiarity with crime scenes.

Two weeks later, the grim scenario was repeated once more, with the discovery of yet another body thirty-five miles southeast of Sacramento, not far from where Stephanie Brown had been found. Dental records identified the victim as Lora Heedick, a twenty-year-old prostitute, and like the others, she had been strangled and her clothes were neatly cut.

On June 21, 1987, in a remote region of Sacramento County called Deer Creek, a fourth woman was found murdered. Karen Finch was age twenty-five, and her car had also been found abandoned on I-5. Her body yielded an important clue: fragments of duct tape in her hair. This explained why Stephanie's hair had been cut: to get rid of tape used to gag her. Apparently the killer carried his own scissors to every crime.

By now the man dubbed the "I-5 Strangler" had become a killing machine. His next victim was Darcie Frackenpohl, a seventeen-year-old runaway from Seattle. In September her remains were found by South Lake Tahoe. Besides the hallmark cuts, she had suffered slow strangulation with a rope and wood garrote. Only this time the killer slipped up: he left an identifiable clue—the rope was the type used in parachutes.

A criminalist, Faye Springer, who had examined the victims for trace evidence, also found two blue nylon carpet fibers manufactured by Dupont on Darcie's dress. What made the fibers even more distinctive was the presence of a fungal spoor. The dress yielded other vital clues: a pubic hair and hair from two different dogs and a cat.

And then in early 1988 a man was arrested in Sacramento after attacking a prostitute in his car. The woman had become alarmed when he'd tried to handcuff her and made her escape. Fortunately, the incident had been witnessed by a passing patrol officer.

Roger Kibbe was age forty-eight at the time of his arrest, twice married, and the manager of some storage units. He also was the brother of a Nevada homicide detective, which may have given him insights into crime investigation. Immediately an item from his past flagged interest: at age fifteen he had been arrested for stealing underwear from clotheslines and cutting the clothes in a random fashion. Significantly, he was an experienced parachutist.

Kibbe owned two cars. One, a sports car, was very similar to the vehicle used to abduct Charmaine; in the other was a rope garrote, handcuffs, and scissors. When Faye Springer examined Kibbe's cars, she found blue carpeting identical to the fibers recovered from Darcie's clothing, even down to the same fungal spoor. A sample of Kibbe's pubic hair matched that found on Darcie's dress, as did hair from the two dogs and a cat he owned.

Springer then had a flash of inspiration. She went back to the earlier cases and noticed that the pantyhose used to bind Charmaine were inside out. When opened up the right way, they revealed fibers microscopically identical to those from Kibbe's car seat.

Finally, she compared pieces of rope found in the car and a storage unit, to that from the Darcie Frackenpohl crime scene. All were made of white nylon with thick fibers running through the cord and contained thirty-two threads per cord. Coincidentally, all three samples showed evidence of red paint staining. Under a scanning electron microscope, ten elements common to red acrylic paint revealed themselves, plus two additional elements—contaminants in the air when the paint was sprayed near the rope. All three pieces of rope showed the same contaminants, linking Kibbe inextricably to the crime scene.

On April 28, 1988, he was charged with two of the I-5 murders. Almost three years later, he was convicted and sentenced to life. It later emerged that, at the time of his arrest, Kibbe had confessed to his wife, Harriet. When she asked him why he had committed such dreadful crimes, he had simply replied, "I don't know."

Knife Wounds

In those countries where the private ownership of guns is strictly regulated, stabbing is the commonest form of homicide. By contrast, in the United States, it accounts for just 15.5 percent of all murders. Since knife wounds also figure prominently in suicide statistics, any corpse displaying obvious signs of mutilation will always receive the closest scrutiny, to determine whether there has been third-party involvement. Particularly close attention will be paid to the type of wounds. They are:

Incised Wounds

These are usually caused by slashing with a razor, the blade of a knife, a jagged piece of metal or a piece of broken glass, and tend to be straight, though this can vary if the weapon's direction is altered, or if the blade has an unusual shape. A curved pruning knife, for instance, may leave a curved pattern as it slices through the skin. Although wounds caused by jagged metal or glass may appear at first to be irregular, closer examination generally reveals the edges to be cleanly cut. Incised wounds usually gape, making it difficult to match the width of the wound to the breadth of the cutting edge that produced it. This problem is exacerbated in a deep wound, where severing of the various muscles, tendons, nerves, and blood vessels may all contribute to making the wound gape even wider.

Punctured Wounds

These are produced by the point of a knife or by any other sharp, narrow instrument such as an ice pick or screwdriver. Punctured wounds can be much trickier to analyze. Should a knife be twisted as it is pulled out after stabbing, it may leave a V- or cross-shaped wound, quite unlike the weapon itself. Similarly, a rounded weapon may produce an elongated wound, not circular at all, caused by the skin splitting in one direction. Even more confusingly, a flat bayonet can produce a triangular laceration, while a square-sectioned spike has been known to leave a cross-shaped wound.

Contrary to popular belief, the external appearance of a stab wound does not necessarily correspond to the shape and dimensions of the weapon. This is due to what are called Langer Lines (or "longers")—named after the nineteenth-century Austrian anatomist Carl Langer—which form the natural grain of the skin. When the skin is cut, as by a knife wound, it pulls back along the Langer Lines. If the wound is lined up with the longers, the wound will appear to be longer than the width of the blade, even with a stabbing wound. If the wound is lateral to the longers, the wound may actually be shorter than the width of the blade.

Not only is the skin the largest organ in terms of surface area in the human body, it also is the toughest. In the course of a lifetime it fends off harmful rays from the sun; keeps us dry in wet weather; and, most importantly, acts as a security shield for all our internal workings. For the most part it is difficult to rupture, but once penetrated, it allows a sharply pointed weapon easy access to the vital organs. Almost no additional force is required to penetrate the tissues, and it is here that punctured wounds do their lethal damage. There may only be a limited amount of external bleeding from a punctured wound, but the internal hemorrhaging in a chest or abdomen wound can be colossal.

Confronted by a dead body with incised or punctured wounds, the medical examiner has to ascertain whether it is a case of homicide or suicide. First he or she will consider the site of the wound. Is it in a position that the victim could reach? If so, further investigation is necessary. The track of the wound in the tissues can be informative. It is easier to stab oneself in a downward or horizontal direction; wounds of this kind may occur accidentally, by running or falling onto the weapon. Upward thrusts generally indicate a homicidal attack. The direction of the wound is also important, as is knowing whether the dead person was left- or right-handed.

Multiple deep wounds are strong indicators of murder, though it is not unheard of for punctured wounds to be found on a suicide victim. Most knife-wielding suicides tend to slash their wrists laterally. Often there are a few "hesitation" or practice wounds on the wrists—generally parallel to one another and quite uniform—made before the decisive blow(s) is struck.

When a right-handed person decides to cut his or her throat, the wound normally begins high up on the left, where it is deep, and finishes lower on the right, where it tails off. Again, hesitation wounds are often found on the victim's neck. The self-inflicted wound is likely to be clean-cut, because the suicide tends to throw back his or her head, stretching the skin of the throat, before slashing. Oddly enough, this is a counterproductive action, as it allows the main arteries to slip back, where they are protected by the windpipe. In such cases, death will result from a combination of bleeding from the cut and perhaps asphyxia if blood clogs the windpipe.

A murder victim taken unawares, in contrast, is usually relaxed, and the skin will typically crumple under the pressure of the blade, giving an uneven margin to the wound. Also, hesitation marks are absent in a homicidal wound, which is likely to be accompanied by other deep cuts on the head or neck. Most attacks of this type tend to come from the rear and, like the suicide, begin on the left with a deep wound, that tends to remain deep and fairly horizontal throughout the entire cut.

When a homicidal attack has originated from the front, in most cases there will be some kind of struggle as the victim attempts to ward off any blows with a sharp instrument or attempts to seize it. This can lead to random defense cuts on the forearms and the palms of the hands. Very often these cuts may appear more severe than the fatal blow itself.

Alexandre Lacassagne (1843–1924)

If ever one person fully deserves the title "Father of Modern Forensic Medicine," then it has to be Alexandre Lacassagne. Although not personally involved in as many actual crime cases as many others mentioned within these pages, it was this stockily built Frenchman with the heavy mustache who laid the tracks for so many others to follow.

He was born at the foot of the Pyrenees in the French town of Cahors. As a young man he attended the École Militaire in Strasbourg before qualifying as a surgeon. He combined these talents by working as an army physician in North Africa, where he soon developed an interest in forensic medicine.

In the slums of Tunis and Algiers shootings were commonplace and so were tattoos. The former gave Lacassagne a priceless opportunity to study gunshot wounds, while the latter intrigued him as a possible means of identification. He soon came to realize the potential importance of forensic medicine in this new age of industrialization and social conflict. In 1878, when his army service ended, he pulled all his thoughts together in a book called *Précis de Médicine,* the outstanding success of which led to him being offered the newly established chair in forensic medicine at the University of Lyons.

His intellectual vitality, personal charm, and comprehensive knowledge of medicine, biology, and philosophy made him, within a few years, more than a match for any of the Parisian school of forensic medicine. Unlike some of his counterparts in the capital, he retained humility and perspective, wryly observing that "history always reminds us of our limitations whenever we are in danger of forgetting them."

His work on postmortem changes in the human body was revolutionary. After prolonged observation, he decided that the dull purple discolorations of the skin that appear on dead bodies—nowadays termed livor mortis, hypostasis, or lividity—resulted from the blood falling to the lowest levels of the body after circulation ceased. This development followed a predictable timescale. It usually began half an hour after death; then, within the first ten to twenty hours, pressing on the spot could make the blotches disappear, because the blood in the capillaries yielded to this pressure. Later, however, as the blood pigment leaked through the walls of the capillaries into the tissues and skin, the blotches became ineradicable.

Such experiments assisted Lacassagne in determining not only the time of death—albeit in a very rudimentary fashion—but also provided important clues as to possible foul play. He found that if a body was moved within a few hours of death, the spots would be displaced, since blood always follows the laws of gravity and flows down into those parts of the body that are lowest after the displacement. Thus marks found on the higher reaches of the body were a sure sign that the body had been moved some considerable time after death. Hours of study in the mortuary provided Lacassagne with the data to establish a fairly predictable schedule for each of these phases.

Rigor mortis and body cooling were just two other postmortem changes that occupied Lacassagne's fertile mind. Both are notoriously difficult, if not impossible, to ascertain with any certainty, especially as a means of establishing **time of death,** as Lacassagne was quick to point out. Always there were environmental variables that needed to be factored into the forensic equation. "One must know how to doubt" was a favorite aphorism of Lacassagne's, and it remained an article of faith that underpinned all his research.

Such skepticism served him well in the Eyraud and Bompard case (see *The Casebook of Forensic Detection,* Wiley, 1996), which brought him international recognition after he salvaged what had been a forensic disaster and turned it into a glittering triumph.

That same year, 1889, Lacassagne broke new ground when, before anyone else, he recognized the correlation between striations on a bullet and the rifling patterns of individual barrels. During an autopsy he had removed a bullet from a gunshot victim and examined it carefully, finding seven longitudinal grooves on its surface. He deduced correctly that these had been made by rifling in the barrel of the murder weapon. Shown a number of pistols owned by suspects, Lacassagne found only one with seven grooves, and on the basis of that discovery the owner was convicted.

Nowadays, of course, no modern court would accept such evidence—it is quite possible that different arms manufacturers could have made several different types of seven-grooved revolvers and that the suspect's gun was not, in this case, the murder weapon—but, as history has shown, Lacassagne was clearly working along the right lines.

He was the first to investigate the possibilities of crime scene **blood spatter analysis** and the need for an adequate means of identifying criminals through a police filing system. In 1898 he conducted the first in-depth assessment of the criminal psyche when he was asked to examine the serial sex murderer Joseph Vacher, who had strangled and raped at least ten, and possibly as many as forty children across southeastern France. Vacher's attempts to feign madness didn't fool Lacassagne. After an exhausting five-month examination, he concluded that the vagrant from southwestern France with a hastily contrived fondness for white rabbit fur hats was "putting it on." When Lacassagne presented his findings to the court, including his theory of exactly how Vacher had committed the crimes, even the defendant was impressed, muttering, "He's very good." Just how good, Vacher discovered on the last day of 1898, when—in a dead faint—he was guillotined.

Lacassagne's work continued without pause. In 1921 he donated his remarkable collection of twelve thousand books, mostly with themes of forensic medicine, pathology, and famous criminal cases, to the medical school at Lyons, where they remain to this day, hallmarking the culmination of a career without parallel in the history of forensic science.

Significant Cases

1889	Michel Eyraud and Gabrielle Bompard
1894	Sadi Carnot Assassination
1897	Joseph Vacher

Kassem Lachaal

Date: 1986
Location: Crawley, England

For centuries, British royalty hunted deer in Ashdown Forest, a huge, sprawling woodland forty miles south of London. On the morning of August 31, 1986, prey of a rather different kind was discovered just off the main Eastbourne-London road. The headless torso had been cut into small pieces, wrapped in blue curtains and a negligee, then buried in two shallow graves. Initial tests suggested that the remains were those of an adult woman and that death had occurred within the past three months.

Once in the mortuary, the pathologist Dr. Michael Heath was able to be far more specific. The woman, he said, had been in her midtwenties, with Mediterranean coloring, of blood group O, about five feet, three inches in height, had given birth to at least one child, and there was a scar consistent with the removal of an abscess. She had died from a frenzied knife attack: her throat was cut; she had suffered numerous stab wounds; and, apart from the heart and lungs, all of her internal organs were missing. A single blue carpet fiber found on the body was logged for future reference.

The absence of the head and hands only magnified the identification problems, but from hundreds of missing-persons reports, the police were able to draw up a possible short list of ten who might be the dead woman. Everything, though, led up a blind alley.

A televised appeal for information about the curtains that specifically targeted mail carriers and delivery drivers failed to produce any worthwhile leads, but it did have one unexpected outcome: a forty-two-year-old Moroccan named Kassem Lachaal contacted a solicitor to explain that his mother-in-law had been pestering him over his wife, Latifa, who had returned to Morocco. He was concerned lest he be connected with the dead woman.

Lachaal had a complicated domestic life. Under Islamic law, he was permitted four wives. He lived with one wife, Fatima, and their children, in Crawley, while a second wife, Latifa, lived close by. He told police that Latifa, age twenty-six, had left for Morocco on August 18 to obtain a divorce. Lachaal sounded credible enough, describing how Latifa had paid cash for her air ticket; how she had left her young son in his charge; and how, on August 18, Lachaal had awoken to find Latifa's house keys pushed through his mailbox.

But when the police interviewed local travel agents, not one had any record of having sold Latifa a ticket. Moreover, passenger manifests for August 18 and surrounding dates showed no one by the name of Latifa Lachaal. Also, Lachaal seemed to be having trouble getting his story straight. Some curious neighbors were told that Latifa had gone to Morocco; others heard tales of an excursion to France.

The police now decided that there was sufficient suspicion to search Latifa's house in Ramsey Court, Crawley. Their search concentrated on the bathroom. Although the bathtub itself had been replaced, the wooden floor and the bath paneling showed tiny stains that were found to be human blood. Altogether, the bathroom yielded 140 separate bloodstains, all type O. Tiny shreds of blue carpet scraped from beneath the bathroom baseboard were found to be microscopically identical to the fiber on the body.

At this time, with DNA testing still in its infancy and prohibitively expensive, most police forces were forced to rely on traditional methods of serological analysis. By obtaining blood samples from Latifa's family in Morocco, scientists were able to establish that the blood from the body, the blood in the bathroom, and the blood from the family were all closely related, as in a family tree.

An invaluable clue came from a family photograph of Latifa, taken while she was standing in front of some blue curtains. Knowing her height, it was possible to calculate their length—exactly the same as the curtains wrapped around the body. The weave in both curtain and photograph appeared to be identical.

There was also a letter, ostensibly written by Latifa to her family in Morocco on August 18. Because it was written in Arabic, assistance was sought from a disputed-documents expert in France, but it was not possible to state that the letter had been forged. What experts did find on the letter, close to a crease in the paper, was Lachaal's thumbprint, in all likelihood made as he folded the letter. By contrast, Latifa's fingerprints were singularly absent.

When a surgeon who had operated on Latifa in Sri Lanka for an abscess was traced, he agreed that the scar on the torso matched the incision he had made for the operation. This gave police the confidence in January 1987 to charge Kassem and Fatima Lachaal with murder. Detectives were convinced the couple had acted together, killing Latifa shortly after inviting her to celebrate the Muslim Feast of Lamb at their house. Even though neighbors told police they had seen Lachaal carrying black plastic bags out to a rental car, there was no concrete evidence that the body was that of Latifa. Then fate played a hand.

In October 1987 a freak hurricane hit southern England, uprooting thousands of trees. As workmen near Crawley toiled to clear the debris, one found a skull in the undergrowth, close to where Lachaal had worked. Although comparison with Latifa's dental records was indecisive, all was not lost. By chance she had attended a local hospital after Lachaal had assaulted her, and they had taken an X-ray of her skull. When the odontologist Bernard Sims compared the photographs with his own X-rays of the skull, and mapped the shapes of the frontal sinus—an air space in the forehead—they matched exactly.

On March 24, 1988, Lachaal was sentenced to life imprisonment. Fatima, acquitted of murder, received eighteen months for perverting the course of justice by helping to dispose of the body.

Marie Lafarge

Date: 1840
Location: Paris, France

Marie-Fortunée Cappelle always was a dreamer. Born into the fringes of the French aristocracy, she liked to hint at royal blood in her lineage, but she always was denied access to the exclusive inner circle. Deprived of what she thought was her birthright, Marie set her sights on marrying a rich landowner. In this task she was ably supported by her parents. They were eager to rid themselves of Marie's highly strung and petulant ways and began trawling various matrimonial agencies. Soon one candidate emerged from the pack.

Charles Lafarge was no great catch—he was coarse and boorish, with disgusting table manners—but the watercolor paintings that he flaunted of his house and estate in the Correze region brought glows of approval to the faces of Marie's parents, who bullied their reluctant daughter into accepting his offer of marriage.

Marie's skepticism proved well founded. Le Glandier, far from being the glittering château depicted in the painting, turned out to be a ramshackle pile, rat-infested and in desperate need of refurbishment. Also Lafarge's much-vaunted iron business was teetering on the verge of bankruptcy and could survive only if he got his hands on Marie's dowry.

It was a marriage made in the depths of hell, and one that Marie instantly regretted. On the wedding night, she locked herself in the bedroom, deaf to Charles's pleading outside the door. Nor was she any better disposed toward her hatchet-faced mother-in-law, who made no secret of her hatred for the haughty coquette who had made her son a local laughingstock.

Desperate to get his hands on the elusive dowry, Charles agreed to revamp the house. First, though, he needed to go to Paris. Before leaving, he and Marie exchanged wills, naming each other as the beneficiary; however, unknown to Marie, at the last moment Charles drafted a new will, which left everything to his scheming mother.

On December 12, 1839, Marie purchased arsenic from a local druggist, saying she was overrun with rats. Simultaneously, she thought it would be a grand idea to send Charles, stranded in Paris over Christmas, a present of some home-cooked cakes. Her mother duly baked a selection of small cakes, which were packaged in front of witnesses and dispatched. But somehow the parcel that Charles received contained just a single large cake, and within hours of eating a slice, he convulsed with stomach cramps. Throughout the holiday he retched repeatedly. On January 3, 1840, he felt well enough to return to Le Glandier and the solicitous ministrations of his young wife. Almost immediately his health nose-dived once again, and on January 14 he died.

Early murmurings of unease became a noisy chorus of suspicion as relatives of the dead man recalled Marie adding a white powder to his food. "Orange-blossom sugar," she cooed, to soothe his irritated stomach. But now thoughts returned to that arsenic Marie had purchased in early December. Every last gram, she insisted, had been made into a paste by one of her servants, Alfred, then laid out for the rats. Alfred agreed that this was true. But Charles's mother had preserved some of her dead son's vomit, together with the dregs of a drink that Marie had prepared for him, and when both these samples were found to contain traces of arsenic, Marie was arrested.

Then came a sensational development. One year earlier, Marie had been under suspicion after a necklace disappeared from the home of her friend Victomtesse de Léautaud. Marie had bluffed her way out of the situation; now, hearing of her arrest, the Léautauds pressed their accusation of theft. When a search of Le Glandier produced the missing necklace, Marie was tried for robbery in July 1840 and sentenced to two years.

With Marie safely behind bars, prosecutors had time to make their case, and in September she was put on trial for her life. The case attracted enormous publicity, splitting the nation in two, as anti-Lafargists clashed bitterly with Marie's supporters. An ominous note was struck with the revelation that the paste was found to be just bicarbonate of soda. Two local chemists were asked to inspect Charles's stomach, using the very latest in poison detection apparatus, the "arsenic mirror" invented by James Marsh just four years earlier (see **toxicology**). Their joint verdict, delivered to a heaving courtroom, caused uproar: there was *no* arsenic present in Charles's stomach!

Marie clasped her hands above her head in triumph as waves of cheering broke out from her supporters. The prosecutors blanched, insistent that such a revolutionary technique demanded elucidation from the man widely regarded as the founder of modern toxicology.

Spanish-born Mathieu Orfila had risen to the rarefied heights of attending physician at the French court, but he would gain international fame as the first person to systemize the study and classification of toxic substances. Through meticulous, often gruesome study on live animals, he was able to correlate the chemistry of a toxin with the biological effects it produces in the poisoned individual.

Orfila agreed to travel down to Tulle, in the province of Correze, from Paris. What he found horrified him. After the initial tests, the stomach, instead of being preserved in a jar, had been thrown into a desk drawer for safekeeping. Orfila demanded that Charles's body be exhumed and fresh samples taken. At the disinterment, he sampled the surrounding soil to ensure that undue amounts of naturally occurring arsenic had not migrated to the body. He found nothing out of the ordinary. Then, watched by the two local chemists, he performed the Marsh test behind locked doors on September 13. He appeared in court the next day to announce his results.

It gave him no pleasure to report that the earlier Marsh test had been botched. This was understandable: the Marsh test was still in its infancy, and neither chemist knew how to properly operate the delicate equipment. In rambling circumlocutory fashion Orfila finally delivered his decision: Charles Lafarge had been deliberately poisoned!

All her life Marie Lafarge had wanted fame; what she got instead was notoriety, as the first person convicted of murder through the Marsh apparatus. Sentenced to life, she was released in 1850 on health grounds—having contracted tuberculosis—and died the following year.

Angelo John LaMarca

Date: 1956
Location: Westbury, New York

Just thirty-three days after being born, Peter Weinberger was kidnapped from the patio of his home on Long Island. His mother, Beatrice, had left her baby for just minutes while she stepped inside to get a diaper. When she returned, the carriage was empty. All she found was a ransom note lying on the floor. Written in green ink, with skillful and highly singular penmanship, on a sheet torn from a student notebook, it read:

> Attention.
>
> I'm sorry this had to happen, but I am in bad need of money, and couldnt get it any other way. Don't tell anyone or go to the Police about this, because I am watching you closely. I am scared stiff, & will kill the baby, at your first wrong move.
>
> Just put $2000 00/xxx two thousand in small bills in a brown envelope, & place it next to the sign Post at the corner of Albemarle Rd. & Park Ave. at *Exactly* 10 o'clock tomorrow (Thursday) morning. If everything goes smooth, I will bring the baby back & leave him on the same corner "Safe & Happy" at exactly 12 noon.
>
> No excuses, I can't wait!

The note was signed, "Your baby sitter."

That day—July 4, 1956—the Nassau County police were notified, and at about 9:00 P.M. news of the kidnapping reached the FBI's New York office. Agents were dispatched to the scene, but because no evidence existed to show that the child had been carried across a state line or that interstate communications had been used by the kidnapper, jurisdiction remained with the local police. In breach of official requests for a media blackout, one newspaper reported details of the ransom note before its demands were fulfilled. This had disastrous repercussions. When Mrs. Weinberger arrived at the drop-off spot with the ransom, hordes of reporters were on hand. So was the kidnapper, but the crowds scared him off. Two days later he phoned the Weinbergers and reiterated his demand.

With the press coverage spinning out of control, what was already a tragedy for the Weinbergers assumed nightmarish proportions as cruel hoaxers bombarded them with calls and threats, all claiming to have their son and demanding money. (Several of these time wasters later faced extortion charges.)

On July 10 the family received a second ransom note from the kidnapper: there was no mistaking that distinctive style of writing. It was penned on the back of an order blank later traced to the Dynalum Window Products Company in Garden City, Long Island. The next day the FBI officially entered the case under the 1934 Lindbergh Kidnapping Act, which provided that after seven days a presumption could be made that the victim had been transported across state lines.

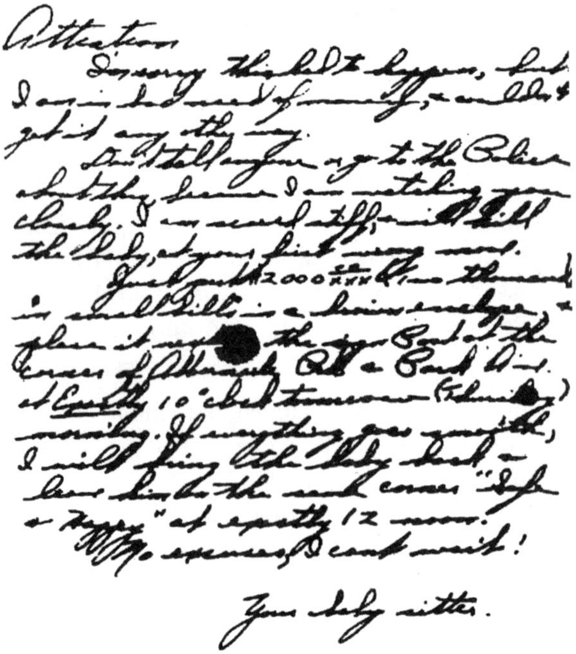

Attention
I'm sorry this had to happen, but
I am in bad need of money, & couldn't
get it any other way.
Don't tell anyone or go to the Police
about this because I am watching you
closely. I am scared stiff, and will kill
the baby at your first wrong move.
Just put $2000.00 (two thousand)
in small bills in a brown envelope, &
place it ne[illegible] the sign post at the
corner of Albemarle Rd. & Park Drive
at exactly 10 o'clock tomorrow (Thursday)
morning. If everything goes smoothly,
I will bring the baby back & leave
him on the same corner "safe
& happy" at exactly 12 noon.
No excuses, I can't wait!

Your baby sitter.

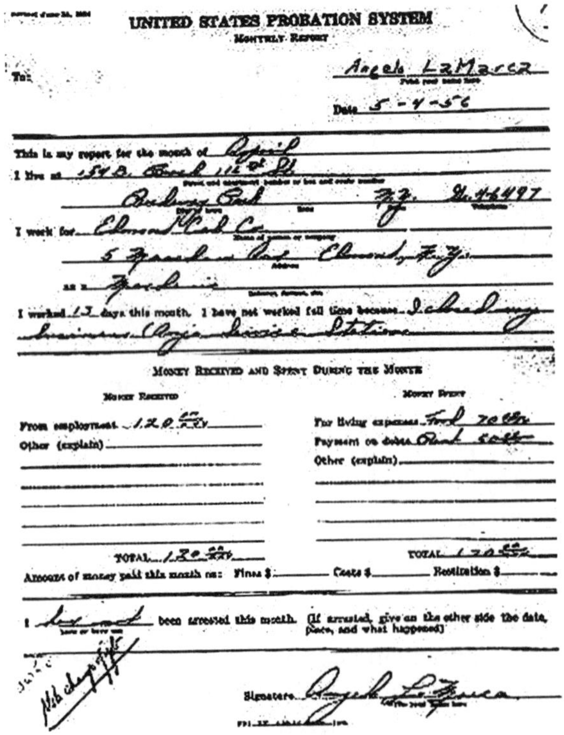

UNITED STATES PROBATION SYSTEM
MONTHLY REPORT

To: Angelo LaMarca

Date 5-4-56

This is my report for the month of April
I live at 154 B. Park 112th St.
Plainview, N.Y. [illegible]
I work for Elmont [illegible] Co.
5 [illegible] Elmont, N.Y.
as a [illegible]
I worked 13 days this month. I have not worked full time because I closed my business [illegible] Station

MONEY RECEIVED AND SPENT DURING THE MONTH

Money Received		Money Spent	
From employment	120.00	For living expenses	Food 70.00
Other (explain)		Payment on debts	Rent 50.00
		Other (explain)	
TOTAL	120.00	TOTAL	120.00

Amount of money paid this month on: Fines $ ______ Costs $ ______ Restitution $ ______

I have not been arrested this month. (If arrested, give on the other side the date, place, and what happened)

Signature Angelo LaMarca

The handwriting on the ransom demand (*above, top*) shows clear similarities to a probation report completed by LaMarca (*right*).

Apart from the taped telephone call, the best chance of identifying the kidnapper lay with the extortion notes. FBI handwriting experts, drafted into the investigation headquarters at Mineola, Long Island, found distinguishing characteristics in sixteen letters of the alphabet. In particular, they noticed the unusual way in which the kidnapper's lower-case script *m* resembled a sideways *z*.

Such quirks convinced investigators that if the kidnapper had ever filled in an official form, they would be able to recognize his handwriting. Working to this end, they initiated a search of all local records. It began with fingerprint cards and files from the Long Island police, then widened to include handwriting specimens from automobile registration forms, post office files, voter registrations, hospital records, every conceivable place where there was handwriting on record. Whenever a signature or a piece of writing even remotely resembling the writing on the ransom demands was found, it was sent to Mineola for closer examination.

On Wednesday, August 22, after seven weeks of mind-numbing drudgery and more than two million handwriting samples, an agent happened to spot a probation violation form filled out by thirty-one-year-old Angelo John LaMarca, who had been arrested in a June 1954 raid on a bootlegging operation. LaMarca had received a ninety-day suspended sentence and probation. Significantly, on July 5—one day after the kidnapping—he had failed to report to his probation officer and did not show until July 28, at which time he filled out the form to explain his absence. The agent looked closely at LaMarca's handwriting: there was no denying its similarity to that on the kidnapping notes. His record was rushed to Mineola, where experts pored over LaMarca's handwritten reports and made a positive identification.

The next day LaMarca, an auto mechanic up to his eyes in debt, was arrested at his home, just five miles from the Weinberger residence. Within hours he confessed. He told agents that he had taken the baby to the ransom drop-off point, only to be scared off by the crowds. In a panic, he had abandoned the baby, leaving him alive in some heavy brush near exit 37 of Northern State Parkway near Plainview. On August 24 the decomposed remains of Peter Weinberger were found in a thicket where LaMarca had said. The baby had perished from starvation and exposure.

At the garage where LaMarca worked, agents found a pad of order blanks imprinted with the name of the same window products company found on the second ransom note. Microscopic analysis showed that the same guillotine had trimmed both pad and note, leaving its telltale markings on the edges of the paper.

Tried for first-degree murder and kidnapping, LaMarca was convicted without any recommendation of mercy. After several stays he went to the electric chair on August 7, 1958.

In the aftermath of this tragedy Congress changed the federal law, authorizing the FBI to enter kidnap cases after just twenty-four hours rather than waiting seven days.

Henry Lee (1938–)

One of the most celebrated and controversial criminalists of recent times, Lee moved at a young age from his native China to Taipei in Taiwan, and there he entered the police force, rising to the rank of captain. In 1965, with just $50 in his pocket, he immigrated to America and soon enrolled in the John Jay College of Criminal Justice in New York. The thorough grounding in forensic science he received there prepared him for his later studies, when he received a doctorate in biochemistry from New York University.

For almost a decade, Lee worked at New York University Medical Center until moving to Connecticut to become director of that state's crime laboratory before assuming the rank of public safety commissioner there.

Media-friendly and blessed with the ability to explain complex subjects in everyday language, he soon became a familiar courtroom figure, the subject of numerous articles and TV programs.

Some of his cases—particularly those involving suspected homicides when the victim had not been found—have become forensic classics (see Tevfik Sivri), but these successes don't convince everyone. Complaints abound that he spreads himself too thinly, that by setting out to appear as a jack-of-all-forensics—blood spatter expert, fingerprint specialist, ballistics expert, his résumé runs to fifty pages—he is actually master of none. How much of this criticism is grounded in professional jealousy must remain a matter for conjecture, but there can be no doubt that many rivals envy Lee's quiet lucidity in front of a jury.

A cornerstone of his philosophy is the absolute need to maintain utter integrity at the crime scene. He has amplified at length on this subject in *Henry Lee's Crime Scene Handbook* (2001), just one of the many books and hundreds of articles he has written.

Each year Lee runs several advanced crime scene symposia, attended by detectives from across the nation. They come to learn the latest forensic techniques, but above all, they come to be imbued with what Lee calls the "logic tree approach," making the theory fit the facts, rather than vice versa.

Sometimes, when Lee can't get to the crime, the crime comes to him via teleforensics. In this new development information is digitized, then transmitted over telephone lines. This allows Lee to study crime scenes even though he might be thousands of miles away, and to make suggestions to his colleagues in situ.

In 1992 he was elected a distinguished fellow of the American Academy of Forensic Science. Nowadays retired, Lee is still consulted on major cases and still lectures frequently at the Henry C. Lee Institute of Forensic Science at the University of New Haven, passing on the knowledge he has gained from four decades of solving crimes.

Significant Cases

1986	Richard Crafts
1986	Robert Chambers
1988	Tevfik Sivri*
1991	William Kennedy Smith
1993	Waco Fire
1993	Vince Foster
1994	O. J. Simpson
1996	JonBenet Ramsay
2001	Rae Carruth

*Profiled in this book.

Edward Leonski

Date: 1942
Location: Melbourne, Australia

For sixteen days in May 1942, the city of Melbourne was terrorized by what the press dubbed "a mad strangler." On May 2 Ivy McLeod was throttled. Eight days later, Pauline Thompson, a policeman's wife, was found strangled in the street. The frenzy peaked on May 18 when forty-year-old Gladys Hosking was seen to take shelter from the rain under an American serviceman's umbrella. Hours later her mutilated body was found dumped in a slit trench close to Camp Pell, a sprawling garrison that housed just some of the fifteen thousand U.S. servicemen stationed in Melbourne at this time.

That same night, Private Noel Seymour, an Australian soldier on guard duty at the camp, had challenged an American GI who tried to gain entrance. Disheveled and out of breath, his uniform soiled with mud, the trooper explained that he had fallen in some mud coming through the park. Seymour let him pass.

When news of the Hosking murder broke, Seymour contacted the police. They linked the incident to two other recent episodes. In the first, a woman had been entertaining a GI in her apartment when he suddenly attempted to strangle her. Her threat to call the police had subdued him, and he'd left. On another occasion, a GI had tried to force a woman into her house, only to be chased off by the woman's uncle.

When all the troops at Camp Pell were paraded, Seymour had little hesitation picking out the soldier he had seen on the night of the murder. He was a twenty-four-year-old Texan with "baby face" good looks, and his name was Edward Leonski.

Fellow soldiers in the 52nd Signal Battalion already knew to give Leonski a wide berth. His manic grin, fondness for pouring pepper into his beer, and a disconcerting habit of walking on his hands when drunk—which was most of the time—had marked him out as decidedly weird. Equally unsettling was the way the oddball Texan liked to gloat over press clippings of the Melbourne murders.

And yet, despite also being identified by the woman's uncle who had chased him off, there was little to say that Leonski was a triple killer. To find the hard physical evidence that would guarantee a conviction, the authorities turned to the local analyst **Charles Anthony Taylor.**

Because the first two murders had been virtually clue-free, Taylor concentrated on the Hosking case. Beside the slit trench where she was found were large piles of yellow ocher mud, and in that mud he spotted the distinctive marks of clawing hands and sliding feet, obviously made by a person or persons as he struggled to clamber free from the gooey mess.

Thoughtfully, he went to Leonski's tent. In opening the canvas flap he replicated what he felt would be the instinctive actions of someone entering the tent, sweeping the heavy flap slightly up and across. Where his hand came to a halt, he looked at the canvas wall of the tent. At that very same spot was a clump of hardened, mustard-yellow mud.

It was a similar tale inside the tent. On either side of the pallet that supported Leonski's bed—where someone might support themselves as they got into bed—Taylor found yellow mud fingerprints, and there also was a seven-inch patch of mud on the blanket.

Leonski tried to explain away the mud by saying it could have been left by anyone tramping in and out of the tent, while the mud and gravel staining on his own clothing was blamed on a fall incurred in the heavy rain that night. But when Taylor visited the spot where Leonski claimed to have tripped, the soil there was much darker in color.

As the grilling got tougher, Leonski eventually admitted to all three murders. By the time of his court-martial, though, he had retracted this confession, saying it had been coerced, and renewed his insistence that the mud had been contracted elsewhere.

Taylor's evidence proved crucial. He told the tribunal that Gladys Hosking had died at Royal Park, an ancient-fossil zone, where the layers of earth were quite distinct from those in other parts of Melbourne. They consisted of a top layer of black earth; a layer of gray clay; one of yellow ocher; and, deepest of all, a stratum of ironstone gravel. The mounds of soil dug from the slit trench lay in reverse order—with the ironstone gravel and the yellow ocher spread on the top, and the gray and black layers well underneath.

Quickly, the defense riposted that away from this trench and nearer the U.S. camp, workmen had recently laid pipes in this same fossil zone; therefore, was it not possible that Leonski could have plastered himself with this yellow ocher mud from these excavations while returning, perhaps unsteadily, back to camp one night?

Taylor shook his head. The pipeline track had been quite shallow, and the lower strata of soil—the yellow ocher and the ironstone gravel—had not been disturbed by the diggers.

Then maybe Leonski could have acquired the mud somewhere else?

Taylor would have none of it. Similar mud did exist in Victoria, most notably the volcanic region of the Western District, but with one big difference: it was smooth in texture. It contained none of the tiny gravel so prevalent at the Hosking trench. That was why the yellow ocher mud in this fossil zone had never been used commercially to make yellow ocher paint. The cost of extracting the gravel would have been exorbitant, and it was that gravel that Taylor's microscope had spotted in the yellow ocher mud on Leonski's clothes and shoes.

Taylor's testimony jerked the noose tight around Leonski's neck. A plea of insanity, claiming he had strangled the women "to get their voices," received short shrift from the court-martial, and, still grinning, he was sentenced to death. Because the murders had created much bad local feeling, the commanding officer of U.S. forces in Australia, General Douglas MacArthur, was in no mood for mercy, and Leonski was hanged.

Edmond Locard (1877–1966)

The celebrated French scientist who, after receiving his early education at the Dominican College at Quillins, attended the nearby University of Lyons. At the time, **Alexandre Lacassagne** was that institute's professor of forensic medicine, and he soon took the young student under his wing. After graduating as doctor of medicine and also licentiate in law, Locard became Lacassagne's assistant, holding the post until 1910, when he resigned to establish what would become the Laboratoire Intérregional de Police Technique in Lyons.

This rather grand-sounding title helped mask the fact that Locard's workplace was a modest two-room operation on the second floor of the courthouse in Lyons and that it housed only two items of equipment: a microscope and a spectroscope. Humble maybe, yet here was the world's first dedicated medico-legal facility, yet another reminder of the trailblazing role played by French crime fighters in the early days of forensic science.

From his Lyons base, Locard began to expand on the ideas that Lacassagne applied to forensic medicine. Locard took a refreshingly eclectic approach, applying his mind to **questioned documents;** poroscopy (detailed analysis in **fingerprinting**); as well as analyses of body fluids, hair, and skin. Nor was he hidebound by academic snobbery; he always urged his students to read the Sherlock Holmes novels, which he regarded as classic exemplars of logic and reasoning.

But it is in the field of trace evidence where Locard gained immortality. His exchange principle—the belief that "every contact leaves a trace"—has become a fundamental axiom of forensic detection. Enter a room, said Locard, and you either leave something there that was previously on your person, or you take something away with you, or both. Millions of rueful criminals can attest to the accuracy of Locard's truism.

One of the earliest, a Lyons bank clerk named Émile Gourbin, had been suspected of strangling his girlfriend but appeared to have an unshakable alibi. However, when Locard took scrapings from under Gourbin's fingernails and examined them microscopically, he found not only skin cells that might have come from the victim's neck but also traces of a fine pink cosmetic powder. When Locard reexamined the dead woman's body, he found this same cosmetic powder on her face and neck. Confronted with this evidence, Gourbin made a full confession.

As Locard's fame grew, so did his responsibilities. He became the founding director of the Institute of Criminalistics. He also taught and wrote voluminously on his subject, and in 1912 he published his monumental treatise *Traite de criminalistique*, which eventually ran to seven editions. Within its pages he argued that proof is established in a criminal trial by confession, presumption, written evidence, testimony, and scientific evidence. The core of his work he summed up in a single, oft-repeated phrase: "To write the history of identification is to write the history of criminology."

Following his retirement in 1951, Locard continued his research and remained active in the crime-fighting community until his death in 1966.

Significant Case
1912 Émile Gourbin

George Mackay (Alias "John Williams")

Date: 1912
Location: Eastbourne, England

On an October evening in 1912 police were summoned to the Eastbourne home of Countess Flora Sztaray to investigate reports of a burglar seen prowling around the property. At 7:40 P.M. Inspector Arthur Walls arrived at the house and ordered the man, still lurking in the shadows, to come out. The reply was two shots, one of which killed the inspector. In the confusion the killer made his escape, leaving just one clue—a fedora hat, size 7¼—lying on the road.

As the inquiry gathered pace, an odious denizen of the local underworld named Edgar Power presented himself to the police, saying he knew the murderer's identity. Power babbled that he had acted as an intermediary between a local burglar named John Williams and his brother in London. John had begged his brother for money to get himself out of a desperate situation. After Power delivered the requested cash—he actually pocketed half himself—he waited for Williams to flee to London, then went to the police.

Power had another reason for betraying Williams. The latter lived with a stunningly beautiful young woman named Florence Seymour, whom Power had long lusted after; here, at last, was a priceless opportunity to get rid of his rival. Coached by the police, Power approached Florence with word that her lover was a murder suspect. Florence panicked and blurted out that she had been with Williams when he buried a gun on Eastbourne's shingle beach.

Power passed this information to the police, and they were lying in wait when Power inveigled Florence to the beach on the pretext that the gun should be relocated to a safer hiding place. Once Florence indicated the general area where the gun was buried, they pounced.

Florence, heavily pregnant with Williams's child and at the end of her emotional tether, buckled beneath a brutal police interrogation. She confessed that on the night in question she had been with Williams close to where the shooting occurred and that at one point he had gone off alone. When he returned half an hour later, he was without his hat and seemed nervous. Then he'd bustled her down to the beach and buried the gun. Officers sifting through the shingle found parts from a dismantled gun, along with a rope, such as might be used by a burglar.

Power wasn't done yet. With one eye firmly fixed on a hefty newspaper reward, he contacted Williams in London and lured him into a police trap at Moorgate Underground Station. Not until much later was it learned that Williams's real name was George Mackay and that he was the son of a Scottish clergyman. This explains why he was charged in the name of Williams.

Although the case was circumstantially strong, it lacked any direct proof. No one identified Williams as the burglar, and the hat found at the scene was of a common type that could have fitted literally thousands of men in the Eastbourne area. Also, his defense argued that Florence had been bullied into incriminating her lover and that her confession—later retracted—was worthless.

So what about the gun? The parts were handed to the gunsmith **Robert Churchill** for inspection. Already at age twenty-six he had made a name for himself in the new field of ballistics analysis, but never before had he been involved in such a notorious case. This was a potential career-maker, and Churchill wasn't about to blow it.

Even though the revolver was incomplete—the smaller parts had apparently been thrown down a drain—he still had a barrel, its cylinder, the hammer action, and the breech to work with. At his London workshop he reassembled the parts, then fitted a new hammer and springs so the gun was once more usable. After test-firing the weapon, Churchill visually compared this bullet to the one that had killed Walls. In his report he wrote: "Not only was the bullet of exactly the same caliber as the suspect revolver, but it also bore the same number of grooves, similar in width and in rifling angle as the test bullets."

But he wanted visual confirmation to put before a jury. Since camera technology of the time precluded the possibility of photographing the inside of a revolver barrel, he and Sergeant William McBride (later chief inspector in charge of Scotland Yard's Photographic Department) devised a method whereby melted dentist's wax was poured into the gun's barrel. Once it hardened, the wax was then eased out of the tubing. By modern-day standards the results were horribly crude: the wax impression of the inner surface of the barrel was in reverse, it was not sufficiently accurate for close measurement, and the wax wasn't sensitive enough to take the significant pits and abrasions in the metal. But it did allow McBride to take clear photographs of the casts.

The pictures that Churchill and McBride produced in court showed an enlargement of the bullet that had killed Walls, mounted above the cast of the revolver barrel recovered from Eastbourne beach. The striations on the bullet plainly matched the twist of the barrel. For comparison purposes, Churchill had photographs of casts taken from numerous other revolvers, with rifling varying from four to eight grooves of various widths and with twists ranging from the extreme left- to the extreme right-hand slant. None looked remotely similar.

Not only had Churchill and McBride discovered a way in which a highly technical matter could be demonstrated at a glance, they also had made British legal history. For the first time, a projectile had been related to a single make of gun. This was still, of course, many years before the comparison microscope, which could tie a bullet to one gun alone, but Churchill's input sealed Williams's fate.

One day before his execution, Williams was allowed to kiss his newborn child. Pressing a scrap of prison bread into the infant's tiny hand, he said, "Now no one can say your father never gave you anything."

Elmer McCurdy

Date: 1976
Location: Long Beach, California

A film crew taping an episode of the popular TV series *The Six Million Dollar Man* at the Nu-Pike Fun House in Long Beach in December 1976 found itself hampered by a painted dummy hanging from the ceiling. Not wanting the dummy in a camera shot, a technician moved it. As he did so, one of the arms came off in his hands. To his horror he saw a human bone protrude from the waxy body.

Dr. Joseph H. Choi, the deputy medical examiner for Los Angeles, examined "John Doe #255" and confirmed that it was human, male, sixty-three inches tall, weighed only fifty pounds, and was entirely mummified. Fusing of the sacrum segments at the back of the pelvis suggested that the man had been about thirty years old at the time of death.

All of the major internal organs were present, although each felt "hard as a rock" due to overzealous arsenical embalming. The amount of arsenic in the tissues was astounding, and it was this feature that first provided an inkling of the corpse's age. Until the turn of the twentieth century, arsenic was the embalming agent of choice throughout America; but by the 1920s its use had been outlawed in most states. Therefore it seemed probable that the corpse was at least half a century old.

Cause of death was a gunshot wound to the chest, the bullet traveling downward into the abdomen. The slug had been removed, but its copper jacket was recovered from the left pelvic region. Ballistics experts recognized it as belonging to a .32-caliber bullet, of a type not manufactured since World War I.

The first clue to identifying the corpse came most unexpectedly. Inside the mouth was a 1924 penny and a ticket stub that read "Louis Sonney's Museum of Crime, So. Main St. L.A." When this was reported in the press, a reader contacted the police, recalling that an "outlaw corpse" had been exhibited at various amusement parks in the 1920s. Another veteran carnival worker remembered a corpse belonging to an Oklahoma bank robber whose name was "Mac-something."

Records at the Oklahoma Territorial Prison soon yielded a more positive identification: Elmer McCurdy. Local historians knew the name well. But how this two-bit outlaw came to be dangling from a beam in a Long Beach fun house was the kind of fantastic story that even Hollywood would have shied away from.

The saga began on October 6, 1911, when McCurdy and two fellow desperadoes robbed a train near Okesa, Oklahoma. Expecting the safe to contain a small fortune that had been earmarked for local Native Americans,

The final resting place in Guthrie, Oklahoma, for Elmer McCurdy, "The Bandit Who Wouldn't Give Up."

the gang was disgruntled to find that it held but $46. Their only consolation lay in a shipment of liquor on board. Before bolting into the night, they grabbed several bottles of whiskey.

The gang split up. McCurdy rode aimlessly around the wilderness, getting drunker by the minute, oblivious to the fifty-strong posse that was hot on his trail. They eventually tracked him down to a ranch in the Osage Hills. By this time McCurdy was so inebriated he couldn't see straight. His warning shots posed few problems for the posse, who merely bided their time and gunned him down at their leisure.

His body was taken to the Johnson Funeral Home in nearby Pawhuska, where the embalmer did such a good job of preserving the corpse that everyone agreed it would be a shame to bury it. For five years the corpse stood, fully dressed and clutching a rifle, at the back of the funeral home, becoming something of a local tourist attraction. Then, in October 1916, a couple of carnies, James and Charles Patterson, showed up, claiming to be cousins of McCurdy. They piously announced that they wished to return their relative to California and give him a decent burial. The corpse was duly released to these "cousins," and for the next several years McCurdy's mummified body was exhibited at carnivals and sideshows all across West Texas and

Oklahoma as "The Bandit Who Wouldn't Give Up." Eventually it wound up on a Long Beach pier, and then went to a storage warehouse for dummies. After that it vanished—until the film crew arrived in 1976.

This, then, was the story; but how to prove definitely that these were the mortal remains of Elmer McCurdy? Despite his colorful past, McCurdy had never been fingerprinted. However, as luck would have it, the Pawhuska embalmer had taken several photographs of the dead outlaw and made copious notes. Among these was an entry recording that on the back of the outlaw's right wrist was a two-inch scar. Sure enough, after scraping off several layers of paint from the mummy's arm, anthropologists found that selfsame scar.

The Oklahoma-based anthropologist **Clyde Snow** flew to California to assist in the project. He and the Los Angeles medical examiner **Thomas Noguchi** worked side by side on the puzzle. Radiographs taken of the corpse's head were superimposed over the 1911 photos of McCurdy's face; then, as a final touch, negatives from the funeral parlor photos were superimposed over the actual head. While bodies may "shrink" in death, the bones remain the same, and in this instance the configurations matched exactly. There could be no doubt about it.

Satisfied at last that the corpse had been properly identified and that all the proprieties had been observed, California authorities issued a death certificate, and Elmer McCurdy—"The Bandit Who Wouldn't Give Up"—was flown to Guthrie, Oklahoma, for interment at Summit View Cemetery. Despite his relative lack of notoriety, he was laid to rest in the cemetery's "Boot Hill" section, alongside another, rather more infamous Oklahoma outlaw, Bill Doolin, onetime leader of the "Wild Bunch."

David Meierhofer

Date: 1973
Location: Bozeman, Montana

What began as a pleasant camping trip in the Montana foothills of the Rockies for the Jaeger family turned to tragedy on a June night in 1973 when someone sliced through the fabric of their tent with a knife and snatched away their seven-year-old daughter, Susan. When she was not found within twenty-four hours her abduction became a federal matter, and the FBI was called in. As agents converged on Bozeman, Montana, the FBI's Behavioral Science Unit (BSU) in Washington, D.C., was asked to prepare a profile of the likely kidnapper. Howard Teten and Pat Mullany sketched out a preliminary report: most likely a young white male, someone local, a loner who had chanced across the family by accident at night. Saddest of all, they seriously doubted whether Susan would be found alive.

The agent in charge of the investigation, Pete Dunbar, soon had a strong suspect: an anonymous caller suggested the name of twenty-three-year-old Vietnam veteran David Meierhofer. Dunbar interviewed Meierhofer and found him polite, exceptionally intelligent, and always helpful. He answered questions readily and without demur. Nothing he said sounded suspicious . . . and yet Dunbar wasn't sure. In broad outline, Meierhofer fitted the profile, but so did hundreds of other young men locally. Without a body or any evidence, there was no justification for holding Meierhofer, and he was released.

As the Jaegers returned home to Michigan, all they took with them was the hope that their daughter was still alive. The slimmest of hopes maybe, but it gave them something to cling to. For Dunbar, there was the frustration of an unclosed file, one likely to stay that way barring any new evidence.

He didn't get any new evidence, but he did get a new crime. In January 1974 an eighteen-year-old woman went missing in the Bozeman area. It transpired that recently she had spurned her boyfriend, told him that she didn't want to see him anymore; from all accounts David Meierhofer had not taken the rejection well. This time when questioned, he volunteered to take a polygraph test and to be injected with thiopental sodium.

Commonly called a "truth serum," thiopental sodium is a yellow barbiturate that can be dissolved in water or alcohol and administered orally or intravenously. Used as a sedative and as an anesthetic during surgery, it depresses the central nervous system, slows the heart rate, and lowers the blood pressure. Patients on whom the drug is used as an anesthetic usually are unconscious less than a minute after it enters their veins. The drug causes only a few minutes of sedation. Because of its effectiveness as a sedative, it is commonly the first of three drugs used by those U.S. states that employ lethal injection as a means of judicial execution.

In milder doses the drug becomes what some call a "truth serum." Those taking the drug tend to lose their inhibitions, become very communicative, and share their thoughts without hesitation. Despite its nickname, thiopental sodium will not make a person tell the truth against his or her will.

It certainly didn't work on David Meierhofer. Nor did the polygraph. He passed both tests with flying colors—so well, in fact, that his attorney pressed for his unconditional release and an undertaking that the authorities would stop harassing him.

But all this time, Meierhofer was feeding extra information to the profilers. They were inclined to disregard the truth serum and polygraph tests. Apart from the fact that people can train themselves to "beat the machine," psychopaths are notorious for an ability to compartmentalize their crimes; and it is this very knack of being able to divorce themselves from their actions that makes them so dangerous to be around and so difficult to catch. As Teten and Mullany learned more about Meierhofer, they felt he was a classic psychopath, quite probably the type who would want to gloat over his crimes and taunt his victims. For this reason the Jaegers were asked to keep a tape recorder by their telephone.

On the first anniversary of their daughter's abduction, Mrs. Jaeger answered a call at her Farmington, Michigan, home from a man who claimed he had whisked Susan away to Europe and was treating her to the kind of lavish lifestyle that the Jaegers could never have afforded. If the caller's intent had been to provoke a torrent of abuse or pleas for help, he had grievously miscalculated. All he heard was a calm, understanding woman who expressed forgiveness for what he had done. Totally thrown by this unexpected reaction, the caller dissolved in a flood of tears and hung up.

Although the call could not be traced exactly, technicians said it appeared to have come from open prairie, possibly from someone tapping into a neighbor's phone line. Meierhofer's service record showed that he had learned this very technique in Vietnam. Other aspects of the tape suggested that Meierhofer had been the caller. Spectrographic analysis of the voice matched that of the chief suspect, but at this time Montana courts were unwilling to admit such evidence.

Mullany's next intervention was controversial. Certain sections of the taped conversation hinted that Meierhofer could well be female-dominated, enough for Mullany to propose that Mrs. Jaeger return to Montana and confront him. She did so at his lawyer's office. Meierhofer's cool air of imperturbability seemed to indicate that the experiment had been a failure, but shortly after Mrs. Jaeger returned to Michigan, she received a collect call from a "Mr. Travis" in Salt Lake City. Travis wanted to explain that he, not someone else, had taken Susan. Mrs. Jaeger wasn't fooled for a minute. "Well, hello, David," she said. Again, the caller broke down and hung up.

Armed with a warrant, agents searched Meierhofer's property and found the remains of both female victims. The ex-soldier confessed not only to those two murders but also to the previously unsolved killing of a local boy. Less than a day after making the confession, Meierhofer, left alone in a cell, hanged himself.

This was a genuine triumph for psychological profiling. BSU doubts about the polygraph and truth serum tests kept Meierhofer's name in the frame, as did their belief that he would eventually succumb to female pressure.

Microscopy

In the late nineteenth century the popular view of scientific crime investigation was embodied in images of that mighty detective of fiction Sherlock Holmes peering intently through a magnifying glass as he combed a crime scene, until he inevitably uncovered the vital clue that had previously eluded those boneheads from Scotland Yard. It was this sense of being able to see the unseeable that invested the magnifying glass with its own special aura.

Nothing has changed. With the possible exception of **fingerprinting,** the magnifying lens has been responsible for jailing more criminals than any other forensic tool. Nowadays, of course, it is more commonly the microscope, in all its shapes and forms, that holds center stage and corroborates the timelessness of **Edmond Locard**'s immortal dictum that "every contact leaves a trace."

In the overwhelming majority of cases, any crime scene where physical contact has occurred will yield some kind of trace evidence. It may be a scrap of fiber, a hair, some grit or powder, a flake of skin, perhaps a pinpoint of mascara . . . the list is endless. What unites them all is their near-invisibility.

Since Roman times, when Seneca noted that letters viewed through a globe of water were "seen enlarged and more clearly," scientists have sought ways of improving visual magnification. No one knows for sure when the first compound microscope was made, but its invention is generally credited to a family of Dutch spectacle makers, Hans Jansen and his son Zacharias, between 1590 and 1608.

It was another Dutchman, Antonie van Leeuwenhoek, who really brought the microscope to the scientific forefront. A successful haberdasher by profession, Leeuwenhoek had the time and the money to finance his all-consuming hobby of grinding high-quality miniature lenses. Unconvinced by the crude compound microscopes then in existence, he built his own, using a single high-quality lens. In 1673 he began writing letters to the Royal Society in London, describing research he had conducted on protozoa, bacteria, and red blood cells, all using his preferred simple microscope. The dramatic nature of his discoveries made him world-famous and led to visits from such notables as Peter the Great of Russia, James II of England, and Frederick the Great of Prussia.

Unfortunately, Leeuwenhoek was obsessively secretive about his methods. How exactly he ground his phenomenal lenses, which achieved a magnification of up to 200X, is a puzzle that has baffled science for centuries. One recent study on the few remaining examples of Leeuwenhoek's microscopes suggests that his very best lenses were blown rather than ground. Apparently he discovered that when a glass bulb is blown, a small drop of thickened glass forms at the bottom of the bulb (much like a drop sits in the bottom of a blown soap bubble). By carefully breaking away the excess glass, this tiny drop can be used as a lens. But in order to observe phenomena as small as bacteria, Leeuwenhoek must have employed some form of oblique illumination, or other technique, for enhancing the effectiveness of the lens, and this remains a mystery. Leeuwenhoek's simple microscope held sway until the nineteenth century, when quantum improvements in the art of lens grinding allowed the compound microscope to regain its former status.

The very best types of modern optical microscopes permit magnifications as high as 2,000X—powerful indeed, but not powerful enough for the requirements of contemporary forensic science. It was this craving for ever higher magnifications that led early-twentieth-century researchers to explore the possibility that cathode rays (or electrons) might be used to increase microscope resolution.

In 1924 Louis de Broglie, a French physicist, suggested that electron beams might be regarded as a form of wave motion. In compound microscopes the magnification, and therefore the resolution, is limited by the wavelength of the visible light; structures that are smaller than the wavelength cannot be seen. Although electrons are considered as tiny particles, they also behave as waves, and their wavelength is very much shorter than that of visible light.

Confirmation of de Broglie's theory came in 1933, when the first true electron microscope was constructed. Within a year it was outperforming the resolution of its optical counterparts, though not without drawbacks. The heating effects of the electron beam meant that the specimen was invariably damaged, and it was some years before this problem was solved.

There are two basic types of electron microscope: the transmission electron microscope (TEM), which can only image specimens a fraction of a micrometer or less in thickness; and the scanning electron microscope (SEM), which is the type most used in forensic examination. In this process a beam of electrons is scanned over the surface of a solid object. The information derived is then amplified by a photomultiplier before being displayed as a three-dimensional enlargement of up to 150,000X on a video display unit, though most forensic samples rarely require such powerful magnification.

Another special type of electron microscope is the electron-probe microanalyzer, which allows a chemical analysis of the composition of materials to be made by exciting the emission of X-rays from the various elements that make up the specimen. These X-rays are detected and analyzed by spectrometers built into the instrument. Once again, the probe microanalyzer produces an electron scanning image on a visual display unit (VDU).

Another significant development, particularly in the field of **ballistics,** was the invention of the comparison microscope in the 1920s. Consisting of two compound light microscopes connected by an optical bridge that allows for the simultaneous viewing of questioned samples—typically bullets, hairs, and fibers—it enables the examiner to compare the microscopic characteristics of the known and questioned samples in one field. The range of magnification used is approximately 40X to 400X.

David Middleton

Date: 1995
Location: Reno, Nevada

A vagrant rummaging through a large Dumpster near Virginia Lake in Reno had his attention drawn to a large, bright yellow package. Untying the ropes that secured it, inside he found a sleeping bag sewn around several black plastic bags. These shrouded the battered body of a middle-aged woman. A missing-persons check yielded several names, and the woman was identified as Katherine Powell, a forty-five-year-old Sun Valley elementary school teacher, who had disappeared on February 3, 1995.

The disposal of the body had been no rushed exercise. Whoever made up the grisly package took his time, and this meant he obviously had somewhere undisturbed to do his work. The rope and wrapping were preserved for later analysis, as were the bluish-green cotton fibers found all over the body, and a single metal shaving lodged in her hair. The types of bruises that covered the body and bite marks to the chest area made it likely that she had been tortured before death. Quite what caused that death was medically unascertainable.

Powell's home showed no obvious signs of forced entry, but family members requested to inventory her belongings did note a missing laptop, printer, and handbag. Since none of the trace evidence from the body came from the victim's home, in all probability she had been killed elsewhere.

Easily the strongest lead came with news that on February 5—two days after her disappearance—someone had used Katherine Powell's credit card at a Reno electronics store to purchase a $1,900 Yamaha stereo system. Because of the size of the purchase, the store clerk had particularly remembered the female buyer, and when shown a photo of the dead woman, the clerk confirmed that the purchaser bore no resemblance whatsoever to Katherine Powell. Staff also noticed that the woman had driven off in a cable TV van, which was soon traced to David Middleton, age thirty-five.

Middleton had a bad record. In 1990, while working for the Metro-Dade police force in Miami, he had been stripped of his badge and jailed for three years for sexually assaulting a sixteen-year-old girl. After leaving prison he'd moved to Colorado, then on to Nevada.

Accompanying him on this interstate odyssey was longtime girlfriend, Evonne Haley. Staff at the electronics store had no hesitation identifying her as the stereo purchaser, and she was subsequently jailed for seven years for credit card fraud. Middleton, meanwhile, was held on a charge of shotgun possession (as a convicted felon, this was an offense in Nevada). Questioned about his contact with the dead woman, he admitted having recently installed cable in Powell's home but insisted that nothing untoward had happened. His denials didn't convince the police. And once they began to comb every inch of his house, Middleton's nerve gave way. In a rush of words he now admitted to an affair with Powell and that one night he'd called at her place and found her dead.

Middleton immediately came to regret this verbal impetuosity when a search of his home failed to uncover a whit of evidence to connect him to the body. Determined not to repeat the mistake, he now clammed up tight.

But it was too late; Middleton's mouth had already undone him in another way. When the forensic odontologist Ray Rawson compared the bite marks found on Powell's body with Middleton's dental impressions, he found them to be identical. The attack had been ferocious. Such bruising, he estimated, would have required Middleton to clamp down with a force of more than 200 pounds of pressure.

It was around this time that an anonymous informant told police of a ministorage unit that Middleton rented in nearby Sparks, Nevada. The almost gothic horror of what confronted detectives as they entered the unit defied belief. They'd walked into a killing factory, complete with ropes, duct tape, handcuffs, and a large refrigerator converted into a makeshift torture chamber, with airholes bored in its sides. Overhead dangled a system of ropes and pulleys sufficient to hoist a body, all the paraphernalia of what prosecutors would later call Middleton's "sexual playpen."

Site attendance sheets recorded Middleton as having visited the unit several times on the day of Powell's disappearance and over the following weekend. Items recovered from the unit included the Yamaha stereo system purchased with Powell's credit card and the computer equipment from her house. Even more critical was the discovery of numerous bluish-green cotton fibers identical to those found on Powell's body, while the metal shaving found in her hair was matched to the airholes that had been bored in the refrigerator. Detectives speculated that the inadequacy of these airholes had caused Powell's death by suffocation. Afterward, they reasoned, Middleton could prepare the body for disposal at his leisure.

Then came a startling development. On April 9 the skeletonized remains of a woman, similarly wrapped in plastic and rope, were found in a marshy area near Verdi, ten miles west of Reno. The body was identified as that of Thelma Davila, a forty-two-year-old casino worker at Circus Circus, who had been missing from her Sparks apartment since August 8 of the previous year—the very day when Middleton first rented the storage unit.

The ropes that bound Thelma's body were identical to those used in the disposal of Powell, and they also matched ropes found at the storage unit. Traces of Thelma's DNA in the form of hair and blood spots were found in the refrigerator. Both women had been murdered, apparently to satisfy Middleton's craving for rough sex. On September 18, 1997, he was sentenced to death.

Middleton is also suspected of complicity in the death of Buffy Rice Donahue, a nineteen-year-old newlywed, last seen alive in November 1993 at a

Wal-Mart store in Montrose, Colorado, where she worked with Evonne Haley. Her body, also wrapped in plastic, was found in May 1995. On June 20, 2000, Haley was convicted of being an accessory to murder in this case and sentenced to eleven years. At the time of writing Middleton has not been charged in this crime and remains on Nevada's death row.

Walter Leroy Moody Jr.

Date: 1989
Location: Birmingham, Alabama

Just before Christmas 1989, federal judge Robert S. Vance received a package at his Birmingham, Alabama, home. As he opened the package, a pipe bomb inside erupted without warning, hurling a murderous salvo of eighty nails at 3,000 feet per second in all directions and killing him.

Two days later, at the Eleventh Circuit Court of Appeals building in Atlanta where Judge Vance had served, a mail bomb was delivered. The package consisted of a brown cardboard box wrapped in brown paper, with excess postage, and a red and white address label. None of the stamps had been licked, so there was no chance of obtaining the sender's DNA profile from any saliva.

The pipe bomb itself was of unusual construction, with flat end caps that had been welded onto the pipe, a design feature that would fractionally delay the explosion and thereby drastically enhance its explosive impact. The workmanship was immaculate and deadly. Some indication of the bombmaker's meticulousness could be gauged from the fact that every square inch of the package's interior had been coated with black enamel paint to mask any possible fingerprints or other trace evidence.

Within twenty-four hours an identical bomb killed Robert E. Robinson, a black lawyer in Savannah, while another was defused at the NAACP headquarters in Jacksonville. Several members of the Eleventh Circuit Court also received threatening letters, signed by a group styling itself "Americans For a Competent Federal Judicial System."

A fingerprint was found on one of these letters, but there was no match in the files. One interesting lead did emerge: the typewriter used to type the letters had an irregular number "1" key. This was found to be a characteristic of a small range of Brother manual typewriters produced between 1961 and 1962. Immediately a search of government documents began, to see whether any had been typed on a similar machine.

The VANPAC investigation—so called because it involved the assassination of Judge Vance with a bomb sent in a mail package—was headed by the FBI, and their scientists set about analyzing the bombs. Each comprised a steel pipe with end caps joined together by a steel rod that ran through the pipe. Nails were tightly packed around this rod, and the device was triggered by a string attached to the packaging.

The detonators from the two unexploded bombs contained a green powder identified as a small-arms primer manufactured by CCI Industries. Uniquely in the industry, CCI primers had a 2 percent aluminum content. A specialized form of analysis—Fourier Transform Infrared spectroscopy—confirmed that the explosive used in the devices was Red Dot double base smokeless powder made by the Hercules Corporation.

Meanwhile, the typewriter provided a strong lead; a similar machine had been used to type correspondence in a bitter insurance dispute. The author of the letter, Robert O'Ferrell, a used-goods dealer in Alabama, vaguely remembered the typewriter in question and claimed it had been sold to a young woman about a year earlier. Investigators combed O'Ferrell's home and property—even excavating the septic tank—but found nothing to connect him to the crime. Moreover, the poor quality of craftsmanship on household repairs was light-years removed from the painstakingly careful bomb construction.

In hopes of breaking the impasse, pictures of the bombs were distributed to no fewer than 217 forensic laboratories nationwide; none reported having seen anything remotely like this bomb before. Then Lloyd Erwin, a chemist with the Department of Alcohol, Tobacco, and Firearms in Atlanta, recalled seeing one just like it back in 1972 in Macon, Georgia. The pipe had been smaller and made out of aluminum alloy, but it had those same distinctive square metal end caps, and four bolts going through it. Erwin recalled that the wife of the man who had constructed it had accidentally detonated the device, injuring herself. Her husband, Walter Leroy Moody Jr., was convicted of making the bomb and imprisoned for six years. (While he was behind bars his first wife, understandably, divorced him.)

Moody had been incensed by the conviction, and after his release he had spent ten years trying to have it overturned, as it negated his dream of going to law school. Significantly, his final appeal had been thrown out by the Eleventh Circuit Court just days before Judge Vance received his deadly package.

Moody was a strange person, highly intelligent, dangerously obsessive, and ultracautious. When agents descended on his house in Rex, Georgia, they vacuumed every square inch of space in an effort to identify some kind of trace evidence that would link him to the bombs but found nothing. With that avenue sealed off, agents targeted Moody's obviously jittery second wife, Susan, twenty years her husband's junior. Under a promise of immunity, she told how Moody forced her to go shopping in hardware stores clear across the southeastern states. On these trips she bought steel pipe, rubber gloves, tubing, and black enamel paint. At one store in Georgia she saw her husband shoplift nails that were found to be similar to those in the bombs. She also admitted buying the typewriter for her husband and having later thrown it away.

Corroboration for her story came from that solitary fingerprint. Once, she had tried to photocopy the letters in a small store in Florence, Kentucky, only to find the copier was out of paper. When a store employee refilled the copier, he left his print on the top sheet of paper. It was this fingerprint that showed on the letter.

In Chamblee, Georgia, investigators found a storage unit rented by Moody, and they uncovered a device constructed from a metal pipe that was similar in construction to the mail bombs. A gun store worker, Paul Sartain, remembered that in December 1989 he had sold Moody a four-pound keg of Red Dot smokeless powder and 4,000 CCI small pistol primers.

In June 1991 Moody's one-man terror campaign earned him, in federal court, seven life terms plus four hundred years. At a subsequent state trial he was sentenced to death.

The Mormon Will

Date: 1976
Location: Salt Lake City, Utah

If the eccentric billionaire Howard Hughes generated a storm of forensic controversy while still alive (see the Clifford Irving entry in *The Casebook of Forensic Detection*), then what followed his death in April 1976 amounted to a category six hurricane. It seemed incredible, but true: one of the world's richest men, with an estate worth about $2.5 billion, apparently had died without leaving a will.

Even setting aside Hughes's legendary antipathy toward his family—in his latter years, he had repeatedly and profanely avowed that his relatives would not inherit a penny of his vast fortune—everyone in the billionaire's close-knit inner circle was convinced that a will *did* exist and that it bequeathed his entire fortune to the Howard Hughes Medical Institute.

Finding that will proved diabolically difficult. Every bank that Hughes had ever dealt with, every hotel where he had stayed, every lawyer, every employee of his myriad companies, all were contacted in the search for the elusive document. Frustrated executives even resorted to consulting a psychic who tried to divine the will's location by contemplating a pair of Hughes's shoes! When this, too, failed to shed any light on the mystery, classified ads were placed in newspapers across the United States.

Journalists were quick to pick up on the story, alerting readers to the possibility that Hughes may have left a "holographic" will—that is, a will written totally by hand, usually in the person's own words without the benefit of an attorney. One lawyer stated that Hughes had twice asked him about the legality of such a document. In the wake of these newspaper accounts came a strange development.

Out of the blue and anonymously, an envelope turned up at the world headquarters of the Church of Jesus Christ of Latter-Day Saints (the Mormons) in Salt Lake City. Inside was a holographic three-page will, replete with spelling errors, allegedly drafted by Howard Hughes, and a note explaining that the document had been found near the home of Joseph Smith (founder of the Mormon Church) and that it should be delivered to the president of the Mormon Church. Since Hughes had surrounded himself with Mormon assistants while in self-imposed seclusion, his sympathy for the church seemed reasonable enough.

What did seem highly unusual, however, was the inclusion in the will of a provision that a one-sixteenth share of the total estate—or some $156 million—should go to a gas station owner named Melvin Dummar.

When contacted at his home in Willard, Utah, Dummar disclaimed all knowledge of the will or how it came into the hands of the Mormon Church. Prior to this incident, Dummar's only brush with fame had been a fleeting appearance on the TV show *Let's Make a Deal* in September 1975. He hadn't fared too well on that occasion, but now it looked as if he had really hit the jackpot.

The story he told had a Munchausenesque quality. Apparently, several years earlier he had stopped in the Nevada desert to pick up a grizzled stranger. As they talked, the hitchhiker gradually revealed his real identity: Howard Hughes. Dummar had dropped him off behind the Hughes-owned Silver Sands Hotel in Las Vegas after giving the man what spare change he had in his pocket. All Dummar could think, or so he told the hordes of reporters laying siege to his gas station, was that Hughes had decided to repay that kindness by remembering him in his will.

While Dummar soaked up the media attention, forensic analysis of the mysterious Mormon Will got under way, and it soon revealed one interesting anomaly: Dummar's fingerprint was on the envelope. Further investigation showed that when the will surfaced, Dummar was a part-time student at Webster University, in Salt Lake City, and in the college library was a copy of the book *Hoax,* an account of the Clifford Irving forgeries. Not only did this book contain many examples of Howard Hughes's handwriting, it, too, had a fingerprint belonging to Melvin Dummar.

When a **questioned documents** examiner opined that the envelope containing the Mormon Will had been addressed using disguised writing, most probably that of Melvin Dummar, the gas station owner was outraged. He hotly denied any allegations of fraud, bellowing that he was a victim of a conspiracy cooked up by Hughes's corporate cronies, but when confronted by the fingerprint and handwriting evidence he began to vacillate. From out of the tangled stories he told, he finally settled on a version that had a mysterious stranger approaching him at his gas station, handing him the envelope and several pages of directions, and instructing him to deliver the will to the Mormon Church.

Still the controversy raged. And it required a seven-month trial to settle the issue. Analysis of the ink used on the will—a standard Paper Mate type made between 1966 and 1972—proved only that it was available when the will was allegedly written, March 16, 1968. This left the battle in the hands of the questioned documents examiners. With three pages of disputed writings, plus a large body of contemporary known writings by Hughes, they had plenty to work with. The Hughes camp was unanimous in its belief that the will was a clumsy forgery, basing their testimony on a little-known fact that the forger had failed to take into consideration: handwriting can be profoundly affected by physical deterioration. In the final years of his life, Hughes had wasted away to little more than 92 pounds. With this emaciation came pronounced changes in his writing habits. Only those closest to Hughes knew what his writing looked like in March 1968, when the Mormon Will was supposedly written, unlike the forger, who had used exemplars from the book *Hoax.*

On June 8, 1978, a jury in Clark County, Nevada, ruled that the Mormon Will was a forgery. No charges were ever brought against any of the principals. Hollywood treated Dummar rather better than did the Nevada courts, with its sympathetic 1980 movie *Melvin and Howard,* a highly fanciful account of this extraordinary case.

Earl Morris

Date: 1989
Location: Cave Creek, Arizona

When Ruby Morris, a well-to-do accountant, failed to show up for a shopping trip on the morning of June 5, 1989, her daughter Cindy was puzzled. Her worries were doubled when she reached the family's palatial home in Cave Creek, Arizona. The place was deserted, with no sign of Ruby, even though her car was still there. Disturbingly, the burglar alarm was turned off and her handbag was missing. The house didn't have its customary neatness: a bathtap was dripping; dirty clothes were piled up on the washing machine; a vacuum cleaner was left out; and, most troubling of all, a .22 pistol, usually kept in the wardrobe, was missing.

After notifying the police, Cindy called her father. Earl Morris, in California, visiting another daughter, promised to return as soon as possible. Car problems meant that the usual six-hour drive took longer than anticipated, and he'd had to rent another car to complete the trip. This sounded reasonable enough until a keen-eyed officer noticed that in the trunk of Morris's car was a suitcase with a baggage claim tag for a recent flight from San Diego to Phoenix.

Passenger manifests had no record of an "E. Morris" on the flight in question, but they did show a "G. Norris," and when cabin crew were shown a photo layout, one flight attendant unhesitatingly picked out Morris because of his unforgettable toupee.

Detectives now returned to the house and this time searched far more thoroughly. Examination of the bedroom revealed that, despite having been cleaned thoroughly, the mattress and carpet were both heavily bloodstained, as was the adjoining bathroom and an outside patio. Most ominous of all, across the bed headboard was a fine mist pattern of blood spots, typical of high-velocity gunshot.

But did this blood belong to Ruby Morris? Because children get half their DNA from each parent, the DNA from a child and one parent can identify the DNA of the other parent, even without a DNA sample from that person. What detectives found here was astounding.

Tests showed that son Randal had one matching band with his mother, but there was no band from Earl Morris. This meant that Earl could not be his father. Family skeletons now began creeping out of the closet. At age fifteen, Ruby had been raped by her own father, Clyde Williams, leading to the birth of Randal. When tests conclusively matched Randal's DNA to that of his grandfather, police in Tennessee immediately charged Williams with incest.

More secrets flowed forth. The children admitted that before her disappearance, their mother had been depressed, because Earl was having an affair with her sister, Peggy Hinton, who lived in Louisiana. On one occasion, Peggy had flown into Phoenix to meet Earl, unaware that Ruby and Cindy were busily snapping photographs of the assignation for use in any possible divorce. When Earl refused to end the affair, Ruby accused him of diverting company funds into Peggy's account and even phoned her sister to confront her.

As far as the police were concerned, here was the motive. Faced by an expensive, possibly ruinous divorce, Morris decided to kill Ruby so he could be with her sister. When interviewed, Peggy said that she'd planned to meet Morris in San Diego that weekend but that she'd missed the flight.

When Morris's El Camino was found in San Diego airport parking lot, an enormous bloodstain on the passenger seat floor—matched to the blood in Arizona—was proof that Ruby Morris was dead. No one could have lost that much blood and survived.

News that the Morrises owned a boat moored at a San Diego marina jarred a few memories. On the morning of June 5 Morris had taken the boat out, and that, too, had disappeared. By chance, that same day the San Diego coast guard investigated a mysterious fire about thirteen miles offshore, when a boat of similar size and description had burned to a cinder before sinking. Its last few minutes had been captured on tape by a passing helicopter TV news crew. Experts who studied this footage were suspicious; the fire seemed to burn from the middle out, whereas boat fires usually begin in the engine room. Unfortunately, the boat was too badly burned to reveal its registration number or name before it sank in 3,000 feet of water, taking with it, in all likelihood, the charred remains of Ruby Morris's body. Local boat rental records showed that Morris had rented a small boat early on the morning of June 5 and had returned it around noon, right when the coast guard spotted the fire.

Faced with this mounting barrage of evidence, Morris now abruptly changed his story. He'd been at home on June 3, he said, and there had been an argument over his ongoing affair with Peggy. At about midnight Morris had gone out to the garage to find a flashlight, when he heard a gunshot. He'd rushed back into the house to find that, in a fit of depression provoked by guilt over her incest and his affair, Ruby had shot herself. At that point he panicked, fearing he would be blamed for her death.

For the next several hours he cleaned up the house; then early on Sunday morning he took off with his dead wife propped up beside him wearing his baseball cap to cover the bullet wound in her head. His original intention was to dispose of the body in a disused mineshaft; instead he changed his mind and drove to San Diego.

But Morris had blundered. In the first place, Ruby was right-handed, and she'd been shot in the left temple; then **blood spatter analysis** showed that two shots had been fired, leaving one spray over another. While it is not unheard of for suicides to shoot themselves more than once in the head, these two findings, plus the overwhelming weight of corroborative evidence, were enough for a jury to convict Earl Morris of murder, and he was jailed for life.

Kevin Morrison

Date: 1996
Location: The Wirral, England

Lying just south of Liverpool, the Wirral is a popular retirement destination for many affluent people seeking sanctuary from the bustle of the big city. Alice Rye was just such a person. A stalwart of the church, this seventy-four-year-old widow was a woman of regular habits, so when neighbors spotted the double gates of her large house inexplicably gaping open one morning, they went to investigate.

Upstairs, sprawled across a bed, lay Alice's half-naked body. Her hands were tied behind her back with blue nylon rope, there was a pink towel stuffed into her mouth, a ligature mark around her neck, and she had been stabbed four times in the heart. As a final indignity, the killer had taken two knives and rammed them into her eyes. Time of death was estimated as the previous day—December 10, 1996—and the motive appeared to be robbery.

Apart from a piece of white shoelace found under the victim's left leg, the crime scene appeared to be devoid of trace evidence. For the first time in Britain, a high-powered inspection light known as a quasar was taken from the laboratory to a crime scene to assist in the search for fingerprints. Quasars can spot fingerprints not visible to the naked eye, and work by fluorescing the ridges of grease and sweat left by a hand as it touches a smooth surface.

Ninety-six prints were found, of which, after eliminating family and friends, nineteen were unaccounted for. As the months dragged on, nothing, not even a substantial reward, loosened any tongues, and eventually newspapers reported that the investigation was being scaled down. It was around this time, May 1998, that a Liverpool detective received an unexpected phone call.

Kevin Morrison was a fifty-eight-year-old informant and petty criminal, and he claimed to have news about that "job on the Wirral." Before speaking further, though, Morrison demanded money, protection, and somewhere to live. Ordinarily, the detective would have paid little heed to Morrison—he was notoriously unreliable—except that he mentioned "two knives," a crime scene detail deliberately withheld from press releases. When interviewed, Morrison told an extraordinary tale.

On the day of the murder, he said, a fellow petty criminal named Keith Darlington had asked him to look after "a bag of stuff from a robbery." Morrison had stashed the package beneath his trailer home, and only later—after discovering that it contained Alice Rye's credit card and a broken, bloodstained knife with a seven-inch blade—did he connect it with the headline-making murder.

Morrison then confronted Darlington, who admitted killing the woman because she wouldn't divulge her PIN number. At the same time, he disclosed that all-important clue about the knives. Then Morrison told police something they hadn't realized: Alice Rye had been tortured. Darlington boasted of having bound her legs together with a long shoelace, and that, before leaving, he had cut the lace, leaving the part found at the scene.

According to Morrison, Darlington claimed that he had found his victim by studying the electoral register at the local library, deliberately hunting out an elderly woman who lived alone, and that he had stabbed Alice Rye's eyes because "they're going to be doing a psychological profile of this guy [the killer]. They won't be looking for me. They'll be looking for a nutter." When Darlington was arrested, he expressed utter amazement at Morrison's claims, bitterly denying every word.

The vehemence of Darlington's denial and the fact that a search of his house revealed not a single clue forced a reevaluation of Morrison's role in this affair. A search of his trailer home uncovered a blue rope superficially similar to that used to bind Mrs. Rye, and also a pocket knife, too small to have been used in the attack, but with a tiny clump of fibers snagged in its hinge.

Morrison continued to embellish his story. After committing the murder, he said, Darlington had washed himself in the bathroom and had used Mrs. Rye's panties to wipe his hands. Rather than leave any DNA evidence at the scene, he had taken these panties with him and disposed of them later. Again, the fact that these panties were missing had not been reported in any newspaper; this was something only the killer, or someone close to him, would have known. Morrison's knowledge of the murder was just too encyclopedic to have been gleaned secondhand, police believed; they reckoned he had betrayed Darlington to claim the reward.

Then came an ironic twist.

Another informant revealed that Morrison had a secret lockup garage some seventeen miles from where he lived. When police raided this garage, they found a bag of women's panties, among which was a pair similar to those worn by Alice Rye. Two DNA profiles were obtained from the panties—one from Rye, the other from Morrison—with a certainty put at 1 in 7.6 million. Morrison's claim that he had bought the panties from a flea market was risible, as was his insistence that he always wore women's underwear because it was cheaper.

An examination of the two pieces of blue rope showed that although they were microscopically dissimilar, each held flakes of identical green paint. Because of their minuscule size, the samples had to be analyzed with an electron probe. This bombards the individual layers of paint with electrons, which causes the paint to emit X-rays. By measuring the energy of the X-rays, it is possible to tell which metals are present in the paint. Here, the presence of chromium, lead, and copper in both samples allowed scientists to say that at some point both pieces of rope had been in contact with the same paint source.

During this investigation more than forty thousand fiber comparisons were made, and the final and most damning piece of evidence came from those fibers found in the knife hinge. In chemical makeup and dye color, they were indistinguishable from fibers found on the cut shoelace. This placed Morrison at the crime scene.

Without Morrison's own initiative in offering information to police, prosecutors admitted that "he would not have been brought to justice." As it was, on July 16, 1999, the killer who convicted himself was jailed for life.

Neutron Activation Analysis

The most powerful and versatile of all the chemical analytical techniques, neutron activation analysis (NAA) can identify trace elements at levels as low as one part in ten billion, or one-billionth of a gram. In addition, because of its accuracy and reliability, it is generally recognized as the "referee method" of choice when new procedures are being developed or when other methods yield results that do not agree.

And yet, despite this astonishing degree of sensitivity, NAA has yet to become a front-line forensic tool. There is one very good reason for this: for the technology to work, it requires access to a research nuclear reactor.

Owing to the dwindling availability of such reactors—half the U.S. university facilities were shut down in the fifteen years prior to 2000—very few scientists have acquired the technical expertise to conduct these tests, a situation that clearly poses problems in the area of peer review and, consequently, courtroom admissibility of NAA testimony. Even with all these drawbacks, there are signs that the vast potential of NAA in criminal investigations is finally being tapped.

The principle of chemical analysis is far from new. It was first proposed in 1936 when the Swedish-based physical chemist George de Hevesy and his assistant Hilde Levi found that samples containing certain rare earth elements became highly radioactive after exposure to a source of neutrons. From this observation they quickly recognized the potential of measuring nuclear reactions to identify both the type and the amount of the elements present in the samples. In order for this principle to be harnessed as an analytical technique, it required the development of suitable electronic equipment. This came about in the 1950s when Dr. Robert E. Jervis, at the University of Toronto, pioneered many applications of instrumental neutron activation analysis (INAA) using the Canadian-designed SLOWPOKE-2 nuclear research reactor.

Shortly thereafter, a string of high-profile cases involving so-called "atomic evidence" catapulted the new technology temporarily into the forensic spotlight. For example, NAA was used to analyze samples of hair from Napoleon, to investigate the possibilities of arsenic poisoning, and to identify the trace elements in bullet lead from the assassination of President John F. Kennedy. However, as other, less expensive analytical tools came on stream, interest in NAA declined.

Neutron activation analysis works because radioactive elements emit three kinds of radiation: alpha particles (helium atoms), beta particles (electrons), and gamma rays (X-rays). The kind of radiation emitted, and its exact energy, is unique to an element, and can be measured by use of a scintillation counter, a device that is triggered by a flash of light. The method can be used to identify extremely small traces of elements, and their proportions, in various materials.

About 70 percent of the elements have properties suitable for measurement by NAA. Even those elements that aren't radioactive—such as sodium, magnesium, zinc, arsenic, cobalt, and potassium—can be made so by being bombarded with subatomic particles called neutrons. The sample is placed in a capsule and inserted into the reactor. When the nucleus of an atom is hit by a neutron, it will often absorb the neutron and become a radioactive isotope of that atom. As a radioactive isotope it then emits gamma rays, which can be measured to determine the identity, presence, and levels of the original trace element in the sample.

Forensic applications for NAA include identifying samples typically found at crime scenes—gunshot residues, bullet lead, glass, paint, soil, and hair, for example. Research suggests it also may be possible to identify paper by batches. One other interesting development is in the always controversial field of determining whether an individual has recently fired a gun. For years law enforcement agencies relied on the dermal nitrate test, where melted paraffin is used to pick up traces of nitrates and nitrites on the hand, after which a chemical test is made for such compounds. Following a recent string of disastrous false positives thrown up by this test, it has now been thoroughly discredited. Use of NAA to detect the presence on the hand of antimony and barium from cartridge primers is much more definitive.

One other area where the use of NAA might be of enormous benefit concerns the identification of elements in bullet lead. For years it was generally believed—and widely testified to in court—that the chemical makeup of the lead used to make a particular batch of bullets was peculiar to that batch alone. Now there is evidence to suggest that this may not be the case. Researchers working at a variety of U.S. smelters have found small but measurable differences in the composition of lead samples taken at the beginning and end of the same batch, probably due to oxidation of the trace elements. This makes it impossible to say whether any two bullets were made on the same day or come from the same box. Further analysis only added to the confusion. Using the FBI's chemical profile standards, it was impossible to distinguish between batches poured *months apart*!

Such anomalies clearly require the most rigorous investigation and highlight the need for the most sophisticated chemical analysis possible. To date this is NAA. Apart from its high-level identification capabilities, it can analyze the smallest of samples; does not destroy the sample; and can run large numbers of samples at one time. Nowadays even the cost—as little as $60 per sample—has been reduced to an economic level. This has prompted a surge in usage. Worldwide, it is estimated that approximately one hundred thousand samples, mostly geological mineral samples, undergo analysis each year, though applications in the fields of archaeology and biochemistry are increasing.

Thomas Noguchi (1927–)

In little more than a decade, Thomas Noguchi rose from being a U.S. immigrant who could not speak English to becoming a globally recognized medical examiner. It was a remarkable climb that began in Tokyo. Like so many pathologists, Noguchi is the son of a doctor, but when he graduated from the Nippon Medical School in 1951, he wanted more than the cozy, well-fed life of the average physician; he wanted a challenge. The following year he immigrated to America and settled in California. Noguchi specialized in forensic medicine precisely because it was such an unpopular field with other medical graduates. Less competition meant more opportunities to shine, reasoned this unabashed overachiever. He applied to the Los Angeles coroner's office in 1960 and was given a position as assistant medical examiner.

For any pathologist with an appetite for public recognition, the glittering sidewalks of Los Angeles provided the perfect springboard, and so it proved. Noguchi's mortuary handled some of the most famous corpses in the world.

Undoubtedly his most notorious case was the death of Marilyn Monroe. In time, Noguchi's verdict that the star had committed suicide would come under attack from all quarters, mostly from crank conspiracists and shysters out to make a quick buck, but his findings have never been seriously challenged.

In 1968 he was appointed chief medical examiner for Los Angeles, but the press preferred to dub him the "Coroner to the Stars," and this was the title by which he became best known. Although universally acknowledged as a superb technician, Noguchi, like so many medical examiners in America, constantly found himself caught in the merciless glare of media scrutiny. He was a lightning rod for criticism. At times the sniping bordered on the surreal. In 1969 he had to fend off bizarre allegations that he had *prayed* for two 707s to collide so he would have more bodies to autopsy!

His career at the Los Angeles coroner's office was punctuated with running battles with the law enforcement hierarchy, who objected to Noguchi's willingness to discuss his cases with the media.

In late 1981 the *Los Angeles Times* began running a series of articles highly critical of the controversial coroner. Disgruntled colleagues leveled charges of egomania—assertions that Noguchi did nothing to deny—and accused him of talking too freely about certain cases to boost his own status.

In the fall of 1982 Noguchi was demoted from his rank of chief medical examiner. Although an independent tribunal later decided that he had been unfairly downgraded, there was no triumphant return to his former post. Noguchi was transferred to the relative obscurity of a teaching position, where he remained until his retirement in 1999. Said by some to have been the inspiration for the TV series *Quincy*, this onetime president of the National Association of Medical Examiners is also a successful novelist.

Significant Cases

1962	Marilyn Monroe
1968	Sirhan Sirhan

1969	Tate-LaBianca murders
1976	Elmer McCurdy*
1981	William Holden
1981	Natalie Wood

*Profiled in this book.

Charles Norris (1867–1935)

With his deep-set eyes, impressive bulk of more than two hundred pounds, and a glossy Vandyke beard, Charles Norris looked more like a stage actor than America's premier pathologist of the early twentieth century. Born in Hoboken, New Jersey, he graduated from Yale and studied medicine at Columbia University before sailing to Europe and the great medical teaching schools of Germany. After spells at Kiel and Göttingen he traveled to Berlin, where he worked under the famed pathologist Rudolf Virchow.

At this time Europe was right on the cutting edge of forensic medicine, and Norris was well placed to take advantage of its offerings. His blueblood background gave him the license to pursue his studies where and when he chose, and in 1894 he moved to Vienna, eager to harvest its rich pickings. Scotland, too, figured prominently in his forensic itinerary.

When he eventually returned to the United States he was appointed professor of pathology at New York's Bellevue Hospital. During his fourteen-year stay at the post he routinely performed autopsies for the police, albeit on an ad hoc basis. By 1917 widespread corruption among lesser pathologists convinced the legislature that a permanent post should be created, and in January of the following year Norris was appointed the first chief medical examiner of (CME) New York City.

His headquarters were originally housed in the Bellevue pathology building, thus beginning that establishment's long association with the CME's office, an association that endures to the present.

Norris set about trying to bring some order to the chaos he had inherited, only to find his reforming zeal thwarted at every turn by politicians out to slash his budget. Often he had to dig into his own pocket to buy laboratory equipment. Slowly, though, headway was made. He established an administrative office in Manhattan, with a telephone switchboard manned round the clock, as well as a branch office in Brooklyn.

There has never been another pathologist quite like Norris. No matter what time of the day or night, he would invariably sweep up to a crime scene in his gleaming, chauffeur-driven limousine, always immaculately attired and with a naturally aristocratic air that tolerated no sloppiness. His days were sharply delineated. Mornings usually found him performing autopsies at the Manhattan morgue; then, barring an emergency call, he would down instruments at noon and head off to some fashionable restaurant for a long and languid lunch.

His staff adored him. When Depression-era austerity brought slashing reductions in what were already meager office salaries, Norris made good the shortfall from his own funds. He never tired of campaigning to improve the lot of his assistants.

Above all, he fought to improve the status of pathology within the medical profession. In his youth most medical schools wanted nothing to do with the "beastly science," but in 1934, just before his death, the New York University College of Medicine created a Department of Forensic Medicine, the first such body in America. Norris's triumph was complete.

Significant Cases

1921	Zelda Crosby
1923	Dot King
1927	H. W. Frauenthal
1929	Jeanne Eagels

Odontology

Of all the components of the human body, virtually nothing outlasts the teeth after death. This durability makes them ideally suited as a means of identification. Indeed, in the aftermath of serious fires, such as the Waco inferno, teeth are often the only means of identifying scorched remains.

Identification by teeth is not new. It dates back to A.D. 49 and the time of Nero. Allegedly, Nero's mother, Agrippina, ordered her rival Lollia Paulina to commit suicide, with instructions for her soldiers to bring back Lollia's head as proof that she was dead. When presented with the head, Agrippina found identification an impossibility until she examined the teeth and, on finding a distinctively discolored front tooth, realized that her hated enemy would trouble her no more. During the Revolutionary War none other than Paul Revere (a young dentist) helped identify war casualties by their bridgework. Almost two centuries later dental records again played a significant part in history, this time to identify the remains of Adolf Hitler at the end of World War II.

It is frequently claimed that no two people have identical teeth; however, it should be remembered that unlike fingerprints, which remain unchanged from birth, dentition achieves its uniqueness through use and wear. For successful identification, both ante- and postmortem records must be available. From such data it is often possible to make an identification from a single tooth.

There are an estimated two hundred different tooth charting methods in use throughout the world. All provide a means of identification that is elegant and almost 100 percent reliable. The American approach, called the Universal System, allocates a different number to each of the thirty-two adult teeth, beginning with the upper right third molar (one), around the mouth to the lower right third molar (thirty-two). Information is recorded about the five visible surfaces of each tooth, from which it is generally possible to complete a dental grid, or odontogram, unique to that individual.

As regular visits to the dentist become a way of life for more people, so the database of fillings, extractions, bridges, dentures, and deformities expands. With every addition comes an increased chance of identification should one ever be necessary.

Teeth have other forensic functions. They can help determine the age of a corpse, especially if the person is young at the time of death. Because the dental tissue growth of four micrometers per day is registered by striations on the tooth, it is possible to estimate the age, within twenty days either side. X-rays of the jaw can reveal other teeth, still developing. The third molars, or "wisdom" teeth, do not usually emerge until the late teens or early twenties. Because these developments are affected by stimuli such as diet, race, and environment, they become less useful with age.

Once all the teeth have emerged, it is possible to make a rough estimate of age by noting the condition of the teeth, their degree of wear, the thickness of the dentine layer, and other indications.

In the 1950s Professor Gösta Gustafson of Malmö, Sweden, devised a six-point system for recording dental changes. It was based mainly on measurements, with changes being noted on a scale of 1 to 4. In one example, wear was scored at 1.5, indicating an age between fourteen and twenty-two; the actual age was eighteen. However, in recent years Gustafson's calculations, particularly his estimated error rates, have been hotly disputed, and this is clearly an area requiring further exploration. Another aging system, developed by French odontologist Henri Lamendin, works by studying the increasing transparency of the root tips as we age.

It should be stressed that all these systems can provide only a very approximate age. When dealing with an adult corpse, even an experienced odontologist would hesitate to hazard a guess beyond an estimated plus or minus forty-two months of the true age.

Bite Mark Analysis

This subdivision of odontology operates on the supposition that no two mouths are alike (even identical twins are different) and that teeth leave recognizable marks. However, a bite mark is not an accurate representation of the teeth. Much depends on the mechanics of jaw movement and use of the tongue. Inside the mouth, the lower jaw (mandible) is movable and usually delivers the most biting force. The upper jaw (maxilla) is stationary, holding and stretching the skin, but when skin is ripped or torn, the upper teeth are involved more deeply.

The first time that such evidence was allowed in a court of law occurred as long ago as 1906. Two English burglars were convicted after one had foolishly bitten on a piece of cheese at the crime scene, and prosecutors showed that the imprint exactly matched his front teeth.

For forensic purposes, bite marks fall into two categories:

1. Human-on-human: where the skin of one or more participants in an assault is penetrated. (This may not always be the victim. Quite often an attacker is bitten by the victim in self-defense.) The primary value of the bite mark is to identify (or exclude) a suspected assailant.
2. Bite marks on food: cheese, chocolate, fruit, etc. This may establish the presence of a person at a particular crime scene.

Of the two, bite marks on humans pose the greater problem, as they may alter with the passage of time. For this reason, such bite marks are routinely photographed over a set period of hours or days, so a permanent record is made. (Ultraviolet light can reveal bite marks even months after they have been inflicted.) If there is no penetration the underlying bruising may take up to four hours to develop in the living, and is clearly visible for up to thirty-six hours. In a dead victim, twelve to twenty-four hours might elapse before the bruise becomes visible. Sometimes it is possible to make a silicone rubber cast if the bite is deep enough. Before this can be done, swab specimens must be taken from the site, as residual saliva can often be detected for blood typing or DNA analysis. Once the cast has been made, comparisons for identification can be made in the usual manner.

Richard Overton

Date: 1988
Location: Dana Point, California

For years Janet Overton had been plagued by ill health, but on the morning of January 24, 1988, she felt well enough to join the rest of her family on a planned whale-watching expedition. No sooner did she step into the driveway of her home at Dana Point, California, than she collapsed. Within hours this forty-six-year-old trustee of the Capistrano Unified School District was dead.

The autopsy found no reason to explain such a tragedy; but there again, Janet had been baffling the medical profession for years. Her health problems dated back to 1983, when she began losing prodigious amounts of weight. The tingling in her fingers, stomach aches, and a strange, reddish-colored rash on her skin had all defied diagnoses. And now she was dead.

As a precautionary measure, blood and tissue samples were put into storage at the coroner's office before her body was released for disposal. Her husband, Richard Overton, a fifty-nine-year-old computer consultant, opted for cremation.

Six months passed, and then the police were contacted by Dorothy Boyer, Overton's first wife. She had a disturbing tale to tell. Her daughter had recently visited Overton and had come across a syringe, rubber gloves, and some mascara hidden behind some books in his library. Such a discovery resurrected memories of a grim episode from Dorothy's past. Twenty years earlier, after divorcing Overton in 1967, her own health had gone into steep decline, so much so that she suspected her ex-husband, who still had access to the house, of poisoning her. Her suspicions had particularly been aroused by a strong sulfuric smell emanating from her shampoo.

Perturbed enough to contact the police, under their supervision she marked the outside of a coffee container, which would reveal signs of tampering. Sure enough, three days later someone had removed the lid. Overton's fingerprints were found on the surface of the container, and analysis of its contents revealed the presence of selenium, a strong-smelling poisonous chemical element, mixed with the coffee.

Overton's protestations of innocence, fiery at first, crumpled under questioning, and he confessed. A deal was worked out: Dorothy agreed not to press charges if Overton stayed out of her life.

But all that was twenty years ago. Was it possible that Richard Overton's warped habits had resurfaced and taken their toll on his second wife?

Initially there appeared to be no reason why he would want Janet dead; the marriage seemed happy enough, he was financially independent, and the proceeds of Janet's life insurance policy went to her son, not him. But slowly reports filtered through of jealousy; Overton resented his wife's political success, and, contrary to popular belief, the marriage was foundering because of Janet's repeated affairs.

Although tests on the mascara from Overton's library did register traces of selenium, the histological samples retained by the coroner's office were clear. But what struck the toxicologist Paul Sedgwick, as he removed Janet's stomach contents from storage, was the distinctive smell of bitter almonds.

The ability to smell the presence of hydrogen cyanide is genetic, restricted to only 40 percent of the population. Fortunately, Sedgwick fell into this category. Because homicidal poisoning is exceedingly rare in the United States (see **toxicology**), unless the medical examiner is specifically checking for some toxic agent during an autopsy, it is easy to overlook. When Sedgwick applied dedicated tests, he found sufficient cyanide in the samples and the stomach contents to change the official verdict on Janet's death to willful poisoning.

One year after the cremation, Overton was brought in for questioning. During the interview, detectives initially kept their knowledge of his tampering record under wraps, as they asked if he had any idea who might have harmed Janet. Overton mentioned that Janet had made a lot of political enemies over the years: one of them, possibly? Then detectives sprang the trap, exposing Overton's tampering background. His response was dramatic: he leaped to his feet and stormed out.

Before leaving, Overton snapped that he had no access to cyanide. However, an acquaintance, who ran a mining operation, admitted that he used cyanide in the extraction of gold and silver from ore and that Overton frequently visited the cyanide store.

Having established that Overton had the means and the opportunity to poison his wife, detectives went searching for motive. They found it in Overton's own writings, a voluminous diary that he kept in both handwritten and computer form. Overton, a mathematician with a doctorate in psychology, had gone to great lengths to cover his tracks, coding many of his diary entries in Spanish and Russian. The handwritten version showed clear signs of alteration; entries had been whited out with typing correction fluid, and the page of his wife's death had been completely removed. But UV light allowed detectives to read through the whited-out passages and discover Overton's fury over his wife's infidelities.

It was a similar story with his computer; files had been changed or deleted. Overton didn't realize that when a file is deleted, only the first letter of its name is changed, telling the computer that this disk space is now available for new data. Until another file overwrites that area, the old file remains intact and can easily be retrieved. Even when the original file *has* been overwritten, all is not necessarily safe—certain ultrasophisticated programs can revive almost anything on the disk. In this case both the hard drive and the 131 disks found in Overton's possession were subjected to the full range of modern data-retrieval software, in the first forensic computer probe in Orange County history.

Hundreds of laboratory hours allowed experts to painstakingly reconstruct Overton's diary, word by word, revealing his innermost thoughts, his profound hatred of Janet, culminating in the chilling entry, made just days before her death, "Something is going to happen."

Bringing Overton to justice proved time-consuming. His first trial ended abruptly in 1992, when his lawyer suffered profound depression and had to leave the case. And there was the problem of finding American expert witnesses with enough experience of poison to testify. In the end, prosecutors turned to Dr Bryan Ballantyne, a British toxicologist, to explain the effects of long-term poisoning. Overton had been poisoning Janet with selenium for years, and then he stopped, allowing the selenium to evacuate her system, before administering the lethal dose of cyanide. He was sentenced to life.

Stanley Patrek and Joseph Stepka

Date: 1945
Location: New York City

Just after dawn on May 29, 1945, Henry Springhorn came downstairs from his janitor's apartment above the Whitestone Savings and Loan Association in Queens to make his customary security checks on the offices below. After satisfying himself that the exterior doors were properly locked, he made his way back upstairs. Although there was no reason for him to do so, had Springhorn entered the office proper he would have realized the futility of his efforts: the safe was already missing. That unwelcome shock was reserved for the manager when he arrived later to open up. He, too, had seen no signs of forcible entry, but when he contacted the police he learned that the safe—minus $6,000—had already been discovered, across the East River, dumped on a Manhattan sidewalk.

Detectives from the city's "Safe and Loft Squad" groaned; this sounded like another score for the Phantom Burglars, a gang seemingly able to get in and out of banks at will, without leaving any clue as to how. Even more galling was the knowledge that the officers almost certainly knew who the Phantoms were and had indeed been tailing them the previous evening, only to lose them in heavy rain and traffic near the Triboro Bridge.

The surveillance had been in place for some weeks now, ever since squad detectives in downtown Manhattan had seen two men loitering outside a bank. One officer recalled seeing this same pair a week before, near another savings and loan institution. Oblivious to the watchful eyes on them, the two men had entered the bank and paused by the door, apparently deep in conversation. The larger of the two seemed to be paying inordinately close attention to the bank's layout, as if "casing" the place. After some time they strolled across to a restaurant opposite. Later they emerged from the restaurant and drove off in a gray Dodge sedan, the license number of which was noted.

A trace on the license plate showed that the car was registered in the name of Stanley Patrek, age thirty-one. The Motor Vehicle Bureau provided details of Patrek's driving license, complete with a physical description that suggested he was the shorter of the two men. In 1935 he had received twelve years for grand larceny, only to be paroled in February 1943, shortly before the "Phantom Burglar" robberies began.

Patrek and his companion were shadowed to a rented garage on Thirty-first Street in Astoria, Queens, and later to their separate addresses. The companion lived close by and was soon identified as Joseph Stepka, age forty. He, also, had a criminal record. In fact, Stepka and Patrek had served time together in Sing Sing. Since his release in March 1941 Stepka had stayed out of the law's way—until now.

The two men were tailed round-the-clock. Both seemed abnormally fond of visiting banks, and not just in the capacity of interested observers. Records showed that they had deposited thousands of dollars in various institutions, usually on days following Phantom robberies (sometimes even depositing the money in the very bank from which it had been stolen!).

On the night of June 1, 1945, Patrek and Stepka again left home late in the evening and went to the Astoria garage. As the Dodge followed a suspiciously circuitous route through Manhattan, unmarked police cars remained in close attendance. When the car swung north it slipped from view, only to be found later parked in the heart of the Yonkers business district. Officers concealed themselves and waited. Sometime later Stepka and Patrek came staggering down the road, both weighed down with heavy objects. Stepka was carrying an oxyacetylene torch, while Patrek was caught with a case containing $15,184, which they had just stolen from the Yonkers Savings and Loan at 28 North Broadway.

The garage in Astoria housed an extraordinary array of the most sophisticated safecracking equipment available. Detectives had seen nothing like it: seven acetylene tanks, five torches, a five-foot bolt cutter, textbooks on welding and metallurgy, wrenches, pliers, keyhole cutters, gauges to determine the combination of oxygen and acetylene gas, and fifty feet of hose to run into a vault from the tanks. Even the Dodge had been specially adapted to accommodate a good-size safe in a concealed compartment. Also recovered were five passbooks showing deposits totaling $27,000 in little more than a year.

Although caught red-handed, there was still no conclusive evidence that Patrek and Stepka were the Phantom Burglars. In efforts to find this proof technical specialists examined every inch of the garage. The floor sweepings showed traces of asbestos—then commonly used as fireproofing in safes—together with metal filings. This evidence was then compared spectroscopically with samples from the Whitestone Savings and Loan safe.

In emission spectroscopy the sample is placed between two carbon electrodes, and a spark is struck between them. Sometimes the energy is generated by heating to high temperatures, or more recently with a laser or electron beam. After passing through a prism, the resulting wavelengths of light split into a spectrum, whose emission lines are recorded on a photographic plate. When this plate is processed a series of lines appears, depicting the sample's component frequencies. Here, it confirmed that filings and asbestos found at the Astoria garage came from the Whitestone safe.

Obviously with an eye to the future, both men refused to answer the question that intrigued everyone connected with the case: how did they manage to "pass through" locked doors? Only later was their secret revealed. In a small box at the garage, detectives found a door lock, together with an extra cylinder—the part the key slips into—and a tiny screwdriver. By inserting the screwdriver into the lock from the interior side of the office, it was possible to loosen a screw in the cylinder, thus allowing that cylinder to later be withdrawn after hours and another cylinder—to which the thieves had the key—substituted. After letting themselves in and rifling the safe, on their way out the robbers replaced the original cylinder, tightened the screw, and left no visible sign of how they had gained access. What the watching detectives had mistaken for "casing" of the bank by Stepka was in fact a subterfuge, whereby he was using his large bulk to shield Patrek while the latter switched lock cylinders.

On March 11, 1946, Patrek was given a lengthy jail sentence. His partner joined him at Sing Sing a short while later. It transpired that Patrek had worked at a plant manufacturing matériel for the war effort in order to learn the latest industrial techniques that could be applied to safecracking. Such dubious application guaranteed the Phantom Burglars' place in criminal history as the fathers of high-tech bank robbery.

Lisa Peng

Date: 1993
Location: Rancho Santa Margarita, California

In the summer of 1993 electronics tycoon Tseng "Jim" Peng appeared to be on top of the world. As the boss of Ranger Communications, a company that made CB radios in Asia, his net worth was estimated at $200 million, he had been married for twenty-two years, and with his wife, Lisa, he regularly shuttled between a home in Taiwan and a luxury house in Rancho Santa Margarita in Orange County, California. At age fifty, Peng was a man who seemed to have it all. Including a secret.

And it was this secret that bore him to an apartment in Mission Viejo, on August 18, 1993. The pudgy multimillionaire was surprised by the lack of response when he rang the bell. Puzzled, he went down to the apartment manager's office to wait. Sometime later—and by now very angry—he returned to the apartment. This time he tried the door handle. To his surprise, the door opened. Stepping inside, he turned on the light. His face froze in horror. Against the couch, framed in a pool of blood, lay the butchered body of Jennifer Ji. She had been stabbed eighteen times.

For three years, Jennifer had been Peng's mistress. They'd met in Shanghai while Peng was on a business trip and, soon after, he had flown her to the United States and set her up in this apartment. In March 1993 Jennifer had given birth to the couple's son, Kevin. Just five months old, he now lay dead in his crib, deliberately suffocated by a blanket.

When the police arrived Peng handed over a button that he had found on the floor. It appeared to have come loose from a woman's dress—not Jennifer's. The victim's body bore all the hallmarks of a savage sexual assault. Her panties were yanked down, and even though vaginal swabs failed to detect the presence of any semen, rape could not be precluded, as many modern-day rapists wear condoms in hopes of defeating DNA technology. Support for the sexual frenzy theory came from a bite mark on her left arm, a common injury in such assaults.

It didn't take long for investigators to clear Peng as a suspect, but as they delved deeper, they learned an interesting fact: just one day before Jennifer was murdered, Lisa Peng had flown back suddenly to the United States, to meet with her husband. When detectives arrived at the Peng household, Lisa had no qualms about allowing them to search for a dress that might be missing a button. They didn't find a dress, but what they did discover were two bags containing women's clothing, underwear, even shoes, all slashed to ribbons.

Shamefacedly, Jim Peng explained. Just one month earlier, Lisa had returned unexpectedly from Taiwan and had caught Jennifer staying at the marital home at Rancho Santa Margarita. In a tormented fury she had thrown Jennifer out of the house, then slashed her remaining clothes to ribbons. Faced with this evidence of Lisa's violent temper, the investigators zeroed in, convinced they were dealing with a slighted wife who'd snapped and murdered her younger rival.

Lisa complied with requests to provide a wax impression of her teeth. An odontologist had no doubts that it matched photographs of the bite mark on Jennifer's arm. Next, swabs from the bite were subjected to DNA analysis. Because the sample was so small, it had to be amplified by means of PCR (see **DNA typing**). This detected a locus common to 20 people in 100. The question now was: did Lisa Peng fall within this grouping? Unfortunately, by this time she had returned to Taiwan, and no blood sample for comparison had been taken before her departure.

It looked like stalemate until one of the forensic experts recalled the wax impression of Lisa's teeth. Was it possible that saliva still existed on this impression, sufficient to provide a DNA profile? Sure enough, it, too, identified the same locus, but the probability remained an inconclusive 20 in 100. A second PCR test identified a different locus. This also gave a match between the saliva from the bite and the wax, with a probability of only 1 in 200. Taking both probabilities together, this gave a figure of 1 in 1,000.

Saliva from the wound had provided enough DNA for the analysts to suggest setting up the more sophisticated restriction fragment length polymorphism (RFLP) procedure. This works by cutting a human DNA sample with a restriction enzyme, thereby creating millions of restriction fragments on gel. The scientist is looking for a single band, or inherited trait. Then it's a question of establishing the frequency of this trait within the population, hence the term "polymorphism."

Lisa Peng, told that the only way she could be eliminated as a suspect was by providing a sample of her own blood, and knowing nothing of the DNA tests, agreed to return to Orange County. The first run of RFLP analysis took nearly a week to complete, during which time Lisa remained in California. The tests gave a match, and she was arrested on January 1, 1994, and charged with murder.

After interrogating Lisa for many hours, detectives encouraged Jim to talk to her in Chinese. During this conversation, which was taped, Lisa burst into tears and admitted biting his mistress in a confrontation before her death. Rather more implausibly, she claimed that Jennifer had accidentally stabbed herself while falling!

After a jury deadlocked in her first trial, Peng was convicted of double murder and sentenced to life without parole on April 25, 1996. But in October 1999 the California Supreme Court reversed this conviction on the grounds that police had compromised her rights by using her husband to elicit incriminating statements.

When a third trial also ended in deadlock, it was time to deal. Peng agreed to plead guilty to two counts of voluntary manslaughter; in return, her sentence was reduced to time served, and she was deported to Taiwan. Although technically liable to be charged in her homeland, thus far no charges have been filed.

Samson Perera

Date: 1983
Location: Wakefield, England

When Dr. Samson Perera, a lecturer in oral biology at the University of Leeds, and father of two sons, decided to adopt a daughter, he returned to his homeland of Sri Lanka. There he found a ten-year-old girl named Nilanthe, whose impoverished family was only too pleased to offer her up for adoption, grateful for the better life she would enjoy in England.

In December 1981 Perera brought Nilanthe back to the family house in Stillwell Close, Sandal, near Wakefield, and the little girl soon became a familiar figure in the neighborhood, with her cheery smile and friendly wave, even if she didn't really seem to be accepted by her new family, who treated her more like a servant than a daughter. Then, in April 1984, she suddenly disappeared. Curious neighbors were rebuffed by Perera's angry insistence that he was keeping Nilanthe indoors until she learned to subdue her flirtatious behavior with the local young men.

Spring passed, still with no sign of the thirteen-year-old. By early summer neighborhood concerns reached official ears and prompted a visit to the house by Inspector Tom Hodgson. Perera said that homesickness had forced Nilanthe's return to Sri Lanka. He had flown with the girl to Sicily, where his brother had taken over for the final leg of the journey home.

Hodgson initiated an inquiry. Airline passenger manifests and contact with the Italian police revealed that Perera had never flown to Sicily, or anywhere else for that matter, with Nilanthe. Gut instinct told Hodgson that Nilanthe was dead. He made no secret of his suspicions at the university, where Perera was deeply unpopular, and in February 1985 a fellow lecturer, who shared a laboratory with Perera, made a startling discovery: inside a desk drawer lay a large brown envelope containing a human jawbone with three teeth and three pieces of a human skull.

Conscious of the official interest in Perera, the lecturer continued looking and found a five-liter glass beaker, a coffee jar, and a shallow stainless steel tray. Each contained small bones and bone fragments, immersed in what proved to be decalcifying fluid that would ultimately have dissolved them completely. As none of the bones was remotely connected with orthodox dental research, the lecturer contacted police.

Hodgson returned to Perera's home. In the hallway he was assaulted by a truly dreadful smell wafting up from three large plant pots. The plants themselves looked sick and anemic. Hodgson studied them more closely and decided that it was time for the house to be searched properly. This was supervised by the Home Office pathologist Alan Usher.

He began with the plant pots, the largest of which, when emptied, revealed a virtually complete human spine coiled around the roots. Inside the other two pots were chunks of decaying human flesh. By now the stench was overpowering. Moving to the kitchen, Usher found a human rib in a butter container filled with methylated spirits.

In the backyard a patch of earth that had obviously been disturbed recently was excavated and found to contain a tooth, a small bone, and a long hank of black, matted hair. All were obviously human. In total, Usher and his team located 105 human fragments that, in their opinion, came from 77 individual bones or parts of bones, recovered from eight sites: four at Perera's laboratory and four at his house and garden. Damning though these discoveries were, there was still nothing to categorically identify them as the mortal remains of Nilanthe.

That task fell to Professor Ronald Grainger, an expert in radiology. Because there was no duplication of bones and because they showed a consistency of size and texture, it was reasonable to assume that they were from just one person. When it comes to determining sex, the skull and the pelvis are generally the best indicators, but in this case both were fragmented.

However, the sciatic notch of the pelvis, through which the sciatic nerve travels, is set at a different angle in females to that in males—61 to 90 degrees in the former, 26 to 65 in the latter—and what remained of the sciatic notch in this skeleton was 80 degrees, well outside the male range.

Normally, various factors are weighed in determining the age of a skeleton—the closing of the skull sutures, for example, the development of the laminal spurs or bony knobs on the spine, and the size of the long bones of the arms and legs. In this instance, matters were complicated by disagreement among authorities about the age at which skeletons of different races mature, and it was left to Grainger, aided by dental analysis, to conclude that the female victim was thirteen to fifteen years of age. At the time of her disappearance, Nilanthe was just thirteen years old.

But when had the girl been killed? The degree of putrefaction found in the plant pot remains suggested that death had taken place at least six months before their discovery, probably longer. However, there was one other clue.

There are more than one hundred thousand types of fly in existence, and each has its own brief season. In this instance, tiny insect pupae found on the remains belonged to a type of fly that thrives in the first and second week of April—exactly when Nilanthe had disappeared.

Perera panicked. First, he blustered that the flesh was pork, used as an experimental fertilizer. Then came an outlandish claim that he obtained the cadaver from a Sri Lankan morgue and brought it to England to aid in his dental studies. A check with all the morgues in Sri Lanka confirmed the falsity of this assertion.

Although never able to ascertain how Nilanthe died, Usher had no doubt that it was as a result of foul play. Why else would Perera have gone to such lavish lengths to dispose of the body? This was the version accepted by the jury, and on March 11, 1986, Perera was jailed for life.

The Persian Mummy

Date: 2000
Location: Karachi, Pakistan

In October 2000, acting on a tip-off, Karachi police raided the home of a tribal chief in a mountainous region of southwestern Pakistan. What they found shook the archaeological world to its very foundations. Encased in a carved stone coffin, inside a wooden sarcophagus, and wearing an exquisite golden crown and mask, lay a tiny mummy—only four feet, seven inches long—resting on a reed mat. An inscription on the breastplate read: "I am the daughter of the great King Xerxes, I am Rhodugune."

This was, potentially, one of the greatest archaeological finds ever. In the fifth century B.C. Xerxes ruled a huge Persian empire that stretched from the Mediterranean in the west, eastward to India, and to Egypt in the south. Now it appeared as though—twenty-six hundred years after death—the mortal remains of his daughter Rhodugune had been discovered.

According to the local chieftain, Sardar Wali Reki, the mummy had been unearthed when an earthquake disturbed an archaeological site, and he admitted trying to sell it on the antiquities black market. The asking price was upward of $20 million, a mind-boggling sum; but this was a truly unique find, one that threatened to rewrite the history books. For decades, historians had declared such elaborate mummification to be an Egyptian monopoly, yet here was a Persian mummy whose internal organs had been removed in identical fashion. Since no Persian mummies had ever been found before, let alone one belonging to a royal princess, it could mean only one of two things: either Egyptian mummifiers had exported their unique skills across the Middle East—a possibility never before considered—or else Rhodugune had died while visiting Egypt, and her remains were mummified before transportation home.

No civilization has ever taken death more seriously than the ancient Egyptians. Because they believed that an entire body was essential for an untroubled passage into the afterlife, they established a complex process of ritual embalmment. Specially trained morticians first removed the internal organs—the lungs, kidneys, liver—everything except the heart, which, as the receptacle for the soul, was left inside the body. Then the body was dried out with a desiccating agent called natron. Once all moisture was eliminated—a process that could take up to seventy days—the body was wrapped in linen and encased in wood, with an effigy of the person carved on the outside. Then the coffin was placed in a sarcophagus. Depending on the status of the deceased, gold or other valuable adornments were added.

Everything about the Persian mummy pointed to Egyptian involvement. How it came to be in Pakistan was unfathomable. The likeliest solution seemed to be that it had been smuggled in from neighboring Iran. Whatever its origins, the mummy was seized by the Pakistani government as a state treasure and housed in the National Museum, to be studied by scholars and scientists. And it was here that the first doubts began to emerge.

When compared to contemporary writings of the Achaemenian period, the cuneiform inscription on the breastplate was found to contain some grammatical errors. This was puzzling but not inconceivable, since most workmen of the time were illiterate and would have been merely copying symbols.

The next step was to submit the mummy to computerized tomography (CT) scans and X-ray photographs. These would permit a detailed analysis of the body inside the shell. The pelvic region showed that the woman—despite her diminutive stature—was a mature adult, aged at least twenty-five, much older than Rhodugune was thought to have been at the time of her death. And the CT scan also revealed irregularities in the way the body had been prepared for mummification. The incision made to access the internal organs was much longer—almost eight inches—than was customary in Egyptian mummification, and the manner in which the brain had been removed displayed a hamfisted clumsiness.

Removing the brain without causing external disfigurement was always the most difficult procedure for Egyptian morticians, one they overcame by inserting a tool through the nose and into the cranium. Once the nasal passage was opened up, another tool was slipped inside the nose, into the brain, and then rotated vigorously. This in effect liquefied the brain, allowing it to drain out through the nose. With the Persian mummy, however, access to the brain had been achieved by crudely driving up under the chin, through the palate, and into the cranium.

Last and most alarming of all, the heart was missing. It was unthinkable that an Egyptian mortician would have excised this most important of all bodily organs.

Such findings fueled suspicion that the mummy might not be of royal origin but rather a lesser person whom black-market dealers were trying to pass off as aristocracy to increase its value.

Then came two stunning discoveries. It suddenly dawned on scholars that Rhodugune is actually a later Greek translation of Wardegauna, the original Persian name for Xerxes' daughter, making it impossible for a contemporary engraver to have spelled out the cuneiform text. Also, pencil marks were found inside the coffin. Since lead pencils were invented only two hundred years ago, this could not be the work of ancient artisans. Obviously, the mummy was a modern fake, concocted to fool the art world and make money. Just how modern became clear when radiocarbon dating of bone and tissue from the corpse showed that the woman had died in 1996.

Then came a revelation darker than anyone had dared imagine: the woman had died from a broken back. Immediately this raised the specter of gangsters murdering women to provide fresh corpses for mummification.

Although no one has thus far categorically proved that this was murder—the body may simply have been exhumed—what is clear is that a sophisticated forgery ring is trying to dupe the art world by faking mummies. Most eyes turn to Iran, a hotbed of art forgery. To date at least two other mummies have been offered to various museums. Inquiries continue into their possible source.

Charlie Phillips

Date: 1980
Location: San Diego County, California

Arson is one of the most reckless and dangerous of all crimes, and one of the worst arsonists ever to plague California began plying his odious trade in June 1980, when a brush fire broke out in eastern San Diego County. Forestry Department investigators combing the source of the blaze found a crude but effective incendiary device made from a book of matches. It had been scrunched up to make it burn more slowly, affording the arsonist an invaluable couple of minutes or so to make his escape before the flames really took hold. Inside of a month, the region was hit by three more fires, all in remote areas and each triggered by a similar matchbook incendiary device, leaving no doubt that the authorities were up against a serial arsonist.

When a fifth blaze erupted near a trailer park, investigators got a break. The incendiary device had not burned thoroughly and still displayed the name of a local bar; furthermore, an informant told police that a woman who waitressed at the bar happened to live at the trailer park. After a few questions, investigators weren't much interested in the woman, but they were intrigued by her husband. Charlie Phillips, age thirty-one, was a volunteer fireman at the trailer park and claimed to have actually witnessed a man running from the scene of the last blaze.

Phillips's cocksure manner, shot through with an air of gloating triumphalism, hinted at some kind of personal involvement, and it was decided to place him under surveillance. Soon afterward he was tracked to a dump site in Harbison Canyon, just a few miles northeast of San Diego, where he was seen to park his truck, vault a fence, then sneak from view down a slope. Just moments later he reappeared, running hard, clambered into his truck, and raced off. Behind him, a telltale plume of smoke rose up from the brush. The fire was extinguished quickly and yet another matchbook incendiary device was recovered. Phillips was placed under arrest, and although suspected of starting numerous fires in San Diego County, he was charged with just the one at the dump site.

To the dismay of prosecutors and the Forestry Department alike, because Phillips had not actually been seen starting the blaze, the jury decided there was a reasonable doubt and acquitted him. Having decided that California was getting too hot for comfort, Phillips upped roots and moved to Texas. With Charlie Phillips out of the way, the number of brush fires in this part of southern California plummeted.

Two years passed, and then Harbison Canyon was hit by a fresh outbreak of suspicious blazes. Alarmed investigators did some checking and found that, sure enough, Phillips was back in town. Moreover, when he moved northward to the Ramona region of San Diego County, the fires went with him, all bearing that trademark incendiary device of the folded matchbook.

This was a frustrating period for the Forestry Department, the prelude to an eight-year war of nerves, with dozens of deliberately set fires and absolutely no evidence against the prime suspect. Then came an unexpected development. Phillips got a job driving a delivery truck for a pharmaceutical supplies company in Ramona, and because he drove the same route all the time, this meant his movements were known and predictable.

In a precedent-setting move, the Forestry Department obtained a court order allowing them to place a concealed video camera in Phillips's van. Never before had the state of California permitted this in a private vehicle. Because agents feared that someone at the pharmaceuticals company might get wind of their intentions and possibly warn Phillips, they entered the company parking lot under cover of darkness and drove off with Phillips's van. That same night a film camera was fitted in the driver's cab, and then the van was returned to its parking spot.

For ten days investigators had to kick their heels in frustration. Then, on September 10, 1996, a fire broke out at 3:17 P.M. on Phillips's delivery route, started by one of those crushed matchbook devices.

Again under cover of darkness, agents returned to the parking lot. It took a few moments to recover the tape. Back at the office, they eagerly gathered around to see what it would reveal. In a twist that might have been devised by a Hollywood scriptwriter, they could only stare in disbelief: Phillips had placed a large package on the passenger seat—directly in front of the camera lens!

Groans turned to cheers of delight when—with the on-screen video clock ticking ever closer to the time of the fire—suddenly the box was shoved out of the way, and Phillips could be seen driving along and winding down the passenger window. There was an eerie predictability to the next few seconds. From a shirt pocket, Phillips withdrew one of those familiar crumpled matchbooks, which he balanced carefully on the steering wheel before lighting it and flicking it out the passenger window. There was no attempt to see the havoc he had wrought; he just drove on.

The video clock showed 3:17:30. Charlie Phillips's sixteen-year reign of terror was over.

After initially admitting his guilt, Phillips withdrew his confession and claimed instead that he was a victim of post-traumatic stress syndrome. According to his lawyer, Phillips's eastern San Diego County delivery route "geographically resembled" the jungles of Vietnam, where Phillips had been ordered to burn brush to clear areas for the passage of military troops and goods.

Since no one could be found who had ever heard Phillips mention Vietnam before, let alone the mental anguish he suffered there, the judge threw out this line of defense. As a result, Phillips pleaded guilty, and on March 5, 1998, he was sentenced to sixteen years' imprisonment and ordered to pay the costs of the investigation, estimated to be in excess of $250,000. Forestry Department officials believe that over the course of two decades, Phillips may have set as many as one hundred fires.

The Phonemasters

Date: 1994
Location: Dallas, Texas

In August 1994 the FBI's Dallas field office received an interesting phone call. A local private investigator said that he had been approached by a young man named Calvin Cantrell, who offered to sell him personal data on anyone he wished. The menu ranged from state motor vehicle records to personal credit reports, all the way up to data from the FBI's very own Crime Information Center. Prices began at $25. For $500, Cantrell promised to deliver the address/phone number of any celebrity or important person.

Intrigued, Michael Morris, the FBI's resident computer expert in Texas, asked the PI to wear a wiretap and meet Cantrell. The information gleaned from those tapes convinced Morris that he had stumbled across something big. He obtained an order permitting the installation of a digital recorder on Cantrell's phone lines. This logged details of all Cantrell's outgoing calls and provided curious results. Cantrell was spending inordinate amounts of time—as much as fifteen hours a day—dialing corporate numbers at telecommunications giants such as AT&T, GTE, MCI, Southwestern Bell, and Sprint. There were even calls to two unlisted numbers at the White House.

Morris was caught in a quandary. Tapping Cantrell's phone lines would only allow him to eavesdrop on spoken conversations, and he doubted that this would provide any usable information. He needed to monitor Cantrell's computer activity, and this meant intercepting the impulses that traveled along Cantrell's phone lines while he was using his computer and modem.

Such a step was fraught with danger. Attorneys at the Department of Justice, understandably concerned at becoming mired in potential invasion-of-privacy lawsuits, pondered the legality of such a request. Eventually, and only after much soul-searching, Morris was given the go-ahead for the first ever federally sanctioned data tap.

Having received the authority, Morris needed a suitable data intercept device. Unfortunately, at this time none existed. Just one year earlier, FBI agents investigating a New York hacking case had experimented with just such a device, only for it to fail dismally. For the scientists at the FBI's engineering lab in Quantico, Virginia, it was back to the drawing board.

While they labored, Morris contacted the telephone companies that he suspected were being targeted. To his surprise he received frosty receptions. Most multinational corporations are extremely sensitive about security lapses. Any hint of a breach could have catastrophic commercial consequences, which is why they prefer to handle such incidents internally, far from the prying gaze of stock analysts or the media.

Fortunately one company, GTE, was only too willing to assist Morris, and together they uncovered another of Cantrell's phone scams. This involved obtaining FBI field office numbers, hacking into the telephone system, and forwarding these numbers to phone-sex chat lines in Europe and Hong Kong. As a result, the FBI was billed for around $200,000 in illegal calls. Elsewhere, Cantrell hijacked a GTE number to generate calls to a phone-sex line, for which he received a $2,200 kickback from a source in Germany.

Meanwhile, engineers at Quantico continued their efforts. Modems take digital data from a computer and translate them to analog signals that can be sent via phone lines. What engineers needed was something that would intercept the analog signals on Cantrell's phone line and convert those impulses back to digital signals so the FBI's computers could capture and record each of the suspect's keystrokes.

By early December 1994 the analog data intercept device was ready. Built at a cost of $70,000, it was installed in a warehouse that stood between Cantrell's home and the nearest telephone central office. A ten-man team of FBI agents settled down to log Cantrell's activities. What they discovered astonished them.

Cantrell was no lone wolf but part of an eleven-strong gang of cyberfraudsters so skilled in manipulating the national telephone systems that listening FBI agents dubbed them the Phonemasters. Beside gaining access to the telephone networks of some of the world's largest companies, the Phonemasters also raided credit-reporting databases belonging to Equifax, Inc., TRW, Inc., and other financial organizations.

Nor was their electronic mischief limited to plundering databases. They also had access to portions of the national power grid and air-traffic-control systems. As mentioned earlier, even the FBI's own Crime Information Center had come under assault. It was estimated that they had the potential to cripple the entire national phone network.

Some idea of the unease that the Phonemasters investigation engendered in legal circles can be gauged from the fact that every ten days Morris had to reapply to the court to prove that his wiretap was yielding evidence. Fortunately, the evidence was multiplying exponentially. Taped conversations soon identified the gang's leader as Corey Lindsley, a student at the University of Pennsylvania. Another major player was San Diego–based John Bosanac.

Unlike most computer hackers, the Phonemasters didn't do it for thrills or bragging rights but purely for money, selling the data they pilfered. Customers included private investigators, so-called information brokers, even the Sicilian Mafia. In the short time they were operating, the gang was estimated to have caused $1.85 million in business losses.

Just after mid-February 1995 investigators got a scare. One gang member informed Cantrell that his home number had shown up in a database of phone numbers being monitored by the FBI. Unwilling to take any more chances, agents swooped. In a joint operation, on February 22, 1995, Cantrell was picked up in Dallas, while Lindsley and Bosanac were arrested in Philadelphia and California, respectively.

Because this was the first data tap case of its kind, prosecutors proceeded cautiously in a case that took years to build. Eventually, when played the incriminating tapes, all three defendants pleaded guilty. In September 1999 the trio were convicted of theft, possession of unauthorized access devices, and unauthorized access to a federal computer. Lindsley, regarded as the mastermind, received a forty-one month prison term, one of the longest sentences for a hacker in U.S. history. Cantrell was sentenced to two years; John Bosanac got eighteen months. Other members of the Phonemasters have still to be charged.

Allan Pinkerton (1819–1884)

Although often erroneously credited with having formed the world's first private detective agency—a distinction that belongs to **François-Eugène Vidocq**—Scottish-born Allan Pinkerton fully deserves recognition as the man who brought method and discipline to the previously haphazard business of fighting crime in America.

Born in Glasgow, a cooper by trade and something of a political firebrand, he immigrated to the United States in 1842, at age twenty-three. He settled in West Dundee, just outside Chicago, where his barrelmaking business became a station on the Underground Railroad for slaves fleeing the South.

He cut his investigative teeth in 1846 by nabbing a gang of local counterfeiters. Three years later, after a spell as deputy sheriff of Cook County, he became Chicago's first police detective, though he was soon on the move again, this time to the post office, where he was asked to solve a series of recent thefts. He soon identified the likely culprit, Theodore Dennison; then, employing the tactic that would become synonymous with his name, he went undercover and infiltrated Dennison's gang. When Pinkerton finally arrested Dennison, he made banner headlines. Riding this wave of favorable publicity, he left the post office and sometime between 1850 and 1852—the exact date is unknown—founded the Pinkerton National Detective Agency.

He was meticulous and innovative. In 1856 he hired Kate Warne as the first female detective in the United States. (By contrast, it would take New York City almost another half century to follow Pinkerton's groundbreaking lead.) Earlier than most, he recognized the usefulness of daguerreotypes and photographs as crime-fighting tools, and he quickly compiled an impressive "rogues' gallery" of miscreants and criminals. Tragically, this collection,

Allan Pinkerton, founder of America's first private detective agency, Pinkertons Inc.

along with the entire Pinkerton archives, was reduced to ashes in the Great Chicago Fire of 1871.

Utterly incorruptible himself, he demanded no less of his agents. Rewards and kickbacks were strictly banned, as was drunkenness. Among Chicago's lowlife he became known simply as the Eye, from which the expression "private eye" is derived, and before long the company motto, "We Never Sleep," passed into American folklore.

The Civil War brought Pinkerton national prominence. In 1861 he foiled a plot to assassinate Abraham Lincoln. Then he organized and directed an espionage system behind the Confederate lines.

During Reconstruction his agents tackled some of the West's most notorious bandits, such as the James Gang and the Reno Brothers, and until the advent of the Bureau of Investigation in 1908 (later the FBI), the Pinkertons operated as a de facto national police force, investigating and solving crimes across the country. This was Pinkerton's great legacy: the recognition that in a huge country such as the United States, interstate crime-fighting skills were not merely desirable but also absolutely essential.

Following Pinkerton's death in 1884, the agency diversified into the security field, an arena in which it is still a world leader.

Significant Cases

1854	Nathan Maroney
1857	Jules Imbert
1866	Adams Express Company Robbery
1868	The Reno Brothers
1873	The Molly Maguires

William Podmore

Date: 1929
Location: Southampton, England

Handwriting analysis had never played a significant role in the British courtroom until the January 1929 discovery of a badly decomposed body in Southampton. It belonged to fifty-seven-year-old Vivian Messiter, an oil company agent, and had been found in the lockup garage that served as a branch of the London-based Wolf's Head Oil Company. Even though Messiter, the firm's local agent and a recently appointed director, had been missing since the previous October, his disappearance had aroused no particular alarm, as he was known to be a wanderer who had spent many years in the United States and Mexico, and relatives merely thought that he had once again departed for more exotic climes.

At first, despite heavy blood staining on the boxes surrounding the body, Messiter's death was attributed to a brain hemorrhage. Only some hours later did a police surgeon highlight the unlikelihood of this, before inadvertently muddying the waters still further with his assumption that a small puncture wound over the left eye was actually a bullet hole. Not until three days later, with the discovery of a hammer stuffed between some boxes and the garage wall, was the genuine murder weapon found. The hammer had a point on one side, and this had made the deceptive puncture wound.

Sir Bernard Spilsbury was asked to perform a second autopsy. He confirmed that Messiter had been battered to death, suffering multiple fractures of the skull in what had been a horrendous assault. Spilsbury had no doubt that the hammer was the murder weapon. Both the shaft and the head were stained with blood, and, embedded on the hammer's face, he found a single eyebrow hair that was microscopically identical to samples taken from Messiter.

Even before Spilsbury's intercession, the local police force had yielded control of the case to Scotland Yard and Detective Chief Inspector John Prothero. His first task was to scrutinize Messiter's papers, both personal and private. Among these was a job application from a W. F. Thomas. Since this name had cropped up elsewhere in Messiter's paperwork, most notably on order forms from companies later found to be bogus, Prothero decided to bring him in for questioning. At the address Thomas gave on his job application, the landlady said that he had left, and she provided a forwarding address in London. When detectives checked this address and found it to be phony, Thomas became a hot suspect.

Newspaper reports of the distinctive hammer produced dividends. A Southampton man who worked at a garage recognized it as one he had lent to a mechanic in October, a man with a scar, and it had not been returned. Responses filtering in from other police forces in southern England suggested that they, too, were searching for a "man with a scar," a con artist who had run numerous low-level frauds on local businesses. Before long, the elusive Thomas was identified as career criminal William Henry Podmore, and he was tracked to a hotel in London.

Podmore made no bones about his larcenous lifestyle, nor did he deny using the alias Thomas, or that he had worked for Messiter in Southampton, but he was vehement in his claims that he had nothing to do with the murder. He had last seen Messiter, he said, on October 30, which, coincidentally, was the last day he was known to be alive.

Podmore's protestations of innocence received a fillip when the person who owned the hammer failed to identify him in a police lineup. Even when Prothero brandished the bogus order forms and growled that these might form an adequate motive for murder if Messiter had discovered their existence, Podmore just shrugged. As a savvy, albeit none too successful criminal, he knew there was insufficient evidence to charge him with murder, and he was quite content to settle for a six-month prison sentence for an earlier offense of car theft.

Prothero took no satisfaction in the fact that Podmore was behind bars. Back at Scotland Yard, he spent hours poring over the evidence from Messiter's office. For what must have been the hundredth time, he plowed through the reams of paperwork, searching for that vital clue. At one point he strolled over to the window, a receipt book in hand. The first nine pages had been torn out, leaving it blank. Prothero was just about to replace the receipt book on the desk when a shaft of sunlight suddenly struck the tenth page. His eyes narrowed. In this light it was possible to discern faint indentations on the page, the legacy of whatever had been written on the preceding receipt.

High-contrast photographs were taken of the page, arranging the illumination so that it shone obliquely across the page. This made the writing legible. It read: "28 October, 1928. Received from Wolf's Head Oil Company commission on Cromer and Bartlett, 5 gals 5/6 commission 2/6. W. F. T."

Not only was Cromer and Bartlett found to be a nonexistent company, but also handwriting experts had no hesitation in stating that this entry had been written by Podmore. This proved that Podmore had been systematically defrauding his employer, and it raised a vital question: who, other than Podmore, stood to gain by ripping out the receipt? Everything pointed to the likelihood that Messiter, having discovered that Podmore was bilking him, threatened to call the police. Podmore, fearful because he was already wanted on other charges, had panicked, grabbed the hammer, and crushed Messiter's head. Afterward, desperate to cover his tracks, he had sought to eradicate all evidence of the fraud, only to leave those telltale traces.

This was the line taken by the prosecution in March 1930, when, fifteen months after the crime, Podmore finally found himself facing a charge of capital murder. The press, as always, reported Spilsbury's involvement in blaring headlines, but he was quick to play down his own contribution to this case, modestly pointing out that the credit for sending Podmore to the gallows on April 22, 1930, belonged almost entirely to a detective who is nowadays scarcely remembered.

Polygraph

Throughout history mankind has searched for ways to trap liars. Priests in India in about 500 B.C. would herd suspected thieves into a darkened room with a "magic donkey," whose tail had been daubed with lampblack. The suspects were then ordered to pull the donkey's tail, having been warned that when the genuine thief pulled the tail, the magic donkey would speak and be heard throughout the temple. When the room was emptied a few minutes later, the person who still had clean hands—having not pulled the tail—was pronounced the thief and punished.

China came up with an even simpler method. Suspected liars were fed a handful of dry rice. If they could spit it out, so the reasoning went, they were telling the truth; if the rice stuck to their tongue, they were thought to have something to hide.

As crude as it may seem, this Chinese "truth test" employed exactly the same principle as the modern polygraph—the notion that when people lie, their body reacts in ways that they cannot control. Whereas Chinese interrogators were on the lookout for a dry mouth as an indicator of lying, the polygraph operator searches for deception by studying changes in blood pressure, rates of breathing, pulse, and perspiration.

The first recorded attempt to construct a mechanical device to measure emotion and determine truth and deception can be traced to the noted criminologist Cesare Lombroso. As early as 1885 he was working with the Italian police, recording changes in blood pressure as suspects were questioned. The next innovation in lie detection came in 1913 when another Italian, the psychologist Vittorio Benussi, published a paper on using breath measurement as a means of determining truthfulness.

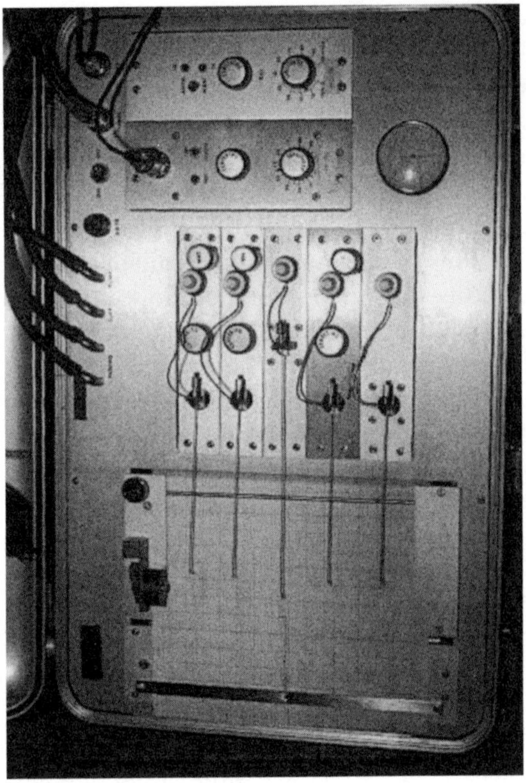

A typical suitcase model polygraph. The pens record breathing rate, galvanic skin response, blood pressure and pulse rate. In essence, this modern machine is very similar to the prototype invented by John Larson in the 1920s.

In World War I an American scientist engaged in counterintelligence, William Marston, took the process one step farther, developing a systolic blood pressure gauge that he tested on German POWs. Unimpressed with his results, Marston discontinued its use.

The undoubted "Father of the Polygraph" was John Larson, a medical student at the University of California at Berkeley. In 1920, working in close conjunction with the local police chief, August Vollmer, Larson built the first machine specifically designed to detect lying through plotting simultaneous measurements of blood pressure, pulse, and respiration on graph paper. Several years earlier a Scottish cardiologist, Sir James Mackenzie, had designed a multifunction heart monitor that he called a *polygraph* (many writings), and Larson decided to appropriate the name.

Although immediately popular with police departments across America, the polygraph suffered a major judicial setback in 1923 when the U.S. Supreme Court, in *Frye v. United States,* ruled that unsubstantiated scientific testimony was legally inadmissible. As a result, the polygraph was largely banished from the courtroom, even as its use in everyday life mushroomed, especially in the arena of job applications. By the 1930s Larson had turned his back on the polygraph, and it was left to his protégé Leonard Keeler to develop what is now regarded as the prototype of the modern polygraph. At the same time, Keeler also founded a school for the proper training of operatives.

The polygraph works by attaching rubber tubes to the subject's chest and abdomen, a blood pressure-pulse cuff to the arm, and small metal plates to the fingers. The examiner then asks the subject a series of questions. The polygraph measures five physical responses:

1. Thoracic respiration
2. Abdominal respiration
3. Perspiration (registered by minuscule changes in skin conductivity of electricity occurring at the fingertip)
4. Blood pressure
5. Blood volume

These five responses are plotted along a horizontal graph, with the location of questions marked at the bottom of the printout. How the questions are framed is critical. Because individuals react differently, the examiner needs to know what triggers a "lie" response in that particular subject. To this end, each test contains certain "control" questions, to which the subject is directed to answer untruthfully. The concomitant anxiety usually shows as a blip on the graph. Once this untruthful benchmark has been established, the actual test can begin.

Numerous questions—some relevant (issues in the case), some not—are fired at the subject. Each response is assigned a number from –3 (indicating a strong negative correlation) to +3 (indicating a strong positive correlation), measured by comparing the relevant response to the previously established "controls." Psychology plays its part, with the skilled examiner constantly reminding the subject of just how accurate the polygraph is in catching any lies told.

Once all the responses are added together, a total score of +6 indicates a strong presumption that the subject is lying. Scores that fall between –5 and +5 are not admissible, because they are not felt to be a strong enough indication of veracity.

While no one disputes that polygraphs measure perceptible changes in human response, there can be no absolute guarantee that these changes are prompted by the act of lying. Because stress plays a big factor in any polygraph test—even truthful subjects occasionally send the styluses haywire—much depends on how the examiner interprets the data. And herein lies much of the controversy. Hand the same polygraph results to two different examiners and, as tests have shown, it is entirely possible that they will reach opposing conclusions as to the subject's truthfulness.

Supporters of the polygraph attribute such discrepancies to poor schooling and lack of experience. A properly trained examiner, they claim, armed with a good instrument, will catch 95 percent of all liars. Critics put the figure much lower and say that with minimal practice, almost anyone can be taught how to "beat the machine" by deliberately manipulating their physiological responses to give false negatives.

Despite these misgivings, the polygraph remains an integral weapon in the American crime-fighting armory. Even the courts are beginning to relax their prohibition. In recent years *Frye v. United States* has come under challenge, and some states now permit the introduction of polygraph results as evidence. Elsewhere in the world, the polygraph has never achieved common usage or acceptance.

Edmond de la Pommerais

Date: 1863
Location: Paris, France

Edmond de la Pommerais was a young doctor in a hurry. In 1859 he purchased a homeopathic medical practice in Paris, only to find that it was not the passport to riches he had hoped for. He also learned that Parisian society looked disdainfully on a struggling physician—especially if he happened to be a serial womanizer with well-publicized gambling debts—which is why, trading on his mother's tenuous connections to the aristocracy, he bestowed upon himself the title of count.

The change of status brought no pecuniary improvement, and in 1861 he was obliged to cast aside his beautiful but impoverished lover, Séraphine de Pawr, so that he might marry a daughter of the wealthy Dubiczy family. Unfortunately for de la Pommerais, his new mother-in-law distrusted him on sight and insisted on retaining tight control of her married daughter's inheritance. Thwarted and frustrated, de la Pommerais set about loosening this grip. Scarcely two months after the wedding, he invited Madame Dubiczy around for dinner, after which she fell mysteriously ill, and within days she was dead. At last de la Pommerais had unfettered access to his wife's newly acquired wealth, which he first used to bail himself out of financial hot water with his creditors, and then to finance a hectic spending spree. He also resumed his affair with the glamorous Séraphine.

Inside of two years every franc had been squandered. As the debts piled up once again in November 1863, Séraphine's health began to slide. Doctors were baffled by her symptoms, particularly an erratic heartbeat, which raced and slowed by turns. She rejected all their diagnoses, insisting it was nothing more than a "light case of cholera" that could be best treated by her lover's homeopathic remedies. Since he had signally failed to save her own late husband, Séraphine's faith was commendable, if somewhat misplaced. After a short illness, plagued by violent stomach pains and vomiting, she died. The death certificate, made out by de la Pommerais, listed cholera as the cause of death, and she was duly buried.

Whispers soon began. Before long an anonymous letter arrived at the Sûreté, hinting that de la Pommerais might have profited from his lover's death. Inquiries revealed that not long before her death, Séraphine had taken out a 500,000 franc insurance policy on her own life, naming de la Pommerais as the sole beneficiary. Although the insurance company had not quibbled over paying, they had been disconcerted by the callous vigor with which the impecunious young doctor had pressed his claim.

Further shocks greeted detectives when they interviewed the dead woman's sister. She mentioned a plan hatched by de la Pommerais with the professed intention of easing *her* financial worries. All she had to do, de la Pommerais had explained, was to take out a large life insurance policy, then feign an illness that he would diagnose as incurable. Upon receipt of his report, the insurance company, desperate to reduce their liability, would jump at the woman's offer to exchange her policy for an annuity payable on a shortened life expectancy. Once the policy was converted, said de la Pommerais, voilà! A miraculous recovery would ensue, leaving the couple free to enjoy a hefty annual income for the rest of their days. So taken was she with the scheme that the woman readily agreed to de la Pommerais's casual suggestion that she make out a will in his favor. Only serendipity, it seemed, had averted a third tragedy.

In light of this statement, an order was obtained to exhume Séraphine's body. As it showed no trace of the supposedly lethal cholera, tests were made for various poisons, notably arsenic and antimony. The analyses were supervised by **Auguste Ambroise Tardieu,** professor of forensic medicine at Paris University. He found no trace of arsenic or antimony but knew that de la Pommerais prescribed a wide range of homeopathic medicines in his practice, including vegetable alkaloid poisons. Unfortunately, Tardieu was hampered by not having a sample of the dead woman's vomit, since such material is likely to contain heavy traces of any poison taken by mouth.

Tardieu decided on a radical step. He injected an extract he had made from the dead woman's organs into the bloodstream of a dog, to see if there was any toxic effect. The poor animal's reactions were dramatic: it vomited, and its heartbeat raced and then slowed, in a replica of Séraphine's symptoms. Clearly, she had been poisoned, but with which poison? As Tardieu searched de la Pommerais' surgery and drug collection, his gaze alighted on a bottle of digitalis.

Extracted from the dried leaves of the common foxglove, digitalis had long been used as a means of regulating the heartbeat. It was first prescribed in 1775 by the English physician and botanist William Withering, who used it in the treatment of edema. His writings emphasized the exceptional care necessary when administering digitalis, as it is lethal at only three times the effective dose.

In minute quantities the drug regulates the rhythm of the heart, but high regular doses have a cumulative effect, slowing the heart to the point of death. Toxic effects occur within two or three hours of taking the poison, and symptoms include nausea, vomiting, diarrhea, disturbed vision, delirium, irregular pulse, and convulsions. Death occurs as a result of cardiac arrest. Tardieu was certain that here was the lethal agent. Then, by a stroke of good fortune, he was able to prove his theory of digitalis poisoning when the police provided him with a sample of dried vomit scraped from the floorboards in the sickroom.

Once again, nineteenth-century French **toxicology** had led the way forward, and now it had trapped one of the most heartless murderers on record. De la Pommerais' protestations of innocence counted for nothing; he was found guilty of murder and guillotined in 1864. Although not charged with the murder of his mother-in-law, it is almost certain that he killed her as well.

Psychological Profiling

Behind every criminal act is the criminal mind. It sounds a simple enough concept, and in seeking to probe the motivations of that mind—and thereby improve their clear-up rate—investigators have increasingly turned for assistance to what is popularly known as psychological profiling. At the heart of this concept is a belief that criminals leave psychological clues at the scene of the crime. By carefully sifting these clues, skilled interpreters endeavor to build up a picture of the likely culprit. Common sense, observation, background knowledge, and geographical considerations play as big a role in this process as does psychology, for only by studying all facets of the crime can the profiler hope to be successful.

The first in-depth analysis of the homicidal mind came in 1930 with Professor Carl Berg's study of Peter Kürten, the so-called Monster of Düsseldorf. However, this was compiled while Kürten was awaiting execution and contributed nothing to his capture. Two years later a rudimentary attempt was made to profile the kidnapper of Charles Lindbergh Jr., but no real headway in this field was made until a Manhattan psychiatrist, Dr. James Brussel, astounded detectives with his uncannily accurate predictions as to the identity of New York's "Mad Bomber" (see the George Metesky entry, *The Casebook of Forensic Detection,* Wiley, 1996) in 1957.

The exciting possibilities provoked by Brussel's success took a serious hit in the aftermath of the Boston Strangler case, where two widely differing profiles failed to indicate the eventual culprit, and it was not until 1969 that psychological profiling again emerged from the shadows.

This time the flag bearer was Howard Teten, an agent at the FBI Academy in Quantico, Virginia. Primed by long consultations with Brussel, Teten started laying the groundwork for the first concerted attempt at predictive analysis of the criminal mind. In 1972 he was joined by Pat Mullany, and together they established the FBI's Behavioral Science Unit at Quantico.

Time and budgetary constraints limited the team to studying only the most serious crimes. This led them to interview a virtual rogues' gallery of America's worst serial killers, men such as Charles Manson, Richard Speck, David Berkowitz, John Wayne Gacy, and Ted Bundy. The results of these interviews were entered on a computer database and then scoured in an attempt to discover similar and repeatable behavioral patterns. An early significant discovery was that most serial killers fall into one of two categories: organized and disorganized. The former are calculating, likely to plan their crimes, whereas disorganized killers are creatures of reflex, impulsive and senseless, with little consideration for outcome or consequence.

As the profilers gained in experience, so their attention turned more to crime scene analysis. They studied photographs, autopsy reports, witness statements, and, critically, any evidence that was left at the crime scene. Factors to be considered included motive, mobility, victim preference, murder weapon, and location, among others.

With this increasing sophistication came the formation of the National Center for the Analysis of Violent Crime (NCAVC), and its offshoot the Violent Criminal Apprehension Program (VICAP), a nationwide attempt to systematically collate and disseminate data related to crimes of violence. Cases typically examined by VICAP include:

- Solved or unsolved homicides, especially those that involve an abduction.
- Murders that are apparently random, motiveless, or sexually oriented; or are known or suspected to be part of a series.
- Missing persons when the circumstances indicate a strong possibility of foul play and the victim is still missing.
- Unidentified dead bodies when the manner of death is known or suspected to be homicide.

The VICAP Crime Analysis Report contains no fewer than 189 questions, ranging from details of the crime and its victims to the modus operandi (MO), autopsy data, and forensic evidence. Once this form has been completed by the investigating agency concerned, VICAP personnel can access the database, seeking out similarities to previous crimes, particularly if it appears as though these crimes may have been committed by the same offender. If patterns are found, the law enforcement agency involved will be notified. It should be stressed that the FBI's role in these cases is that of an adviser unless a federal crime is involved. Otherwise, actually solving a crime and apprehending the perpetrator are very much the preserve of the local investigating agency.

Since 1990 the Behavioral Science Unit has been renamed Behavioral Science Services. There are currently just over thirty agents qualified to work on VICAP, and each year they receive more than one thousand profiling requests from law enforcement agencies, not only in America but around the globe as well.

It is fair to say that psychological profiling is more entrenched—and certainly better organized and funded—in the United States than it is in Europe, where profound doubts persist. Critics highlight one spectacular British catastrophe in 1994, when a murder trial was halted after the judge decided that there was not a shred of evidence—other than a highly tenuous profile—to link the defendant to the crime. The profiler in question, who was perceived to be quarterbacking the entire investigation, was lambasted as a "puppetmaster" who had overseen "a blatant attempt to incriminate a suspect by . . . deceptive conduct of the grossest kind."

More recently the Washington, D.C., sniper case—where a bewildering array of "experts" flooded the airwaves with a bewildering array of profiles that were not only wildly disparate but also positively dangerous in the way that they diverted police resources—has further fueled complaints that too many profilers are too slavish in their devotion to databanks and sound bites.

By its nature, psychological profiling tends to be retrospective, and while solutions to crimes of the present may be suggested by crimes of the past, the shrewd profiler needs to be aware that mankind's capacity for evil is as innovative as it is infinite. As an adjunct to traditional investigative techniques, profiling undoubtedly has a part to play, but there can be little doubt that its current popularity owes more to media hype than it does to putting a significant dent in the crime figures.

Questioned Documents

Although the work of the questioned document examiner is multifaceted, requiring knowledge of ink, paper, and typography, the sequence of events involved in the preparation and handling of a document, the alteration of a document, and its age, at its heart lies the examination of handwriting, with the intention of ascertaining authorship of a document.

The first person to systematically study handwriting and its related issues was Albert S. Osborn, whose *Questioned Documents* (1910) and *The Problem of Proof* (1922) quickly became recognized texts, accepted and acknowledged in courtrooms across America. In 1942 Osborn founded and became the first

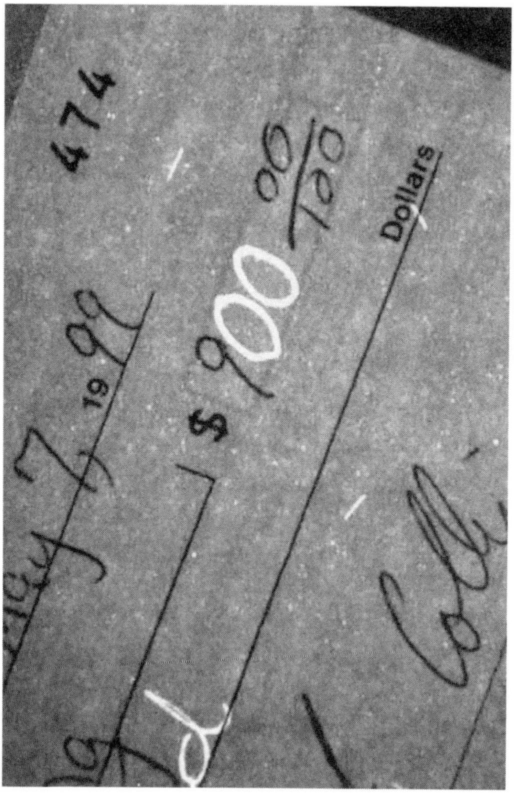

Through its use of infrared luminescence, the video spectral comparator shows clearly how this check has been fraudently altered to increase the amount.

president of the American Society of Questioned Document Examiners. Since that time the society's membership has grown to more than one hundred.

Like all other evidence, handwriting is identified on the basis of individuality. Children may be taught a specific way of forming letters, but they rapidly begin to inject their own quirks and idiosyncrasies. By the time a person reaches maturity, so the theory goes, his or her handwriting has acquired sufficient peculiarities so as to be identifiable.

If only it were that simple. In truth, our handwriting is rarely static. Fluctuations can occur, often from day to day. Mood, the position in which we sit, our physical well-being—all of these can affect the way we put pen to paper. But to the accomplished examiner, there is, beneath these superficial deviations, a unique style that shines through, defying any attempt at disguise. It might be the angle of writing, its uniformity across the page, or the manner in which letters are formed, such as whether letters such as *g* and *h* are looped. Such analysis requires vast experience and a large investment of time before a considered opinion can be given.

A forged signature presents very specific problems. Phony signatures based on memory tend to contain a combination of the forger's own writing habits and his or her recollection of the victim's habits. Often the discrepancies will be manifest. On the other hand, when the perpetrator makes a careful drawing of the victim's signature or traces an authentic signature, while the forgery may be exposed, identifying the perpetrator is next to impossible, since two individuals making careful tracings of the same signature can produce virtually identical drawings.

Besides handwriting analysis, the questioned document examiner is frequently called on to identify a source of mechanical writing, such as a typewriter or a computer printer. Here, reference files and differentiation charts hold the key, listing, as they do, every kind of typeface design. A specific typewriter can be identified if it contains sufficient individuality, based on broken or tilting characters, badly aligned characters, characters that print more heavily on one side than on another, and rebounding characters. Since it is virtually impossible to reinsert a document into a typewriter in its exact former position, a skilled examiner, by using a ruled screen, can ascertain whether a document has been prepared at one sitting or is the product of multiple insertions.

Building on this mechanical expertise, the examiner also needs a knowledge of the history of print technology. Say, for example, a document was purportedly written in 1912, yet records showed that the machine upon which it was typed was not manufactured until 1938, then that document must be viewed with the utmost skepticism.

Other factors to be considered are ink and paper. In the 1920s the U.S. Secret Service acquired the International Ink Library from the police in Zurich, Switzerland. Nowadays the library contains the chemical composition and other information, such as date of formulation, of more than seven thousand types of ink. The library also maintains a watermark collection of more than twenty-two thousand images, as well as collections of toners and computer printer inks. Although ink comparisons may provide invaluable evidence, it is not possible to individualize ink—that is, identify it as coming from a unique source.

Papers can be identified on the basis of fiber, filler, and sizing constituents. Fibers can be identified by differential staining and microscopic examination. Fillers can be identified by X-ray diffraction because they are crystalline substances. Chemical tests are used for the identification of sizing constituents. Research with **neutron activation analysis** suggests it may even be possible to identify paper by batches.

Determining whether a document has been altered is usually possible through electrostatic detection apparatus (ESDA). A document is placed on top of an electronically charged metal mesh, then tightly covered with a thin plastic film. As the document and the film are sucked tightly onto the mesh, a mixture of photocopier toner and fine glass beads is applied, which cling to those electrostatically charged areas. When the original document is removed, all of the indentations on the film may be read. By matching all suspect original pages against each image, investigators can determine whether changes have been made.

Questions concerning the sequence of writing—for example, if the ink signature is over or under the typewritten portion of a document—can be vital in proving the authenticity of a document. In this and related problems, such as deciphering and restoration of eradicated or erased writing, most examinations are nowadays carried out primarily using computer-based technology.

The latest weapon in the FBI's questioned documents arsenal is the video spectral comparator 5000 (VSC5000), an extraordinarily sophisticated imaging device that allows an examiner to analyze inks, visualize hidden security features, and reveal alterations on a document. Using the VSC5000's infrared radiant energy source and filters, the examiner is able to see through inks to reveal objects that are obscured to the naked eye. But it has a variety of other uses.

The specimen is first subjected to a variety of light sources, while cameras and filters record the effect on a VDU. Software enables the examiner to manipulate the image for easier viewing. It allows images to be overlaid or compared side by side, useful in performing torn edge comparisons on sheets of paper, and in determining whether a page has been added or replaced in a multipage contract. It can even aid the examiner to sort shredded pieces of paper, allowing the reconstruction of a readable document. Such advances make the field of questioned documents one of the most dynamic in the whole forensic science arena.

Dennis Raso and Stephen Azzolini

Date: 1978
Location: Hoboken, New Jersey

On June 22, 1978, Dennis Raso, a twenty-five-year-old New Jersey contractor, filed a missing-persons report with local police, saying that his wife, Rosa, had disappeared. He told how, two nights previously, he and Rosa had gone out partying. After visiting several bars, they wound up at a disco; both were badly drunk, and a fight broke out between them. Rosa brought the skirmishing to a close by storming off alone, while Raso kept on drinking until he fell asleep. When the club closed, he was thrown out, at which point he went home to his house in Hoboken. Since then he had seen and heard nothing of his wife.

Police checked their records and learned that their counterparts in New York City were investigating the death of a young woman whose body had been found in a FedEx car lot the previous day. She had been brutally murdered, her throat slashed so deeply that the head had been almost severed. When shown a photo of the dead woman, Raso tearfully identified his wife, Rosa. As he talked, it became increasingly likely that Rosa had been murdered for money. When found, there was no trace of the expensive jewelry she habitually wore on nights out. This tallied with the medical examiner's finding of a thin, distinctive ligature mark around the neck, possibly made by a gold chain yanked tightly. Petechiae found in the dead woman's eyes strongly indicated that she had been partially strangled before the killer finished her off by cutting her throat. The only other evidence of any consequence found on Rosa's body were some small particles of carpet fiber beneath her fingernails.

When Rosa's family heard of the tragedy, they instinctively smelled trouble. They knew Dennis Raso as a brutal, wife-beating thug who on one occasion had thrashed Rosa so badly that she needed hospital attention. In spite of this, and against the wishes of her family, she refused to leave her husband, convinced that, deep down, he loved her.

It didn't take long for the police to share the family's suspicions, especially when they discovered that on the night of Rosa's disappearance, and after being thrown out of the disco, Raso had gone home and seduced the baby-sitter, in what turned into an all-night sex marathon. Judging from the baby-sitter's statement, Raso wasn't expecting to be disturbed anytime soon, almost as if he knew that Rosa wouldn't be returning.

Rosa's family kept up the pressure. They told police that a van used by Raso to deliver flowers had gone missing. Eventually it was traced to an isolated part of Brooklyn. The interior was marked with specks of blood, of the same type as Rosa's. At the same time, experts recovered carpet fibers microscopically identical to those beneath Rosa's nails.

Although the police strongly suspected Raso of close involvement in his wife's death, there was nothing to physically connect him with the crime; and his alibi for the night in question was bulletproof. Reluctantly they had to release him on bail.

Then came a curious turn of events. Two weeks later a young woman named Mary Ellen Azzolini, who was seven months pregnant, was shot to death at her apartment in Hoboken. It might only have been coincidence, but detectives were struck by the fact that Mary Ellen was the wife of disco-loving Stephen Azzolini—who just happened to be Dennis Raso's best friend.

A search of the crime scene revealed two pairs of sunglasses. One pair belonged to the victim; the other—with highly unusual frames—was traced to a Hoboken ophthalmologist, whose records showed that they had been sold to Dennis Raso. When confronted by this evidence, Raso folded fast. He admitted killing Mary Ellen but insisted that he had nothing to do with Rosa's death. That, he said, had been carried out by Stephen Azzolini. Further questioning revealed that the two men had entered into an unholy pact: each would kill the other's wife, allowing that man to establish an impregnable alibi.

Stephen Azzolini proved to be cast from more durable stuff than his erstwhile partner. Flashy and confident, he held up well under questioning, claiming that Raso had murdered Mary Ellen to silence her, because he feared she was about to spill details of how he had killed Rosa. As for Raso's claims that he, Azzolini, had murdered Rosa, he just laughed. In fact, Azzolini kept laughing all the way out of the Hoboken police station.

One officer watched his swaggering exit with undisguised contempt. Azzolini was very much a product of the disco era, and his macho appearance—complete with bushy hairdo, tight pants, and unbuttoned shirt—led the detective to comment sourly that the only item Azzolini seemed to be lacking was the obligatory gold chain. At this, two other officers glanced sharply at each other. Each was certain that when the interview began, Azzolini did indeed have a gold chain around his neck. Well, not now, commented the first detective.

This triggered an immediate search of the interview room. Nothing was found. As the search widened without any success, frustration grew until, several days later, in the police station bathroom, a gold chain was found stuffed behind some pipes.

Friends soon identified this chain as having been worn by Rosa on the night of her disappearance, and the medical examiner was able to match it indisputably to the ligature marks around her neck. Greed and stupidity had floored Azzolini. After semistrangling Rosa with the chain, then slashing her throat, he had been foolish enough to wear the chain to the police station, only realizing later that the crucial piece of incriminating evidence was hanging around his own neck.

The penalty for this breathtaking stupidity was a sentence of twenty-five years to life. One year later, in December 1981, Raso, who readily admitted his part in both murders and who agreed to testify against his former partner in crime, received a lesser sentence of twenty to life.

James Robertson

Date: 1950
Location: Glasgow, Scotland

The short Scottish summer night was just beginning to lighten as a taxi driver motored along Prospecthill Road in South Glasgow on July 28, 1950. Suddenly his headlights picked out a woman's body in the road. To the inexperienced eye, she appeared to have been the victim of a hit-and-run, but to the first police officer on the scene, Constable William Kevin, a man with considerable experience of road accidents, things were not so clear-cut. He saw none of the debris normally associated with such crashes, broken headlight glass and the like; and tire marks on the road appeared to show that the vehicle had been traveling in two different directions. Taking into account the woman's massive injuries, which he later described as "the worst . . . I've ever seen in a road accident," Kevin concluded that the woman was already lying on the road when first struck. Apparently she had been trapped beneath the car and dragged along the road; then the car had stopped and reversed over her several times in a figure-eight maneuver. When Kevin shared his suspicions with his superiors, they examined the evidence and agreed. Everything pointed to this being a rare case of homicide by automobile.

The autopsy, carried out by Professor Andrew Allison, confirmed that the injuries were inconsistent with a road accident; and there was a bruise on the skull that had been incurred before death. It didn't take long to identify the victim. Catherine McCluskey was an attractive forty-year-old blonde, unmarried, with two children and many male admirers. Just recently she had griped to acquaintances that the father of her second child, a police officer, had refused to pay child support.

That officer, James Robertson, a thirty-three-year-old constable already under a cloud for suspicion of dealing in stolen cars, immediately became the number one suspect. On the night of the killing, he had bragged to a fellow officer that he was "going to take a blonde home." He later attributed his absence from duty between 11:00 P.M. and 1:00 A.M. to car problems.

Inquiries showed that this car, which Robertson had been driving for several weeks, was stolen. He claimed to have found it abandoned and had appropriated it for his own use after checking police records and then changing the license plates. (The worth of this story can be gauged from the fact that investigators found no fewer than fourteen stolen sets of car registration documents at Robertson's house.) The car's underside, when examined, revealed clear traces of blood and hair.

Robertson was arrested and searched. In his uniform pocket was a rubber blackjack, stained with blood but not enough to provide usable test results. He made no attempt to deny meeting Catherine McCluskey on the night of her death; in fact, he was quite expansive on the subject. She had been annoyed, he said, because she was locked out of her own house and wanted him to drive her to a friend's place, some fourteen miles away. When he had refused, saying that he was still on duty, an argument had broken out, and Robertson drove off. One hundred yards down the road he underwent a change of heart and put the car in reverse to offer her a ride. But unbeknownst to him, Catherine was standing in the road, and he backed right over her. When he tried to drag the blood-drenched woman out from underneath the car, her clothing caught in the driveshaft, forcing him to shunt the car backward and forward until she was free. Then he had panicked and fled.

But would Robertson's version of events stand up to close scrutiny? The pathologist **John Glaister,** professor of forensic medicine at Glasgow University, and one of the foremost medico-legal experts of the time, didn't think so. The more he studied the circumstances of Catherine McCluskey's death, the more obvious it became to him that she had been the victim of deliberate murder. In the first place, she did not have a single injury to her legs, such as would have been sustained had Robertson knocked her down in the manner he described; second, on this particular vehicle the driveshaft was enclosed and therefore could not have caught her clothing, as he had alleged.

Nor could Glaister make any sense of Robertson's claim that he had attempted to drag Catherine out from beneath the car. Had this been the case, the evidence should have been all over his uniform. Yet Glaister was not able to find a speck of blood on Robertson's clothing. Glaister was a strong believer in the maxim that negative evidence is the best evidence of all. If the facts don't fit the story, then something has to be wrong. And as James Robertson found out, usually it's the story.

The scenario that prosecutors painted at Robertson's trial was of a ruthless man motivated by a determination to avoid paying child support for the child he had fathered. First he had clubbed Catherine unconscious, then he deliberately drove his car over her, time and time again, until he was sure she was dead. Robertson's initial cockiness on the witness stand wilted horribly under cross-examination, when he was trapped in one lie after another. It came as no surprise when the jury returned a verdict of guilty, and he was sentenced to death.

While awaiting his date with the gallows, Robertson repeatedly bragged to the death house guards that his former occupation would guarantee a reprieve. "They'll never hang a copper," he boasted. On the morning of December 16, 1950, the full enormity of that misapprehension was brought home to him.

Keith Rose

Date: 1981

Location: Budleigh Salterton, England

Juliet Rowe was a timid woman, much given to concerns about personal security, which was why her home at Budleigh Salterton, Devon, was fitted with a panic button that triggered an alarm at the local police station. At about 3:00 P.M. on September 21, 1981, the alarm suddenly shrilled. When police reached the Rowes' residence some minutes later, they found the front door locked but one side window open.

Juliet Rowe lay in the hallway. She had been shot four times in the back, then finished off with close-range shots to the head and heart. Although nothing was taken, everything bore the hallmarks of a robbery gone wrong. It appeared as though Juliet, age forty-two, had surprised a burglar, only to be cruelly cut down as she fled. Her husband, Gerald, a self-made millionaire who owned eighteen supermarkets, had been away from the house on business at the time of the crime, an absence that did nothing to quell local gossip. His outgoing ebullience had always seemed at odds with his wife's shy, retiring nature, and soon the inevitable rumor mill was grinding remorselessly. These suspicions were not shared by the police. They still firmly believed that this was a bungled robbery.

More than three hundred fingerprints were lifted at the house. After painstaking elimination of relatives and acquaintances, just one—a left thumbprint—remained unidentified. Attention then concentrated on the murder weapon, a .22-caliber pistol. Every registered firearm of that type in Devon and Cornwall was seized and test-fired. None produced a match. Gradually the search extended to the rest of the country. Thousands of weapons, including many illegally held firearms, were test-fired; still the murder weapon—which by now had been identified as a Colt Woodsman—remained elusive.

Despite a huge commitment of officers and resources, the investigation foundered, and as the months and then years drifted by, it began to look very much as though the killer of Juliet Rowe would never be found.

Eight years passed. And then in August 1989, Victor Cracknell, age thirty-two and the son of a food millionaire, was spirited away from his Surrey home by kidnappers who demanded a £1 million (about $1.587 million in 1989) ransom for his safe return. Cracknell was driven two hundred miles across southern England to a remote location in Devon. His captor—a lone man, apparently—first gagged and blindfolded his victim, then secured him by slipping a wire noose around his neck. Any attempt to escape could result in strangulation or even decapitation. At one point the sadistic kidnapper taunted Cracknell with a choice of deaths if things went wrong: either the noose or a motorcycle crash helmet that had been specially wired to deliver a lethal electric shock at the touch of a button. (Fortunately, Cracknell managed to break free from his bonds and escape; otherwise police are convinced he would have starved to death.)

Following the ransom drop, undercover police tracked the kidnapper across southern England all the way to Devon, where he was captured as he parked his Porsche outside a house in Exeter. Inside the car was the ransom money. His name was Keith Rose, a thirty-nine year-old failed businessman, and he received fifteen years for kidnapping. Such a crime—exceedingly rare in Britain—made every TV station, and among those watching news of Rose's conviction was Gerald Rowe. Instantly his mind flew back a few months. He recalled being in an Exeter pub when a stranger had approached and introduced himself, saying, "I'm Keith Rose. Did you know that I was pulled on your wife's murder because I belonged to a gun club?"

Rose had then inquired if anyone had ever been arrested for the crime. Rowe, appalled by the insensitive boorishness of such an approach, had brushed the man off. Now he immediately contacted the police.

They checked their records and confirmed that Rose, a member of various gun and rifle clubs, had indeed been interviewed at the time of the Rowe murder, because he was the registered owner of a Colt Woodsman pistol. However, when detectives called, Rose had produced the weapon in pieces, saying it was unusable, and the officers had taken him at his word. Also, he appeared to have a sound alibi. (Only later was it realized that Rose's alibi cunningly referred to events one day after the crime.)

Devon police now contacted their Surrey colleagues and requested copies of Rose's fingerprints. After eight long years, they finally had a match for that mysterious left thumbprint.

Unbelievably, Rose still owned the Colt Woodsman, though it was now too heavily corroded and with too many missing parts for an effective ballistics comparison to be made with the bullets that killed Juliet Rowe. But all was not lost. The gun was shipped to the United States, where a firearms expert in New England had a solution. He noticed that the Colt had a faulty magazine retaining clip that pushed the magazine too high in the breech. This meant that, as the shell casings were ejected, they hit the lip of the magazine case and sustained an unusual marking—just like the shell casings found at the Rowe murder scene. It was the final piece in a puzzle that had taken eight years to solve.

At the time of the Rowe murder, Rose had been up to his eyes in debt; his newly established detergent company in nearby Crediton was sinking under debts of £80,000 ($170,000 in 1981) and he was in hock to the bank for £20,000 ($42,500) more. But Rose was no more successful as a kidnapper than he had been in business, and when Juliet Rowe had fled, he panicked and gunned her down in cold blood.

Convicted and sentenced to life on March 19, 1991, Rose was not yet through with headline-making. In January 1995 he and two other convicts succeeded in breaking out of the high-security Parkhurst Prison on the Isle of Wight. Although they remained at large for only five days, their high-profile escape ruined several prison department careers. For his efforts, Rose received another three years in prison.

Darlie Routier

Date: 1996
Location: Dallas, Texas

To most onlookers, Darlie and Darin Routier embodied the American dream. Still in their twenties, they had three great sons, owned a fine house in the exclusive suburb of Rowlett, just outside Dallas, and drove imported sports cars, while Darin's thriving business—his company repaired mainframe computers—had netted him $100,000 in 1995. Then, in a few short minutes on June 6, 1996, the dream turned into the worst nightmare imaginable.

Sometime after 2:00 A.M., an intruder broke into their house and crept into the living room where Darlie and her two eldest boys, Devon, age six, and Damon, a year younger, lay fast asleep after watching TV. The first Darlie knew of this intrusion was when she felt a knife at her throat. Her first thought was that the intruder was trying to rape her—her panties were missing—and she felt "some pressure down there."

After stabbing Darlie twice, the intruder ran off. She called 911. Both boys had been butchered, and Darlie was rushed into surgery to repair a wound that had missed the carotid artery by less than an inch. A rape test proved negative. She described her assailant as a white male, about six feet tall, wearing a black shirt, jeans, and a baseball cap.

At the house, a slashed window screen in the garage signified the intruder's apparent entry point. In a nearby alley was a sock, probably dropped as he fled. Detectives studied the scene quizzically. The crime seemed motiveless; and why kill the children and let the only witness live?

Darin, upstairs asleep with another son at the time of the attack, offered his own theory for the attack, saying his wife was a "good-looking blonde with thirty-eight-inch double D's."

Ignoring this crass remark, investigators concentrated on some puzzling anomalies. For some reason, bloodhounds—with a sense of smell two hundred times more acute than that of humans—were unable to track the scent beyond where the sock was dropped. So either the killer had vaporized, or he had backtracked to the house.

Also, there were holes in Darlie's story. She said she had chased the intruder through the kitchen, where he knocked a wineglass on the floor; but glass fragments were found *on top* of the blood drops, and Darlie's bare feet had somehow negotiated this carpet of broken glass without sustaining a single cut.

She also said the assailant had dropped the murder weapon—a ten-inch kitchen knife—by the door before fleeing through the garage. She'd then picked up the knife and placed it on a counter. This accounted for her fingerprints on the knife, but **blood spatter analysis** expert Tom Bevel could find no evidence to support the claim that the knife had been dropped on the kitchen floor. Although Darlie's blood was found on a vacuum cleaner, the spatter wasn't consistent with someone running past, as she'd claimed. All the spots were circular, which meant they were deposited by someone either standing still or walking very slowly. Running produces a different pattern, more of an elliptical shape, usually with a tail indicating the path of the person.

With the investigation narrowing its focus at every turn, investigators recalled that when Darlie was first interviewed, she was holding a wet towel to her neck wound. Was it possible she had used this to clean up the house before they arrived? To find out, they sprayed the scene with Luminol, a compound that luminesces when it comes into contact with blood—even if those traces are years old. It is so sensitive, it can detect blood at one part per million, even after a cleanup has occurred.

With the kitchen light turned off, a bloody footprint glowed bluish-green in front of the sink. Beneath the sink more blood was found, suggesting that someone had stood still while bleeding. DNA tests confirmed all the blood to be Darlie's. It was the same with all the bloody footprints—every one belonged to Darlie. And yet, on the sofa where she said she had been attacked, there was not a trace of blood.

Nothing in the house indicated the presence of an intruder.

If the blood raised doubts, then it was the taped 911 call that made a liar out of Darlie Routier. She had always insisted that she had phoned from the kitchen, and didn't enter either the living room or the garage. But Barry Dickey, a forensic audio expert, knew differently. Sound is either absorbed or reflected by the various elements in a room; generally, soft surfaces tend to soak up sound, while hard surfaces such as glass and stone bounce the sound around. By eliminating all background noise, Dickey was able to isolate Darlie's voice, the varying wavelengths of which told him that the call had come from at least three rooms. Detectives reasoned that as she sobbed out her 911 story, Darlie rushed from room to room, wiping away, or so she thought, the evidence of her misdeeds.

The clinching evidence came with the discovery of a minute glass fiber rod and some rubber dust on a bread knife found in the kitchen. When examined microscopically, the cut screen in the garage was found to be made from polyvinyl chloride (PVC) bundles, the interior core of which was composed of glass fiber rods identical to that found on the knife. And the rubber dust was consistent with having come from the cut PVC screen. This meant that whoever slashed the screen had already been inside the house.

On June 18 Darlie was charged with double murder. Background checks revealed a family in financial crisis; they were behind in their mortgage, and just days before the killings, they had been turned down for a $5,000 loan. (Coincidentally, each child had a $5,000 insurance policy on his life.) Prosecutors portrayed Darlie Routier as a premeditated killer who had acted alone and slaughtered her children for money. On February 1, 1997, she was convicted and later sentenced to death.

Stephen Scher

Date: 1976
Location: Montrose, Pennsylvania

The evening shadows were lengthening as Martin Dillon and Stephen Scher made their way back to the hunting cabin that Dillon kept just north of the small Pennsylvania town of Montrose. They had been skeet shooting and were now heading home. Suddenly Dillon spotted a porcupine. "Wait right here!" he yelled, grabbing Scher's shotgun and dashing back up the path to where a skeet firing device was sited. Moments later, Scher heard a shot. Then all fell quiet.

Scher called out and, not getting any response, went to investigate. He found Dillon slumped on the ground, by the edge of a clearing, blood pumping from a shotgun wound to the chest, caused by the very weapon he was carrying.

Being a doctor, Scher tried CPR, getting splashed with blood in the process, then realized the hopelessness of the situation and ran for help. He soon returned with a neighbor. In a theatrical and very public fit of rage, Scher grabbed his shotgun and smashed it against a tree, crying, "This gun will never kill anybody again!"

When the police saw Dillon's untied right boot lace, they figured that here was the cause of the trip and fall that led to the thirty-year-old lawyer accidentally shooting himself. The autopsy was performed the next day—June 3, 1976—by a local doctor, who noted that the wound was oval-shaped, "about 1½ inches in length and roughly 1 inch in width." He also found evidence of "powder burns." With nothing to arouse suspicion, the death was recorded as accidental.

Eager to put the tragedy behind him, Scher left Montrose and moved to North Carolina. After filing for divorce, he remarried, and this was where his problems really began, for his new bride was none other than Dillon's widow, Patricia. Even before the tragedy, local gossip had linked the two in a steamy affair; now suspicion hardened that all was not right about the death of Marty Dillon.

No one held this view more strongly than a police officer named Francis Zanin. He had shot photographs of the scene and felt it looked phony. Yes, Dillon's shoelace was undone, but the top of the boot was still pressed tightly against his shin. If he'd been running, surely the boot would have flopped open? Also, Dillon's pants were hitched up, as if he been squatting next to the skeet machine, not chasing some porcupine.

Someone else profoundly suspicious of Scher was Dillon's father, Lawrence. For more than a decade he had hounded the authorities and gotten nowhere. Then, in 1988, he hired Warren Stewart Bennett, a former police officer now working as a "forensic reconstructionist," someone who re-creates suspicious deaths, to see if he could shed any light on the mystery.

At issue was one central point: was the gun barrel touching Dillon's body when it discharged? If it was a contact wound, then Scher's story held water. If not, he might well be lying.

The barrel of Scher's 16-gauge shotgun was approximately dime-size and round; and yet the wound, according to the original autopsy report, was a gaping oval, about 1½ inches in length, with "scalloped" edges. Since scalloping is caused by the pellets fanning out after leaving the barrel, it is not customarily seen with a contact wound. To replicate the wound, Bennett stretched pigskin—chosen because it has properties similar to human skin—over a mannequin. Using the same model shotgun as the one that killed Dillon and identical ammunition, he first set the skin at contact distance, then six inches, twelve inches, and so forth.

For the gun to produce an oval, similarly sized wound to that found in Dillon's chest, Bennett had to fire at a downward angle of forty-five degrees, from a distance of between three and five feet. Add the distance to the shotgun's trigger—at least another forty inches—and it meant that Dillon would have needed arms almost *seven feet long* to shoot himself!

Despite these inconsistencies, the authorities were defiant and unmoved until 1992, when, under mounting pressure, they sent all the evidence—including Scher's boots and the tree stump, both of which had tested positive for blood in 1976—to the FBI, which passed it to the renowned forensic expert Herb MacDonell.

His results were devastating. Scher's boots, besides showing splashes of blood that had dripped from Dillon, displayed clear evidence of "blood spatter," the fine mist of droplets that sprays out when a body is struck by a bullet or pellets. This spatter placed Scher within touching distance of Dillon when he died, not one hundred feet away, as he'd claimed. Similar spatter on a tree stump standing next to the skeet machine, and on the bottom of Dillon's boot, indicated that Dillon may have been sitting on or near the stump when he was shot and not running. Finally, there was blood all over Dillon's head, and on the ear protectors found nearby, yet none on his ears, making it virtually certain that the protectors had been removed after death as Scher attempted to stage the "accident."

In 1995 Marty Dillon's body's was exhumed and reautopsied by Dr. Isidore Mihalakis. He could find no powder burns around the wound and declared this a clear case of homicide. After twenty years Scher was charged with murder. In court he finally admitted that the porcupine story had been a lie and that he and Dillon had argued over Patricia. They had fought over the shotgun, Scher said, and it discharged accidentally, killing Dillon.

The jury didn't believe a word of it, and in October 1997 Scher was convicted of murder and given life without parole. In a stunning turn of events, this verdict was overturned twenty months later, when a judge decided that the lengthy delay had tainted the evidence and violated Scher's right to a fair trial. Scher was set free. His flirtation with liberty ended in August 2002, when the Pennsylvania Supreme Court reinstated the original verdict and he was returned to prison.

John Schneeberger

Date: 1992
Location: Kipling, Canada

In the small town of Kipling, Saskatchewan, Dr. John Schneeberger was a well-liked and highly respected physician. Since migrating from his native South Africa in 1987, the thirty-one-year-old had built up a solid practice in this largely rural community, and among his roster of patients was a young woman whom Schneeberger had been treating for more than a year. In January 1992 he had even delivered her baby. But there were emotional difficulties for the woman, and she was in a highly distressed state when she called at Kipling Memorial Union Hospital on the night of October 31, 1992.

Schneeberger, solicitous as always, lay the woman down on an examination table and gave her what he described as a calming sedative shot. But the drug was far more powerful than the woman had expected, and she soon found herself sliding in and out of consciousness. During her lucid moments, she became vaguely aware of someone removing her underwear. Moments later came the horrific realization that she was being raped. Unable to fight or resist, she could only lie helpless. Eventually the light was switched off and she was left to fall asleep in the darkness. The following day, when Schneeberger made a duty call, he asked if she had had any "wild dreams" before discharging her.

Three days later she went to the police, brandishing the semen-stained panties she had worn on the night in question; evidence, or so she believed, that Schneeberger had raped her. But when tests were run, the rapist's DNA and that obtained from a sample of Schneeberger's blood were found to be totally dissimilar. Most in the closely knit community were delighted by the finding, convinced this was just one more example of an overwrought female patient bringing unsubstantiated charges against an innocent doctor. Schneeberger went back to his work, and the pace of life in Kipling resumed its normal leisurely gait.

But the woman, humiliated and furious that no one would believe her, refused to quit without a fight. In March 1996 she approached a private investigator and asked if there was any way that he could obtain another DNA sample from Schneeberger. Larry O'Brien knew that under Canadian law even evidence gleaned without a search warrant was still admissible in court, and this led him to break into Schneeberger's car, where he found an almost new Chap Stick. O'Brien carefully stroked the Chap Stick three or four times across the inside cellophane portion of a window envelope. He sealed this envelope, signed and dated it, placed it inside another envelope, and mailed off the whole packet to a DNA testing laboratory. As he'd hoped, there was enough saliva on the Chap Stick to provide a strong DNA profile, which matched that obtained from the rapist's semen, with a certainty put at 1 in 76 million.

When told of this finding, the police had no alternative but to test Schneeberger again. On November 20, 1996, he provided a second DNA sample. In the videotaped procedure the lab technician can be seen having difficulty inserting the needle into Schneeberger's left arm just below the elbow. Eventually a sample was drawn. But once Schneeberger had left the room, the technician began to express doubts about what had happened. She studied the sample quizzically. "This blood doesn't look really fresh," she said. A serologist later agreed, calling it "very dark, almost black," almost as if it had been drawn from a dead person.

The Royal Canadian Mounted Police, who by now were handling the investigation, decided that another test was called for, but before this could be performed, events took a startling turn. Schneeberger's wife came forward with accusations that he had twice sexually abused her fourteen-year-old daughter: once in 1994 and again in 1995.

This revelation forced the issue and allowed the RCMP to obtain a court order compelling Schneeberger to provide further samples, this time by cutting twenty-five strands of hair from his head, taking saliva swabs from inside his cheek with a cotton bud, and by extracting blood from the tip of a finger on his right hand.

In January 1998 the results came back from the lab: Schneeberger's DNA and that of the original rapist were a perfect match.

Arrested and charged with double rape, Schneeberger finally admitted how he had fooled the authorities for so long. Back in 1992, fearing that he might have to provide a DNA sample, he had drawn blood from an unwitting male patient, filled a five-inch-long rubber tube called a Penrose drain with this blood, then surgically inserted this tube into his arm, beside the artery. It was from this tube that the first sample was drawn.

Anticipating that a second test might be required at some point, he had removed the tube and stored the rogue blood in a refrigerator. When, four years later, he was asked to provide another sample, he went through the whole gruesome procedure again, reinserting the blood-filled tube into his left arm and keeping it there long enough for the skin to heal around the operation. Then he had given the sample as before. Unfortunately, he had failed to appreciate how much blood changes color with age and that to a trained observer his deception would be obvious.

At his trial, prosecutors claimed that Schneeberger paralyzed his victim with the powerful sedative Versed, which leaves someone unable to move or speak and which is known to cause amnesia in some people, so he might achieve sexual gratification.

Schneeberger fought back with a cynical defense, claiming that the woman patient, driven by spite because he had refused her advances, had broken into his home and stolen a used condom from the garbage. She had then smeared its contents over her panties in order to frame him. All he had done, he claimed, was to protect himself against the false allegations of an embittered woman.

Dismissing Schneeberger's claims as "inventive, fanciful, imaginative . . . preposterous," Judge Ellen Gunn sentenced the disgraced doctor to six years' imprisonment. In November 2003 Schneeberger was released from prison. The following month his citizenship was revoked, and he now faces deportation.

Serology

Next to impossible to clean up or eradicate entirely, bodily fluids come right at the top of the trace evidence pecking order, for the way in which they can link victim to suspect, and suspect to crime scene. Blood is the most plentiful, the best-known, and the most important bodily fluid. The average adult has about ten pints of the stuff gurgling through his or her system, so it's little wonder that when punctured arterially, the human body has a tendency to spray its contents like a water fountain.

Although scientists in the nineteenth century recognized that blood consisted of various types, not until 1901 did Karl Landsteiner, a Viennese immunologist, standardize the modern ABO system. By separating the serum from red blood cells in a centrifuge, then adding red blood cells from different people to the serum, he found that two distinctively different reactions occurred. In some cases the serum seemed to attract the red blood cells, but others it repelled. One lot of cells agglutinated, or clumped together; others didn't.

Landsteiner labeled these two blood types A and B, only to soon realize that there was a third type that didn't react like either A or B but that showed characteristics of both. This he called C, though it soon became more popularly known as O. One year later an assistant discovered yet another serum type that did not agglutinate with either A or B. This was labeled AB. Allowing for some racial and geographical variation, blood types are normally distributed in the population as follows:

O	A	B	AB
43–45%	40–42%	10–12%	3–5%

In the mid-1920s Landsteiner, with his colleague Philip Levine, discovered a different grouping system as a result of injecting rabbits with human blood. This produced M and N groups; a person could be either M or N, or a combination of the two, MN. Modern science has continued Landsteiner's work to the point where there are now 257 antigens and no less than 23 blood group systems based on association with these antigens.

The next great advance came in 1949, when two British scientists observed that the nuclei in cells of female tissue usually contain a distinctive structure that is rare in males. It was called the Barr Body, after one of its discoverers, and is most noticeable in white blood cells. The presence of this "female only" structure is accounted for by the differences in chromosomes between males and females.

Although initially conducted to eliminate the dangers of indiscriminate blood transfusion, Landsteiner's research, and that of his followers, has had an enormous bearing on the course of medical jurisprudence to the present day.

When confronted by a suspect stain, the serologist must ask five distinct questions:

1. Is the sample blood?
2. Is the sample animal blood?
3. If animal blood, from what species?
4. If human blood, what type?
5. Can the sex, age, and race of the source of blood be determined?

The first question is answered by employing color or crystalline tests. Benzidine, a colorless, crystalline solid, practically insoluble in water, was popular for a while, until its toxicity—it can cause dermatitis and bladder tumors—was discovered. It was replaced by the Kastle-Meyer test, which uses the chemical phenolphthalein. When it comes in contact with hemoglobin (and sometimes other organic matter), phenolphthalein turns the sample a bright pink color. By contrast, a similar test, using the chemical orthotolodine, produces a vivid blue color in the sample. Even stains invisible to the naked eye cannot escape detection. For this there is Luminol, a chemical that when sprayed on walls, floors, and furniture reveals a slight phosphorescent light in the dark where bloodstains (and certain other stains) are present.

To answer questions 2 and 3, forensic scientists use antiserum or gel tests. The standard test—called the precipitin test—involves injecting an animal (usually a rabbit) with human blood. The rabbit's body creates antihuman antibodies, which are then extracted from the rabbit's serum. If this antiserum creates clotting, you know the sample is human.

The answer to question 4 depends on the sample being both adequate and of sufficient quality. If so, direct typing using the ABO system is done.

Indirect typing would have to be done on severely dried stains, and the most common technique is the absorption-elution test. This is performed by adding compatible antiserum antibodies to a sample, heating the sample to break the antibody-antigen bonds, then adding known red cells from standard blood groups to see what coagulates.

Question 5 is the most contentious. Various color and nitrate tests as well as heredity principles are used to estimate variables such as age, sex, and race. While no exact determinations are possible, clotting and crystallization help estimate age; chromosome testing may help to determine sex (75 percent of males have a Y chromosome in their red blood cells); and certain racial genetic markers involving protein and enzyme tests can help determine race within certain very broad limits, though this procedure is the subject that has attracted great controversy.

Blood at the crime scene can be in the form of pools, drops, smears, or crusts. Of these, wet blood has the most evidentiary value because more tests can be run. For example, alcohol and drug content can be determined from wet blood only. Blood begins to dry after three to five minutes of exposure to air, and as it dries, it changes color toward brown and black.

Besides blood, forensic serologists analyze semen, saliva, and all other bodily fluids. Such diversity inevitably leads them into the associated discipline of **DNA typing,** and occasionally **blood spatter analysis** as well, though this has tended to become more of an independent specialty.

Roger Severs

Date: 1993
Location: Hambleton, England

When Derek Severs and his wife, Eileen, went missing in late 1993, other residents in the small Leicestershire village of Hambleton, where they lived, soon became worried. It wasn't like the sixty-eight-year-old retired executive to just go off and leave their home, nor was Eileen the type to abandon the charitable work that had formed such an important part of her life. They'd last been seen on Saturday, November 13. Eileen had spent the morning helping out at a church bazaar, until lunchtime, when she went home. Derek had left his local pub at around 3:30 P.M., also homeward bound.

On the following Thursday police made a routine call at the family residence. They were greeted by Roger Severs, the couple's only son, and a source of constant worry to his parents. On the rebound from a disastrous relationship with a woman who had borne his child, he couldn't hold down a job, and at age thirty-seven still relied on handouts from his wealthy parents. He breezily explained that his parents had decided to spend some time in London and that he was expecting them back soon. A cursory search of the house—it was nighttime—revealed nothing out of the ordinary. Still, this didn't satisfy the neighbors, whose relentless pressure prompted a second police visit, this time in daylight.

In the bathroom, on the side of the tub, they found traces of blood, and a large number of green fibers in the hallway. Similar fibers cropped up in the trunk of Derek's car—which was still at the house—and on a pair of pants that Roger wore. What made these fibers especially significant was that they had not come from inside the house. There was more blood on the backseat of Derek's car, together with signs of blood spatter on the inside of the garage door.

With the benefit of daylight to assist them, officers now saw that the back garden showed signs of having been dug recently and that there had been a fire. Scans with ground penetrating radar failed to uncover anything suspicious, but the fire did betray traces of carpet and clothing. The search radiated outward from the house, into some woodland, even to a large nearby reservoir. Divers and sonar combed the murky depths, all to no avail.

These events jogged memories. Prior to the missing persons report being filed, a police officer had seen a man whom he now realized matched Roger Severs's description in a local wooded area after dark. When questioned, the man claimed he was collecting leaf mold for his garden. A search of this area did uncover a towel—stained with blood—that matched other towels at the Severs residence, but nothing more.

The critical breakthrough came when a detective, studying case photos, noticed something odd: the family car showed traces of a light mud, unusual in this area. Dr. Tony Brown, geologist, was asked to examine the vehicle. He scraped mud and debris from all four wheel arches. The mix of soil and vegetation included moss, leaves, and grass, which together suggested a shade/light combination he thought most likely to occur either on the edge of woodland, or in a small clearing. There also was a small quantity of fishing line, hinting at an area where anglers parked.

Of greater significance was the fact that he found more than twenty different types of pollen among the debris. Because of their remarkably symmetrical structure and surface patterns, pollen grains are readily recognizable under the microscope, and their high resistance to decay makes them first-class items of evidence.

Brown needed to isolate the microscopic pollen granules, and he achieved this through a process of filtration, then by soaking the sludge with hydrofluoric acid. This washed away the mud and left just pollen. Most of the pollens were of common types—oak, elm, and hawthorn—but he found one that initially defied analysis. After hours spent rummaging through numerous reference books, he found it—horse chestnut, an exceptionally rare tree in this part of the English countryside.

Because horse chestnut pollen is very heavy, it tends to fall straight to ground, rather than being borne on the wind; therefore its incidence is highest closest to the tree. Since there was horse chestnut pollen in all four wheel arches, Brown reasoned that at some time recently the car had been parked very close to such a tree.

Using local maps, Brown was able to identify five possible locations where this horse chestnut pollen might be found. A search of the first area, closest to the house, proved fruitless, but the second zone, in Armley Woods by the reservoir, paid off when a policeman prodding the ground with a stick, suddenly found little resistance. After three weeks, the bodies of Derek and Eileen Severs had been found.

Both had been bludgeoned to death. Now they lay, side by side, wrapped in a green blanket—the same green blanket that had left those telltale fibers in the house and car. Analysis of leaves piled on top of the bodies showed them to be from the wooded region where Roger Severs had been seen, while roof tiles from a batch found at the Severs's house had been used to shore up the sides of the grave.

Police speculated that after a day spent drinking at numerous pubs, Severs, enraged by his parents' refusal to keep on bailing him out financially, went to the house and attacked his mother in the bathroom, fracturing her skull with eight blows. He wrapped her body in the green blanket and carried it to the kitchen, then lay in wait for his father, battering him to death in the garage. After binding his father's body with belts and string, he placed it on the backseat of the car, stuffing his mother into the trunk.

At his trial, Severs admitted killing his parents with a wooden steak mallet but pleaded diminished responsibility. On December 6, 1994, the jury rejected this defense and found him guilty of murder.

Keith Simpson (1907–1985)

No forensic pathologist in history has performed more autopsies than British-born Keith Simpson. As early as 1966 he brought gasps to the Steven Truscott review tribunal (see *A Question of Evidence,* Wiley, 2003) by modestly putting the number at one hundred thousand, and he was to remain in harness for another seventeen years. Such experience gave him unrivaled authority on the international stage. The breadth and depth of his knowledge were outstanding. He was a pioneer in the field of odontology and one of the first to recognize "battered baby syndrome," but it was in the antiseptic tranquillity of the mortuary where Simpson ruled supreme.

Born on the south coast of England, where he attended Brighton and Hove Grammar School, he bypassed university entirely and, at age seventeen, went straight to Guy's Hospital Medical School in London, the institution that would provide the backbone of his professional life. After a glittering studentship during which he won five major prizes including two gold medals, he graduated in 1930 and was immediately appointed to a teaching post.

Oddly enough, it was squeamishness that steered Simpson into pathology. He found the often ghastly ailments that afflict the living, especially the young, too upsetting to countenance, and far preferred patients whom he could, as he said, "put back into the refrigerator . . . if their illness is perplexing."

Throughout the 1930s Simpson gradually eased himself into forensic pathology. Most of the prize plums still fell in the lap of the chief Home Office pathologist **Sir Bernard Spilsbury,** but Simpson's reputation prospered. During World War II he performed literally thousands of autopsies on victims of German bombing, and then, in 1947, following Spilsbury's death, Simpson finally stepped out of the shadows and into the media spotlight.

Though he would never achieve the public acclaim of his illustrious predecessor, Simpson's standing among the police and the courts was second to none. Juries approved of his clear explanations, delivered without any hint of condescension, and the way in which he was always willing to admit to any gaps in his knowledge. More than once in his career he would look up from the corpse he was dissecting, shake his head, and frankly admit that he had no idea what had caused death. After the self-assumed omnipotence that had tarnished Spilsbury's later years, such modesty was as healthy as it was welcome.

Besides teaching at Guy's, he also passed on his knowledge in a string of textbooks that are models of lucidity and scholarship. He was a member of the Société de Médicine Légale and of the American Academy of Forensic Sciences. **Milton Helpern** called him "the doyen of British legal medicine." Few would disagree.

Significant Cases

1942	Harry Dobkin
1942	Samuel Dashwood and George Silverosa
1942	Bertie Manton
1943	Harold Loughans
1944	Arthur Heys
1946	Neville Heath
1946	Sidney Sinclair
1946	Thomas Ley and Lawrence Smith
1947	Joe Smith
1949	John Haigh*
1949	Margaret Williams
1949	Frederick Radford
1953	John Armstrong
1957	Gordon Hay
1960	Arthur Jones
1961	James Hanratty*

1964	William Brittle
1966	Steven Truscott
1966	Kray Brothers
1972	Abdul Malik (Michael "X")
1982	Roberto Calvi

*Profiled in this book.

Paula Sims

Date: 1989
Location: Alton, Illinois

As Paula Sims was carrying out the garbage at ten-thirty on an April night in 1989, a gun-carrying assailant in dark clothes and a ski mask forced her back into the house. Once in the kitchen, she was felled by a blow to the back of the neck; then everything went black. She was still unconscious when her husband, Robert, arrived home just after 11:00 P.M. After rousing his wife, he searched the house and found that their six-week-old baby, Heather, was missing.

Detectives summoned to the house in Alton, Illinois, were immediately suspicious. For someone who'd been unconscious for forty-five minutes, Paula seemed remarkably unscathed and very lucid. Also, there was no sign of an intruder, nothing had been taken, the area around Heather's bassinet was eerily tidy, and there seemed to be no reason why anyone would want to kidnap the child of a family so patently unable to pay a ransom.

Right: The roll of garbage bags found in Paula Sims' house. *Facing page:* Analysis of die lines in the plastic showed that the garbage bag used to wrap the body of Heather Sims matched the roll of bags found in her mother's kitchen.

90509026 K-4
FBI
LABORATORY

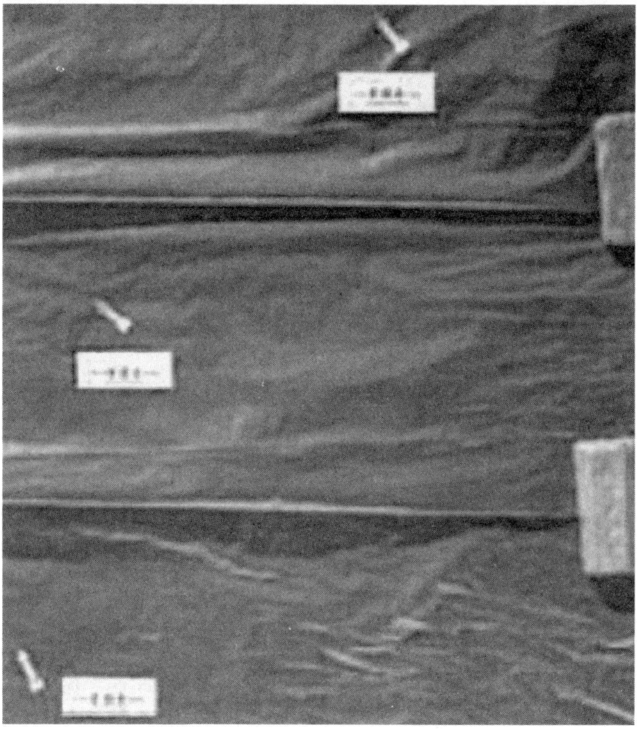

The following Wednesday, a man fishing the Mississippi River, some two miles away, paused to drop some garbage into a trash can. Noticing a large, black plastic bag, he looked more closely. One peek inside left him little doubt that he'd found Heather Sims.

When Detective Mick Dooley studied the well-preserved remains, his first instinct was that Heather had been killed recently; but he then noticed that lividity, which usually becomes fixed some eight to twelve hours after death, was on the front of the face, and Heather was found lying on her back. And there was a bright red mark on the baby's cheek, such as might be caused by freezer burn. His immediate conclusion was that whoever had killed Heather had first stored the body in a freezer, then dumped it in the garbage can shortly before its discovery.

The medical examiner Dr. Mary Case confirmed Dooley's suspicions about the freezing, adding that abrasions inside the mouth were consistent with Heather having been suffocated. What was an already bizarre case assumed surreal proportions with the astonishing revelation that Paula Sims had gone through all this before.

Almost three years earlier, on June 17, 1986, while living in nearby Jersey County and while Robert was at work, Paula claimed that a masked intruder had broken into her house at gunpoint and snatched her twelve-day-old baby, Loralei. One week later the baby's skeletal remains were found in a thicket behind the Sims's residence. Despite deep official misgivings, the indeterminate cause of death made it impossible to make a case against Paula, so no charges were leveled.

Was it possible that some phantom kidnapper was targeting the Sims family and that lightning really had struck twice? Mary Case didn't think so for one minute. Besides being a medical examiner, she was also a specialist in neuropathology and understood the effects of head trauma on the nervous system. A blow hard enough to render Paula unconscious for almost an hour would cause the brain to collide with the skull. Such an injury generally destroys all memory of the incident, yet Paula claimed to have a clear recollection of all details of the attack. This didn't make sense.

As detectives probed the relationship between Paula and her husband, they uncovered some deeply disturbing facts. They suspected that Paula had killed Heather to regain the sexual affections of a man who loathed daughters. Twice Paula had come back from the maternity hospital with a little girl, and on each occasion Robert had banished her from the marital bedroom, forcing her to sleep with the infant. Only when the baby was dead was Paula welcomed back into his bed.

The police believed that Paula suffocated the baby, drove across town to her parents' house, knowing they were away that weekend, and stored the baby in their freezer. Afterward, she had returned to the house and faked the incident. The following day, once the police had finished searching her house, she had retrieved the baby from her parents' freezer and kept it in her own basement freezer until that Wednesday, when she had made the two-mile drive to the parking lot and dumped the frozen body.

All this was, of course, conjecture. There was still nothing concrete to connect Paula to the murder of her daughter until detectives noticed a roll of black Curb Side garbage bags in Paula's kitchen.

They were manufactured by Poly Tech, Inc., in Minneapolis for Kmart, and in make, size, and color the bags were identical to that found with the body. When FBI agents learned that Poly Tech made more than a million such bags every day for Kmart, they wondered if there were any characteristics that might identify different batches. Because of the stretching that occurs in tearing off each bag, the cut edges were unsuitable for this purpose; however, the heat-seal process used during manufacturing did offer possibilities.

Garbage bags are made from huge sheets of melted plastic that pass over rollers. In one procedure a blade makes the perforations that enable the bags to be ripped from the end of the roll; elsewhere on the production line, a heat seal melts the bottom of the bag and seals it tightly. With millions of feet of plastic processed daily comes an inevitable buildup of debris on the heat seal, thus ensuring that, while bags made within seconds of each other are microscopically similar, bags made at either end of the working day will display markedly different heat-seal characteristics.

Heather's bag had a slight puncture hole caused by roller debris and a tiny opening on the heat seal where the plastic had not melted thoroughly. When compared microscopically, the bags in Paula's kitchen displayed identical flaws, leading the FBI to calculate that the bags were made within ten seconds of one another.

To narrow the time frame even farther, agents examined yet another characteristic that accrues when plastic is pulled over production line rollers. A very slight stretching occurs, leaving marks that are called die lines. When the die lines on Heather's bag were compared with the next bag on the roll in the Sims's kitchen—much like the way in which ballistics experts compare the striations on bullets—they matched exactly.

Such evidence was sufficient for a jury to find Paula Sims guilty of murder. Following her conviction, she admitted that she also had killed Loralei.

Udham Singh

Date: 1940
Location: London, England

There was no real mystery about who assassinated Sir Michael O'Dwyer. On March 13, 1940, the former diplomat was just one of several notables who had gathered for a public meeting at Caxton Town Hall in the heart of London, when a gunman of Asian appearance leaped onto the platform and opened fire, hitting several of those present. As O'Dywer fell to the ground mortally wounded, his killer was quickly subdued and arrested. What baffled the authorities, however, were three questions:

1. Why had the killer taken such murderous action?
2. What was the killer's real name?
3. Last and most puzzling of all: how was it possible that so many people could be shot at point-blank range and survive?

For the answer to the first question, it was necessary to go back twenty-one years, to April 13, 1919, when British troops sent to put down an uprising in the Punjab town of Amritsar, opened fire on a crowd of about 10,000 unarmed Indian protesters. In a few bloody minutes an estimated 379 people were slaughtered, with a further 1,000 seriously injured. The shooting was followed by the proclamation of martial law, public floggings, and other humiliations.

In Britain, news of the massacre caused an outrage, with most of the condemnation being directed toward the commanding officer, Brigadier General Reginald Dyer. But in India, blame for the Amritsar Massacre was laid squarely at the door of another man, Punjab's lieutenant governor at the time: Sir Michael O'Dwyer. Vows of revenge were sworn. But for more than two decades, O'Dwyer had been untroubled by the events of his past—until he attended a meeting of the East India Association and the Royal Central Asiatic Society at Caxton Town Hall.

The gunman was an enigma. He gave his name as Singh Azad, but an exhaustive police inquiry revealed him to be Udham Singh, a forty-year-old Bolshevik from the Amritsar region who'd served prison time in his home country. As early as 1927, Singh was on record for having threatened to murder the imperialist Europeans who ruled India. Now he had made good on that threat.

For the ballistics expert **Robert Churchill,** the case was one of the most intriguing of his career. The circumstances of the assassination might have been plucked from the pages of a mystery novel. Singh had leaped onto the platform as the meeting broke up and emptied all six rounds from his revolver at a group of men gathered around O'Dwyer. These included Lord Zetland, then secretary of state for India; Lord Lamington; and Sir Louis Dane.

Singh had fired twice at O'Dwyer, hitting him in the back. Zetland, too, was struck by two bullets; Dane and Lamington were each hit once. Yet, apart from O'Dwyer, the other three men were astonished to find that all of the bullets had bounced off their bodies and then fallen at their feet. What made the incident doubly fantastic was the fact that each man had been fewer than *eighteen inches* from the assassin when the shots were fired!

Churchill was asked to explain how this could have happened. His first thought was that the powder charge in the cartridges had been deliberately reduced, perhaps by as much as three-quarters, to diminish the penetrative force of the bullets. This could have a twofold impact. On the one hand, it suited defense claims that the whole incident had been more of a publicity stunt than an assassination attempt: Singh hadn't meant to kill anyone, just make a point. On the other hand, professional killers often tend to prefer low-powered weapons that leave the bullet inside the victim rather than careering on.

In the event, neither solution was an option: the cartridges had plenty of powder. Churchill needed to look elsewhere. He eventually told the jury at Singh's trial how the "impossible" had happened. The weapon, he explained, was an American six-chambered Smith & Wesson, .455 caliber, made for the British government in World War I. After the armistice, thousands of these weapons passed into private hands as war relics, and few were ever used again. Although poorly maintained, this particular revolver was in reasonable working order. When Churchill examined the bullets recovered from the crime scene, he found something unusual: they were smaller in size than the barrel of the gun. The ammunition—.40 caliber—was very uncommon in England, loaded with black powder and a pure lead bullet. Churchill reckoned it was thirty years old at least.

He testified that these cartridges formed such a loose fit in the chamber of the revolver, that when one was fired it would wobble its way along the barrel without engaging the rifling grooves. This sloppy fit allowed the propellant gases to escape around both the case and the bullet to such a degree that accuracy and penetration were wholly unpredictable.

One bullet, which had hit Lord Zetland over the heart, appeared to have cartwheeled through the air, penetrated ten thicknesses of handkerchief in his breast pocket, holed his shirt and undershirt with a sideways hit, and then dropped to the ground. Sir Louis Dane's jacket had a bullet hole in the right sleeve, but the projectile penetrated only the cloth, leaving him with a broken arm. Lamington suffered a superficial injury to his right wrist. According to Churchill, it was "just rank bad luck that O'Dwyer caught one which flew straight and hard."

Churchill's finding sealed Singh's fate. He went to the gallows on July 31, 1941, bemoaning the fact that he had only killed one person.* For Zetland, Lamington, and Dane, it had been a tremendously lucky escape. Few have survived a well-aimed bullet at such close range. For three people to do so without sustaining anything more than minor injuries almost defies belief.

*In 1975, at the Indian government's request, Udham Singh's remains were returned to his homeland.

Tevfik Sivri

Date: 1988
Location: Meriden, Connecticut

Sometime on the morning of April 18, 1988, Carla Almeida, a twenty-two-year-old masseuse who lived in Meriden, Connecticut, got a call from the escort agency that employed her, saying that a one-hour appointment had been booked at midday with a client who lived in Trumbull, about thirty miles away. When she failed to return by four o'clock that afternoon, concerns at the agency mounted. Eventually they phoned the client, Tevfik Sivri, who claimed that Carla had shown up as arranged, stayed the allotted time, then left. He professed ignorance of her present whereabouts.

When the police were eventually informed of Carla's disappearance, they obtained a search warrant for Sivri's home. The twenty-nine-year-old house painter repeated his earlier insistence that he had not see Carla since the appointment, and a search of his home seemed to support his claim that nothing untoward had happened. Nothing was out of place, nothing suggested any evidence of foul play. For ten hours the police searched the house from top to bottom, all to no avail. But there was something in Tevfik's manner that aroused suspicion, enough for investigators to request the assistance of **Henry Lee,** director of the state's crime laboratory, and one of the country's top criminalists.

There was just one problem: Lee was in Washington, D.C., giving one of his many lectures. When contacted by phone, he listened to what the officers had to say and agreed to return that same night. From the airport he was whisked to Sivri's home. Like the other investigators, he, too, was struck by its immaculate tidiness. In fact, he thought it looked suspiciously clean. Working his way slowly though the house room by room, searching for anything that might be a clue, he tried to compile a mental picture of what might have happened, only to be thwarted at every turn. Like the officers before him, he found the uncanny tidiness a difficult hurdle to overcome. And then he reached the basement. Instantly he bent down and examined the carpet, then looked up at the detectives. "Put your cheek against the carpet," he said. It was a strange request, but all of the officers complied. Only now did they realize that it was damp. Someone had gone to a great deal of time and trouble to shampoo the carpet thoroughly.

Lee ran a filter paper across the carpet's pile, then applied a solution of orthotolodine to test for blood. As he suspected, the paper turned a brilliant blue color, a sure indication of blood. The carpet was cut away, and beneath the padding, a large pool of blood could be seen clearly.

Proving that this blood belonged to Carla Almeida was straightforward—DNA comparisons with samples provided by her parents left no doubt on this matter—but what Lee needed to know was whether the amount of blood present in the basement was sufficient for him to prove that Carla was dead.

Some years previously, in 1979, he had published a paper that dealt with this very subject. In it, he presented a formula for estimating the volume of blood loss from quantities present at a crime scene. Applying those calculations to the blood found in Tevfik's basement, Lee estimated that approximately two liters—or roughly one-third the average human blood volume—had been spilled. For a woman of Carla's size and age such a catastrophic blood loss, in what had obviously been a very short period of time, would result in certain death.

Tevfik, meanwhile, remained uncommunicative, even when a spot of Carla's blood was found in the trunk of his car. His reticence meant that prosecutors were trapped in a dilemma. Like the investigators, they believed that Tevfik had murdered Carla, but they were uneasy about going to trial. Proving murder without a body is always fraught with danger. And these were the very early days of **DNA typing;** not everyone was convinced by the new technology.

It was January 1992 before the state felt confident enough to take this case before a jury. After much deliberation, Judge Joseph T. Gormley ruled that the testing procedures used by the DNA laboratory concerned were reliable and admissible. This was a tremendous breakthrough. In what was Connecticut's first murder trial to rely almost exclusively on DNA evidence, the assistant state attorney Jonathan Benedict made an overwhelming case in favor of homicide having occurred, while Lee amplified on his previously expressed opinion that no one could lose that much blood, so quickly, and survive. By contrast, the defense argued that without a body it was impossible to prove that Carla Almeida was dead. In the end, the jury agreed with the state. They convicted Sivri of murder, and he was subsequently sentenced to life imprisonment.

Unsurprisingly in such a contentious case, the legal wrangling continued, and in August 1994 the state Supreme Court overturned the guilty verdict on grounds that the judge had misdirected the jury. A new trial was ordered. It began in June 1995. This time, however, there was one fundamental difference: the body of Carla Almeida had been found.

Just six months after Tevfik's original conviction, skeletal remains were discovered at a Christmas tree farm on Route 111 in Monroe, fewer than ten miles north of where Carla had last been seen. The skull showed evidence of a single bullet hole. Once again, DNA profiling provided the identification. Samples taken from the long bones matched samples from Carla's parents.

At the second trial, all doubt was removed. After just four and a half hours of deliberation, the jury convicted Sivri of murder and he was again sentenced to life.

Dennis Smalley

Date: 1991
Location: Lincoln, England

There seemed to be no earthly reason why anyone would have wanted to kill Fred Maltby. The reclusive seventy-five-year-old lived alone in a small farmhouse on the outskirts of Lincoln, and there he was found on October 2, 1991, slumped in his favorite armchair, his head crushed by four pulverizing blows. With no sign of a break-in and nothing of any great value having been taken, the only clue was a bloodstain on the sofa, which showed the clear silhouette of an ax, made apparently by the killer laying the murder weapon down briefly before taking it with him when he left. The senselessness of it all initially hampered attempts to solve this crime.

Four months later, the normally peaceful city of Lincoln was shaken by yet another brutal ax murder. This time the victim was a sixty-year-old bookmaker named Joe Rylatt, found lifeless on the floor of his betting shop with the same ugly pattern of jagged wounds to his head. The door of his safe hung open, and it was later estimated that more than £3,000 (about $5,550 in 1992) was missing.

Rylatt was a dubious character in more ways than one. Besides being a serial womanizer—in itself a possible motive for some jealous attack—he supplemented his bookmaking income by acting as a fence for local thieves. A roundup of local burglars failed to find anyone prepared to admit to a grudge against the dead man. Even the discovery that Rylatt had also been running a lucrative loan-sharking business produced no obvious suspects.

Just about the only clue came from the wounds in Rylatt's scalp. Embedded in his brain were traces of a mysterious gray substance left by the ax as it performed its murderous work. Experts at the British Paint Research Foundation (BPRF) in southwest London confirmed that it was paint, but nothing like they had seen before. Once again the Lincoln ax murderer had apparently defeated his pursuers.

And then a few months later, some locals out boating on a nearby lake happened to moor at a small island. There, half hidden in the undergrowth, lay an ax. Recalling the double murders, they took their find to the police.

Not only did the ax display traces of Rylatt's blood, but also there was that distinctive gray color. Detectives theorized that this was the ax that also killed Maltby, and that after that murder, the killer had painted over the bloodstains in a failed attempt to conceal them. Visual confirmation that this ax was a dual murder weapon came from a reappraisal of the bloodstained sofa. This showed that the murder weapon had been placed on the cushion twice, then moved in a wiping motion. An outline of the ax, drawn onto paper and also positioned twice on the sofa, overlay this stain exactly.

Even with a larger paint sample to analyze, the BPRF was still unable to positively identify the paint, other than to say it was extremely unusual in that its zinc base had come from reconstituted zinc rather than from new. What they could identify was the binding agent used to hold the paint together—Epoxyester D4. This was traced to a factory in Essen, Germany. From there, the company's distribution lines were tracked to paint manufacturers right across Europe—to Germany, France, Belgium, and Holland. At each stop, detectives asked the same two questions: Do you use this binding agent in a paint that has reconstituted zinc? And do you export it to Britain?

After months of arduous and frustrating investigation, they finally struck lucky in Roosendaal, Holland, at a factory that manufactured Rust-Oleum 2165. A single shipment had been sent to Britain. The importing agents checked their records and found only one customer in the Lincoln area, a building supplier named Hykeham Forum on the outskirts of the city.

Of the thirty-six cans that Hykeham Forum had ordered, twelve were still on the shelves; the remainder had been sold to a company next door. When that company's employee list was checked, the name of Dennis Smalley, a forty-nine-year-old welder, stood out, as someone who had been known to borrow money from Joe Rylatt.

Smalley's arrogant manner when interviewed at the time of Rylatt's death had irked police, but as he appeared to have a rock-solid alibi—babysitting while his wife was out at work—he was crossed off the list of suspects. Now, further digging uncovered another connection: Smalley had once worked part-time for Fred Maltby.

A search of Smalley's house and garage revealed three cans of Rust-Oleum 2165 paint that he had stolen from work. It was also learned that at the time of the Rylatt murder, Smalley was heavily in debt, with collectors pushing hard; yet just days later he was able to pay £2,000 (about $3,700 in 1992) into a savings account. The circumstantial evidence was damning, but still there was the problem of his alibi.

That was exploded by a neighbor. Following Smalley's arrest, she came forward to say that, worried by his habit of going out at night and leaving his young children, she had kept a log of his nocturnal movements. On the night Rylatt died, Smalley left home at 8:05 P.M. and returned at 9:50 P.M. As Rylatt was known to have been murdered between 8:30 P.M. and 10:00 P.M, Smalley's alibi was in shreds.

Almost a year after the death of Joe Rylatt, Smalley was finally charged with double murder. He had gone to Maltby's house in hopes of stealing some of the £250,000 (about $440,000 in 1991), that the old man had allegedly pocketed after selling a piece of farmland, only to find that the rumors were untrue and that Maltby had not sold any land at all. Had Smalley not painted the ax to cover the bloodstains and left those telltale gray fragments in Rylatt's brain, he would most likely have evaded justice. As it was, this misjudgment cost him a life sentence.

Sir Sydney Smith (1883–1969)

From the abundance of outstanding forensic experts who emerged in the first half of the twentieth century, Sydney Smith has strong claims to be regarded as the greatest of them all. Certainly he was the most versatile. The fund of knowledge that this globetrotting New Zealander acquired in more than forty years of crime-solving gave him unparalleled insights into the catastrophes that can befall the human body. Not only were his diagnostic skills absolutely first-rate, but also his contributions to **toxicology, microscopy,** and particularly **ballistics** were more than enough to earn him a place at the very pinnacle of forensic science. Such all-round brilliance did not go unrecognized: law enforcement agencies on four continents had good reason to be grateful for the assistance they received from Smith in their attempts to solve baffling crimes.

As a teenager on New Zealand's South Island, he studied pharmacy in the small town of Roxburgh, and there he might have remained had it not been for a speculative boom in local gold mining stocks. Fortunes were being made overnight. Although not a gambler by instinct, Smith took the plunge, and just like that other great forensic pioneer **Edward O. Heinrich** he got lucky in the market, soon accumulating enough money to put himself through college, where he gained a medical degree. Restless and ambitious, in 1908 he journeyed halfway around the world to Scotland and the University of Edinburgh, where he continued his studies. His intention after graduating in 1912 was a research scholarship in ophthalmology; instead, almost by accident, he fell under the spell of Professor Harvey Littlejohn.

Nowhere in the world at this time was forensic medicine taken more seriously or taught with more panache than in Scotland. Littlejohn, right in the vanguard of this movement, needed an assistant and offered the post to Smith. In something of a blur, Smith accepted.

His early brilliance in a string of difficult cases marked him out as a man with a future and in 1917 he accepted the position of principal medico-legal expert to the Egyptian Ministry of Justice. (He later founded the chair in forensic science at the University of Cairo and became its first professor.)

These were tempestuous times in the Middle East, and political conflicts were often settled in lethal fashion. Since a high percentage of these killings involved the use of firearms, it gave Smith an unprecedented opportunity to study the effect of bullets on the human body, a pursuit that eventually led to him being regarded as one of the world's great authorities on gunshot wounds and firearms.

Sir Sydney Smith, the brilliant New Zealand–born pathologist who solved crimes on four continents.

Being so far removed from the academic and scientific mainstream meant that Smith was forced to improvise much of his own equipment. Earlier than most, he became fascinated by the possibilities of bullet identification, and to this end he made a rudimentary attempt to construct a comparison microscope, only to learn that the American ballistics pioneers Philip Gravelle and Calvin Goddard had beaten him to it. Never one to bear a grudge, Smith appreciated the superiority of the Gravelle/Goddard design and wasted no time in acquiring one of their instruments.

Unusual for this period, Smith was not afraid to ruffle official feathers. Even though he worked for the Egyptian government, he twice pointed the finger of blame at his embarrassed employers over their blatant misreporting of certain crowd disturbances. In one instance he discovered that several locals killed in a riot had been shot with square-tipped bullets of a kind issued only to the Ghaffirs, an irregular force attached to the police. Then, sometime later, rioters in Alexandria were gunned down by British army-type .303 bullets, which were peculiarly distinctive. On both occasions the facts had been buried beneath an official cover-up. Smith was furious. His reports suffered a similar fate, but that didn't prevent him collating information and fulminating over these injustices.

The eleven years that Smith spent in Egypt were among the most productive and rewarding of his life, and ended only with the death of Littlejohn in 1927. Smith returned to Edinburgh to take up the vacant chair at his old university, a position he held for the next twenty-six years.

During this period he figured prominently in some of the most notorious murder trials of the age, always giving his evidence fairly, always ready to fight for the underdog. Evenhandedness was the watchword. Early on, he became uncomfortable with the oppressive cult of personality that had sprung up about his great contemporary from south of the border, **Sir Bernard Spilsbury.** Smith abhorred the way in which juries blithely accepted Spilsbury's testimony as canonical truth, and he never shirked from tackling the great man in court. The two clashed often, with honors about even. Spilsbury didn't approve of such impudence. A notoriously bad loser, he refused, after one stinging defeat, to even talk to Smith.

Unlike some of his contemporaries, Smith was no empire-builder. He had an unquenchable enthusiasm for his job, and a genuine delight in sharing whatever knowledge he gleaned with his many pupils. In 1925 he published his groundbreaking *Textbook of Forensic Medicine,* which with its lavish illustrations and controversial insistence that ballistics should be treated as a science would go on through several printings to become the greatest authority in its field.

In 1947 Smith was knighted for his services to forensic medicine, and he retired from the chair at Edinburgh University six years later. According to **Keith Simpson,** "No expert in the art of medical detection has ever enjoyed the respect and affection of his fellow pathologists as Sydney Smith did, and few can have extracted so much fun from a macabre profession." It was a fitting epitaph for a quite remarkable man.

Significant Cases

1913	Patrick Higgins
1924	Sir Lee Stack*
1926	Donald Merrett
1929	Sidney Fox
1930	Annie Hearn
1931	Peter Queen
1934	Jeannie Donald
1935	Patrick Brady
1935	Buck Ruxton
1938	Johnny Ramensky
1952	Regina v. Sathasivam
1954	James Wilson

*Profiled in this book.

Clyde Snow (1928–)

Born in Texas, the man who would go on to become the world's foremost forensic anthropologist had his first encounter with skeletons at age twelve on a hunting trip, when his father, a doctor, helped identify some mysterious bones as belonging to a man who had been missing for some years.

There was little in Clyde Snow's youth to suggest the triumphs to come. Kicked out of high school in his sophomore year, he struggled at the New Mexico Military Institute in Roswell before flunking out of Southern Methodist University in Dallas. Eventually the wildness subsided enough for him to earn a master's in zoology from Texas Technical University. After a spell in the U.S. Air Force Medical Service Corps at the Histopathology Center, he enrolled at the University of Arizona in 1958 to study archaeology. He later switched to anthropology, and received his Ph.D., studying the growth of Savannah baboons.

One of his first jobs was at the Federal Aviation Administration, where he investigated airplane crash fatalities. His greatest challenge was the May 1979 crash of American Flight 191 in Chicago. Using a handheld computer to record such data as height, weight, racial characteristics, dental work, previous injuries, signs of disease, right- or left-handedness, jewelry, and clothing worn, Snow was able to compare his database to the passenger manifests and details supplied by relatives. This allowed him to identify 234 of the 273 victims. (Astonishingly, no fewer than 10 victims were identified from previous gunshot wounds!)

An earlier success in the Elmer McCurdy case had helped raise his profile beyond the world of aviation, increasing demands on his time as a forensic anthropologist, which in turn fueled his restlessness. Temperamentally unsuited to the demands of a rigid bureaucracy—some of his internal memos at the FAA achieved legendary status—in 1979 he left the organization to focus solely on forensics and teaching.

In recent years he has applied himself to the area of human rights abuses. "Of all the forms of murder," he says, "none is more monstrous than that committed by a state against its own citizens." Investigation of suspected atrocities has taken him to South America, Africa, and Europe.

Much of this work involves searching for reputed mass graves. Before excavations begin, preparatory work has to be done to determine the actual size of the grave, soil density, and hardness. A typical method used to search for bodies is to take a T-shaped steel probe, thrust it into the ground, then remove it to smell for the telltale odor of decaying flesh. Since the positioning of bodies provides numerous clues that can reveal a number of factors in the deaths, it is important to dig slowly.

Snow prefers to call his work "osteobiography," saying, "There is a brief but very useful and informative biography of an individual contained within the skeleton, if you know how to read it."

Significant Cases

1976	Elmer McCurdy*
1978	John Wayne Gacy
1979	Chicago DC-10 crash
1984	Argentina "missing"
1985	Josef Mengele
1993	Vukovar Massacre excavation
1995	Oklahoma City bombing

*Profiled in this book.

Timothy Spencer

Date: 1984
Location: Arlington, Virginia

When Susan Tucker was found strangled inside her Arlington condominium on December 1, 1987, something about the way she had been hogtied with rope resurrected memories of an eerily similar murder that had occurred just four blocks away a few years earlier. In January 1984 Washington lawyer Caroline Hamm also had been strangled and bound with rope by someone who had broken into her bedroom. On that occasion the case had been solved with a minimum of fuss or delay. David Vasquez, a borderline mental defective seen nearby at the time, was taken into custody, interrogated, and soon confessed. To escape the death penalty, he had pleaded guilty to second-degree homicide and burglary. In return he received a thirty-five-year prison term that he was still serving. Concerns now surfaced that Vasquez had operated with an accomplice and that this killer was still on the loose.

One hundred miles to the south, police in Richmond also feared that they were hunting a serial killer. A spate of murders had broken out on that city's South Side, beginning on September 18, 1987, when Debbie Davis was raped and murdered in her Westover Hills apartment. Two weeks later, just a few streets away, Dr. Susan Hellams also was found raped and strangled. In November the man dubbed the "South Side Strangler" struck again, this time killing fifteen-year-old Diane Cho. Like the victims in Arlington, each woman had been attacked in her own bedroom, each had been tied with her hands behind her back, each had been raped, and each had been strangled with a rope.

Oblivious to the murderous events in Richmond—because the crimes occurred in different jurisdictions, neither law enforcement agency made the connection between the two murder sprees—Arlington detectives pursued their belief that the Hamm and Tucker cases were related, a possibility that increased significantly when the forensic scientist Deanne Dabbs analyzed four semen stains found on Susan Tucker's bedding. These turned out to be type O, with a particular enzyme profile that matched just 13 percent of the population—including the killer of Caroline Hamm. Also found at the Tucker crime scene was a pubic hair that appeared to have come from an African American.

Recent developments in the field of **DNA typing** encouraged investigators to submit all these samples to the Lifecodes laboratory in Stanford, Connecticut, in hopes that a profile could be obtained. In the meantime someone recalled that back in 1983 an uncaught rapist had terrorized the neighborhood where Susan Tucker was murdered, using an identical means of incapacitating his victims. Was it possible that the rapist had now graduated to murder? A new round of inquiries was initiated. As neighborhood memories were revived and jogged, one name kept cropping up: Timothy Spencer.

He was a loner, someone whom people instinctively didn't trust. But there was just one problem: Spencer was already behind bars. At the end of January 1984, shortly after the Hamm killing, he had been arrested on a burglary charge, found guilty, and jailed. It looked like another dead end until a closer check of the prison inmate records in Virginia showed that Spencer had become eligible for a halfway house scheme, whereby he was allowed out of prison on a temporary basis, prior to making his application for full parole.

What really set investigative pulses racing was the realization that the privately run halfway house where Spencer was registered lay on Porter Street in South Richmond, adjacent to the area where the latest killing binge had occurred. Moreover, at the time of Susan Tucker's murder, Spencer had been granted a furlough to visit his mother, who lived in Arlington, very close to where the killing had taken place.

On January 20, 1988, Spencer, age twenty-five, was placed under arrest. His clothes, when combed for trace evidence, yielded several glass fragments. Glass refraction analysis of these fragments—achieved by directing light from several different points on the spectrum through the particles to see how the sample bent the beam, then plotting these results on a graph—gave a result that matched broken glass found at the Tucker crime scene.

In isolation this would not have been sufficient to guarantee a conviction, but DNA fingerprinting was now starting to make headlines worldwide, and prosecutors were convinced that this revolutionary technology held the key to convicting this savage serial killer. Spencer's defense team fought hard to prevent their client from having to provide samples of blood, hair, and saliva, only to be denied by a court order. The test results were better than anyone had dared hope. Spencer was judged to be the person who had murdered Susan Tucker and Debbie Davis, with a certainty put at 1 in 135 million.

Even more significantly, Spencer's DNA also branded him—and not David Vasquez—as the killer of Caroline Hamm. As it soon became apparent that no vestige of a link existed between Spencer and David Vasquez, and because the FBI's Behavioral Unit believed that the highly distinctive modus operandi in all five murders, including the Hamm case, was strongly indicative of a single killer, an immediate appeal was lodged on behalf of Vasquez.

At times the wheels of justice grind with unfathomable, almost cruel slowness, and another year would pass before Vasquez was granted a full pardon and released after spending five years in prison for a crime he did not commit.

By this time Spencer, in two separate trials, had twice been condemned to death, and on April 27, 1994, he went to the electric chair, the first killer in the United States to be executed through the use of DNA evidence. In recent years Virginia has become a leader in the use of genetic material to solve crimes. Its DNA database of nearly 177,000 convicted felons is one of the largest- and longest-running in the United States.

Sir Bernard Spilsbury (1877–1947)

No one in the history of forensic science has exerted more influence or commanded as much awe as Bernard Spilsbury. A legend in both the laboratory and the courtroom, it was in the latter where he really shone. No one has ever testified better than Spilsbury. Assured, lucid, always in full possession of the facts and blessed with Olympian self-confidence, this son of a Warwickshire pharmacist dominated the British legal system for close to forty years. He arrived at an opportune time. Forensic medical testimony was in the doldrums, still struggling to recover after a string of high-profile fiascos, when Spilsbury made the switch from attempting to cure patients to deciding what had killed them. In 1905 he was appointed resident assistant pathologist at St. Mary's Hospital in Paddington, London, and three years later he was elected to the Medico-Legal Society. He first stepped into the limelight at the 1910 trial of Hawley Harvey Crippen, and there he remained for the rest of his life.

His eye-catching performance on that occasion—devoid of the outlandish speculation that had plagued so many of his Victorian predecessors—made a massive impression on both jury and press alike, and set the template for decades to come. Newspapers of the era reported murder cases at huge length, and Fleet Street quickly realized that here was a genuine star. They devoted thousands of column inches to his exploits, finding that modern miracles of science and a highly photogenic young doctor did wonders for flagging circulation. *"Hanged by a Hair!"* the headline would scream, and

Implacable and deadly in the witness box, Sir Bernard Spilsbury virtually invented the role of the modern "expert witness."

underneath, an awestruck public could gaze upon the latest image of Spilsbury, imperious as ever, by his microscope.

Behind all the media hoopla were some impressive credentials. Spilsbury was a superb diagnostician, and his brilliance was all the more remarkable when one considers that he was fumbling around at the very genesis of forensic pathology. He had no vast literature on which to draw; indeed, pathology was still viewed with profound distaste by most of the medical profession. This meant that Spilsbury had to devise his own experiments, make calculations in the dark, draw conclusions based on his own, rather than empirical, knowledge. Oddly enough, these shortcomings worked in his favor. Because there was no great fount of alternative information, Spilsbury became very much a law unto himself.

As the Home Office pathologist he was privy to situations and cases that no other medical examiner had seen. This gave him an enormous advantage in court. Because he never published any findings—all his cases were filed on a card index kept at his Gower Street laboratory in North London—he was virtually immune to serious cross-examination. One of his favorite devices when testifying was to refer to some vague case in the past, a case that only he had seen, and explain how it informed his current opinion. Nowadays such a tactic wouldn't survive five minutes, but Spilsbury operated in a different, more reverential era, and he evinced absolute certainty. It oozed from every pore. Opinions coalesced into facts with scarcely a quibble, as the prosecution, the bench, and above all, the jury, accepted his word as Gospel truth.

Such implacable self-belief made him a terrifying opponent for defense counsel and defendant alike. Literally dozens of killers heard their last hopes of escaping the gallows dashed by the deadly testimony of the tall, immaculately attired figure with the ever-present red carnation. In 1923 he was knighted for his services to forensic pathology, and soon the cry of "Call Sir Bernard Spilsbury," echoing along oak-paneled corridors, became the inevitable precursor to a sharpening of pencils in the press gallery and a sinking of spirits in the dock.

As the legend grew, so did his reputation for infallibility. The view expressed by Judge Charles Darling, referring to Spilsbury as "that incomparable witness," overwhelmingly captured the prevailing mood. However, such an unquestioning reliance on the word of one expert witness could not last forever. Timidly at first, then with greater vigor, counsel began to probe Spilsbury more sternly. He was not amused. In his later years, as ambitious newcomers muscled in on what had previously been his exclusive territory, he even found his opinions being openly contradicted in court. No matter how heated the exchanges, Spilsbury's icy composure always remained intact, but once outside the court he was not above rebuking these young upstarts for their impudence, then stamping off in a fit of pique.

As far as the public was concerned, he remained the master. And he was, indisputably, a great pathologist. He took what had been derided as "that beastly science" from the wings to center stage and made it a branch of medicine to be proud of. Over a long career he carried out more than twenty-five thousand autopsies, including some fifty or so on the very murderers he had condemned to the gallows. Spilsbury was always fascinated by judicial execution, and close study of the effects of hanging on the human neck led him to recommend that the length of all drops be increased by three inches. (Incidentally, Albert Pierrepoint, the public hangman, turned a blind eye to the recommendation, preferring to rely on his own unique experience, and continued to perform his duties with sublime efficiency.)

By the end of World War II overwork and personal crises—he never recovered from the tragic death of two sons—had worn Spilsbury to a shadow, resulting in hesitancy at the mortuary table. Far too astute not to notice this decline, his response was typical. On December 17, 1947, after mailing off a letter to his close friend Dr. Eric Gardner, informing him of his intentions, Spilsbury went to his laboratory, locked the door, and gassed himself.

Significant Cases

1910	Hawley Harvey Crippen
1911	Frederick Seddon

1915	George Joseph Smith
1917	Louis Voison
1922	Frederick Bywaters and Edith Thompson
1922	Herbert Rowse Armstrong
1924	Patrick Mahon
1924	Norman Thorne
1924	Jean-Pierre Vacquier
1926	John Donald Merrett
1927	John Robinson
1929	William Podmore*
1929	Sidney Fox
1930	Alfred Rouse
1937	Leslie Stone
1939	Joseph Williams
1942	Gordon Cummins
1947	Christopher Geraghty, Charles Jenkins, and Terence Rolt

*Profiled in this book.

Sir Lee Stack

Date: 1924
Location: Cairo, Egypt

In the early 1920s Cairo was a cauldron of political unrest, with assassinations an everyday occurrence. For **Sir Sydney Smith,** the newly appointed professor of forensic science at the University of Cairo, such upheaval provided a unique opportunity to pursue one of his passions: forensic ballistics.

His greatest triumph had its genesis on November 19, 1924, when the sirdar, or commander in chief of the Egyptian army and governor-general of the Sudan, Sir Lee Stack, was ambushed in broad daylight as he drove through the streets of Cairo. A gang threw a bomb and opened fire. Stack was hit in the stomach and died the next day from his injuries. His aide-de-camp and driver also sustained fatal injuries.

Smith was asked to investigate the incident. At the crime scene he found nine cartridge cases, all .32-caliber, though three different guns had been used, one of which, judging from extractor and ejector marks, was a Colt automatic.

The actual bullets were even more informative. Five of them, including the one that killed Stack, had crosses filed into their tips to convert them into dumdum bullets. Outlawed by the Geneva Convention, such bullets expand on hitting a target, hugely multiplying the impact and causing massive injury. From the grooves and direction of twist, Smith deduced that the bullets had been fired from a Colt automatic, a Mauser automatic, and either a Browning or a Sûreté automatic.

Stack had been killed by a shot from a Colt. Under the microscope, the slug's rifling marks were very faint, indicating considerable wear, but there was one distinctive flaw: a scratched groove. Smith peered more closely. He'd seen this groove before on other bullets recovered from political assassinations, and he had little doubt that the gun had murdered several people. He felt confident that if the Colt were found, he would be able to identify it.

Meanwhile, the Cairo police were making headway in rounding up the killers. The cabdriver who had ferried the gang away from the ambush, Mahmoud Saleh, was tracked down, and under rigorous interrogation admitted that he could identify the assassins. Ultimately his information led to the conspiracy's ringleader, a radical lawyer named Shafiq Mansur, who had twice run for Parliament and twice been disowned by his party.

Other names mentioned included the Enayat brothers, Abdel-Hamid and Abdel-Fattah. Without any firm evidence against the Enayats, the Cairo police opted for an unorthodox ploy. A spy was introduced into the gang, with disinformation that the police were on the verge of making a string of arrests. He urged the Enayats to flee to Tripoli for safety. The hope was that if the brothers did flee the country, they would, in all probability, take the murder weapons with them.

The plan worked to perfection. On February 2, 1925, the Enayats boarded a train from Alexandria to Mersa Matrouh, en route to Libya. They were quickly seized and searched. But not until a guard accidentally kicked over a basket of fruit did officers find four hidden handguns.

They were dispatched to Smith for examination. Two, being of .25-caliber, he immediately eliminated. The others, a Colt and a Sûreté, were .32-caliber, and both contained dumdum bullets. Smith had no trouble linking the Sûreté to three of the murder bullets, and after test-firing the Colt, he found that telltale groove on each bullet. As promised, he had identified the weapon that had been used in so many previous unsolved murders.

Faced with a mountain of evidence, the Enayat brothers confessed and implicated a Cairo engineer named Mahmoud Rashed. Disregarding Rashed's protest that he "couldn't kill a chicken," searchers tore his house apart and uncovered a vise and several rasps—all the equipment necessary to manufacture dumdum bullets. Microscopic inspection of dust in the crevices of the vise showed particles of lead, copper, zinc, and nickel indistinguishable from filings from the murder bullets. Smith held his elation in check; any engineer might have such filings in his tools, and he doubted that this would be enough to convict Rashed, who still proclaimed his innocence.

His downfall came about when Mansur suddenly decided to confess. He admitted his part in the assassination and told police that the murder weapons had been stored in Rashed's house, in a hidden compartment in a door panel.

Sure enough, the compartment was just where Mansur had claimed. The fact that it was empty scarcely mattered, since Smith spotted several interesting dents in the wood inside. By placing the Colt into the compartment, he was able to line up the foresight and backsight of the pistol so they corresponded exactly with the indentations. Even with the Colt in place, there was still room to comfortably conceal the other weapons, just as Mansur had stated. Rashed just crumpled when confronted with this evidence, and his full confession came in a rush.

The trial began at the end of May 1925, and Smith was the principal medico-legal witness. With so many of the confessions having been repudiated, his evidence was crucial, as he demonstrated how the dumdum bullets were made. Using the very tools found at Rashed's house, he produced just such a bullet in seconds. He also explained the significance of the bullet striations, and finally he demonstrated just how the guns had been hidden in the door.

At this time few courts in the world had heard such convincing and comprehensive ballistics testimony. Smith was an apostle of the new technology, and this was one of his finest hours. On June 7 the court returned guilty verdicts for all eight defendants. Seven were sentenced to hang; only Mahmoud Saleh, the cabdriver, was shown leniency, with a two-year sentence.

Smith, delighted by his first major success in the ballistics field, contributed a paper on the Stack case to the *British Medical Journal,* and that same year he devoted a section of his *Forensic Medicine and Toxicology* to ballistics, the first medical jurisprudence volume to contain such an entry.

Barbara Stager

Date: 1988
Location: Durham, North Carolina

An emergency phone call to the authorities in Durham, North Carolina, on February 1, 1988, included garbled details of what appeared to be a dreadful accident. Officers summoned to the home of Russell and Barbara Stager heard Barbara tearfully explain how she had been asleep in bed when she thought she heard a burglar. Groggily, she had reached for the .25-caliber pistol that she and Russell kept beneath the pillow for protection. Somehow her finger brushed the trigger, causing the gun to discharge and shoot Russell in the back of the head as he lay sleeping.

The forty-year-old baseball coach at Raleigh High School was in an irreversible coma and, later that day, Barbara signed a consent form to switch off the life support system that ended their nine-year marriage. With nothing to suggest foul play—a spent .25-caliber shell casing had been found on the bed beside Russell—the police were ready to close the case as an accident. Until they were contacted by Russell's previous wife.

Since the divorce she and Russell had remained on good terms, and she now told police how unhappy life with Barbara had made him. He'd been especially worried about Barbara's financial extravagance and on occasion had even expressed fears for his own life.

As police delved into Barbara's background, they uncovered a woman hungry for extramarital affairs and high living. She had a long history of bouncing checks and thought nothing of forging her husband's name on loan applications, convinced that when found out—as she always was—she could somehow manage to scrape together the money to pay off disgruntled creditors and avert legal action.

News that Russell was a firearms instructor and obsessively cautious around guns added another dimension to the case. It beggared belief that he would have slept with a gun beneath the pillow, cocked and with the safety off, which is what must have happened if Barbara's story were true.

But what really lit a fire under the inquiry was the revelation that ten years earlier, Barbara Stager's first husband had died in shockingly similar circumstances. Just after midnight on March 22, 1978, Larry Ford also had been found shot to death, with a .25-caliber pistol purchased the day before. Despite some misgivings, that had been ruled an accident.

Ever resourceful, Barbara had drawn on that personal tragedy to write a novel called *Untimely Death,* about a man who'd accidentally shot himself, and sent the manuscript to the publishing house of Doubleday. When they sent back a form rejection letter, Barbara used the Doubleday logo to forge another letter, this time saying that the novel had been accepted for an advance of $25,000. Offering this letter as security, she obtained a $25,000 loan from a local bank. Only when a friend contacted Doubleday to find out when the book was scheduled for release was the scam exposed. Eager to hide its embarrassment and happy to get its money back, the bank declined to press charges. Once again Barbara Stager had gotten away with fraud. Was she now trying to get away with murder?

To assist police, she agreed to reenact the incident on video, and it was here that inconsistencies appeared. She showed how, after realizing what she had done, she had cradled her husband's head in her lap and attempted artificial respiration. Paramedics disputed this. When they found Russell, he'd been lying as if fast asleep, with no evidence of having been moved.

Also, Barbara's claim that she had been holding the gun at mattress height when she fired was demonstrably false. There were no powder burns on the sheet, and, according to the medical examiner, Dr. Thomas Clark, Russell had been shot from above and at least two feet away, with a downward trajectory, whereas it should have been slightly up had Barbara been telling the truth.

Slowly a motive began to emerge. Russell was carrying life insurance policies in the sum of $200,000 when he died, all payable to Barbara, and within just hours of her husband's death she had presented his will for processing. Although it had been signed by Russell, all the witnesses were members of Barbara's immediate family.

With suspicion mounting, the will was passed to the **questioned documents** section of the North Carolina State Bureau of Investigation for scrutiny. Because handwriting can vary slightly depending on mood, or medications taken by the writer, ideally several samples are needed to make a valid comparison. It is also desirable to obtain samples written as close to the disputed time as possible, as signatures tend to vary with age.

In this instance, after comparing the signature on the will with known exemplars of Russell's writing, the head examiner Durward Matheny had no hesitation in declaring it a fake. He was similarly emphatic that a $1,500 check, signed by Russell and made payable to Barbara just days before his death, also had been forged.

Elsewhere in the SBI's Raleigh headquarters, experts in the Ballistics Department found that in test firings of the gun that killed Russell, shell casings were thrown at least three and a half feet. Had the gun discharged in the way Barbara claimed, the shell casing should have ended up on the floor, not on the bed beside Russell.

Perhaps the most powerful evidence, though, came when Frederick Evans, a student at Russell's school, was clearing out a gym locker and found a cassette tape. On it, in vivid and emotional language, Russell Stager poured out his innermost fears: how he thought Barbara had murdered her first husband and was now planning to kill him. When played in court, it pointed a damning finger at the accused.

The prosecution had little trouble in successfully portraying Barbara Stager as a heartless murderer for profit. Having dug an enormous financial hole for herself, killing Russell was her only way out. Originally condemned to die, Stager spent four years on death row until her sentence was commuted to life imprisonment.

Patricia Stallings

Date: 1989
Location: Hillsboro, Missouri

Just before putting her two-month-old baby to bed on Friday, July 7, 1989, a young Missouri mother, Patricia Stallings, gave him his evening bottle. Little Ryan immediately threw up. The next day he seemed to improve, but by Sunday morning his condition had deteriorated to the point where Patricia made arrangements to meet a doctor at the emergency room of Children's

Hospital in St. Louis. In her agitated state, Patricia got lost and ended up at Cardinal Glennon Hospital.

There the staff, suspicious about the baby's symptoms, ran tests that indicated a high level of ethylene glycol in Ryan's blood. Ethylene glycol is a toxic, colorless liquid used in the production of man-made fibers, some explosives, and, most commonly, auto antifreeze. The tests had been conducted by two laboratories, SmithKline Beecham and the **Toxicology** Department of St. Louis University. Each was adamant that peaks on the graphs produced by their tests matched the retention time for ethylene glycol.

As it seemed impossible for a two-month-old baby to have ingested antifreeze accidentally, all the signs indicated deliberate poisoning. When Ryan was discharged on July 17, he was placed in a foster home pending further investigations.

On September 4, following a visit from his mother, Ryan was hospitalized a second time. A second test found even higher levels of ethylene glycol—911 micrograms per milliliter of blood serum. The next day, Patricia, whom investigators believed had poisoned her son during the visit, was arrested. A search of her home found a half-empty container of antifreeze. When Ryan died on September 7 Patricia Stallings found herself facing a charge of murder.

At the time of her arrest, Patricia was pregnant, and five months later she gave birth to her second son, David Jr. He, too, was placed in foster care. Soon it became clear that something was amiss with David, and in April 1990 he was diagnosed with an extremely rare genetic disorder, methylmalonic acidemia (MMA), which affects 1 of every 48,000 children and inhibits the body's ability to process food, especially protein. It also produces toxins in the blood. When Children's Hospital diagnosed David with the disease, experts said there was a 1-in-4 chance that Ryan, too, had suffered from the rare genetic disorder.

Two pieces of medical evidence, though, seemed unassailable, First, there was the finding of ethylene glycol in Ryan's body by both SmithKline Beecham and St. Louis University. Even if Ryan suffered from MMA, this could not account for the levels of ethylene glycol found in his blood. Nor could it account for the autopsy's finding of apparent calcium oxylate crystals in the child's brain and other body organs, traces consistent with ethylene glycol poisoning.

On top of that, traces of ethylene glycol also had been found in the bottle Patricia had used to feed Ryan shortly before he was admitted to the hospital the second, and final, time. In light of these findings it was hardly surprising that Patricia's attorney was unable to find any expert to testify that Ryan might have died of MMA, and that he was not poisoned at all, much less by his mother. In February 1991 Patricia Stallings was imprisoned for life without parole.

But help was at hand. Dr. James Shoemaker, a young scientist who had just set up a genetic testing laboratory at St. Louis University—ironically, the very institution that had found ethylene glycol—ran extra tests on Ryan's blood. Using a test designed to detect MMA in urine, he discovered that Ryan Stallings had, in all likelihood, suffered from MMA.

And when Shoemaker analyzed Ryan's blood for retentions times, he found not ethylene glycol but proprionic acid, which has a retention time similar to that of ethylene glycol. Significantly, proprionic acid is often produced by MMA sufferers. Superimposition of a graph over the original database printout showed clear disparities in peaks. As for the contaminated baby bottle, Shoemaker strongly believed that it was sterilization that had produced a trace reading of ethylene glycol.

He sent his findings to Dr. Piero Rinaldo, a world-renowned genetics expert from Yale University. Rinaldo was flabbergasted by what he found. He described the quality of the test results generated by SmithKline Beecham and St. Louis University as "unbelievable; out of this world. . . . I couldn't believe that somebody would let this go through a criminal trial unchallenged."

In independent tests Rinaldo found no evidence of ethylene glycol in Ryan's blood. Nor was there anything in the baby bottle to indicate the presence of ethylene glycol. Rinaldo went further: Cardinal Glennon Hospital's treatment of Ryan—treatment that included fasting and the use of ethanol to limit the effects of ethylene glycol poisoning—were inappropriate for a child with MMA. As for those mysterious crystals found in Ryan's autopsy, in all likelihood, said Rinaldo, the crystallization had been caused by the ethanol drip used in the hospital to treat Ryan's suspected ethylene glycol poisoning.

Such was Shoemaker's unease at these findings that he conducted an experiment, sending samples of blood spiked with proprionic acid to seven laboratories. To his horror, no fewer than three misidentified it as ethylene glycol. Also, a reexamination of the original data revealed yet another extraordinary blunder: for Ryan to have 911 micrograms of ethylene glycol in his system, he would have had to ingest more than *80 gallons of antifreeze,* a clearly absurd amount.

There had been no murder, just bad science. Fortunately, better science was at hand, and Patricia Stallings was freed in September 1991 and all charges against her were dropped. Numerous lawsuits against various parties were settled out of court.

It is sobering to reflect that had Patricia Stallings not been pregnant, and had David Jr. not exhibited the symptoms of MMA, she probably would still be behind bars. This highlights the need for constant vigilance. As courts come to rely ever more on the testimony of forensic experts, the quality of their work must be scrupulous and beyond reproach. Nothing else is acceptable.

Kenneth Starrs (1931–)

Although he has no formal qualification in forensic science, Starrs—a larger-than-life law professor at George Washington University (GWU)—has made himself one of the most visible players on the contemporary American forensic scene. This has largely been achieved by a series of highly publicized exhumations of famous or infamous figures from history, always seeking to question the official version of their deaths, and from his reinvestigations of several notorious American crimes.

After returning from the Korean War, Starrs became a lawyer but found the work unchallenging from an intellectual standpoint. When, in 1968, he was asked to establish a forensic science program at GWU, he jumped at the chance.

He first came to national prominence in 1989 with the case of Alfred Packer, the so-called Colorado Cannibal, a mountain guide convicted for the 1874 killings of five fellow travelers who became trapped in a Rockies snowstorm. Although Packer freely admitted cannibalizing the bodies, he always claimed that another explorer had actually killed the victims. When Starrs's team of forensic scientists, geologists, and anthropologists exhumed the bodies of the five victims, the angle and consistency of the skinning knife marks on the bones were enough for Starrs to confidently assert that Packer himself was the actual murderer, though this finding has been hotly disputed.

In the wake of this expedition came a string of highly publicized ventures to other historical gravesites, the most notable of which, in Kearney, Missouri, belonged to the train robber and gang leader Jesse James. Through the use of DNA, Starrs was able to state, with "99.7 percent certainty," that the remains were indeed those of the notorious outlaw, and not an impostor, as had been claimed.

Not all of Starrs's efforts have been as successful or even appreciated. In 1992 he was refused permission to exhume the body of Meriwether Lewis, the nineteenth-century explorer who, history records, committed suicide; Starrs thinks the death might have been a homicide. And he later had to endure a barrage of hooting derision when he made some outlandish speculations regarding the death of J. Edgar Hoover. Dissatisfied by the official verdict that the seventy-seven-year-old director of the FBI died of a heart attack, Starrs argued that a new autopsy might reveal evidence of poisoning.

Such claims, often made on the flimsiest of evidence, have prompted accusations that Starrs is motivated more by self-promotion than by scientific curiosity. Certainly he is unencumbered by false modesty, insisting that his mingling of science and the law makes him unique. "There's really nobody else in the world who can do it," he says.

A fellow of the American Academy of Forensic Sciences, Starrs records his findings in a quarterly newsletter, *Scientific Sleuthing Review*. In recent years, as the pool of potential exhumations has inevitably shrunk, he has assisted on computer simulations in such notorious cases as O. J. Simpson and the Menendez brothers.

Significant Cases

1989	Alfred Packer
1991	Carl Weiss
1992	Meriwether Lewis
1993	Menendez brothers
1994	O. J. Simpson
1995	Jesse James
2000	Albert DeSalvo

Auguste Ambroise Tardieu (1818–1879)

A benign and kindly figure, Tardieu was one of the principal medico-legal experts in nineteenth-century France, contributing to many of that country's greatest causes célèbres. Although well versed in all aspects of forensic investigation, he is chiefly remembered for having undertaken the first exhaustive study of the effects and indicators of asphyxia, and for landmark research in the subject of child abuse.

Tardieu was born in Paris and received his doctorate in 1843, writing a dissertation still considered a classic in its field. National celebrity came in 1847 with his involvement in the notorious du Praslin murder case (see **Charles-Louis Theobald**). He followed this with a string of courtroom successes. When someone was needed to investigate the botched 1858 assassination attempt on Napoleon III that had left several bystanders dead and scores injured, Tardieu was the logical contender. He oversaw the investigation that eventually led to the arrest and execution of the bomb plot's leader, Italian revolutionary Felice Orsini.

His academic career was no less glittering. In 1861 he was appointed professor at the University of Paris, where he eventually became dean of the faculty of medicine. The year 1867 brought double honors: first he became chairman of the French association of physicians, then he was awarded the presidency of the Académie de Médecine.

Besides being a city magistrate, he was also a frequent medical witness in court. But it was through the efforts of his pen that he gained forensic immortality. A veritable blizzard of monographs and papers flew from his desk. He left no area of criminology untouched: **microscopy,** infanticide, **toxicology,** and criminal insanity were just a few of the topics to come under his critical review. As an aid to identification, he recorded the recognizable physiological changes to people following some forty-eight different trades.

Auguste Ambroise Tardieu, the French medico-legal expert who revolutionized the study of asphyxia and child abuse.

Then came an example of his humanity, with a paper outlining the deleterious effects on inmates of unduly harsh imprisonment.

Undoubtedly, though, his greatest work was *Étude Médico-Légale sur la Pendaison, la Strangulation, les Suffocations* (1870), which dealt with every aspect of death by asphyxia. It was Tardieu who first identified the ecchymoses or petechial hemorrhages in the face, neck, and lung areas that frequently accompany strangulation or suffocation. To this day they are still called Tardieu spots.

Another discipline in which Tardieu earned an eponymous attribution was in the hitherto disregarded subject of child abuse. Tardieu's syndrome alerted the entire medical profession to the need to check for repeated and unaccountable examples of physical maltreatment, such as bruising confined to the buttocks and lower back, trauma by the use of heat and water, cigarette burns, and injuries to the liver or spleen. Nowadays more popularly called Battered Baby Syndrome, the effects are just as pernicious and sinister as when Tardieu first investigated them. But it is thanks to this brilliant Frenchman that they are more generally understood.

Significant Cases

1847	Charles-Louis Theobald*
1863	Edmond de la Pommerais*
1868	Pierre Voirbo

1869	Jean-Baptiste Troppmann
1870	Pierre Bonaparte

*Profiled in this book.

Charles Anthony Taylor (1885–1965)

Nicknamed "The Cat" because of his initials, Charles Anthony Taylor was Australia's premier forensic scientist of the early twentieth century. He was a genuine Renaissance man, much in the mold of his great American contemporary **Edward O. Heinrich.** Each possessed the same nose for crime-solving and extraordinary deductive skills that seemed more akin to detective fiction than to real life. In those prespecialization times, forensic experts were expected to turn their hand to almost every discipline—**toxicology, fingerprinting, ballistics,** and **microscopy**—and Taylor was good at all of them, though it was as an analytical chemist that he achieved his greatest successes.

He grew up in the small town of Maryborough, in central Victoria, and proved to be a precocious learner. By age fourteen he could identify every local wildflower and orchid, and he took this inquisitive nature to the School of Mines at Ballarat to study geology. But the thriving gold boom that had put this region on the map was fizzling out, and with it disappeared Taylor's hoped-for career in gold exploration. With a heavy heart he took up a poorly paid position as a science teacher in a Melbourne school, though he soon managed to obtain a position on the staff of the Gordon Institute of Technology at Geelong. Then came his big chance, when the government analyst Charles Price took him on as his deputy.

Before long, Taylor reached the senior rank, a position he was to hold for some thirty years. During this time he figured prominently in many of Australia's most notorious cases, often trekking hundreds of miles into the outback in pursuit of some arcane clue. He sweated alongside the aboriginal trackers, who could follow a suspect over some of the harshest and most unhelpful terrain on earth, wedding their almost supernatural tracking skills to his own rationalist analysis. It was an unlikely alliance that solved dozens of major crimes.

Like most forensic scientists who made their name in this era, Taylor shone in the witness box, giving his evidence firmly and well and, once he had made up his mind, without a shred of self-doubt. Nowadays such emphatic dogmatism is unfashionable and would certainly be more readily challenged, but Taylor was merely a product of his age, and as his record shows, he never once suffered the sting of courtroom defeat. A quiet family man—he had six children—who rarely talked of his cases, he was content to let the Australian press chronicle his exploits, which they did in lavish, often lurid detail. In later years he came to regret the way in which forensic medicine increasingly intruded on his analytical work, preferring the sharper demarcation characteristic of the 1920s. Pathologists, he felt, should stick to pathology, and leave laboratory analysis to those trained in the practice of "pure science." It is a gripe that resonates to the present day.

Significant Cases

1921	Colin Ross
1936	Arnold Sodeman
1938	George Green*
1939	Raymond White*
1942	Edward Leonski*

*Profiled in this book.

Erich Tetzner

Date: 1929
Location: Leipzig, Germany

Late one night on a Munich road, a car carrying businessman Erich Tetzner spun out of control, hit a roadside marker, and burst into flames, incinerating the driver. The next day—November 26, 1929—Emma Tetzner was brought from Leipzig to view the blackened remains. Through tear-filled eyes, the bereaved widow identified her late husband. That same day she filed insurance claims on Tetzner's life totaling DM145,000 ($29,000), a huge amount for someone of Tetzner's relatively modest means. Alert to the possibility of suicide—the policies had been in effect only a few weeks—cautious claims adjusters told Frau Tetzner that an autopsy would be necessary.

Richard Kockel, of the Institute of Forensic Medicine at the University of Leipzig and Germany's leading criminalist, went to the funeral chapel where the body was awaiting burial. Several features about the blackened corpse disturbed him. Inexplicably, the cranium and both legs from the thigh down were missing: neither, Kockel thought, was likely to have been consumed in the fire. And the twenty-six-year-old Tetzner had been described as burly and muscular, yet these remains were decidedly those of a slim, light-framed male; also, cartilage that normally disappears in the male no later than age twenty-three was still present. If these discrepancies alone were sufficient to put Kockel on his guard, then what he found, or rather didn't find next, set alarm bells ringing: the respiratory passages were entirely free from the kind of sooty deposits customarily associated with smoke inhalation.

Most fire deaths are caused not by flames or heat but from the effects of carbon monoxide. The blood turns a bright cherry color and may retain detectable amounts of the lethal gas for up to six months after death; but in this instance, when Kockel tested blood samples, none showed carbon monoxide contamination. This meant that the victim was already dead when the car burst into flames. But what form had that death taken? Eliminating stroke or coronary failure as being most unlikely in someone so young, Kockel considered two alternatives: trauma sustained in the accident, or foul play.

Although gutted by fire, the car was still intact and did not appear to have sustained the kind of damage that would instantly kill its driver. At this point the missing section of skull took on a more sinister light. Kockel wondered if it had been removed before the fire because it showed telltale signs of physical distress, a suspicion strengthened by the discovery of part of the dead man's brain on the road, almost two yards from the driver's seat.

As the inconsistencies mounted, so did Kockel's certainty that the dead man was some unfortunate, murdered as part of an insurance swindle. Tetzner, he was sure, was still alive and in hiding, and it would only be a matter of time before he contacted his wife.

Frau Tetzner was immediately placed under round-the-clock surveillance. When it was noticed that she seemed to be using a neighbor's phone with more than usual frequency, a tap was placed on the line. On the morning of December 4, a listening detective heard the operator connect a long-distance call from Strasbourg, just across the border in France. The caller gave his name as Stranelli. Posing as the man of the house, the detective quickly cut into the line, saying that Emma Tetzner would not be available until six o'clock that night and asking the man to call back. He managed to keep Stranelli on the line long enough for the call to be traced to a public phone booth in the Strasbourg main post office. That night, at a few minutes before six, a bulky man in his midtwenties entered the Strasbourg telephone booth. No sooner had he asked the operator for the number in Leipzig than the door flew open. So great was Erich Tetzner's surprise at being arrested that he immediately admitted his true identity.

That night he made the first of numerous confessions. He had been planning the fraud for some time, encouraged by an unrelated insurance windfall. Just a few months earlier, his mother-in-law had announced that she was suffering from cancer; her only hope rested with an operation in which chances of survival were rated at no higher than 50 percent. Tetzner argued against the procedure just long enough to insure her life for DM10,000 ($2,000)—he would have made it more, but the insurance companies declined to offer further coverage—then persuaded her to undergo the operation after all. The gamble paid off. The mother-in-law died and Tetzner got his money, unable to believe how easy it had been.

Flushed with success, he resolved to try again, this time for much higher stakes. He would stage his own death. He originally considered resurrecting a body from a graveyard but decided that fresher was better. His first murder attempt was foiled when the intended victim, a man of similar build, managed to fend off the wrench-wielding Tetzner. Finally he picked up a hitchhiker, a wiry young man about twenty-one years old. Tetzner had waited until the hitchhiker fell asleep, then doused his car with gasoline and tossed in a match.

Not true, said Kockel: the victim was already dead by that time. Moreover, why, if he had fallen asleep in the passenger seat and supposedly burned to death there, was he found in the driver's seat? Aware that he had been trapped in an obvious lie, Tetzner abruptly changed his tale. His next version had him accidentally running down the hitchhiker in the dark. Only after picking up the stranger and placing him in the car did he realize that he was dead. Suddenly an idea occurred to him, and he perpetrated the swindle.

Again Kockel was ready for him. Why, in that case, remove the missing body parts? It was one question too many. On May 2, 1931, Tetzner was executed at Regensburg. Just before walking to the scaffold, he gave his final version of the unknown hitchhiker's last few minutes. It tallied exactly with Kockel's.

Although rarely used as a means of homicide, fire has obvious attractions for someone seeking to destroy an unwanted body. However, recent advances in medical technology—it is now possible to ascertain whether burns were sustained ante- or postmortem—virtually guarantee detection.

Charles-Louis Theobald

Date: 1847
Location: Paris, France

Fifteen years of marriage, during which she produced no fewer than nine children, had left Altarice Sebastiani, a daughter of one of Napoleon I's generals, utterly exhausted. Her husband, Charles-Louis Theobald, the snobbish Duc de Choiseul-Praslin, only added to Altarice's misery with his relentless complaints that she was neglecting their children's education. A succession of governesses came and went at the couple's fashionable Parisian residence or at their castle in Melun. The last of these was a beautiful young woman named Henriette DeLuzy Deportes.

The children took Henriette to their hearts, and so did Theobald. When the duchess found out, she demanded that he fire Henriette. Theobald refused point-blank. Furious, the duchess took matters into her own hands and dismissed Henriette without so much as a reference. Henriette packed her bags and left for Paris, where she found work in a boarding school.

Theobald, utterly besotted, openly visited his mistress at every opportunity. In June 1847 the duchess announced that she intended to seek a divorce, on the grounds of her husband's adultery. Facing public disgrace, Theobald panicked. On the evening of August 17, 1847, after visiting Henriette, he returned to his house on Rue Faubourg de St. Honoré. A heated exchange with his wife ended when Theobald retired to his separate bedroom.

At around daybreak, a piercing scream, followed by urgent ringing on the maidservant's bell, brought staff running to the duchess's bedroom. But the door was locked. A loud crash from inside only elevated their anxiety. Despite repeated knocks, no answer was forthcoming. It was the same when they tried another door. That, too, was locked. Racing out into the garden, they peered upward just as the bedroom shutter flew back. There, framed in the window, was Theobald, moving frantically. All they could think was that he was tackling some intruders.

Another headlong dash upstairs brought further mystery: the bedroom door was now unlocked. Inside, the scene defied belief: furniture hurled everywhere, splashes of blood across the walls. In the midst of this chaos lay the duchess, throat slashed, her face bruised and battered. She had succumbed to seven blows in all, some from a *poignard* (a sharp-pointed dagger), others from a clubbing instrument. Just then the duke appeared at the door, claiming to have just been awoken by the alarm. He howled with anguish when he saw his wife and ran to her side, crying for the doctor to be called.

Within the hour, the house was full of police officers. Theobald's claim that this must have been the work of burglars fell some way short of the facts: the duchess's jewelry was on full display and untouched, and beneath a sofa, a bloodstained pistol was found.

Asked if he recognized the gun, Theobald nodded, saying that, upon hearing his wife's cries for help, he had brought it from his own bedroom. He must have dropped it as he bent to raise his wife, an explanation that also accounted for his blood-drenched clothing. When officers pointed out a trail of blood spots that led to Theobald's bedroom, he said they must have occurred when he returned to wash himself after finding his wife. What he could not explain was the discovery in his bedroom of a bloodstained handkerchief, a broken *poignard* hilt, and the severed end of the bellpull from the duchess's bedroom.

Despite Theobald's lofty claims of immunity, he was arrested and bundled off to the Palace of Luxembourg. His guilt seemed inescapable. But the police knew that someone with Theobald's enormous influence—he was a cousin of the king—could pull all manner of different strings, certainly enough to convince a gullible jury that his servants had been confused in their observations and timings of events.

It was to allay these fears that the police enlisted the assistance of **Auguste Ambroise Tardieu,** a young pathologist, whose glittering doctoral dissertation had already marked him out as a forensic pioneer. In particular he was asked to concentrate on the bloodstained pistol. At issue was whether the pistol had been dropped in the duchess's blood, or used as a weapon to batter her to death.

Tardieu studied the pistol, first under a magnifying glass, then with a microscope. His first discovery was a chestnut hair adhering to the butt (the duchess had been redheaded), and then, near the trigger guard, he found fragments of what looked like skin tissue. Further microscopic examination revealed a human hair root and more fragments of flesh. When Tardieu held the pistol butt against the contused wounds on the dead woman's forehead, he got a perfect match. Everything pointed to the duchess having been battered to death with the pistol.

Next, Tardieu drew up the likely murder scenario. He believed that Theobald had intended it to look like the work of burglars. Originally, he slipped into his wife's bedroom, intending to slash her throat with one stroke of the *poignard*. For whatever reason—either his nerve failed, or perhaps she awoke as he bent over her—it all went horribly wrong. The blade made a deep but only partial cut in her throat. Deafened by her screams, he thrust again and again with the dagger, then pummeled her with the pistol butt as she struggled on the floor. A row of deep teeth marks in Theobald's leg revealed the extent of her resistance.

Such bedlam had, by now, aroused the whole house. With servants knocking at the door, Theobald's scheme was in tatters. His hasty improvisation, throwing open the window to make it appear like burglars, had backfired badly when he was seen by the servants. His subsequent actions—the disappearance, his reemergence, and his hysterical response to his wife's demise—had fooled no one, least of all Tardieu.

Four days later, sensing that he was doomed and unable to face the ignominy of the guillotine, Theobald committed suicide by swallowing a dose of arsenic.

Time of Death

Nothing in forensic science is trickier—or has been the cause of more bitter disputes—than the problem of establishing the time of death in murder victims. It is a fiendishly difficult business, made harder still with each passing hour that the body remains unfound, until eventually a point is reached where associated or environmental evidence, rather than anatomical changes, is likely to furnish more reliable data. Here, though, we shall confine ourselves to the corporal evidence.

Traditionally, three indicators are used to determine how long a person has been dead: rigor mortis, hypostasis (livor mortis), and body temperature (algor mortis). A fourth, putrefaction, must be considered when dealing with bodies found some considerable time after death. None is wholly reliable, and, as we shall see, all are subject to huge variations.

Rigor mortis is a stiffness of the body caused by muscles contracting after death, as glycogen is converted into lactic acid. It usually begins to show three hours after death in the muscles of the face and eyelids, and then spreads slowly through the body to the arms and legs, taking about twelve hours to complete. In the majority of cases the process begins to reverse after approximately thirty-six hours, until the body is soft and supple again. However, temperature and climate affect this. Heat accelerates the process and cold slows it down. In extremely hot climates, the onset of putrefaction may completely displace rigor within nine to twelve hours of death.

Prolonged muscular activity—such as exhaustion caused by fighting for one's life or convulsions—shortly before death will not only make the onset of rigor more rapid but also shorten its duration. Conversely, a late onset of rigor in many sudden deaths is sometimes explained by the lack of muscular activity immediately prior to death. Such a wealth of variables has led some medical examiners to entirely discount rigor mortis as a means of estimating the time of death; for others it remains an invaluable if highly contentious tool.

Hypostasis (lividity) is a dark discoloration of the skin resulting from the gravitational pooling of blood in the veins and capillary beds of the dependent parts of the body following cessation of circulation. The process begins immediately after the circulation stops and is present in all bodies, although it may be inconspicuous in some and thus escape notice. Lividity, too, develops in a time sequence, and is first apparent about thirty minutes after death. As the red cells break down, evacuate the capillaries, and enter the body, dull red patches or blotches appear on the skin beneath, which deepen in intensity and coalesce over the succeeding hours to form extensive areas of reddish-purple discoloration, a process that generally takes six to ten hours. The color then becomes fixed. If a person dies in bed lying on his or her back, the discoloration would normally be found on the back. Any lividity found on the front part of the body would indicate some postmortem movement.

The third, and probably the most useful indicator of time of death—especially if the victim has been dead for fewer than twenty-four hours—is body temperature (algor mortis). After death, when oxygen is no longer fueling the body and keeping it warm, the body temperature falls until it reaches the temperature of its surroundings. Musculature and ambient temperature play significant roles. An obese person will cool much more slowly than someone who is lean; children lose heat more quickly than adults; while someone who dies in a warm room will retain more body heat than someone who succumbs outdoors in cold weather. Clothing, too, is important. According to **Keith Simpson,** cooling of a naked body is half again as fast as when clothed.

On balance, algor mortis is more reliable in temperate or cool climates. Tropical climates may cause only a minimal fall in body temperature, while in exceptionally hot countries, the corporal temperature may even rise after death. Various formulas have been devised in an attempt to provide a mathematical means of calculating time of death. The following is fairly typical:

$$\frac{\text{normal temp. } (98.6^{\circ}\text{F}) - \text{rectal temp.}}{1.5} = \text{approx. hours since death}$$

In recent times, medical examiners have tended to shy away from the mathematical model because of the bewildering number of variables.

These, then, are the conventional means of establishing time of death, but there are others.

Putrefaction is the postmortem destruction of bodily soft tissues caused by the action of bacteria and enzymes. This results in the gradual dissolution of the tissues into gases, liquids, and salts. The main changes that can be recognized in the tissues undergoing putrefaction are changes in color, the evolution of gases, and liquefaction. Environmental temperature has an enormous effect on putrefaction. In a temperate climate the degree of putrefaction reached after twenty-four hours at the height of summer may require as many as two weeks in the depth of winter. High humidity also aids putrefaction.

One recent addition to the medical examiner's armory, so-called eyeball chemistry, works by measuring the rate at which potassium from the red blood cells enters the vitreous fluid of the eye. Various studies of this technique have produced widely divergent results, and the jury is still out on whether this will ever enter the forensic mainstream.

Other factors useful in estimating the time of death—such as stomach contents, insect infestation, and **anthropology (forensic)**—are dealt with elsewhere in this book.

Again, it cannot be emphasized strongly enough that none of the above tests is anything like 100 percent accurate. Only by factoring in all the data can a likely time of death be estimated.

In 2001 scientists at Oak Ridge National Laboratory in Tennessee released details of a planned scanner that incorporates mass spectroscopy and gas chromatography and that can be passed over a corpse to detect and analyze the chemicals of decomposition. The belief is that these chemical "signatures" can be analyzed to give a time of death with only a two-day margin of error for every thirty days of decomposition. Research on this project is still continuing.

Toxicology

Poisons have been the subject of folklore and myth since ancient times. Their systematic study can be traced to the sixteenth century, when the German-Swiss physician and alchemist Paracelsus first stressed the chemical nature of poisons. It was Paracelsus who introduced the concept of dose and studied the actions of poisons through experimentation, and it was Paracelsus who summed up his findings in the memorable aphorism "All substances are poisons; there is none which is not a poison. The right dose differentiates a poison and a remedy."

Even armed with this knowledge, there was absolutely nothing anyone could do to curb a resolute Renaissance poisoner. Poisons were, quite simply, undetectable. For this reason they became indispensable tools in the politics of Europe, nowhere more so than in Italy, where powerful dynasties such as the Borgias and the de Medicis kept professional poisoners on the payroll to eliminate political and social obstacles.

Overwhelmingly, the poison of choice was arsenic. Nicknamed "inheritance powder" for the way in which it adjusted family fortunes, arsenic was readily available; virtually tasteless in food; killed with symptoms sufficiently similar to countless natural ailments to avoid suspicion; and was, of course, impervious to detection. But the winds of forensic change were beginning to blow.

Some time around 1790 a chemist named Johann Metzger discovered that if substances containing arsenic were heated and a cold plate held over the vapors, a white layer of arsenious oxide would form on the plate. While this "arsenic mirror" could establish whether food had been laced with arsenic, it could not tell if a body had already absorbed arsenic.

The solution to this problem was provided by Dr. Valentine Rose of the Berlin Medical Faculty in 1806. He took the corpse's stomach with its contents, cut them up, and boiled them into a kind of stew. After filtering the stew to remove any remaining flesh, he then treated the liquid with nitric acid. This had the effect of converting any arsenic present into arsenic acid, which could then be subjected to Metzger's "mirror" in the usual way.

By far the greatest toxicological leap forward came in 1836 when James Marsh, a London chemist, invented a means of detecting even the smallest quantity of arsenic. It was similar to Metzger's method, but instead of allowing the vapors to rise to the cold metal plate—with most of the gases escaping into thin air—the whole process took place in a sealed U-shaped tube that only allowed the vapors to exit via a small nozzle. The suspect material was dropped onto a zinc plate covered with dilute sulfuric acid to produce hydrogen. Any arsenine gas was then heated as it passed along a glass tube, condensing when it reached a cold part of the tube to form the "arsenic mirror." In a refined form, the Marsh test is still used today.

Elsewhere, Mathieu Joseph Bonaventura Orfila, a Spanish physician who acted as attending physician to Louis XVIII of France and occupied a chair at the University of Paris, was adding enormously to the overall knowledge of this complex subject. In thousands of grisly experiments on dogs, he recorded the effects of different poisons. Fascinated by the possibilities of combining chemistry and jurisprudence, he was the first to recognize the importance of obtaining autopsy specimens to detect accidental and intentional poisonings. Little wonder, then, that Orfila has been dubbed "The Father of Forensic Toxicology."

Toxicology is the science of adverse effects of chemicals on living organisms. Broadly speaking, a toxicologist detects and identifies foreign chemicals in the body, with a particular emphasis on toxic or hazardous substances. Toxic reactions fall into one of three categories: pharmacological—injury to the central nervous system; pathological—injury to the liver; and genotoxic—creation of benign or malignant tumors (usually very long-term, from twenty to forty years).

Toxic materials exist in many forms (gaseous, liquid, solid, animal, mineral, and vegetable) and may be ingested, inhaled, or absorbed through the skin. Poisons generally enter the body in a single massive dose, or accumulate over time. The latter method is most commonly employed by the deliberate poisoner, a stealthy erosion of the victim's health to the point where death is both expected and nonsuspicious.

Of the many confirmation tests for poison, mass spectrometry—with its ability to determine the organic structure of a sample—is considered the most preferable, since each toxin has a known mass spectrum, or "fingerprint," which is infallible proof of its presence at the chemical level.

How many people are murdered each year by poison is unknown. Confirmed cases make up a minuscule percentage of the annual homicide rate. Data compiled by the FBI show that out of 15,517 homicides in 2000 just 8 were poison victims. Given the extraordinary sophistication and range of modern detection techniques, one can only marvel that poisoners persist in their attempts to fool the laboratory. But their advantage lies in the fact that before it can be detected, poison first has to be suspected, and while the symptoms remain so tricky to diagnose, it is safe to say that poisoning will remain with us.

The following is a list of the most common poisons and their typical symptoms:

Acids (nitric, hydrochloric, sulfuric)—burns around mouth, lips, nose
Aconite—numbness and tingling in extremities
Arsenic—acute, unexplained diarrhea, Mees lines
Atropine (belladonna)—pupil of eye dilated
Carbolic acid—odor of disinfectant
Carbon monoxide—skin is bright cherry red
Cyanide—quick death, red skin, odor of almond
Metallic compounds—diarrhea, vomiting, abdominal pain
Nicotine—convulsions
Opiates—pupil of eye contracted
Oxalic acid (phosphorous)—odor of garlic
Strychnine—convulsion, dark face and neck
Thallium—hair loss

Jack Unterweger

Date: 1991
Location: Vienna, Austria, and Los Angeles

In 1991 polices forces on two continents were struggling to catch a serial killer, each unaware that they were pursuing the same man. In California, over a twenty-day period beginning June 20, the bodies of three prostitutes were found in Los Angeles County. All three killings were eerily similar: each girl had been strangled with her own bra, which had been tied with a distinctive knot, then each had been dumped, either nude or half nude, in some remote rural region far from the city lights where they had hustled a living.

Details of the killings were fed into the FBI's Violent Criminal Apprehension Program (VICAP) database. This operates on the principle that crime signatures—the manner in which crimes are committed—can be almost as individual as a fingerprint, with each killer displaying his own distinctive quirk or pattern of quirks that highlight his individuality. Ordinarily VICAP can be expected to highlight the ten closest matches from known previous crimes; here it drew a blank. The L.A. killings were so distinctive that they only resembled each other.

Half a world away, in Austria, the Viennese police were equally baffled. Since the turn of the year, that city's red-light district had been paralyzed with fear. Four prostitutes had been strangled in five months. Only grudgingly did the police accept the fact that they were dealing with a serial killer, a phenomenon hitherto virtually unknown in that country.

A retired detective living in Salzburg, disturbed by newspaper accounts of the crimes, contacted officers working the case and reminded them of a 1973 murder he had investigated involving a female Yugoslav factory worker who had been dragged from Lake Salzach. By the time he had amassed enough evidence to charge his prime suspect, the man was already serving a life sentence for murder, so he was ordered to drop the case. Now the ex-detective had made an unnerving discovery: Jack Unterweger was a free man.

At the time of his 1975 conviction for strangling a female neighbor, Unterweger had been described by a prison psychologist as "enormously aggressive with sexually sadistic perversion . . . incorrigible." The assessment had ended with a chilling prediction: "Recidivism has to be expected with certainty."

And yet, despite this warning, Unterweger, now age thirty-eight, was out walking the streets, feted as a celebrity. While behind bars, he'd discovered a genuine talent for writing: plays, poetry, and a novel flowed from his pen. The Viennese literati took him to their heart, heralding him as a model of rehabilitation and campaigning noisily for his parole. This came in September 1990. Television appearances followed, as did radio work and journalism, and it was in the latter capacity that allowed him to cover the red-light murders in

Vienna from a unique perspective, ensuring that his radio interviews with police officers and prostitutes alike received big ratings.

In the summer of 1991 Unterweger was commissioned by a magazine to write about prostitution in Los Angeles. Shortly after his arrival in California, streetwalkers began dying. His return to Austria coincided with another spike in the red-light killings. Then a young Graz prostitute told police how a client had driven her out to some woods, paid her, then handcuffed her. When she became frightened and started to cry, he inexplicably released her. From the personalized license plate on the car—JACK 1—police had no difficulty tracing the driver.

Unterweger became the center of a huge surveillance operation. Credit card bills placed him in Graz, Vienna, and Vorelberg at the time of the murders. Attempts were made to trace his cars—he had owned six in two years—but each had been methodically cleaned and offered no evidentiary assistance. The Austrian press, by now in a frenzy, prematurely announced that a warrant had been issued for Unterweger's arrest. Unterweger, in Switzerland at the time, fled, first to Paris, then to the United States.

Street maps of L.A. found in his Vienna apartment soon established a link between the Austrian and American killings, and Unterweger had stayed in hotels immediately adjacent to the areas where the L.A. victims had gone missing. When the FBI ran the Austrian killings through VICAP, using six indicators—female, prostitute, age nineteen to thirty-five, found nude or seminude, ligature-strangled, body disposed in remote wooded area—it located four matches. One, an unrelated crime, had been solved; the other three were the murders in L.A. On February 27, 1992, Unterweger was arrested in Miami.

Although there was a very strong circumstantial case against Unterweger on two continents, it was by no means cast-iron. Desperate not to let him slip through their fingers, the Austrian authorities contacted Interpol and requested details of all similar murders anywhere in the world.

This led them to Prague. On September 14, 1990, a young woman named Blanka Bockova had stormed out of a bar after arguing with her boyfriend. At the same time, at the other end of Wenceslaus Square, Unterweger just happened to be wishing a friend good night. The next day Blanka's strangled body was found in some woods. Oddly enough, the Ford Mustang that Unterweger drove on his Prague trip was the only one of his cars that detectives had failed to trace, and they wondered if it might hold a lead. Finding that car proved nightmarishly difficult. Eventually, after two years of painstaking effort, it was traced to a Linz garage.

On the passenger seat was a single hair. It was sent to a lab in Berne, Switzerland, for DNA analysis. Because DNA from hair can only be extracted from the root—and they had only one—it made for some extraordinarily delicate testing. In the end it yielded just *9 billionths of a gram* of human DNA!

It was enough. After complex PCR sampling, scientists were able to state, with a certainty of 1 in 2.1 million, that this hair had come from Blanka Bockova.

Charged in Austria with the murder of eleven women in three countries, Unterweger was convicted and sentenced to life without parole. Fewer than twenty-four hours later, using a rope fashioned from shoelaces and a track suit cord, this extraordinary international strangler hanged himself.

Willem van Rie

Date: 1959
Location: Boston, Massachusetts

Lynn Kauffmann was a twenty-three-year-old divorcée from Chicago who worked as a secretary for a St. Louis professor. When the professor and his family took a sabbatical in the Far East, Lynn accompanied them. In August 1959 the party joined the Royal Dutch Steamship Company's *Utrecht* in Singapore for the thirty-three-day voyage to Boston. It was a small ship, with just nine passengers, a perfect forum for Lynn's vivacity. By all accounts she was the life and soul of the party—until the ship docked in Boston on September 18. On that day she suddenly turned morose and refused to leave her cabin. Even the ship's radio officer, Willem van Rie, who had become friendly with Lynn, failed to coax her from her lethargy.

At 6:15 P.M. the ship steamed south for the short voyage to New York. Forty-five minutes later Lynn was still refusing to leave her cabin, saying that she didn't feel well enough to eat. When she had failed to put in an appearance at nine o'clock, the purser, together with van Rie, went to her cabin. They found it empty. Although both portholes were open and Lynn's dinner dress hung unused on a hook, there was little immediate cause for concern. The high rail that protected the companionway outside Lynn's cabin made it almost impossible for her to have fallen overboard accidentally.

But when a search of the ship and a lifeboat drill failed to flush her out of hiding, the captain was forced to accept the inevitable. At midnight he radioed the U.S. Coast Guard with his suspicions that a passenger had vanished overboard. As a precautionary measure, he also had the cabin locked.

When the *Utrecht* docked the next day in New York, Lynn had already been found. Her seminude body had washed up on Spectacle Island, a ninety-seven acre outcrop in Boston Harbor. Initial police inquiries suggested that an unwanted change in her employment circumstances had led to depression and suicide.

In the meantime, an autopsy was performed by Dr. Michael Luongo, the Suffolk County, Massachusetts, medical examiner. Apart from unmistakable signs of drowning, there were small areas of hemorrhage on the membranes of the brain and a number of bruises on the body. Drawing on this evidence—and this evidence alone—he ruled the death a homicide.

The police were thrown into a quandary. They still thought it was suicide, but Luongo's intransigence triggered a change of heart. Fresh inquiries targeted van Rie, and soon various anomalies appeared. His coat was found in Lynn's cabin, and on the evening of her disappearance, his weather report to the bridge had been delayed and there were some inaccuracies in his radio log.

When questioned, van Rie had answers for all these minor inconsistencies, and he also confirmed what shipboard gossip had long suspected: he and Lynn had been sleeping together. Under a brutal interrogation, he made a statement—later disputed—that he had visited Lynn to ask if she was pregnant. Prosecutors speculated that this had triggered a violent quarrel during which the radio officer savagely beat Lynn, then threw her overboard. He was charged with murder.

Desperate to fend off bad publicity and a possible civil suit, van Rie's employers contacted **Milton Helpern,** New York's chief medical examiner. They wanted to know if it was possible to say that someone had been murdered purely on the evidence Luongo uncovered in his autopsy. Helpern had his doubts and agreed to review Luongo's findings.

What he found startled and unnerved him. Yes, Lynn had drowned; yes, she had a head injury; yes, she had widespread bruising on her body. But there was absolutely nothing to prove homicide. Helpern based his opinion on the fact that nearly all the injuries were confined to the left side of the body, and he couldn't imagine any way that a struggle of the kind described by prosecutors would produce such uniform marks. What he could picture was the very strong likelihood that most of these left-sided injuries had been caused by Lynn hitting the water with colossal impact.

Falling some forty feet from a ship traveling at sixteen knots, Helpern estimated, would produce a collision impact of between thirty and thirty-five miles per hour. At that kind of speed water can be as hard as concrete. In addition, he felt that a folded gangplank projecting from the ship's side beneath Lynn's cabin might well have contributed to the overall bruising.

At the trial Luongo insisted that Lynn's injuries had all been inflicted in the cabin, that she had been rendered unconscious, then thrown overboard.

Helpern was horrified by such arrogance: nothing in the autopsy permitted such conclusions. When he himself took the stand, he said it was perfectly possible for this woman to have fallen or jumped overboard. Asked if she could have been pushed, he replied, "Yes, sure she could—but you have to prove that some other way; you can't tell that from an autopsy." He went on to explain how, in addition to the injuries sustained in the fall, Lynn's body had been washed back and forth among the rocks on Spectacle Island before discovery. All the other minor injuries to the body could have been sustained at this point.

Prosecutorial belligerence at this perceived interloper from New York City meant that Helpern was given a hard time on the stand, but he refused to budge. "If you've ever seen a body falling," he told the assistant district attorney, "you'll know there's a lot of action. It doesn't fall like a statue . . . the body is folded, the limbs are flexed, the head is moving. The impact is not single, it's composite. As soon as it strikes it gets thrashed about."

Despite sustained and sarcastic attempts by the state to undermine Helpern's testimony, it obviously impressed the people who mattered most. On March 2 the jury acquitted van Rie, who renounced the sea and returned to his native Holland. Helpern went back to New York, nursing suspicions about what he termed the "vengeful nature" of New England justice that never quite left him.

Darren Vickers

Date: 1997
Location: Manchester, England

The disappearance of eight-year-old Jamie Lavis from his home provided a rallying call for the whole community of Openshaw, Manchester, and among the many well-wishers who called at Jamie's house the next day was Darren Vickers, a twenty-seven-year-old bus driver who lived three streets away. Vickers offered more than just sympathetic encouragement: he told police he was certain that Jamie had been on his bus on May 5, 1997, and he wanted to do everything possible to assist the inquiry. A statement was taken. Although previously a stranger to the family, Vickers wormed his way into their good graces to the point where he actually moved into the family house and attended the emotion-packed press conferences, even accompanying Jamie's mother to scenes of alleged sightings.

Right from the outset, detectives distrusted Vickers. But the family would hear none of it. So far as they were concerned, their newfound ally was "a pillar of strength," someone they had come to trust and rely on in their hour of need. Such loyalty badly hampered the police, making them reluctant to share any leads with the family in case they got back to Vickers.

CCTV security footage at the bus station where Vickers was based showed Jamie playing and meeting Vickers. As had happened on several occasions before, Jamie had ridden Vickers's bus for several hours until, said Vickers, the boy disembarked.

Although profoundly suspicious of Vickers, investigators found nothing tangible to link him to Jamie's disappearance. Vickers, meanwhile, reveled in the media coverage. As the months passed and his confidence grew, he even organized ad hoc search parties to look for the boy. Twice he led separate groups of teenagers to some woodland adjoining a local golf club, only to return empty-handed.

Coincidentally, police officers had already earmarked this wooded stretch as one area in which Vickers, if he was the killer, might have disposed of the body. A prolonged and thorough search finally paid off on October 23 with the discovery of bone fragments. Laboratory tests confirmed that these were human remains, though animal depredations had left precious little to analyze. Because the killer had hacked off the limbs and most of the skull—the jawbone was the largest bone found—it made identification almost impossible.

A uniform decomposition rate, the fact that the bones were of similar age, and the absence of duplication gave the pathologist Dr. John Rutherford enough confidence to state that the bones were from one individual, aged between six and eleven. But he could not determine the sex of the victim, nor could he offer any opinion as to time of death, except to say that the total absence of soft tissue suggested exposure to the elements for several months.

Even the victim's teeth—often a prime source of identification—proved infuriatingly ambiguous. An odontologist named Judy Hinchcliffe studied X-rays of the jawbone and saw that the first molars had developed, the premolars were waiting in the jawbone, and sockets at the front were of teeth lost after death. She estimated that the jaw was from a child aged between seven and nine. However, while dental records strongly indicated that it could have belonged to Jamie, a positive identification was impossible because children's teeth change so rapidly.

In situations like this, forensic laboratories nowadays turn to DNA to provide proof positive of identification. But DNA testing works best on soft tissue that has cellular material from which DNA can be extracted. Here there was no soft tissue. Further frustration followed. Sometimes DNA can be extracted from the marrow of the long arm bones and leg bones, but these were missing. Despite an overwhelming likelihood, there seemed to be nothing to say categorically that this was the body of Jamie Lavis.

Eventually it was decided that there was reasonable cause to arrest Vickers on a charge of abduction. Numerous passengers on the 209 bus that day told of seeing the boy either sitting in the cab or else taking fares. Some mistook Vickers to be the child's uncle, with one person observing to the driver that he had his "little helper" with him again.

Vickers was steadfast in his denials of both abduction and murder. But under constant questioning, holes began to appear in his story, and he eventually admitted giving the boy a ride in his car after finishing his shift.

Just when it seemed as though Vickers might elude justice, a new breakthrough in DNA technology offered a ray of hope for the beleaguered investigators: scientists managed to extract dental pulp from the premolars. Because it is free from natural contamination, dental pulp is one of the most informative sources of DNA. For this reason, scientists investigating the Black Death that ravaged Europe in the fourteenth century, killing more than twenty million people, have begun using tooth pulp from victims to investigate the possible causes of this outbreak.

The big drawback of tooth pulp is that it yields only minuscule amounts of DNA. Therefore, the sample must first be amplified using PCR. In this case, the results were sufficient to match the DNA of the victim in the woods to the grieving parents.

Jamie Lavis had been found and identified.

Although prosecutors had no idea when or how Vickers murdered young Jamie, they were adamant that this was no spur-of-the-moment assault. For weeks, they said, Vickers had been "grooming [Jamie] for sex," regularly inviting him onto his bus, gaining the youngster's confidence. On May 5 all his plans had come to fruition. Afterward he had hacked the boy's head off—it was never found—and then dumped the body.

At his trial—and without a whit of evidence—Vickers attempted to shovel all the blame onto Jamie's father, but it was a heartless ploy that failed to convince the jury. On April 23, 1999, he was jailed for life. After being convicted, Vickers wrote a sanitized confession in which he admitted killing Jamie Lavis, claiming that it was a tragic accident.

François-Eugène Vidocq (1775–1857)

A former lawbreaker who became the founder of modern criminal investigation, François-Eugène Vidocq was born in Arras, in northern France. In 1792, at age seventeen, he fled his hometown after killing his fencing master—whether by accident or in a duel is uncertain—and thereafter pursued a life of mostly petty and unsuccessful crime.

After several stints behind bars and one spectacular escape, he wearied of the brutal galley ships and rat-infested jails and offered his services as a police spy in return for amnesty. The offer was accepted. He prospered in his new role, and in 1810 was placed in charge of the newly formed Sûreté in Paris. Adopting the philosophy that to catch criminals one had to think like a criminal, Vidocq recruited a network of spies and informants, and sent them into the teeming streets of the capital. In 1817, with only twelve full-time assistants, he was responsible for more than eight hundred arrests. Many of those arrested were offered a stark choice: prison or turncoat. Most

François-Eugène Vidocq, the former thief who went on to head the Sûreté before establishing the world's first private detective agency.

opted for the latter, adding to Vidocq's growing army of underworld spies. Some even became bona fide detectives.

Although Vidocq was a ruthless self-promoter who hired ghostwriters to record and embellish his achievements in a string of highly popular books, there can be no doubting his pioneering flair. Besides being a master of disguise and surveillance—traits he encouraged among his staff—he was also the first to introduce systematic record keeping into police work, imposing a card-index system to keep track of the flood of tips and information that at times threatened to overwhelm the Sûreté. His evidence-harvesting techniques were equally revolutionary. It was his agile mind that saw the possibilities of using plaster of Paris to make casts of foot/shoe impressions left at crime scenes.

Despite these groundbreaking advances, Vidocq was restless and hungry for money. In 1827 he resigned from the Sûreté to start a paper and cardboard mill, staffed in the main by former convicts. But cash flow problems ruined him, and he was obliged to again become chief of the Sûreté's Detective Department.

Scandal was never far removed from Vidocq, and in 1832 allegations that he had organized a theft forced his removal from office. This time the break was irrevocable, and that same year he created Le Bureau des Renseignements (Office of Information), the world's first private detective agency. Even in his days at the Sûreté, he had undertaken private cases to boost his paltry income; now it became his life. To make ends meet, he diversified. An annual subscription of 20 francs bought clients access to a blacklist of convicts and fraudsters that Vidocq had compiled, a forerunner of the modern credit check.

Although Vidocq's agency dwindled to nearly nothing and he died in poverty, his memory lives on at the Vidocq Society, an informal gathering of forensic and law enforcement professionals that regularly meets in Philadelphia to discuss old unsolved cases and to apply the same deductive principles first introduced by the brilliant detective from France.

The Vinland Map

Date: 1965
Location: New Haven, Connecticut

In 1965 a document came to light that threatened to turn history upside down. Drawn on a single vellum sheet measuring eleven by sixteen inches and folded down the middle, it purported to be a medieval map of the Old World. In the western Atlantic it depicted a large island called Vinilanda Insula (island of Vinland, land of vines), the Vinland of the Norse sagas, and what is unmistakably the northeastern coast of North America.

Bound to the map was a single tract of medieval Latin text, dated circa 1440, that described how Leif Eriksson, a Viking mariner, had traveled to this new land around the year 1000. Both map and tract appeared to suggest that Europeans—not just the Vikings—were aware of the New World a full fifty years before Christopher Columbus made his epic voyage of discovery in 1492.

But one big question remained: was the Vinland Map genuine?

Ever since medieval times the antiquities/art market has provided an irresistible lure to forgers. When one considers the sums of money involved, this is scarcely surprising. In the mid-1990s even the most conservative estimate valued the Vinland Map at more than $20 million.

Such valuations—and the insurance premiums that accompany them—mean that museums and other repositories set great store by provenance. Originally the map had been offered to the British Museum in 1957 by an unspecified source. Uncomfortable with the map's murky past and certain irregularities with the binding, the museum had rejected the item, and it remained in private hands until 1965, when the philanthropist Paul Mellon donated it to the Beinecke Rare Book and Manuscript Library at Yale University. Archaeological discovery in the early 1960s of a Norse settlement in Newfoundland only heightened the map's relevance.

Doubts about its authenticity persisted, however, and in 1972 Yale commissioned the Chicago chemist Walter McCrone to microscopically analyze the map. McCrone found that whoever drew the map first used a yellow ink,

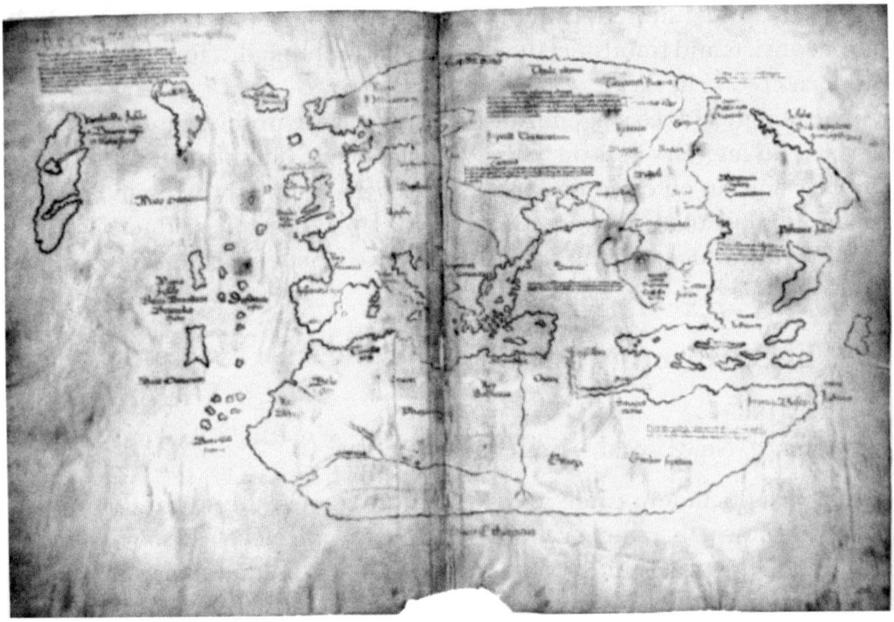

The Vinland Map: a genuine treasure or a brilliant fake? Arguments rage to the present day.

then carefully superimposed a black ink line over this. The black outer layer was actually flaking off, but the yellow ink still adhered firmly to the surface, and it was this yellow ink that raised doubts. In it, McCrone detected the presence of anatase, a form of titanium dioxide. Anatase does occur in nature, but only in small amounts and then in jagged, irregular crystals—not the round, uniform crystals that McCrone found here. As far as McCrone was concerned, this form of anatase could have originated from only one source: modern ink. In 1923 ink manufacturers began adding just such uniform crystals of anatase to their products; this was evidence enough for McCrone to declare the Vinland Map a twentieth-century fake.

McCrone, a scientist of profoundly skeptical views, most notorious for his debunking of the Turin Shroud, was a natural lightning rod for criticism, and in 1995 his findings came under attack from a team led by Thomas Cahill, a professor of atmospheric science and physics at the University of California. Their analysis concluded that most of the crystals McCrone found were not anatase and that a third of the ink contained no titanium.

The war of words continued to rage. In July 2002 supporters of the map received a boost when a Smithsonian Institute–backed radiocarbon dating of the parchment came up with a date of approximately 1434, well within the time frame of when the map was supposed to have been drawn. After all, said the research chemist Jacqueline Olin, "It's not a trivial thing for a forger to get a parchment [from that time period]."

By coincidence, on that same day, researchers at University College in London also revealed the results of *their* investigation into the Vinland Map, and these provided unequivocal support for McCrone.

Using a Raman microscope, which employs a laser beam that scatters molecules as radiation with different colors, Professor Robin Clark and Katherine Brown found that anatase was detected solely in the yellowish ink lines and not elsewhere on the parchment. Since yellow lines are sometimes left behind when medieval ink made of iron gallotannate degrades, Clark said a forger would know about the yellow residue and try to reproduce it. But the black ink on top of the yellow ink was found to be carbon-based, not iron gallotannate, so no yellow residue should be present.

Most likely, both teams are correct: the parchment is fifteenth-century vellum, and the inks are indisputably modern. Whoever faked the Vinland Map was clearly an expert in his or her field, and in August 2002 the author Kirsten Seaver pointed the finger at a most unlikely culprit.

Father Joseph Fischer, who died in Germany in 1944 at age eighty-six, was an authority on medieval cartography. As a young man he had discovered the first map, dated 1507, to name America—it was bought recently by the Library of Congress for $10 million—and it was Fischer's obsession with achieving firsts, according to Seaver, that prompted the fake. She believes that Fischer succumbed to serious depression after his credentials came under attack in 1934, and that at about the same time he acquired a volume of fifteenth-century manuscripts into which was bound a loose leaf of a piece of parchment dating from the 1440s, and he decided to fool the world.

Seaver claims to have analyzed the record of every other scholar in the field between 1920 and 1957, and insists that the circumstantial evidence points overwhelmingly to Fischer. His handwriting corresponds to that on the map; the incorrect Latinate spellings are what one might expect of a scholar who was proficient in Latin but ignorant of Old Norse; the tract bears the remains of a faded stamp similar to one used by the Jesuit college of Stella Matutina at Feldkirch, Austria, to which Fischer was linked; and even the fact that the map showed the world as round told against Fischer. Seaver says that Fischer was alone in realizing that medieval mapmakers utilized the Ptolemaic knowledge that the world was not flat.

Whether Seaver's allegations stand the test of time remains to be seen. But for now, the evidence is strongly in favor of those who believe the Vinland Map to be a highly skilled forgery.

Voiceprints

In 1941 the possibility that someone could be identified solely by the sound of his or her voice led scientists at Bell Telephone Laboratories to develop the sound spectrograph. First used by World War II intelligence services to identify voices broadcast by German military communications, the technology fell into disuse until the early sixties, when the FBI began to investigate its forensic applications. The Bell engineer Lawrence Kersta became convinced that voice spectrograms—or "voiceprints," as he called them—could provide a valuable means of personal identification.

First he needed to examine what it is that gives our voices their seemingly unique aural characteristics. It is mostly a result of physiology—the size of the vocal cavities such as the throat; nasal and oral cavities; and the shape, length, and tension in an individual's vocal cords in the larynx. As air passes over the vocal cords, the vocal cavities act as resonators, much like organ pipes, shaping and amplifying the sound.

Then it is the turn of the "articulators," those muscles of speech that come into play when an individual is talking. These include the lips, teeth, tongue, soft palate, and jaw muscles. They, too, add uniqueness. Once the resonators and articulators have done their work, we have intelligible speech. Given the seemingly infinite number of variables inherent in such a physical setup, the chances of two people having an identical configuration would appear to be very remote.

Kersta realized that the human voice is incapable of producing just one pitch at a time. Instead, it produces a simultaneous series of fundamentals and overtones. Some overtones are random; others are multiples of the fundamental, called harmonics. Of all the characteristics of voice, two of the most important ones are frequency and intensity. Frequency is the speed at which air particles vibrate, measured in centimeters per second. Humans can only produce and hear frequencies in the range of 60 to 16,000 cycles per second. Intensity is the amount of energy (volume) in a sound wave or pulse. Variation in intensity does not affect frequency, but no two sound waves (even those produced by the same individual) will have exactly the same frequencies and intensities—that is, a sound, once made (even by the same individual), can never be exactly replicated in all its characteristics. Over four years, Kersta studied recordings of fifty thousand different voices, many of them apparently similar. He then submitted them to spectrographic analysis.

The spectrograph records a 2.5-second band of speech on tape, which is then scanned electronically, a process taking some 90 seconds. The output is next recorded on to a rotating drum. As the drum revolves, a filter adjusts the various frequencies, enabling a stylus to record their intensity, and producing a printout that looks similar to recordings of earthquake tremors. These printouts are sliced into 2.5-second segments called spectrograms, and they portray three spectra: time (horizontal axis); frequency (vertical axis), and intensity (degree of darkness in the ink—the denser the print, the louder the tone). Two kinds of voiceprint can be obtained: bar prints and contour prints. The former are used for identification; the contour version is suitable for computerized filing.

Kersta found spectrographic differences in all fifty thousand experiments. Even professional mimics, asked to record imitations of individuals, were unable to fool the machine, producing results on graph and screen that were markedly dissimilar from those they were imitating. The findings encouraged Kersta to branch out on his own, marketing both the principle and the equipment necessary for its implementation.

He found critics at every turn. Naysayers contend that conventional voiceprints make little allowance for bodily or environmental changes. A tooth extraction or the wearing of dentures can drastically affect the vocal cavities, while aging affects all the muscles associated with speech, possibly producing spectrographic changes. Also, someone's manner of speech may alter significantly if he or she changes locality and acquires a regional accent. Without empirical evidence—and there have been no broad-based studies thus far—the impact of these changes is impossible to gauge.

Today, use of the term "voiceprint," with its misleading association to fingerprinting, has fallen into disfavor, as some fear that it invests the technology with more scientific credibility than it deserves. "Spectrograph voice recognition" is now the most commonly used description. The change in nomenclature has done little to advance the technology's acceptance in American courtrooms, where it has still to find universal acceptance, even though law enforcement agencies have found it to be a valuable investigative tool for screening potential suspects.

In many respects this legal reticence is baffling. Elsewhere, voice individuality is increasingly used in many areas of daily life. The U.S. military, in the search for ever more efficient ways of improving national security, now use voice recognition as a means of monitoring access to restricted areas. Computer programmers, desperate to find the "killer ap" that will enable the human voice to replace the keyboard and the mouse, have made quantum leaps in voice recognition software.

"Voiceprints are as unique as fingerprints," boasts one California-based voice recognition software developer. But this is to patently overstate the case. Fingerprints are static: if someone makes five prints of his right thumb, they will all match. However, if that same person makes five voiceprints of him saying "Put one hundred thousand dollars in unmarked bills in a brown paper bag," each voiceprint will be different. This is because voices are dynamic. The voice you use first thing in the morning—before a cup of coffee, say—will be different spectrographically from your voice later that morning. For this reason, the experienced examiner will insist on obtaining several repetitions of a speaker's voice, saying the same thing, so the full range of variations can be found.

Despite all these safeguards, error rates in excess of 6 percent have been recorded in some voice spectrographic tests. Although a skilled examiner could probably make significant inroads into that failure rate, chances are that spectrograph voice recognition will continue to struggle to escape the shadow of the **polygraph,** and is therefore likely to remain a peripheral forensic discipline.

Albert Walker

Date: 1996
Location: Devon, England

When John Copik, a commercial trawlerman working the southern Devonshire coastline, hauled in his nets on July 28, 1996, he made a gruesome discovery: among that day's catch was a dead male body. A deep cut to the back of the head and another gouge on his hip were the only injuries, though neither wound was thought suspicious, both being consistent with either having struck a rock or having been hit by a boat propeller. There was nothing about the body to aid identification—except a Rolex wristwatch and a small tattoo on the back of the right hand.

Rolex factory records logged the service serial number to a Ronald Joseph Platt, who was traced to a rental address in Chelmsford, Essex. The landlords of the property were unable to help with Platt's current whereabouts, but they did direct police to a friend of the missing man.

David Davis lived in nearby Woodham Walter; however, when a detective visited Davis's farmhouse, he called at the wrong house, only to be told that he must be mistaken—nobody named Davis lived next door, but there was an American named Platt. A string of background checks soon revealed the startling truth: for the past three years, Davis had been living every aspect of his life as Ronald Platt!

When officers did gain access to the nondescript farmhouse, they just looked around in amazement. It was stuffed with gold bars, oil paintings, and a huge selection of false identity documents.

David Davis, age fifty, shifted and quibbled, but gradually the truth began to emerge. His real name was Albert Walker, and he was not American but Canadian. Nor was he any run-of-the-mill expatriate: in 1990 he had fled Ontario to escape thirty-seven charges of theft, fraud, and money laundering involving millions of dollars. By the time of his arrest, he had risen to number four on Interpol's most-wanted list.

Walker had arrived in Britain with his daughter Sheena, then age fifteen, in December 1990. Courtesy of countless false identities, he continued to launder his stolen millions through a bewildering maze of accounts. Then, in late 1991 he met Ronald Platt, a gullible dupe with dreams of living in Canada. When Walker offered to finance his ambition, Platt jumped at the opportunity and took off for Canada, blissfully unaware that as soon as he left, Walker assumed his identity.

Living as Ron and Noelle Platt, husband and wife, Walker and his daughter had not attracted suspicion. Indeed, they prospered, and might have continued to do so had not Platt returned, penniless, to England in 1995. Police suspected that with this unexpected reappearance, Platt unwittingly signed his own death warrant. Walker, now well established as a financial adviser, was prepared to pay any price to preserve his new identity, even if that meant killing Ronald Platt.

But was there any evidence to say that Platt had actually been murdered?

More in hope than expectation, detectives reinterviewed the trawlermen and learned that a separate anchor had been dragged up with the body. Since there was no rope attached to either the body or the anchor, and since it appeared to be an unrelated find, it had been disposed of at a secondhand sale. After three months of laborious searching, police finally managed to track down the missing anchor.

Then came a flash of deductive brilliance. What if, said a junior officer, Platt had been rendered unconscious, and the anchor had been hooked over his belt before he was thrown in the water? Might such a scenario account for that hip injury? Sure enough, when samples from belt and anchor were analyzed, both were found to contain similar traces of speckled zinc.

The investigation now gathered pace. It was learned that on July 8, 1996, someone had gone into a ship chandler's shop in Devon with a credit card in the name of R. J. Platt and purchased an anchor identical to that used to weigh down the body. This credit card was found in Walker's possession when he was arrested.

On Walker's boat the *Lady Jane* was a bag with the dead man's fingerprints, and a cushion that harbored three individual samples of Platt's hair (DNA analysis had confirmed the identification). Walker smoothly admitted that he and Platt had gone sailing on July 7 and that a large wave had caught the boat awkwardly, sending Platt sprawling and banging his head.

Walker's story seemed unbreakable, as did his insistence that he had been nowhere near the spot where Platt's body was found, until searchers visited a storage unit that Walker had rented. Hidden inside was a global positioning satellite (GPS) navigational system.

The GPS system has revolutionized navigation on sea and land. At its heart is a network of orbiting satellites, whose locations are continuously monitored by stations around the globe. The satellite transmits a radio signal at a steady frequency. A stationary observer detects a higher frequency as the satellite approaches and a lower one as it recedes. Measuring the speed of this frequency drop determines the distance of the observer from the satellite's track.

At the instant of the satellite's closest approach, the observed frequency is the same as that transmitted, so at that time the observer must be somewhere along the line at right angles to the satellite's track. Since this track over the Earth's surface is accurately known at all times, this reading, combined with the distance measurement, pinpoints the observer's position.

Walker's GPS system proved to be his undoing. A computer download was able to display the last known coordinates of where that handset had been turned off. These plotted the position of the *Lady Jane* at about three miles off the south Devon coast—right where the body was found—at 2059 hours on July 20, 1996.

A ten-pound anchor was more than sufficient to take Platt's body to the bottom, and experts conducted experiments to see if currents in that area were sufficient to move such a weighted body. They concluded that the body had been dumped where it was found.

All this information had come from a single watch. Had Walker ditched the Rolex, he would have gotten away with murder. Instead he got life imprisonment.

Delbert Ward

Date: 1990
Location: Munnsville, New York

The Ward boys were an eccentric bunch, whose existence owed more to frontier times than it did to their native upstate New York in the 1990s. The quartet of brothers—all bachelors—ranged in age from fifty-nine to seventy, and they lived together in a run-down four-room shack with no indoor plumbing on the outskirts of the town of Munnsville, where they made their living tending cows.

Although not the oldest, Bill, age sixty-four, was by common consent the leader of the Ward clan. He was the smartest and the strongest, even if he did complain constantly of stomach cramps, headaches, and swollen feet. On the morning of June 6, 1990, Bill's chronic suffering came to an end when he was found dead in bed by his youngest and closest brother, Delbert. The autopsy was performed at the Onondaga County medical examiner's office by Dr. Humphrey Germaniuk, who refused to declare a cause of death pending further investigation, because he had found signs of petechiae on the body.

Petechiae are tiny hemorrhages, pinpricks of blood caused by burst capillaries. They happen when the heart is unable to do its job properly. Ordinarily the heart keeps the body supplied with the oxygen and other elements it needs to survive. If something happens to impede that pumping, the blood backs up in the veins and begins to exert pressure on the capillaries, the smallest of the body's blood vessels, causing them to erupt and form petechiae, most often in the whites of the eyes. In dead bodies this reaction is very often an indicator of asphyxia.

Because of the medical examiner's doubts, the Ward brothers were taken that same night to the sheriff's office in Munnsville. After prolonged and vigorous questioning, Delbert signed a confession to the effect that he had smothered Bill by placing his hand over his brother's mouth and nose for about five minutes until he was dead, as he thought he would be "better off away from his pains." Disturbingly, once Delbert confessed, Germaniuk reclassified the death certificate to read "homicide."

But local townspeople were concerned. Delbert, a simple soul, was known to be highly suggestible, and the mood was that he had been browbeaten into confessing. It just didn't seem possible for such a little guy to suffocate his much bigger and stronger brother with his bare hands. However, when the full autopsy report confirmed the presence of petechiae in both eyes and the mouth, and insufficient evidence of organic disease to account for death, prosecutors decided they had enough to charge Delbert with second-degree murder.

One person who had followed this high-profile case with keen interest was the pathologist **Cyril Wecht.** While aware that petechiae were generally caused by asphyxia, he also knew that they could occur naturally, so when he was asked by the defense to review the autopsy notes, he readily agreed. What he found troubled him profoundly. When a person is abruptly deprived of air, the survival instinct goes into overdrive as the body does whatever is necessary to obtain oxygen. Unless the person is either infirm or heavily drugged, this usually means a violent struggle. Even though smothering can occasionally leave little external evidence of trauma—in babies, for instance—the forceful closure of the air passages more often than not results in some hemorrhaging and tearing of the inner linings of the mouth and nose. Yet here, the autopsy report indicated that the deceased's air passages were free from trauma or blood.

Another telltale sign in a suspected case of asphyxia is evidence of regurgitation, brought on by the combined physical effect and emotional stress of struggling for air. Just before retiring for the night, Bill had eaten a large clam supper, yet none of it had been found in his esophagus, trachea, or mouth. Nor was there a thinning of the blood or a bluish-purple appearance to the skin, two other quite common symptoms of asphyxial deaths.

The more Wecht studied the report, the more baffled he became by Germaniuk's finding that there was little evidence of organic disease. Not only were the liver and spleen both enlarged, but also the heart weighed 420 grams, more than one hundred grams above the average weight for a man of Ward's size and age, and atherosclerosis—fatty degeneration—had caused a 20 percent blockage of the coronary arteries.

Also, the respiratory system displayed clear evidence of abnormality. The right lung weighed almost twice as much as the left, and the lower part of the left lung was covered with scar tissue. Even more importantly, both lungs showed "prominent arteriosclerotic plaques" of the pulmonary arteries—another sign of cardiopulmonary disease.

As far as Wecht was concerned, there was plenty to suggest that the physical ailments that had so plagued Bill in life could be attributed to an inadequate blood supply. All it would take was for some kind of cardiac arrhythmia—an irregular heartbeat—and Bill would have died a natural death. This was a set of circumstances regularly found in autopsies performed on people of Bill's age. Wecht could find nothing in the report to indicate murder.

Because of its unusual nature, the case attracted plenty of media interest, most of it highly favorable to the defendant. Perhaps for this reason, New York State prosecutors went after Delbert Ward with a particularly mean-spirited tenacity.

Despite Germaniuk's astonishing courtroom admission that without Delbert's confession he would not have changed the death certificate, the state refused to recant and instead launched a bitter counterattack. Wecht bore the brunt of their wrath. Brought in as a defense witness, he slugged it out with the prosecutor in a bruising, often abusive contest, holding fast to his position that nothing in the autopsy indicated an unnatural death.

Wecht battled his way to a points victory. On April 5, 1991, Delbert Ward was cleared of all charges and freed.

Cyril Wecht (1931–)

Cyril Wecht typifies a new breed of forensic pathologist—those whose prominence has chiefly been gained through reviewing the efforts of their peers. By its very nature this is a line of work peppered with controversy and animus, and Wecht has left a trail of crushed toes in his professional wake. He can be ultraprickly, and with his aggressive style of testifying, born out of a distaste for bullying attorneys who attempt to browbeat witnesses and ride roughshod over their evidence, he has never been reticent about expressing an opinion informed by the experience of more than thirteen thousand autopsies.

He was born in Bobtown, Pennsylvania, and attended the University of Pittsburgh, where he decided to explore the possibility of legal medicine as a career. At the same time, he undertook a course in law. A two-year stint in the air force was followed by research work at the Baltimore medical examiner's office. He also passed the state bar exam, and with this under his belt, he took a job with a Pittsburgh law firm.

In 1963 he became assistant district attorney and medico-legal adviser in Allegheny County, Pennsylvania. Six years later he took on the position of county coroner. When he joined the department it didn't even own a microscope; when he left, in 1979, it was among the best-equipped and most respected facilities in the country.

But Wecht's fame extends far beyond state boundaries. He first came to national prominence when he openly questioned the findings of the Warren Commission's conclusion that Lee Harvey Oswald was the sole gunman who killed President John Kennedy. An ardent and vocal detractor of the notorious "single-bullet theory," Wecht has no doubts that a conspiracy of some sorts initiated that fateful day in Dallas, and that Oswald really was, as he famously declared to reporters, "a patsy." Such high-profile misgivings made Wecht a natural fit when Hollywood director Oliver Stone was casting around for consultants to his movie *JFK*.

Wecht is equally controversial when it comes to the 1968 assassination of Robert Kennedy, insisting that convicted murderer Sirhan Sirhan could not have fired the gun that killed the senator because he simply didn't get close enough (smoke blackening around one bullet wound suggested the gun was no more than two inches away when fired).

In the wake of these incidents, Wecht has been asked to reinvestigate some of the most infamous crimes in American history. Critics often accuse him of reading more into the evidence than is really there—particularly with his startling conclusions in the JonBenet Ramsey case (he believes she was an accidental victim of a "sex game" gone wrong, played by the parents).

After a long period spent writing and consulting, Wecht returned to public office in 1997, when he was once again elected coroner in Allegheny County, a position he holds to the present time.

Significant Cases

1963	John F. Kennedy
1968	Sirhan Sirhan
1969	Chappaquiddick incident
1969	Tate/LaBianca murders
1975	Charles Friedgood
1977	Elvis Presley
1980	Claus von Bulow
1980	Jean Harris
1986	Karen Diehl
1987	Jack Davis
1990	Delbert Ward*
1991	Joann Curley*
1991	Arthur Jones

1994	O. J. Simpson
1996	JonBenet Ramsey
1998	Sandy Murphy and Rick Tabish

*Profiled in this book.

Raymond White

Date: 1939
Location: Walwa, Australia

It was just before ten o'clock at night on Shelley Road, high in the rugged Australian Alps region of north Victoria, and Raymond White and his wife, Elizabeth, were driving back to their three hundred–acre homestead just outside the small town of Walwa. Suddenly a sheep darted out in front of them. White yanked the steering wheel to one side, only to lose control of the car, which flipped into a roadside culvert.

According to White, he was hurled from the moving car, then beaten back by flames as he rushed to free his trapped wife. And yet minutes later, when a nearby farmer reached the scene, he was struck by how unruffled White looked following such an ordeal. Why, he was still wearing a hat! Setting aside his misgivings, the farmer joined White in futile efforts to free Elizabeth. Only much later were her virtually unrecognizable remains finally extricated from the smoking ruin.

A local constable was the first to sound warning bells. Studying the dusty roadway above the culvert, he saw no skid marks—indeed, the path of the vehicle into the culvert appeared quite uniform—nor was there any sign of sheep or sheep tracks.

The next day—February 20, 1939—news of the incident reached Melbourne, where it was deemed sufficiently suspicious to warrant the dispatch of a full investigative team, among whom was the government analyst **Charles Anthony Taylor.**

This wasn't the first time that Taylor had brushed up against the oddly incident-prone Raymond White. The two men had crossed paths just after World War I. Then White had worked on a struggling dairy farm, whose owner had decided to cut his two-man staff by 50 percent. One evening, the other employee, after complaining that the stew prepared by White tasted strangely bitter, left it for the dogs. The next morning they were found dead.

When Taylor analyzed the dogs' organs, he found strychnine of a particularly coarse-grained type, one rarely seen in Australia. He hazarded that it had been manufactured in Madras, India. A can of strychnine subsequently found at the dairy confirmed the accuracy of Taylor's guess and, for a while, White was held on suspicion of attempted murder, only to be freed due to a lack of evidence.

Following this, White found work on a farm some twenty-five miles along the valley just outside Walwa. It belonged to the Brennan sisters Elizabeth and Johanna. Of the two, Johanna was much the more attractive, and she soon became the target of White's amorous advances, which she coquettishly deflected. Undeterred, he switched his attentions to the older and plainer Elizabeth. Infuriated at being rebuffed, Johanna left the farm in a snit. When she deigned to return, the couple had married. To show that she harbored no ill feelings, Johanna even changed the terms of her will so that her half of the farm would go to Elizabeth.

Just a few months later, on April 25, 1928, Johanna accompanied her brother-in-law on a duck-hunting expedition. The way White told it, Johanna tripped and fell into a gully, discharging her rifle with lethal results. The gunshot wound behind her left ear was ruled accidental, and meant that sole ownership of the farm now passed into Elizabeth's hands.

By local standards she was now a wealthy woman, with a farm worth £A5,000 ($20,000), and a substantial bank account. Initially she remained circumspect: under the terms of her will, her husband would receive only a life interest in her assets, but in December 1938 Elizabeth drew up a fresh will, making White joint owner of her property and joint drawer on her bank account.

Two months later, she was dead.

Charles Taylor smelled trouble. According to the hospital reports, the cuts on White's chest appeared self-inflicted—his undershirt was undamaged—nor was there any trace of the gravel rash consistent with having been thrown from a moving car, as he claimed. Taylor returned to the accident scene and scoured every inch. Suddenly a faint gleam on the ground caught his eye. He bent down and picked up a small fragment of metal. A moment's cleaning revealed a tiny nugget of gold. Drawing on his mining background, Taylor realized it wasn't alluvial gold, but a misshapen piece of jewelry, possibly a ring.

A frisson of triumph coursed through Taylor: this was no ordinary auto fire. To generate the 1,064 degrees Celsius necessary to melt gold, some accelerant must have been employed. Elizabeth had been killed—most likely shot, he thought, though the body was too badly burned to tell—and then the crash was faked to cover up her murder.

Search efforts now concentrated on the shell of the front seat. After several hours of sifting, two .22-caliber bullets were found buried deep in the ashes. When someone noted that locals often carried bullets in their car, which might have exploded in the fire, Taylor snorted his derision. Just the two bullets? And both discovered adjacent to the victim's body?

He found what he was looking for beneath the passenger seat—a disconnected fuel pipe. Once the car flipped over, gasoline would flood directly onto the body, stoking the funeral pyre to more than one thousand degrees Celsius, hot enough to melt even a gold ring and turn a human body to ashes. Such experience with high temperatures, Taylor reasoned, suggested a mechanical background, possibly a ships' artificer. Checks showed that White had indeed worked as an engine room petty officer. It also revealed that his real name was Edgar Farrell, and that he had deserted from the Australian navy in 1919.

When police searched White's property they found a .22-caliber pistol at the bottom of a lake. But they couldn't find White. He was eventually traced to the bustling town of Albury. There, at the base of the Soldier's Monument, he wrote one last note. It was no confession, just a stated desire to be with his "dear wife." Then he took a shotgun and blew out his brains.

Gustav Wilson

Date: 1963
Location: San Francisco

In February 1968 Steven Sheldon went out to the shed behind the house he had just bought at 1710 Oakdale Avenue in San Francisco, undid the padlock, and stepped inside. Seconds later he was rushing back toward the house. His emergency call triggered a swift response. Two officers arrived within minutes. Ashen-faced, Sheldon led them out to the shed, opened the door, and pointed. On the floor, half hidden beneath some old camping equipment, lay a lumpy, bloodstained sack. Protruding from one end was a human foot.

Inside was a woman's body. The cause of death was plain enough—the head had been crushed to a pulp—but what made this corpse so unusual was the fact that it was entirely mummified. The shed's low ambient temperature and even lower humidity had drained every drop of moisture from the skin, giving it the appearance of wrinkled leather. The medical examiner concluded that the woman was in her midforties and had died no later than 1964. Judging from the broken fingernails and other injuries to her desiccated body, she had fought frantically for her life. Following that struggle, the killer had stuffed her clothes underneath the body, but only after removing all the manufacturer's labels.

Even the fingerprints, usually the best means of identification, seemed to offer little hope; the skin was so shriveled that not a single ridge could be seen. But all was not lost. By restoring the skin's suppleness, it was just possible that an identifiable print might be achieved. After amputation at the first joint, the fingers were soaked in a solution of glycol, lactic acid, and distilled water. In extreme cases this procedure can take weeks and always carries the risk of failure. Closely controlled conditions are paramount, as any undue fluctuations in solution strength or temperature can have devastating consequences. In this instance, two of the fingers were also injected with glycerin to expedite the process.

While the technicians labored, detectives checked the property tax rolls. This led them to Gustav Wilson, a fifty-nine-year-old butcher, who had owned the building from 1952 until 1964. He admitted living there with his wife, Emma, until their divorce; afterward he had moved and had not returned to the house since.

Newspaper accounts of the grim discovery brought another lead. A man named Thomas Green contacted the police, wondering if the body might be that of his sister Kathleen, who had vanished in November 1963. After several months of fruitless searching, he had filed a missing-person report on May 24, 1964. As that report now revealed, the missing woman's name was listed as Kathleen Wilson, wife of Gustav. And yet Wilson had not mentioned anyone named Kathleen. Confirmation of a second wife's existence came from Emma, who told police that after their divorce, Wilson had remarried in 1962.

Meanwhile, after days of conscientious experimentation, the laboratory team managed to obtain a set of clear fingerprints. Tempering official elation, however, was the knowledge that if Kathleen Wilson's prints were not on record, all that work would have been in vain. A check of the San Francisco Police Department fingerprint files came up blank, and frustration was beginning to set in when Thomas Green suddenly recalled that sometime in the early 1960s his sister had been arrested—he couldn't remember where—following some minor infraction.

Every city and town in the Bay Area received photographs of the prints, with a request to check their records. The response was fast and positive. One day later Redwood City, just south of San Francisco, reported that Kathleen Wilson had been arrested in 1962. Their fingerprint file corresponded exactly with the photograph.

Now that they had identified the body, detectives moved fast to arrest Wilson. While the case against him was strong, it was purely circumstantial. His insistence that he had not been at 1710 Oakdale Avenue since early 1964 sent investigators back to the house searching for clues, and in the same shed that had housed Kathleen Wilson's body for so many years, they found the evidence that proved her husband a liar.

A wooden box that stood on the floor had been thoroughly searched before but never moved. Now, as a detective rummaged through the shed, he happened to push the box to one side. His eyes fell on a sheaf of grubby papers. Tucked among these was an opened letter addressed to Gustav Wilson, postmarked January 1968. When examined, the letter revealed three latent fingerprints—all Wilson's. The final clinching proof came from Wilson's current home: hidden under his bed they found a small metal key that fitted the shed lock. For whatever reason, even after selling the house, he was drawn back to that shed in the garden, and now it had exposed him as a callous murderer.

This was the line that prosecutors took at Wilson's trial, portraying the defendant as a violent, abusive husband. Defense witnesses refused to believe a word of it. According to their testimony, Wilson wouldn't harm a fly. In this instance the jury chose to believe the state, and on July 11, 1968, they found Wilson guilty of second-degree murder. He received a life jail term.

Obtaining fingerprints from mummies has always posed problems, but solutions are never far away. In one method a special quick-drying dental putty is applied to the finger. After it hardens, the putty is peeled off and the inside painted with several coats of acrylic. Once removed, the dried paint gives an accurate cast of the fingerprint, which can then be printed by the usual inked pad method.

Paul Wolf

Date: 1982
Location: Santa Rosa, Texas

On a searing South Texas day in July 1982, police were called to a car perched precariously on the edge of a drainage ditch near the sleepy town of Santa Rosa. The inside of the vehicle had been gutted by fire, and when the car was hauled onto level ground, it became obvious that a large stone had been placed on the gas pedal in a failed attempt to drive the car into the water. Registration records showed the owner as a local man named Billy Staton, who along with his girlfriend Leticia Castro hadn't been seen for ten days. A wide-ranging search of the canals and brushland that interlace this region of the Rio Grande valley failed to provide any other clues.

Leticia's brother had last seen the couple on July 16, the day they left to pick up Staton's nine-year-old daughter from his ex-wife. He explained that Staton was caught up in a long-running custody battle for the child and that things had been getting ugly of late. When detectives called on Staton's former wife, Sherry, and her new husband, Paul Wolf, they heard that the couple had suddenly moved on July 17, one day after the disappearance. The Wolfs were traced to nearby La Feria. Both insisted that Staton had never arrived to pick up his daughter.

Official antennae were now twitching. A search of the Wolfs' former residence disclosed a damp spot in the middle of the living room carpet. Underneath the carpet a large section of the floor had been painted over. Analysis of this stain confirmed the presence of blood, but the high level of paint contamination made it impossible to type. Even so, there was no hiding the fact that a great deal of blood had been spilled at some time in this room, a feeling strengthened by the subsequent discovery of tiny, almost unnoticeable flecks of blood spatter on the walls. These told of some brutal struggle.

Out in the yard there was an area of freshly turned earth, such as might be made if a stone or a rock had been pulled from the ground. When the large stone used to weight down the gas pedal was fitted into the empty space, it was like slotting the last piece in a jigsaw puzzle. In the face of this development, Wolf abruptly changed his story.

He now admitted that Staton *had* shown up on the day in question, ready to take his daughter on a picnic, only to turn apoplectic when told that Sherry and the child were not at home. Staton had come at him, swinging punches, said Wolf. By the greatest of good fortune Wolf happened to have an iron bar handy, which he used to defend himself. A flurry of blows left Staton motionless on the carpet. Moments later, Leticia burst in, saw what had happened, and she, too, had attacked Wolf. For the second time in a matter of minutes, Wolf was obliged to employ the iron bar in self-defense, with equally lethal results.

Panic-stricken, Wolf asked a local farmer and close friend, Glenn Henderson, to help dispose of the bodies. They first dumped the bodies in a drainage ditch, then rested the stone on the gas pedal of Staton's car, only for the engine to stall at the water's edge. The next day Wolf had gone back and torched the vehicle.

Wolf said where the bodies could be found. Leticia was recovered from a canal, twelve miles away from the car, with her head stoved in. A farther ten miles away, Staton's body was found, partially submerged in a canal. His head was similarly crushed. But there was one glaring discrepancy in Wolf's story: besides being bludgeoned with a bar, Leticia also had been shot in the head. And there was something else that Wolf had not bargained for.

Taped to Billy Staton's stomach was a minicassette recorder, used on the advice of his lawyer, to gain evidence of Sherry's foul-mouthed and malicious obstructionism whenever he came to pick up his daughter on weekends. Had it now been a witness to murder?

Even though the tape had been submerged in water for several weeks, hopes were still high that it was usable. It was sent, still in water, to the FBI laboratory in Washington, D.C., for processing. Ten days later it was back in Texas.

The tape provided what prosecutors would later call "twenty-three minutes of murder," a fuzzy but audible account of double homicide. It allowed investigators to go back to the house, and by comparing times and distances with the blood spatter on the walls—which by now had been typed to Staton—work out exactly what had happened.

Far from being bad-tempered, Staton had been quite calm as Wolf invited him in. Sherry, too, was not away from the house, as Wolf had claimed, but clearly audible on the tape, talking to her doomed ex-husband. Early on, Wolf made an excuse to take out some garbage; he needed to know if Leticia was waiting in the car outside. Once her presence was established, he picked up an iron bar and returned to the house. By this time Sherry had gone, and taken the child with her. Without any warning or provocation, Wolf clubbed Staton to death in a sudden, frenzied attack.

Then, demonstrating the premeditated nature of the crime, he called out to Henderson, who had been lurking in another room. Together they went out and murdered Leticia.

All the while the tape kept rolling.

Later, when the two men were in the act of dumping the bodies, came a startling realization: Leticia was still alive. A single shot can be heard. Thirty seconds later, the tape ran out.

On April 20, 1983, Paul Wolf was convicted of murder and sentenced to life imprisonment. The following month, Henderson pleaded guilty and also received a life term. The final member of this murderous trio, Sherry Wolf, failed in her attempts to convince the jury that she had been an innocent bystander, and on July 29, 1983, she, too, was found guilty of murder and jailed for life.

William Zaph

Date: 1861
Location: Joliet, Illinois

Right after the outbreak of the Civil War, the city of Joliet, Illinois, was a wild place to be—a haven for draft dodgers, bounty hunters, and other assorted desperadoes. Law-breaking was a way of life for many of these interlopers, and yet, curiously enough, the crime that would forever stamp the city's name in the annals of forensic history concerned a couple of locals.

Benjamin Pickles was a blacksmith, affluent enough to afford a fancy Italian-style home, one of the largest houses in the city, and he ran a thriving business on Eastern Avenue. With a building boom under way, Pickles frequently worked late at his blacksmith's forge, fashioning ironwork for the many fine houses. One such evening was Friday, December 6, 1861. Pickles and his two teenage sons were eager to finish up some railings before heading home for supper. The job was just about done when Pickles happened to pass close to the window. Suddenly a shot rang out. He fell as if poleaxed. A bullet, fired from outside, had struck him in the head, close to the left ear. His sons froze for a moment, then rushed to their father's side. Once they realized the hopelessness of his plight, they cautiously inched their way out into the bitter winter night, only to find that the killer had vanished.

Daylight brought a significant clue. The city marshal Anthony McNerny, investigating the crime scene with a thoroughness not often found in those less sophisticated times, found his attention drawn to some footprints in a patch of mud beneath the window. Bending down, he studied them closely, impressing their distinctive pattern in his memory. Then he interviewed the deceased's family. They soon came up with a strong suspect. For years there had been bad blood between Pickles and his brother-in-law, William Zaph, and just recently the feud had worsened, with Zaph openly threatening to harm the blacksmith.

That same day Zaph was arrested and thrown into jail. Before locking the cell door, McNerny demanded that the prisoner surrender his shoes. Zaph, a cobbler by trade, looked instantly anxious. He explained how, to save on expensive leather, he had mended the shoes with half soles, the pattern of which, McNerny noticed, looked remarkably similar to that found in the muddy footprints. McNerny hurried back to the blacksmith's shop. Because of the frigid weather, the footprints were still intact, and when he carefully placed one of the shoes into a print, it fitted perfectly.

Suspicious though this was, on its own it scarcely merited bringing a charge of murder against Zaph. To gain a guilty verdict prosecutors needed more, and they found it when county coroner Charles Demmond performed the first close examination of the victim's body. Inside the left ear was a small scrap of newspaper, evidently the remains of wadding used in the pistol that had fired the deadly bullet.

Wadding is the material placed between the propellant and the projectile. Nowadays it is used almost exclusively in shotgun shells, since all modern handguns, both revolver-style and semiautomatic, use metal cartridge ammunition that does not require additional packing. Most pre–Civil War revolvers, however, required that each cylinder be loaded by hand. This involved six steps:

1. Measure the quantity of powder.
2. Pour the powder into the chamber.
3. Insert the ball or bullet.
4. Seat the ball on the powder.
5. Place wadding over the ball.
6. Cap the pistol.

It sounds like a laborious, time-taking procedure, but under battle conditions, an experienced soldier could reload all six cylinders in less than a minute. Besides acting as packing for the ball or bullet, the wadding also afforded the user some protection from any gun flame. Usually, when the gun was fired, the wadding would fall away harmlessly, a few feet in front of the muzzle; but at close range, a solid chunk of wadding could often end up inside the actual bullet wound.

Which was what had happened here. Besides revealing that Pickles had been shot at close range, the scrap of newspaper yielded one other vital clue: it was written in German.

Sure enough, when McNerny searched Zaph's home, he found a German newspaper, with one page torn. By carefully unfolding the wadding that had been removed from Pickles's ear, he matched it to the torn page. This was landmark detective work, the first time that such a technique had been employed in America, but still McNerny was not satisfied. Hearing that Zaph's wife had asked to talk to her husband in jail, he came up with an idea. He ordered one of his subordinates, Constable Thomas O'Brien, to hide beneath a large couch in the room that had been set aside for the meeting. As soon as Zaph saw his wife, he confessed to the shooting, blithely unaware that his every word was being overheard by O'Brien.

The skilled forensic work, coupled with O'Brien's testimony, was enough for the jury, which promptly found Zaph guilty of murder. But irregularities discovered late in the proceedings prompted the judge to declare a mistrial. A second trial, in January 1863, produced an identical outcome: guilty, quickly followed by a mistrial.

Undaunted, the state tried once more, and this time Zaph couldn't find any legal loopholes through which to crawl. The summer of 1863 found him convicted of murder and locked away in the county jail, pending sentence. Under few illusions as to what that sentence might be—he looked certain to hang—Zaph took matters into his own hands. On the night of July 24, 1863, along with five other inmates, he dug a hole in the southern wall of their second-floor cell, then lowered himself on bedding that had been tied together. Once on the ground, William Zaph disappeared into the night. Neither he nor his fellow escapees were ever seen again.

Landmarks in Forensic Science

3rd century B.C. The Alexandrian physicians Erasistratus and Herophilus conduct the first autopsies.

44 B.C. Antistius performs an autopsy on Julius Caesar.

1194 The Office of Coroner originated in England, first referred to as *custos placitorum* ("keeper of the pleas") in the Articles of Eyre. The name was originally "crowner," or "coronator," derived from *corona,* meaning "crown."

1248 A Chinese book, *Hsi Duan Yu* (The Washing Away of Wrongs), contains rudimentary descriptions of how to distinguish suspicious deaths. This is the first recorded application of medical knowledge to the solution of crime.

1447 Missing teeth are used to identify the body of the Duke of Burgundy in France.

1507 The first European book to acknowledge the usefulness of physicians in legal cases, *Constitutio Bambergenis Criminalis,* is published in Bavaria.

1663 The Danish physician Thomas Bartholin devises a test to establish if a dead baby had been stillborn or the victim of infanticide. Air in the lungs would be proof that the baby had breathed.

1670 The first simple microscope with powerful lenses is created by Anton Van Leeuwenhoek of Holland.

1775 The body of U.S. General Joseph Warren is identified by the engraver Paul Revere, who had made his false teeth.

1813 Mathieu Orfila publishes *Traite des Poisons ou Toxicologie General.*

1817 Francois-Eugène Vidocq forms the first police detective bureau in Paris, the forerunner of la Sûreté.

1823 The first paper to discuss the nature of fingerprints is published by John Evangelista Purkinje, a professor of anatomy at the University of Breslau, Czecheslovakia.

1829 Scotland Yard is formed.

1835 Henry Goddard, a Scotland Yard detective, begins to make comparisons between bullet striations and the rifling in gun barrels.

1836 James Marsh develops his "mirror" test for arsenic poisoning.

1851 Jean Servais Stas becomes the first to identify vegetable poisons in body tissue.
1858 Sir William Herschel requires natives in the Hooghly district in India to affix fingerprints to contracts as a means of identification.
1859 Spectroscopy is developed. Gustav Kirchoff and Robert Bunson show that substances give off a spectrum of light that identifies elements in the substance.
1865 Alfred Swaine Taylor publishes *The Principles and Practice of Medical Jurisprudence.*
1879 The system of identifying people by taking several body measurements (anthropometry) is developed by Alphonse Bertillon.
1880 Henry Faulds publishes a paper in the journal *Nature,* suggesting that fingerprints at the scene of a crime could identify the offender.
1884 Chicago creates the first municipal Criminal Identification Bureau.
1888 Alphonse Bertillon develops full-face and profile photographs as mug shots and the "portrait parle" (speaking likeness) of suspects.
1891 The first murder conviction is obtained through the use of fingerprints by Juan Vucetich in Argentina.
1892 (Sir) Francis Galton publishes *Fingerprints,* the first comprehensive book on the nature of fingerprints and their use in solving crime.
1893 Hans Gross publishes his seminal work, *Criminal Investigation.*
1897 The National Bureau of Criminal Identification is established by the International Association of Chiefs of Police (IACP) in Chicago.
1900/1 Paul Uhlenhuth develops the precipitin test to distinguish human blood from animal blood.
1901 Karl Landsteiner discovers human blood groups.
1901 Sir Edward Henry, commissioner at Scotland Yard, advocates the adoption of fingerprint identification to replace anthropometry.
1902 A burglar, Harry Jackson, becomes the first British person to be convicted on fingerprint evidence.
1903 The New York State prison system begins the first systematic use of fingerprints in the United States for criminal identification.
1905 The Bureau of Investigation (later FBI) is established.
1910 Edmond Locard sets up the world's first forensic laboratory in Lyon, France.
1910 The American handwriting expert Albert S. Osborn's pioneering *Questioned Documents* leads to the acceptance of such testimony in court.
1915 The first antibody test for ABO blood groups is developed by Leone Lattes in Italy.
1915 The International Association for Criminal Identification (to become the International Association of Identification) is organized in Oakland, California.

1921 John Larson and Leonard Keeler design the polygraph.
1923 Calvin H. Goddard refines Phillip O. Gravelle's comparison microscope for use in ballistics examinations.
1925 The Bureau of Forensic Ballistics is founded in New York City by Charles Goddard, Phillip Gravelle, Charles E. Waite, and John H. Fisher.
1930 The national fingerprint file is set up in the United States by the Bureau of Investigation.
1932 The Bureau of Investigation crime laboratory is established.
1935 The Bureau of Investigation is renamed the Federal Bureau of Investigation (FBI).
1941 Voice spectography study begins at Bell Labs.
1945 Frank Lundquist, working at the Legal Medicine Unit at the University of Copenhagen, develops the acid phosphatase test for semen.
1952 The gas chromatograph is invented by A. T. James and A. J. P. Martin.
1953 Paul Kirk publishes *Crime Investigation,* one of the first comprehensive criminalistics and crime investigation texts.
1967 The FBI National Crime Information Center (NCIC) becomes operational.
1971 Photo-fit process, enabling eyewitnesses to piece together facial features as a means of identification, is developed by the photographer Jacques Perry.
1977 Masato Soba invents the "Superglue" fuming method of developing latent fingerprints in Japan.
1978 The Electrostatic Detection Apparatus (ESDA), used to expose invisible handwriting impressions on paper or any other surface, is developed by Bob Freeman and Doug Foster.
1986 In the first use of DNA to solve a murder, (Sir) Alec Jeffreys uses DNA profiling to identify the killer of two young girls in the English Midlands.
1987 Tommy Lee Andrews, a rapist, becomes first American convicted through the use of DNA profiling.
1991 Integrated Ballistics Identification System (IBIS), an automated imaging system for the comparison of the marks left on fired bullets, cartridge cases, and shell casings, is launched.
1999 The FBI introduces the Integrated Automated Fingerprint Identification System (IAFIS), which allows storage and search capabilities directly to the national database.
1999 The video spectral comparator is introduced, providing enhanced computerized means of examining questioned documents.

Index